Vol. 559
No. 10

Monday
5 December 1994

PARLIAMENTARY DEBATES
(HANSARD)

HOUSE OF LORDS
OFFICIAL REPORT

CONTENTS

Questions—Crown Post Office Services [Col. 787]
—London Foot Hospital and School of Podiatric Medicine [Col. 789]
—Inland Revenue Offices [Col. 790]
—Green Belt Planning Policy: Religious Institutions [Col. 793]

Ministerial and Other Salaries Order 1994—Motion for Approval [Col. 796]

Industrial Training Levy (Engineering Construction Board) Order 1995—Motion for Approval 1995—Motion for Approval [Col. 798]

Industrial Training Levy (Construction Board) Order 1995—Motion for Approval [Col. 801]

Legitimated Persons: Succession to Titles—Motion for a Humble Address [Col. 802]

Unstarred Question—Western Sahara: Conflicts [Col. 802]

Written Answers [Col. *WA 61*]

LONDON: HMSO
£4·20 net

Lords wishing to be supplied with these Daily Reports should give notice to this effect to the Printed Paper Office.

The bound volumes also will be sent to those Peers who similarly notify their wish to receive them.

No proofs of Daily Reports are provided. Corrections for the bound volume which Lords wish to suggest to the report of their speeches should be clearly indicated in a copy of the Daily Report, which, with the column numbers concerned shown on the front cover, should be sent to the Editor of Debates, House of Lords, within 14 days of the date of the Daily Report.

PRICES AND SUBSCRIPTION RATES

DAILY PARTS

Single copies:
Commons, £7·50; Lords £4·20

Annual subscriptions:
Commons, £1,275; Lords £615

WEEKLY HANSARD

Single copies:
Commons, £22; Lords £9·00

Annual subscriptions:
Commons, £775; Lords £310

Index—Single copies:
Commons, £6·80—published fortnightly;
Lords, £1·90—published weekly.

Annual subscriptions:
Commons, £120; Lords, £65.

LORDS CUMULATIVE INDEX obtainable on standing order only.
Details available on request.

BOUND VOLUMES OF DEBATES are issued periodically during the session.

Single copies:
Commons, £90; Lords, £68.
Standing orders will be accepted.

THE INDEX to each Bound Volume of House of Commons Debates is published separately at £9·00 and can be supplied to standing order.

WEEKLY INFORMATION BULLETIN, compiled by the House of Commons, gives details of past and forthcoming business, the work of Committees and general information on legislation, etc.
Single copies: £2·30.
Annual subscription: £88·80.

All prices are inclusive of postage.

© Parliamentary Copyright House of Lords 1994
Applications for reproduction should be made to HMSO

HMSO publications are available from:

HMSO Publications Centre
(Mail, fax and telephone orders only)
PO Box 276, London SW8 5DT
Telephone orders 0171 873 9090
General enquiries 0171 873 0011
(queueing system for both numbers in operation)
Fax orders 0171 873 8200

HMSO Bookshops
49 High Holborn, London WC1V 6HB (counter service only)
0171 873 0011 Fax 0171 831 1326
68-69 Bull Street, Birmingham B4 6AD 0121 236 9696 Fax 0121 236 9699
33 Wine Street, Bristol BS1 2BQ 0117 9264306 Fax 0117 9294515
9-21 Princess Street, Manchester M60 8AS 0161 834 7201 Fax 0161 833 0634
16 Arthur Street, Belfast BT1 4GD 01232 238451 Fax 01232 235401
71 Lothian Road, Edinburgh EH3 9AZ 0131 228 4181 Fax 0131 229 2734

The Parliamentary Bookshop
12 Bridge Street, Parliamentary Square
London SW1A 2JX
Telephone orders 0171 219 3890
General enquiries 0171 219 3890
Fax orders 0171 219 3866

HMSO's Accredited Agents
(see Yellow Pages)

and through good booksellers

ISBN 0 10 701095 x
ISSN 0 309-8834

Printed in England and Published by HMSO

House of Lords

Monday, 5th December 1994.

The House met at half-past two of the clock: The LORD CHANCELLOR on the Woolsack.

Prayers—Read by the Lord Bishop of St. Albans.

Crown Post Office Services

Lord Skelmersdale asked Her Majesty's Government:

What services are available in Crown post offices that are not available in sub-post offices.

The Minister of State, Department of Trade and Industry (Earl Ferrers): My Lords, there are principally three major services which are not universally available in sub-post offices but which are available in Crown post offices. Those are motor vehicle licences, British Visitors' Passports and passport application forms, and Datapost.

Lord Skelmersdale: My Lords, I am grateful to my noble friend for that answer. My interest is in the middle category of those which my noble friend enumerated. Why is it impossible to obtain a passport application form, as opposed to a British Visitor's Passport, from a sub-post office?

Earl Ferrers: My Lords, there are a number of different passport application forms. There are those for new applications, those for amendments, those for children under 16 with their own passport, and British Visitor's Passports. The forms are frequently amended considerably and it is not cost effective to make all those forms available throughout more than 19,000 post offices. They are made available where they are mostly required. Where they are not available, Post Office Counters offers a help line, at local call rates, to advise customers of the nearest post office where British Visitor's Passports or passport forms can be obtained.

Lord Dean of Beswick: My Lords, is the Minister not aware that there is a service which smaller post offices provide for the public which cannot be listed? That service is providing personal contacts in their area for people such as the ageing and disabled. It is often their one point of contact. Will the Minister ensure that the Government bear that service in mind if they discuss the future of the small post offices again?

Earl Ferrers: My Lords, the noble Lord, Lord Dean of Beswick, is often right, and he is on this occasion. That is an important part of the post office system. Nineteen thousand of the 20,000 post offices are in private ownership. They serve the needs of the populace according to their ability, and very successfully.

Lord Haskel: My Lords, all post offices are part of a network. Does the Minister agree with me that restrictions on investment in a rural post office reduce the effectiveness not only of that particular post office but also of the entire network, particularly where information technology is concerned?

Earl Ferrers: My Lords, that is why we consider it desirable that they should be in private ownership. That is why they are in private ownership. I agree with the noble Lord, Lord Haskel, that there are tremendous opportunities for the Post Office in the future. That will require a good deal of investment. That is why we wanted to see that that investment would be available to the Post Office.

Lord Geddes: My Lords, now that post offices no longer have the burden of issuing game licences, thanks largely to the efforts of my noble friend the Minister, does that not mean there is more time to issue passport applications?

Earl Ferrers: My Lords, that depends upon the amount of time that was spent issuing game licences. According to my noble friend and some of his noble friends, that was not as great as it should have been.

Lord Dixon-Smith: My Lords, will my noble friend the Minister consider the matter of the hours that post offices may be open? It is increasingly the custom today to find post offices in supermarkets which can be open all hours of the day and night and at weekends, whereas post offices generally are still restricted.

Earl Ferrers: My Lords, my noble friend Lord Dixon-Smith touches on a very pertinent point. Crown post offices used to close at 12.30 on Saturdays but are now open until 7 o'clock in order that people—of whom I am sure my noble friend Lord Dixon-Smith will be one—should be able to purchase their lottery tickets.

Earl Russell: My Lords, will the Minister give a little more thought to the point made by the noble Lord, Lord Haskel, about rural areas? It is highly inconvenient to be as much as 12 miles from the nearest Crown post office. Before the Minister again invokes cost effectiveness, will he consider that it is not cost effective to have us all living in conurbations either?

Earl Ferrers: My Lords, I shall need a little time to work that question out. The fact is that country post offices are required and are available. It has been found that they are more suitable when they are in private ownership. Of the 20,000 post offices, 19,000 are in private ownership. I quite agree with the noble Earl that if people wish to have more sophisticated services, they will have to go to a Crown post office. If that is 12 miles away, so be it. It would be unreasonable to expect all post offices of all natures to provide all services even though the majority of the services may not be required.

Lord Skelmersdale: My Lords, I quite agree with my noble friend. However, where a sub-post office postmaster finds a need, for example, for passport application forms, should he not be able to obtain them even if a small charge is levied?

Earl Ferrers: My Lords, if I may say so, the answer is quite simple. The passport application forms are available at most post offices. But the fact is that there

[EARL FERRERS]
are a number of different passport applications. Over the past few years there have been a great many alterations in the types of passport. The Post Office charges for storing and moving those forms about. It is only realistic that the forms should be available where the demand is greatest. I quite understand that my noble friend might like to see those different forms available in all post offices. However, if only one a year is required, even my noble friend might consider that that was a slight extravagance.

Lady Saltoun of Abernethy: My Lords, does the noble Earl really believe that selling a road tax fund disc is a sophisticated service which is not required by a great many people all over the country?

Earl Ferrers: My Lords, Post Office Counters acts as agent for the Driver and Vehicle Licensing Authority. It limits the facilities to 4,000 of the post offices. If more post offices dealt with the licences, it would result in higher cost but no extra revenue. I can assure the noble Lady that the forms can be obtained at all post offices; it is merely the issuing of the licences which will be restricted to 4,000 post offices.

London Foot Hospital and School of Podiatric Medicine

2.45 p.m.

Baroness Seear asked Her Majesty's Government:

Whether the London Foot Hospital and School of Podiatric Medicine is threatened with closure because of a projected cut of between a quarter and a third of its budget, and what effect this will have on the quality of training of future chiropodists.

In so doing, I declare an interest as a grateful patient.

The Parliamentary Under-Secretary of State, Department of Health (Baroness Cumberlege): My Lords, the London Foot Hospital and School of Podiatric Medicine combine the provision of high quality comprehensive foot care with education, training and research. Local discussions are taking place which aim to retain those attributes but to achieve better value for money.

Baroness Seear: My Lords, I thank the noble Baroness for her relatively encouraging reply. However, will she assure us that she recognises that practical training in chiropody is of the greatest importance? While it is desirable that chiropodists understand about feet, it is even more important that they know how to deal with them. It is essential that good practical training be closely related to theoretical training. Where the two aspects are connected geographically, it makes the matter a great deal easier than if the training is widespread. Training in any profession is a special skill. It is not satisfactory to assume that because a person is a good chiropodist he or she can also be a good trainer.

Baroness Cumberlege: My Lords, the noble Baroness is absolutely right.

Baroness Jay of Paddington: My Lords, I, too, must declare an interest as another grateful patient of the London Foot Hospital which has made it possible for me, through what I believe is now called podiatry, to enjoy long country walks again. Is not this centre of excellence now being squeezed by the internal market? Is it not another example of the way in which the internal market is reducing services to patients?

Baroness Cumberlege: My Lords, no. The hospital and training centre are unique in that the training is done through the trust which runs the services. In every other instance there is separation between the training of the chiropodist or podiatrist and the services given. The discussions taking place at present are to prevent the unit remaining isolated and to incorporate it into the university, as is the case with every other centre.

Inland Revenue Offices

2.48 p.m.

Lord Boyd-Carpenter asked Her Majesty's Government:

Whether the payment of income tax should be made more convenient for the taxpayer by ensuring that the offices from which the Inland Revenue collect it are located closer to the taxpayer's place of residence.

The Parliamentary Under-Secretary, Ministry of Defence (Lord Henley): My Lords, the Inland Revenue maintains an extensive network of local offices. This is at present being restructured to reduce costs and improve services.

Lord Boyd-Carpenter: My Lords, I thank my noble friend for that somewhat platitudinous reply. Is he aware that some of us who live in London and in the south of England have found our tax affairs transferred to Inland Revenue offices in such places as Walsall, with payments sometimes having to be made to Glasgow? It is an extraordinary inconvenience if one wishes to discuss one's tax affairs with the responsible office. Why is it necessary to transfer the tax affairs of people in the south of England to Walsall?

Lord Henley: My Lords, I start by saying that there is nothing wrong with Walsall. I can assure my noble friend that again it matters little where the payment of taxes is made, because I believe that there is probably a letterbox not far from him. However, I understand the problem that he sets out. What I can say is that most self-employed people—and they are the ones who usually have the most complex tax affairs—will be dealt with by the office nearest to their own business. That is important for them.

I appreciate that those—and for all I know, my noble friend might be one of them—who are termed "multi-sourced" and who have various different sources of income might be dealt with by a number of different offices. I can tell my noble friend that there are historical reasons for this, but the Inland Revenue recognise that it can be confusing and can provide a poor service. As a result of restructuring, we hope that from April 1997 most people will deal with only one office in respect of all their sources of income. With the new technology being introduced, they will be able to deal with an office near them which will be able to access their own records, even if those are dealt with by another office.

Lord Bruce of Donington: My Lords, is the Minister aware that, contrary to popular supposition, local inspectors of taxes—as distinct from collectors of taxes—prove extremely co-operative when taxpayers call at the offices to discuss their tax affairs so that they do not have to incur the expense of going to accountants? Will the noble Lord therefore ensure that the service provided locally by inspectors of taxes is not reduced to the point where it becomes almost impossible for local people to make the appropriate tax inquiries in order to clarify their taxation problems?

Lord Henley: My Lords, I am grateful to the noble Lord for paying tribute to the service that is provided by many local offices. I think that the noble Lord deserves credit for not taking the opportunity to advertise his own profession—accountancy. I shall certainly take note of what he has said and I can confirm that so far as possible we would like to be able to provide the appropriate local advice from appropriately qualified local inspectors.

Lord Peston: My Lords, I hasten to add my words of support on what a good job the Inland Revenue is doing, particularly the inspectors. Can the noble Lord tell me what kind of people visit tax offices? I have been paying income tax for about 40 years. When I have problems, I ring up the inspectors; when they have problems, they write to me and I send them a cheque. It has never occurred to me to visit them. Is there any indication of what fraction of the tax-paying public makes use of the excellent service to which my noble friend referred? Is it usual and is it to be encouraged?

Lord Henley: My Lords, I think that it depends very much on the nature of the sources of income and the complexity of the matters of the individual. It may be that many self-employed people, particularly in small businesses, who do not wish to employ an accountant but find the whole process of self-assessment, or whatever it is, over-complicated, might prefer to make use of the advice that they can get from the tax office. They might therefore prefer to make a personal call. Certainly, the Inland Revenue can cope with that and will continue to provide that service. I cannot give figures as to what percentage of taxpayers like to call on the local tax inspector and make his acquaintance, but I shall certainly look into the matter. If I can provide the figures for the noble Lord, I shall do so.

Lord Monson: My Lords, will the noble Lord agree that it is a disgrace that taxpayers now have officially to be discouraged from posting cheques to the Inland Revenue because so many cheques are apparently stolen and the payee's name altered? Will the Minister agree that, in the absence of a repeat of the Great Train Robbery, there are only two places where the thefts can take place? The first is the Post Office and the second is the Inland Revenue itself. Can the noble Lord say what action is being taken to track down those responsible?

Lord Henley: My Lords, I cannot answer the noble Lord's question, but what I can say is that it is still possible for the noble Lord to pay his taxes by post. The Inland Revenue has no objection to him doing so. If he wishes to continue to pay by post, he may, but there are other means by which he can pay his taxes.

Baroness David: My Lords, may I say how helpful it is that I can include my income tax payments with my other bills and pay them all at the bank in one go? It is very simple, I get an envelope marked "free", with a first-class stamp on it, and it is sent to Glasgow. It is much more convenient and I am grateful that one is able to do that at one's local bank.

Lord Henley: Again, my Lords, I think that the Inland Revenue will note what the noble Baroness said and be grateful for her tribute to the services which it offers.

The Countess of Mar: My Lords, the noble Lord might be interested to know that I have had cause to call on my local tax inspector on my husband's behalf and I was dealt with politely. Is there any way in which the two systems of computers which the Inland Revenue has—in other words, the computers which make the assessments and those which make the demands for payment—could be made to talk to each other? Then one will not be asked for a payment and be given a refund about two weeks later.

Lord Henley: My Lords, I shall certainly make inquiries about the latter point, which I am afraid I cannot answer immediately at the Dispatch Box. As regards the first point which the noble Countess made, I am sure that the noble Lord, Lord Peston, noted that at least one Member of this House visits the local tax office.

Lord McIntosh of Haringey: My Lords, can the Minister say whether any progress is being made in the Inland Revenue on encouraging the instruction of taxpayers in completing their forms? I think in particular of the possibilities of interactive CD-ROMs or interactive videos which would be even more helpful than trying to deal with problems after they have arisen.

Lord Henley: My Lords, as regards new IT of that sort, I am afraid that I cannot answer the noble Lord's specific point. However, I shall certainly make inquiries as to whether greater progress has been made. I can assure the noble Lord that the Inland Revenue is committed to providing the best possible service it can to those who pay it tax.

Lord Boyd-Carpenter: My Lords, does my noble friend's supplementary answer mean that in 1997 responsibility for dealing with taxpayers who live in the south of England will be transferred back from Walsall to an office in the south of England?

Lord Henley: No, my Lords. What I said is that from that date most people will deal with only one office,

[Lord Henley]
particularly those who are multi-sourced. It might still be the Walsall office that deals with my noble friend's taxation, but a local office will be able to deal with him when he goes to make inquiries. By means of the new technology which is being introduced, my noble friend's records and papers will be accessed by a tax inspector in an office near my noble friend.

Lord Mackie of Benshie: My Lords, is the Minister aware that I have had much to do with tax inspectors? They have always been polite to me and invariably I have come off worst. Will the noble Lord assure us that the Government are not paying tax inspectors by results on the way to tax farming?

Lord Henley: My Lords, I can assure the noble Lord that there is no tax farming.

Lord Barnett: My Lords, perhaps I should declare an interest. I received a tiny perk for having recently opened a tax office in Manchester. Is it a coincidence that many bills from the Inland Revenue arrive just before Christmas?

Lord Henley: My Lords, I think that that is in the nature of things and I can assure the noble Lord that it is a coincidence.

Green Belt Planning Policy: Religious Institutions

2.57 p.m.

Lord Stallard asked Her Majesty's Government:

Whether, in the forthcoming revision of Planning Policy Guidance Note 2 (Green Belts), they propose to maintain the special provision for development accorded to religious institutions and foundations.

The Parliamentary Secretary, Ministry of Agriculture, Fisheries and Food (Earl Howe): My Lords, there is no special provision for development by religious groups in the existing Planning Policy Guidance Note 2.

Lord Stallard: My Lords, I thank the noble Earl for that fairly disappointing reply. In the existing PPG2 there is provision which has existed for 40 years or more for religious organisations or places of worship under the category of institutions in extensive grounds. That has existed so that custom, practice and precedent have been well established over a long period. I accept that the definition is perhaps imprecise and not perfect: that is what has caused so much trouble. Nevertheless, successful applications which have gone through have welded and moulded the existing PPG into practice. Does the noble Earl accept that successful applications have resulted in improving many derelict sites in the green belt, much to the enthusiasm and acceptance of the local authorities and the neighbourhoods, as well as providing much needed places of religious worship and teaching for the present and future moral welfare of the nation?

Earl Howe: My Lords, the noble Lord is quite right that the existing PPG2 states that development for institutions standing in extensive grounds is not subject to the general green belt presumption against development. However, research on the effectiveness of green belts published by the Government last year recommended that this special treatment should end because it conflicted with the fundamental green belt aim of keeping land permanently open. It had also, as the noble Lord himself indicated, proved unclear in operation and had provoked extensive litigation. Those are the reasons why, in the consultation document that was issued by the Government earlier this year, a reference to institutions standing in extensive grounds was deleted.

Lord Williams of Elvel: My Lords, will the noble Earl accept that, if the provision under the old PPG2 was unclear, the Government should clear up the matter; that it should not be left in abeyance and it should certainly not be simply eliminated from the new draft just because the Government cannot be bothered to deal with it?

Is it not also the case that, in the new draft guidance, if no land is available elsewhere, green belt can be used for park-and-ride facilities? In what sense are park-and-ride facilities better than religious institutions in green belts?

Earl Howe: My Lords, first, the Department of the Environment has already clarified what it means by the phrase "extensive grounds", which is the phrase that has caused most difficulty. I am afraid, however, that that has not prevented the arguments from continuing. As has already been said, those arguments have caused a considerable delay for the applicant; they have been expensive both for him and for the taxpayer.

With regard to the noble Lord's second point, the Government propose that institutional development in green belts should require very special circumstances if it is to proceed. We have considered all the responses to the consultation document and we expect to publish the revised PPG2 shortly.

Lord Simon of Glaisdale: My Lords, is the noble Earl aware that in a number of cases the place of worship has been built on derelict land which has been subsequently landscaped by the congregation?

Earl Howe: My Lords, I am aware of a number of such instances, and I am sure that noble Lords will be aware of several others. It would not be appropriate for me to comment on the worth or otherwise of particular developments. What I can say is that we come back to the difficulty that I mentioned earlier of defining what we mean by "extensive grounds". For those reasons, the consultation document proposed that development which is otherwise considered inappropriate for the green belt could nevertheless take place in very special circumstances. Of course, the nature of those circumstances would fall to be decided by the local authority.

Lord Elton: My Lords, as my noble friend referred to both the consultation and the publication of the revised document, can he kindly tell us, first, whether in the consultation the question was ever addressed as to whether or not to change or preserve the fifth stated aim of green belt policy—namely, to assist in urban regeneration? Secondly, can he tell us when "shortly" will become "now"?

Earl Howe: My Lords, I would like to be as helpful as possible to my noble friend. As I said earlier, the intention is to publish the revised PPG2 shortly. I am afraid that I cannot give him a precise date. We are in the process of dotting one or two "i"s before publication is possible. With regard to my noble friend's other question, I hope that he will allow me to write to him.

Lord Williams of Elvel: My Lords, I am grateful to the noble Earl. However, does he agree that institutions which have been in PPG2 since 1955 as being proper occupiers of green belt land subject to all the appropriate restrictions, are now to be ruled out? The categories of institution include places of religious worship. Would it not be sensible for the Government to divide institutions between those which have virtue—such as places of religious worship—and those which do not, both in the new consultation and in the new draft PPG2?

Earl Howe: My Lords, the institutional category started off as a recognition of the fact that institutions such as Victorian mental hospitals were located in areas which subsequently became green belt. However, as time has gone on, it has been increasingly used to justify new institutional development. I have to say that it is difficult to reconcile that with maintaining the openness of the green belt, which is of course the central theme running through all green belt policy.

Lord Stallard: My Lords, will the noble Earl concede that there have been many successful applications under the existing PPG2? Surely that creates a precedent. Does he agree that, if there have been successful applications, then somebody in the legal world accepts the interpretation that has been put forward by religious organisations and others? Does the Minister see that by deleting this from the new planning guidance he is likely to cause more problems than he solves; that difficulties will be created where they do not exist at the moment? Would it not be far better to leave it in and tidy up the wording of the PPG?

Earl Howe: My Lords, I accept that a number of applications have succeeded on appeal, as the noble Lord indicated. But that was within the terms of reference of PPG2 as it now stands. I have to say to the noble Lord that, in our consultation document, a tightening up of the definition of what new development should be allowed in the green belt was favoured by a number of respondents—in particular the Association of District Councils and individual local authorities, which felt that the provision had too often been used to legitimise what would ordinarily be seen as inappropriate development in the green belt.

The Lord Bishop of St Albans: My Lords, can the noble Earl give any hope to those large religious institutions—I think particularly of retreat houses, theological colleges and so forth—which may be left with extensive grounds for historical reasons and yet because of financial stringency are having to look again at their resources? Such institutions find themselves restricted by planning laws—understandably—and yet, because of the restrictions, may well be forced out of business.

Earl Howe: My Lords, I hope that I can be helpful to the right reverend Prelate. Planning Policy Guidance Note 12 states that development plans should provide for places of worship. The development plan process affords full opportunities for public consultation. Religious groups should therefore involve themselves in the plan preparation and, where they consider it necessary, seek provision for places of worship.

Lord Stoddart of Swindon: My Lords, does the noble Earl agree that many religious organisations, and indeed many religious buildings, add to the beauty and effectiveness of the green belt itself? Will the Government therefore reconsider their position, especially bearing in mind that it may be for the betterment of people's lives and souls if they are able to attend a religious organisation which is put in an appropriate place given the money that is available to that organisation and where it would be pastorally correct?

Earl Howe: My Lords, I would not take issue with the noble Lord about the value of religious practice. As I said earlier, the consultation document, despite the tightening to which I referred, still proposed that development which would otherwise be considered inappropriate for the green belt could nevertheless take place in very special circumstances. It is worth reminding ourselves that the green belt was put there for a purpose. The chief purpose is of course to protect the countryside, particularly for access from large conurbations and as a way of checking urban sprawl. I believe that that is something that the public values highly.

Ministerial and other Salaries Order 1994

3.8 p.m.

The Lord Privy Seal (Viscount Cranborne) rose to move, That the draft order laid before the House on 22nd November be approved [*1st Report from the Joint Committee*].

The noble Viscount said: My Lords, I beg to move the Motion standing in my name on the Order Paper.

The draft order gives effect to the arrangements described on this corresponding occasion last year by my noble friend Lord Wakeham for the annual uprating of the salaries of Ministers and other office holders. The new salaries under this order are the result of applying the procedures set out by my noble friend then.

With your Lordships' permission, I should like to touch briefly on recent history. Members in another place and Ministers and other office holders accepted a freeze on their salaries in 1993 following the introduction of public sector pay restraint. In doing so, they forwent their entitlement at that time under the links that, up to then, had applied with the Civil Service, and indeed, had applied since 1987.

[VISCOUNT CRANBORNE)]

When the linkage was re-established last year for the 1994 salary review, it was agreed that the basic increase would be paid in two stages: the first stage was to be of 2.7 per cent. payable from 1st January 1994; and the second stage, also of 2.7 per cent., on 1st January 1995. Last year's Ministerial and other Salaries Order gave effect to the first stage. The second stage is included in the order that is before your Lordships today.

In addition, it was announced last year, as part of those arrangements, that the 1995 uprating would reflect the increases in the salary received by middle ranking civil servants during 1994—by "middle ranking civil servants" I mean Grades 5 to 7. Those civil servants received a settlement worth 2 per cent. with effect from 1st August 1994. The same 2 per cent. will be paid to Ministers and other office holders in respect of their 1995 settlement with effect from 1st January 1995, if this order is approved. This is also included in the figures appended to the order.

So far I have spoken in terms of the basic ministerial salaries under the principles which were established last year, principles whereby Ministers and others covered by the Ministerial and other Salaries Order can normally expect to receive the same percentage increases as Members of Parliament. Your Lordships will be aware that the salaries of Members of Parliament are in turn linked to the pay settlements in the Civil Service. However, I should remind noble Lords of one other feature of the arrangements which is of particular relevance to Ministers, the Leader of the Opposition and the Opposition Chief Whip in this House. Since Ministers and office holders in this House do not receive the reduced parliamentary salaries payable to Ministers in another place, the procedure is that they should receive the same cash increase as their counterparts in the other place, taking account of their combined ministerial and reduced parliamentary salaries.

Finally, I should stress that the overall increases of 4.7 per cent. for most Ministers and the cash equivalent for Ministers in your Lordships' House, which is worth more in absolute percentage terms, are not out of line with other settlements or indeed with economic conditions generally. Perhaps I may suggest to your Lordships that it would be worth bearing in mind that more than half of the increase is a deferred payment and that that deferred payment is part of last year's settlement, not part of the new settlement. As a result of that deferment, Ministers and other office holders have lost considerable sums in comparison with the salaries that would have been paid if the link with the Civil Service salaries had been maintained throughout. These amounts will not be recovered by the office holders concerned by re-establishing the link. The 1995 settlement itself is 2 per cent., in line with the pay settlement in the Civil Service, and therefore fully in accordance with the Government's approach to the public sector pay.

I hope that that will be a sufficient and—I hope your Lordships will agree—severely factual explanation of the circumstances that lie behind the order. I believe that the draft Ministerial and other Salaries Order provides for a realistic settlement in accordance with agreed arrangements for Ministers and for Opposition office holders in both Houses of Parliament. I commend the order to the House.

Moved, That the draft order laid before the House on 22nd November be approved [*1st Report from the Joint Committee*]. —(*Viscount Cranborne.*)

On Question, Motion agreed to.

Industrial Training Levy (Engineering Construction Board) Order 1995

3.14 p.m.

Lord Inglewood rose to move, That the draft order laid before the House on 17th November be approved [*1st Report from the Joint Committee*].

The noble Lord said: My Lords, it may be for the convenience of the House if I speak to this order and the following order together.

The proposals before your Lordships this afternoon seek authority for the Construction Industry Training Board and the Engineering Construction Industry Training Board to impose a levy on the employers in their industries to finance the operating costs of the boards and to fund their range of training initiatives, including grants schemes.

Provision for this is contained in the Industrial Training Act 1982 and the orders before your Lordships would give effect to proposals submitted by the two boards. Both proposals include provision to raise a levy in excess of 1 per cent. of an employer's payroll. The Industrial Training Act 1982 requires that in such cases the proposals must be approved by affirmative resolution of both Houses.

In each case the proposals are exactly the same as those approved by your Lordships last year. As in previous orders they are based on employers' payrolls and their use of sub-contract labour. Both have special provision for excluding small firms from paying levy.

For the CITB the rates are 0.25 per cent. of payroll and 2 per cent. of net expenditure by employers to labour-only sub-contracting. Employers with a combined payroll and labour-only payments of less than £61,000 a year are exempt from paying levy.

The ECITB treats its head offices and construction sites as separate establishments and applies different levy rates which reflect the costs and the different arrangements for training particular workers. For head offices the rates are 0.4 per cent. of payroll and 0.5 per cent. of net expenditure by employers on labour-only sub-contracting. Firms employing 40 or fewer employees are exempt. The rates for sites are 1.5 per cent. of payroll and 2 per cent. of net expenditure by employers on labour-only sub-contracting, with exemption for employers with a combined payroll and labour-only payments of £75,000 a year or less.

In each case the proposals have the support of the employers in the industry, as required by the Industrial Training Act, and have the full support of the respective boards, which consist of senior employers, trade unionists and educationalists.

Your Lordships will know that the CITB and the ECITB are the only two statutory industry training boards. Most other sectors of industry are covered by independent, non-statutory arrangements. In those two industries employers and their representative organisations have remained firm in their support for a statutory levy system.

Both boards have recently undergone major reviews of the need for their continuance. Following those reviews, we reconstituted each of them for a further term of office up to 1998. In doing so, we recognise the strong feelings of the employers and the performance and achievements of the boards.

The draft orders before the House will enable the two boards to carry out their training responsibilities in 1995 and I believe it is right that the House should agree to approve them. I commend them to the House. I beg to move.

Moved, That the draft order laid before the House on 17th November be approved [*1st Report from the Joint Committee*]. —(*Lord Inglewood.*)

Baroness Turner of Camden: My Lords, I thank the Minister for his explanation of the two orders. As he rightly said, they are very similar to the orders that were discussed in this House last year. We approve and support them on this side of the House.

However, I am concerned that there is still a terminal date, so to speak, of 1998 in respect of the continuance of those training boards. It would be very much better, since both boards do an excellent job of work and are acknowledged by everyone in the industry to do an excellent job of work, if they had a little more assurance of continuity than a term point of 1998 put upon their future existence. We raised the matter earlier. In fact, I raised it last year when I said that it was necessary for continuity and a feeling of security among staff, who do a very good job working for the boards. I still feel that it is a pity that 1998, although some time in the future, should be put as a term when the boards may face discontinuance. They are both very necessary.

The other point that I should like to make, which I also raised last year, concerns the small firms exemption clause. I know that it has been agreed, but it has always seemed to me necessary for small firms to have trained personnel. It is perhaps an even greater necessity for small firms than for larger ones which may have in-house training schemes anyway. In the construction industry in particular, as everyone knows, there are inherent dangers; a high rate of industrial accidents and so forth. No matter what is done it is likely to remain an inherently hazardous industry. It is all the more necessary therefore that small firms should have trained staff capable of coping with safety provision. In that case it is unfair that they should be exempted from the need to pay the levy. I know that that has been generally agreed and that we have raised the matter on past occasions. Nevertheless, that is still my view. Having said that, I offer no objection to the orders.

Baroness Seear: My Lords, we too welcome the continuation of the work being done by the two training boards and support what the noble Baroness said in relation to the exemption of small firms.

Industry as a whole is woefully undertrained and we are facing reductions rather than increases in government spending. That makes it all the more important that the training boards should continue and, as the noble Baroness, Lady Turner, said, that there should be confidence about their continuing into the future.

Throughout industry we are suffering from under-training. It is one of the most serious obstacles in the way of recovery. It is therefore extremely welcome that the boards will be able to raise the money in order to carry out the training needed. However, it raises the broader question of whether the Government were ever right to stop putting charges of this kind on industry as a whole. I dare say it is a forlorn hope, but I shall not lose the opportunity of saying that we would welcome the Government reconsidering the question of how the money for training, which is at present so woefully inadequate, should be raised. That money, if we are to have any future as an industrial country, needs to be greatly increased.

Lord Monkswell: My Lords, in rising to support these measures perhaps I can ask the Government one question. One of the benefits of the industrial training levy is that it involves firms directly in the whole training regime. Having paid the levy they then have an incentive to get something out of it either through being involved in training or undertaking other activities which bring them into the system. One of the difficulties of not imposing a levy on small firms is that they are then not within that regime. Can the Minister say what efforts the Government are making to ensure that small firms are involved in training regimes, either as providers of training or in the use of trained personnel?

Lord Inglewood: My Lords, the proposals before the House relate to the construction and engineering construction industries. Both industries have specific training problems due to a largely mobile workforce, the prevalence of small firms and the use of labour-only sub-contractors. The employers believe they need collective funding with the statutory underpinning provided by the levy system. They feel strongly that any other solution would be unrealistic and lead to a shortage of skilled labour in those sectors.

The noble Baroness, Lady Turner, asked about the conclusion date for the boards of 1998. There is no magic in the date of 1998. It is merely that any such board should from time to time be reviewed. The noble Baroness may recall that last year the term of the Construction Industry Training Board had been agreed but not that for the Engineering Construction Industry Training Board. In the circumstances, because they are similar to each other, it seems sensible for the two boards to be reviewed at the same time.

I hasten to add—without wishing to pay tribute to the work the boards are doing because it was after all the collective view of all those involved in the industries that the boards, in the specific circumstances, played a useful role—that it is accepted by the Government that, while we are not in favour of statutory boards in general, these specific boards should continue.

[LORD INGLEWOOD]

In relation to the small firms' exemption—as the noble Baroness said, it is a point she raised last year and I reiterate the remarks of my noble friend Lord Henley on that occasion—we are anxious to see small firms thrive in this country. We believed that on balance it was better not to impose this burden on small firms in this sector. But merely because small firms are not paying a levy does not mean that they are not thereby able to avail themselves of the services provided by the boards. When one looks at the range of courses provided by TECs throughout the country, a considerable amount of help is available to the construction industry, using the word in the widest sense. It is important that that continues for reasons, not least, of health and safety, as mentioned by the noble Baroness.

The noble Baroness, Lady Seear, commented on the reduction in spending by the Government on training. In this case it is important to recognise that the Government are ever more carefully focusing the expenditure they devote to training. As a result we believe that we shall be able to provide at least as good a training as we have done in the past at less cost. That is extremely important. Again in that context it is worth recalling that while government provide of the order of £2 billion a year on training, that is matched by provision and funding from the private sector of a further £20 billion or so. It is a mistake to see that simply as an exercise in provision by the Government. It must be looked at in a much wider context.

The noble Lord, Lord Monkswell, remarked on the involvement of small firms in the training process. That is a matter for the proprietors and managers of small firms, bearing in mind the circumstances of their businesses. A whole variety of initiatives, such as Investors in People, are available for small firms to use if they wish to go further in that direction.

The proposals have the support of the respective employers and have been approved by the boards. I believe that it is not in dispute that they should be approved by your Lordships, and I commend the order to the House.

On Question, Motion agreed to.

Industrial Training Levy (Construction Board) Order 1995

3.27 p.m.

Lord Inglewood rose to move, That the draft order laid before the House on 17th November be approved [*1st Report from the Joint Committee*].

The noble Lord said: My Lords, I beg to move that the Industrial Training Levy (Construction Board) Order 1995 be approved.

Moved, That the draft order laid before the House on 17th November be approved [*1st Report from the Joint Committee*].—(*Lord Inglewood.*)

On Question, Motion agreed to.

Legitimated Persons: Succession to Titles

3.28 p.m.

Lord Kilmarnock: My Lords, I beg to move the Motion standing in my name on the Order Paper.

Moved, That an Humble Address be presented to Her Majesty praying that Her Majesty may be graciously pleased to allow that Her undoubted Prerogative may not stand in the way of the consideration by Parliament during the present Session of any measure providing for an amendment of the law relating to the succession of legitimated persons to dignities and titles of honour.—(*Lord Kilmarnock.*)

On Question, Motion agreed to and it was ordered that the Address be presented by the Lords with White Staves.

Western Sahara: Conflicts

3.29 p.m.

The Earl of Winchilsea and Nottingham rose to ask Her Majesty's Government what action they are taking as a member of the United Nations Security Council to resolve conflicts in the Western Sahara and other areas of tension in the African continent.

The noble Earl said: My Lords, since 1986 I have become closely associated with the last remaining colonial problem in Africa—that of the Western Sahara. I propose therefore to confine my remarks to that continuing, if unresolved, conflict.

Because I am the founder and trustee of a registered charity which exists solely to provide humanitarian aid to the 200,000 or so refugees who were forced to flee from that unfortunate country in 1975/76, due to the brutal invasion of it by Morocco in that year, I have always tried to confine my activities to the humanitarian aspect and steer clear of the political aspects.

I hope that the Charity Commission will note that I have tried to be a good boy. But when I was told that there may be a slot available for this Unstarred Question today and that the Minister was also available, the temptation was altogether too much to resist, even though I was thrown into an immediate panic by the shortness of time between last Wednesday, when I was told, and this afternoon to prepare a speech worthy of your Lordships' House. Nevertheless, I am extremely grateful for this opportunity, not because I enjoy making speeches, which I do not, but because this problem has always been and remains largely ignored by the world and its media.

Very few people know anything about this remote and long-standing tragedy which has now been festering for 20 years. Any news of it which occasionally gets into print is confined to a tiny paragraph buried on page 9 or wherever, and yet, when exactly the same thing happened to an oil-rich country like Kuwait, where we have considerable economic interests as well as a dependency on its product, the media were full from front to back for many months of the gross violations of basic human rights by Saddam Hussein that were taking place in Kuwait and Iraq. Very little was said about the gross violations of human rights in Kuwait before the

Iraqi invasion. Sadly, it seems that human rights carry a price tag, along with everything else these days. We are prepared to protect them only when there is something in it for us. I had that said to me quite candidly last year by our foreign affairs Minister in his office in Whitehall.

That attitude of total cynicism is something which we have created ourselves in our cosy world and I maintain it is because we feverishly seek excuses to hide behind in order safely to distance ourselves from any responsibility in disputes which are not of our making and where our wallets are unaffected. It would be a very different story if the Western Sahara was floating in oil, or had other commercially desirable minerals in abundant quantity. If that had been the case, no doubt the United Nations' response would have been vastly different, and the problem would have been swiftly solved within six months of the Moroccan invasion taking place, instead of the 20 years it has taken so far. By any yardstick, that length of time is obscene, but it becomes especially obscene if you are the unfortunate victim.

The Saharawis were forced out of their homes by bombs being dropped on them, bombs manufactured in the United States, the home of the free and the brave. The bombs were dropped by units of the Moroccan air force and consisted of napalm bombs, cluster bombs and phosphorous bombs. The planes pursued the civilian population into the open desert, where they had set up some temporary refugee camps, and bombed those camps as well. Thousands were killed, maimed, and injured. They had no option but to flee across 700 miles of open, hostile desert, to the sanctuary of neighbouring Algeria, where they arrived exhausted, dehydrated, starving, destitute and suffering from severe exposure. Many of them were carrying dead children in their arms.

They have since been forced to exist in exile, in terrible conditions, which they have tried largely by their own efforts to improve, and all of this without a mention, let alone a headline, and certainly never a murmur of condemnation of the aggressor, the Kingdom of Morocco, from any of the five permanent members of the UN Security Council, of which the UK is one. It is my own view that if a full member of the UN breaks the UN Charter which it has sworn to uphold, then that member should be expelled until he mends his ways. The threat of public humiliation of that kind could be more than enough to convince wrongdoers of their sins and crimes.

So why has Morocco been allowed to get away with this act of international terrorism? Well, my Lords, we are back to the price tag again, aren't we? Morocco had something we wanted; it was of great geographic and strategic importance to NATO; it has a king who is seen to be pro-Western; it has unlimited quantities of high-grade phosphates; and it is a nice place to go for a holiday or to shoot a TV commercial or a Hollywood feature film. It also produces nice oranges. Never mind its appalling record of gross human rights abuses; or the rejection by the International Court of Justice of the claim of territorial sovereignty of the Western Sahara submitted by Morocco; or the fact that Morocco's invasion of the Western Sahara has also been roundly condemned by the Organisation of African Unity.

So where are we now? What is the UN actually doing to try to bring an end to this illegal occupation by Morocco of the Western Sahara? Are we going to see another Israel and West Bank situation being repeated in the Western Sahara? Do the Saharawis have to remain in the wilderness for the obligatory 40 years, or will we graciously allow them to return to their country and homes after a mere 20 years of misery? The decision is ours in that we have a collective responsibility to humanity in our position as one of the five permanent members of the UN Security Council. Will we see the UN taking some firm, courageous and unbiased action to bring a just and fair referendum to the people of the Western Sahara, something that was originally promised to them by Spain, when she withdrew from her colonial territory back in 1975?

The way things are going, I doubt it. The UN has shown itself to be greatly lacking in resolve and impartiality in seeking an acceptable solution in the Western Sahara. The present Secretary-General is known to have Moroccan sympathies and leanings; so did his predecessor. There have been recent confirmed press reports of UN officials, tasked with organising the referendum by the UN, being arrested by the Spanish authorities for massive drug smuggling on their way from Morocco to New York, and being mysteriously reinstated by the UN after being in prison for five months.

A blind eye is turned to the 400 or so violations by Morocco of the cease-fire, currently shakily in place, which was initiated by the Saharawis three years ago in an effort to encourage the peace process, and there has been only a muted response from the UN to the outrageous demands from Morocco for an additional 120,000 names to be added to the list of those entitled to vote in the referendum, which is based on the last population census carried out by Spain in 1975.

On top of all this, as if the Saharawis have not enough to bear, their four refugee camps, each holding approximately 50,000 people, were very badly damaged, with one camp being totally destroyed, leaving about 55,000 people, mainly women, children and the elderly, without any form of shelter. In two days at the end of October, more than three feet of rain fell, and more was to come in a second wave of storms which hit the camps at the beginning of November.

All the infrastructure which they had so laboriously created through their own efforts at self-help was severely damaged or washed away. Gone are their schools, hospitals, clinics, kindergartens, day-care centres, and the protective walls around their horticultural establishments which had been growing a wide variety of fruit and vegetables where nothing ever grew before. I have witnessed these achievements on my 15 visits to the refugee camps since 1986. In spite of this latest disaster, our Government still refuse to send direct aid to these refugees, preferring instead to continue making anonymous contributions through the UN High Commissioner for Refugees in Geneva for general distribution. That is because the British Government maintain that they have always adopted a position of neutrality in the dispute and that to aid one side would offend the other. Therefore our aid to the

[THE EARL OF WINCHILSEA AND NOTTINGHAM]
refugees has to be covert and indirect in nature. But what about the considerable sums that we openly give to projects in Morocco which benefit the Moroccan king and his people? Would that not offend the refugees who would be bound to see Britain aiding Morocco in this direct fashion as being extremely one-sided and unjust?

The noble Baroness the Minister knows that I have applied through her office on more than one occasion for a modest amount of ODA funding for humanitarian projects in the Saharawi refugee camps. She also knows that my applications have always been refused on the grounds that to grant them would be to violate Britain's position of neutrality. She attempts to justify British aid to Morocco, which last year amounted to just over £9 million, by saying that none of it reflects any opinion on Morocco's policy towards the disputed territory of the Western Sahara, and it is all of a developmental nature anyway.

I am sure that ways could be found of getting direct aid to the refugee camps—aid which is crucially and urgently needed after the recently disastrous flooding—without offending Morocco. Anyway, if Morocco did get upset with us for sending aid to the Saharawis, I am sure that we could weather that storm. But the Saharawis were not able to weather the storms that hit them and they need to know that there are people out there who do care about them. So I submit that direct aid needs to be sent from Britain, and it needs to have a symbolic Union Jack on it.

I also submit that the very least that this country must do as a founder member of the UN is to take a much more robust role in encouraging the peace process in the Western Sahara. It would only need a sharp word from Britain on the floor of the UN in New York to achieve a shift in Moroccan intransigence and evasiveness. We are still admired around the world as being the mother of parliaments and one of the founders of democracy and champions of liberty and freedom. Why do we not practise what we preach?

3.41 p.m.

Lord Wise: My Lords, I have travelled with the noble Earl, Lord Winchilsea, on, I believe, three occasions to the Western Sahara. I have been associated with him in the sterling work he has done and is doing for those people. He must be one of—if not the—finest friends which they have in the western world. I want to support him very briefly in what he has been saying.

As he said, in a few months' time 20 years will have elapsed since Morocco invaded the Western Sahara. We all know that it was a far from peaceful invasion, as the noble Earl has told us. I shall not reiterate all that he has said about the horrific and gruesome details and the sufferings endured by the defenceless Saharawi people. Suffice to say that those who survived eventually managed to trudge the 700 miles across the desert into Algeria where, with Algerian help, they set up the camps, where they remain to this day.

However, the Polisario did fight back and, as we all know, a bitter war raged right up to, I believe, the unofficial ceasefire negotiated in 1989. The ceasefire was going to be made official in 1991 to mark the beginning of the operation of the settlement plan leading up to the free and fair referendum which was to be held in January 1992, to which Morocco had agreed. The original United Nations settlement plan, which was agreed by the United Nations Security Council, Morocco, the Polisario and the Organisation of African Unity, identified a census of the Western Sahara population carried out by Spain before it left its former colony in 1975. That was going to be identified as the starting point for the electoral register.

It was agreed by all, including Morocco, that the electoral roll would consist of all of the Saharawis listed in that census plus their descendants. However, at the last moment and, not unsurprisingly, Morocco decided not to honour the agreement and then sent tens of thousands of new settlers into the Western Sahara, claiming their right to vote on the territory's future. It renewed air strikes against the Polisario. As the noble Earl has pointed out, the United Nations report stated that there had been frequent air strikes and many other violations of the ceasefire by Morocco. But that seems to be just another story of Morocco's complete disregard of international opinion or the authority of the United Nations.

It is now three years since the referendum should have taken place. The United Nations Mission for the Referendum in Western Sahara, called MINURSO, is still trying to progress in the identification and registration process. It is a pretty thankless task, greatly aggravated by Morocco's procrastination and intransigence and its insistence on the addition of between 120,000 and 150,000 names over and above the original agreement. That is the main sticking point. It is obviously completely unacceptable and it is the root of the current crisis.

The United Nations Secretary-General, Boutros Boutros-Ghali, had hoped to report in August last that the referendum would take place in February of next year. However, when he finally produced his report on 9th November it indicated that February 1995 was not going to be the date for the referendum after all. Again, that is hardly surprising.

The noble Earl's Question asks what action Her Majesty's Government, are taking, as a member of the Security Council, towards the resolution of the conflict. I hope that my noble friend the Minister will assure us that, even though we have withdrawn our personnel, we shall not allow MINURSO to be disengaged. It is seriously undermanned in both civilian and military sections. Owing to the sheer frustration of the whole situation, I believe that there is a real danger of it being abandoned. If that happens another horrific, full-scale war will undoubtedly erupt.

The Secretary-General, Boutros Boutros-Ghali, is dispatching a technical team to the field to reassess the logistic and other requirements for the deployment of MINURSO at the full strength that was originally intended. He is asking for this full-strength deployment, and I hope that Her Majesty's Government will urge that this should be done. MINURSO is an essential instrument in the quest for peace and stability in the area. If it is brought up to full strength it will speed up the process of identification and registration.

I believe that the Security Council and the United Nations must assert its authority. It has to bring the two sides together for dialogue in conjunction with the United Nations and the OAU. That is the only way in which the conflict can be resolved peacefully, if at all. It is not going to be easy. If the United Nations has any credence at all it must honour its obligations to the Saharawi people for their right to self-determination.

The noble Earl spoke of the devastation in the camps following the terrible and unprecedented floods. I also implore my noble friend the Minister, whom we all know to be a very kind and compassionate lady, to use all her powerful influence to try to get direct aid sent from Britain to alleviate the immediate problems. To say that the situation is appalling is a gross understatement: it is absolutely catastrophic, as the noble Earl has said. These people desperately need help and I am sure that if the will is there we can send help directly to them from this country—and I trust that we shall.

3.48 p.m.

Viscount Waverley: My Lords, the number of speakers today is not indicative of the importance of the subject of conflict resolution. Indeed, the House should be grateful to the noble Earl, Lord Winchilsea, for his initiative. I listened with great interest to the contributions which addressed the Western Sahara dispute. I understand that the noble Lord, Lord Redesdale, will concern himself with the United Nations role in Africa. Therefore, I wonder whether I might broaden the debate.

Conflict prevention and resolution are complex but essential. The unfolding events in what was Yugoslavia are ample evidence of that. The Stockholm International Peace Research Institute illustrates the gravity by determining that, of 34 major armed conflicts in the world last year, seven were in the African continent.

If those conflicts are to be prevented, it is essential to understand their root causes. In Africa poverty, for example, has a devastating effect on the continent, with half of the entire population living below the poverty line. Fifty per cent. of total African external earnings is required to service their external debt. Declining income with the fall in commodity values—the continent's principal export—and a corresponding increase in the cost of manufactured products have all led to extreme difficulties. Structural adjustment programmes and inward investment are vital.

Population pressures, with falling food production and desertification, are threatening the food-producing areas at the rate of 6 million hectares per year. A combination of drought and unsuitable agricultural practices have increased the misery. Insecurity and instability along borders, sometimes caused by not negotiating shared resources, precipitate tensions in neighbouring countries, with the risk of armed confrontation and, as we know from recent events, they can give rise to refugees. The list goes on: illiteracy, with a staggering 165 million still illiterate; illegal immigration; gun running and drug trafficking compound the difficulties. It is a grim picture.

African initiatives undertaken by Africans are politically essential. Regional co-operation, as a confidence-building measure, sustains friendly relations and peace. That is illustrated in the work of such regional bodies as the Organisation of African Unity. The countries of Africa constitute one-third of the membership of the United Nations. That partnership has contributed positively to efforts to resolve conflicts, although such bodies tend to work more closely on preventive diplomacy by promoting African unity and tackling the continent's economic problems.

Among the principles of the OAU Charter is a mechanism for preventing, managing and resolving conflicts in Africa. It is prepared to undertake peace-making functions. The OAU has been given a shot in the arm by President Clinton's negotiations to set up an African peace-keeping force, which could also be called upon by the United Nations. Last month the United States Congress passed an African Conflict Resolution Act which will set aside foreign aid for that purpose. I urge Her Majesty's Government to take a proactive interest in that initiative. Perhaps the Minister can tell the House how much information about funding initiatives is passed between the donor nations in order to achieve the maximum, and avoid duplication, from scarce resources.

The Southern African Development Community divides sectors of responsibility among member nations. The new remit for politics, democracy, human rights and security has not yet been allocated. That will shortly be forthcoming, and is welcome. South Africa, as a newly admitted member, could possibly be a suitable candidate. Certainly the Mandela-Mugabe axis makes for a formidable team and much can be expected from their endeavours to keep peace in the region. Angola, Mozambique and Lesotho were three countries where immediate attention needed to be directed. That was done effectively by the two presidents.

The Commonwealth Secretariat is proactive in the peace process. That is to be encouraged when the opportunity presents itself. The Secretary-General, with two highly regarded unsung members of his staff, Mr. Gaylard and Dr. Anafu, twice successfully defused tension in Lesotho and Natal. The Secretary-General actively works for the promotion of democracy, human rights and conflict resolution through preventive diplomacy. The secretariat's election monitoring mission underpins the democratic process. The outcome of elections determines whether democracy will take root. The secretariat currently has a team in Namibia.

Finally, the application of the Parsons principle in crisis diplomacy establishes a contact group or diplomatic presence to monitor a crisis and to take the opportunity of any opening to negotiate with the parties concerned. Our Prime Minister, in a recent speech in Cape Town, declared:

"an entirely new effort at preventative diplomacy is long overdue. With our friends in Africa and with their agreement and their participation, Britain wants to develop new mechanisms to head off conflicts".

The Foreign Secretary developed those ideas in a speech to the United Nations General Assembly on 28th September.

[VISCOUNT WAVERLEY]

It seems to me that regionalisation is the key to future stability and should be encouraged. The European Union, MERCOSUR in the southern countries of South America, NAFTA and APEC are evidence of such regionalisation. It is becoming generally accepted that the Lomé Convention will be replaced by entirely different arrangements. Future arrangements will possibly be region specific as part of the overall European development policy. Political leaders will therefore be made to communicate with each other if they are to benefit from bilateral aid. That is not to suggest that the work of the noble Lord, Lord Judd, and myself as officers of the All-Party Lomé Group diminishes. On the contrary, our duty is to ensure that existing benefits are not eroded under whatever new arrangements are set up. That will help, in a small way, the preventive process.

However, more is required. Constant confidence-building processes are necessary, and it must never be forgotten that the essential ingredient for the peaceful process is negotiation through continuous debate and consultation.

3.57 p.m.

Lord Redesdale: My Lords, I thank my noble friend Lord Winchilsea and Nottingham for tabling this Unstarred Question. Perhaps I may mention his role in helping the Saharawi people through Rainbow Rovers. On my visit to the camps in southern Algeria I saw many indications that my noble friend had been there. No one who has been to see the polisario camps can fail to be impressed by the people's tenacity and ingenuity in surviving that very harsh environment. I was distressed to hear of the storms that have caused so much devastation.

The conflict has been going on for a long time and needs to be resolved as quickly as possible to help the Saharawi people. Ultimately, the United Nations has a large part to play in resolving the conflict. However, the difficulties faced by the United Nations in enforcing Resolutions 658 and 659 in the Western Sahara are a striking example of the problems of inadequate resources and ambiguity of mandate that can often undermine the effectiveness of the United Nations. In April this year, total contributions outstanding to the MINURSO special account amounted to approximately half the total annual cost of its present deployment of 40 million dollars. The United Kingdom has a good record for paying its assessed contributions to the United Nations on time. But other member states' failure to pay on time is a serious obstacle to the fulfilment of the organisation's role. As the noble Baroness has said previously, the United Nations is the sum of its parts. It is only as effective as its members allow. The Foreign Secretary has commented on the need for reform of the UN's financing system. Will the Minister say what action the Government have taken to put that suggestion into effect?

I do not intend to address the numerous areas of tension in Africa but to confine myself to three present conflicts—Somalia, Angola and Rwanda—because they seem to me to exemplify the limitations of the United Nations and hence the need for substantial reform. Essentially, that is where the United Kingdom can take action by pushing for effective reform at the international level.

Since the end of the cold war, the type of conflicts that prevail today result from numerous complex and historical factors including political instability, ethnicity and religion. The definition of what constitutes "conflict" and at what stage the international community should step in has been the crux of the dilemma about foreign intervention in today's conflicts. The UN Secretary-General, Boutros Boutros-Ghali, helped to clarify the types of conflict and the consequent changing demands on the UN in his document *An Agenda for Peace*. Among his recommendations is the idea of preventive diplomacy, a concept that is really at the heart of the founding purpose of the United Nations. The vision expressed in 1946 at the opening session of the UN Security Council centred not so much on how to respond to future conflicts but how to prevent their very occurrence.

In *An Agenda for Peace*, Boutros Boutros-Ghali spoke also of the need for peacebuilding and reconstruction in post-conflict areas. Without the foundations of a peace-building strategy, which take into account the necessary political, social and economic changes in order to create an environment for stability, the international community has been only partially successful. That means that in future the assistance provided by UN agencies and other agencies not usually associated with peacekeeping—such as the International Monetary Fund, the World Bank and the private sector—should be tailored to both short and long-term needs.

UN operations in Somalia, Rwanda and Bosnia have demonstrated the urgency of institutionalising preventive diplomacy. An integrated early warning system for those crises could well have limited civilian casualties. Active UN diplomacy in Somalia did not begin until 1992, 15 months after the conflict began. Had the UN responded earlier, it is likely that much suffering could have been avoided. In Rwanda, UN troops were withdrawn from the area in April when evidence showed clearly that the crisis had mounted into genocide. The United States' reluctance to become involved in another Somalia, for whose failed and questionable military strategy the US lost face and which further damaged the credibility of the UN, meant US obstructiveness was a contributory factor to the UN's delayed response to the unfolding tragedy in Rwanda. Despite appeals from African nations to act, and the provision of a 5,500 African peacekeeping force, the logistical support was not forthcoming. By the end of May, the Secretary-General issued a strong criticism to member states:

"We must all recognise that ... we have failed in our response to the agony of Rwanda, and thus have acquiesced in the continued loss of human lives. Our readiness and our capacity for action has been demonstrated to be inadequate at best, and deplorable at worst, owing to the absence of collective political will".

UNOSOM II, the UN's second operation in Somalia, launched in May 1993, was to some extent an experiment drawing the UN into peacemaking rather than peacekeeping activities. "Peacebuilding operations" were the pretext under which the US military-dominated command pursued General Aideed only to end in defeat and the further loss of life. The lack of a clear mandate in Somalia contributed to the UN's ineffectiveness in many of its initial aims.

The political impasse in Somalia continues despite the considerable reduction in UN forces in the course of this year. It appears that the balance of power is once again in the hands of the faction leaders. There is fear that a new federal government could collapse if the fragile arrangement between Ali Mahdi Mohammed and his allies and the SNA is not accepted; at worst that could re-ignite the war. The cost of UN peacebuilding in Somalia has already set the UN back some 1 billion dollars a year. If the Nairobi Declaration were to disintegrate, it is doubtful whether the political will would exist for another attempt by the international community to resolve the conflict in Somalia. Moreover, the perceived partiality of UNISOM may well mean that the validity of its mandate to try to forge a political solution has long expired. Will the Minister commentd on any recent developments in Somalia; the United Kingdom's position regarding any new outbreak of conflict; and the value of the United Kingdom's contributions to Somalia since 1991?

I move on to Angola. The ceasefire in Angola has raised hopes for an end to the conflict, often referred to as the worst war in the world. Although the peace accord has a fragile base, the chance for reconstruction and peacebuilding in Angola is an opportunity which should be encouraged by every means possible. Angola is a country rich in resources and its prospects are good. But much support in the way of foreign investment and long-term development initiatives is needed. As at 30th April 1994, total contributions outstanding to UNAVEM I and UNAVEM II were approximately 31 million dollars. Would the Minister consider channelling the amount outstanding to meet the needs of reconstruction?

A further problem is that although long-term agricultural potential in Angola is large, an estimated 10 million to 20 million landmines are scattered across the country, preventing agricultural workers returning to the field. That leads me to ask what steps the United Kingdom has taken to ratify the 1981 UN Inhumane Weapons Convention or to impose a ban on the production and export of landmines which continue to inflict civilian suffering in many regions of post and present conflict in Africa?

I say a final word on Rwanda. The conflict in Rwanda bears some of the most serious criticisms that can be levied against the UN, because of its delayed response to the reported genocide. If nothing else, it sets the most recent case for an immediate call to strengthen the UN's ability to undertake preventive action. Until such structural changes to the UN organisation are introduced, in particular the establishment of a UN rapid deployment force and including human rights monitors, the UN is unequipped to do its job. Quite apart from the compelling moral case of the international community's responsibility to uphold respect for human rights, the costs in terms of global security are not to be diminished. I wish to refer to a recent report by Saferworld, an NGO, which focuses on issues of international security, entitled *The true cost of conflict*. It summarises the costs incurred in a number of conflicts, not just in terms of the financial deficit of member states, but in the long-term wasted potential of the afflicted country and its bearings on regional and international levels of stability and prosperity. It states:

"International peacekeeping represents a real investment ... if moral reasons do not give rise to the political will needed, then national self-interest should".

As the Minister will appreciate, the United Kingdom has the opportunity to convey that message in the UN Security Council conference in January.

I conclude with a reference to the peace settlement in Mozambique. I recently had the opportunity to witness the elections in Mozambique. I was amazed by the degree of organisation and the peaceful nature of those elections. Mozambique summarises what can be achieved by the UN if it has the will to undertake such activities.

4.10 p.m.

Lord Judd: My Lords, the noble Earl, Lord Winchilsea and Nottingham, spoke with compassion and conviction rooted in his first-hand experience of the Western Sahara and his exemplary commitment to the Saharawi people. However, as was argued by the noble Lord, Lord Redesdale, his Question has a relevance which stresses way beyond the Western Sahara. It is highly pertinent to next year's 50th anniversary of the United Nations. There will be much international debate about the future of the UN. Part of that debate will concern the future of the Security Council.

Were the Security Council being formed today, it is hardly conceivable that the United Kingdom would be offered permanent membership. However, permanent membership is what we have inherited based on the world as it was in 1945. If we want to retain that permanent place we must justify it. In our post-imperial, post-colonial era, the way in which we can best look to our interests is to be second to none in our commitment to international institutions, which are vital for effective global governance.

It is by our demonstrable internationalism that we shall maximise our influence on world affairs. Part of this will be our contribution to international peace-keeping. But more important than that by far will be our lead in building up the resources for pre-emptive diplomacy and conflict resolution.

There are those—and I am sure that the Minister is not one—who will argue that the United Kingdom has no interest in the Western Sahara. In our closely-knit interdependent world, with all the unpredictability of knock-on effects, that argument is dubious. But that is not the point. Such cynicism ill befits a nation wanting to retain its permanent membership of the Security Council. That status is not simply to pursue narrow UK interests; with it goes the task of shouldering our share of responsibility for security throughout the world.

The noble Earl reminded us of the brutality of the displacement of the Saharawi people. Amnesty International reports that, despite the presence of UN monitors, they still suffer disappearances, political

[LORD JUDD]
prisoners and torture at the hands of the Moroccans. In the past some have been held for up to 16 years without charge or trial and no explanation has ever been offered. Human rights, guaranteed under the implementation plan agreed by the UN in co-operation with the Kingdom of Morocco and the Polisario (the political resistance movement of the Saharawi people), are not yet respected. I am afraid that, although Polisario does not yet itself have an unblemished record—and Amnesty International has certainly drawn attention to its prisoners of conscience—it has never resorted to international terrorism.

The Saharawi people do try to operate under broadly democratic principles, with the objective of one person, one vote and government by elected representatives. They aspire to religious freedom. In the main, women enjoy comparable rights with men. Priority is given to education and a 95 per cent. illiteracy rate has been transformed into a 95 per cent. literacy rate.

As was indicated by the noble Earl and the noble Lord, Lord Wise, the UN supervised referendum to determine the future of the Saharawi people, which was promised 20 years ago, has still not happened, and the implications of the UN Secretary-General's report of last November suggest that inevitably there will be another postponement beyond the expected date of February next year. The choices on offer are, after all, for a referendum without agreement on the electoral roll, for the UN to drop its presence and to withdraw the proposal for the referendum and for the parties to continue talking until June in the hope of compromise.

As the noble Lord, Lord Wise, stressed in his remarks, there are already acute anxieties about the manipulation of the voter registration process, with reports of intimidation by the Moroccans and of thousands of new settlers being sent into the region by Morocco. In all these circumstances, it is hardly surprising that the Saharawi people are rapidly losing faith in the UN—or, as the Minister reminded us in the debate on the Queen's Speech, in us—for there is no United Nations other than its member states.

The noble Baroness will need to convince us that the Government, as one of the five permanent members of the Security Council, are taking the lead that they should be taking to resolve the impasse and to bring about the direct dialogue between the parties for which the United Nations General Assembly has called.

Meanwhile, as the noble Earl so graphically described, the four Saharawi refugee camps adjacent to Tindouf were a month ago the victims of catastrophic floods. He told us that 50,000 people have been made homeless, infrastructure has been wrecked, all schools are closed and 20 years of hard work lie ruined in mud. The overstretched United Nations High Commission for Refugees is trying to respond, but special assistance is clearly needed at once. We look to the Minister to reassure us that it is being provided.

The Question tabled by the noble Earl refers to Africa as a whole. The cost of failure to resolve or forestall conflict in that continent has been horrendous. The accumulated evidence of the Horn, Somalia, Sudan, Mozambique, Liberia, Angola and, indeed, little Gambia is grim. Surely the inescapable lesson is that, as in the Western Sahara, the priority must be to address the causes of conflict and to act in time.

We have been reminded that in Rwanda, for example, there was no shortage of warnings. As one of the five permanent members of the Security Council, we must take very seriously our share of the responsibility for the failure to take pre-emptive action on the basis of the special rapporteur's report and, when conflict erupted, for the failure of the wider world to provide troops or even to provide sufficient logistic support in time to back up the African troops who had been offered. In other words, the issue was a lack of will.

In a age of revolutionised communications, with so much more information available, the predominance of reactive diplomacy is a sad commentary on political culture. It is all too often not a matter of whether the international community will intervene but of when it will be compelled to intervene—probably too late, at greatest expense and when least can be achieved. Repeatedly we cobble together the resources—far from sufficient—for the UNHCR to meet the latest refugee crisis; but how much do we spend on preventing the crisis developing in the first place? We agonise about GATT and the need to expand world trade; but how often do we count the cost to world trade of the failure to prevent conflict?

Governments speak of pre-emptive diplomacy—and, as was pointed out by the noble Viscount, Lord Waverley, the Secretary of State when he addressed the UN General Assembly spoke of his intentions to promote this in Africa—but what in the Government's thinking really is the priority for pre-emptive diplomacy? According to the latest's estimates, annual global military expenditure is of the order of 1,000 billion US dollars. The total annual UN peace-keeping budget, inadequately struggling to cope with failure, is by comparison only some 3.6 billion US dollars. But resources for pre-emptive diplomacy and conflict resolution barely register in the shadow of the these incredible figures. The Government like to claim a radical sense of purpose. Real radicalism in foreign affairs cannot leave these skewed priorities unaddressed.

In the African context this very day the world's attention, led by the Security Council, on which the UK is so determined to serve, should, for example, be tirelessly focused on Kenya, with all its sinister, incipient violence and cynical manipulation of ethnic differences—its disappearances, assassinations, hundreds of documented cases of police torture, judges directed by government, the media intimidated, MPs needing permits to hold political meetings and 36 of the 85 Opposition MPs gaoled in 1993 for varying periods of time. Those facts were all admirably rehearsed in the Queen's Speech debate in the other place.

Attention should similarly be focused on Zaire and Nigeria, where there have been 24 years of military dictatorship and denial of human rights and where, as tension mounts, the United Kingdom still inexplicably and dangerously maintains its arms supplies to the regime, including, significantly, Vickers battle tanks. It does that despite the European Union's curbs on arms sales and IMF anxiety about the level of arms expenditure by the Nigerian regime.

Attention should also be given urgently to the renewed dangers in Rwanda demonstrated in the refugee camps, where an international police force is urgently required, and to the dangers in Burundi where the failure of the international community to provide the number of monitors called for by the UN Commissioner for Human Rights and many non-governmental organisations is frankly a disgrace, not least when the cost of not supplying them may well yet prove to be disastrous by comparison.

As I emphasised in the debate on the Queen's Speech, it is lamentable that, with all the talk of the importance of good governance, democracy and human rights, we have appeared impotent in the face of the wanton destruction of democracy in little Gambia by a handful of ambitious, power-hungry army officers.

In the debate on the Queen's Speech, my noble friend Lady Blackstone called for an early debate on pre-emptive diplomacy and the reform of the UN system. The question raised by the noble Earl today and the significant and thoughtful contribution by the noble Lord, Lord Redesdale, underline the importance of that proposal. Apart from the case for a rapid deployment force at the disposal of the Security Council and the Secretary-General to contain situations before they escalate out of control, the case for earmarked stand-by forces in member countries of the UN to be called up by the Security Council and Secretary-General when required, and the case for a proper, responsible system of financing UN peace-keeping operations, there is the crucially important issue of establishing clear guidelines and principles for UN pre-emptive intervention, let alone military action.

Recent history has been a disturbing story of tardy arbitrariness. The debate for which my noble friend called will, I suggest, need to examine arrangements for petitioning the international community by groups at risk; for early warning; for the use of the specialist knowledge and insight of non-governmental organisations, academics and other similar sources without—a vital point—compromising their ability to act as genuinely independent impartial agents. It will need to consider whether an office for preventive diplomacy, preferably on the 38th floor of the UN, might have a powerful part to play. It should look at experience of sanctions and how in future they might be better targeted and refined to achieve their objectives with minimum adverse effect on the innocent. It would be sensible too to review the contribution of safe havens.

The debate will not be able to dodge the issue of the arms trade—the crude fuel of armed conflict—the degree to which it is exploited ruthlessly by immoral profiteers and merchants of death and, equally significant, the degree to which large numbers of decent people in otherwise civilised countries have, through no fault of their own, become dependent, together with their national economies, on arms manufacture and exports. I hope that the debate will grapple with how, in the name of humanity, governments can together make the arms trade more accountable and transparent and how they can together work at massive programmes of substitution for arms manufacture.

Meanwhile, one astounding and profoundly worrying statistic cannot be too often repeated; namely, that almost 90 per cent. of the arms sold to the third world are sold by the permanent five members of the Security Council. Above all, however, in Africa, as the noble Viscount, Lord Waverley, suggested in his powerful contribution, we must never overlook the reality that among the root causes of conflict have been the problems of land distribution, grinding poverty, debt, adverse terms of trade and insensitive economic restructuring demanded by wealthy nations of the world. In that respect Rwanda's story was far more complex than just ethnic conflict alone.

With all that in mind, latest budget indications for the future of the aid programme, when aid is already at an all-time low as a percentage of gross national product, are candidly depressing. With his unrivalled insight into the Western Sahara, the noble Earl has helped to demonstrate today that viewed from another galaxy the priorities of humankind are indefensible. Indeed, we prepare like giants for war and like pygmies for peace.

I cannot say often enough that the Minister is personally a genuine humanitarian. I have no doubt that she will convince us of that once more this evening. On all sides of the House we must work with her to build a strategy to transform the myopic preoccupations of government so that rationality is asserted, so that we think ahead and so that we free ourselves from the horrific consequences of fatalism. Nowhere is that more important than in our policy towards Africa. The story of the Western Sahara is all too symptomatic of the absence of commitment to effective global governance.

4.25 p.m.

The Minister of State, Foreign and Commonwealth Office (Baroness Chalker of Wallasey): My Lords, I begin by congratulating the noble Earl, Lord Winchilsea and Nottingham, on choosing this subject for debate. He is absolutely right to say that it is often forgotten. But it is certainly not forgotten by the Foreign Office and the ODA, as I hope to demonstrate, despite the fact that he was critical of me, as is his right.

However, at the beginning I wish to say to your Lordships that we must be realistic in what we demand of the United Nations and in what can happen. I am beginning to believe that there are some parts of the world where people, quite frankly, do not want to stop fighting, whatever is done by others outside those groups. The sufferers are the women and children and some of the men who genuinely do not wish to fight.

Therefore, let us have a reality about the situation before we get into the "something should be done" mode, which is all too easy to do. However, we must find out what will be appropriate and what will work at a reasonable cost. When I say "a reasonable cost", I mean that I am not unwilling to spend money on peacekeeping; in fact, I am extremely willing to spend money on conflict prevention and resolution. But let us understand that sometimes the costs that will be put

[BARONESS CHALKER OF WALLASEY]
upon the giving nations, which may still be thrown back in their faces by the warring nations, may be too great for the giving nations to continue providing. We need to have that very firmly in our minds.

The noble Earl's remarks concentrated almost entirely on the subject of the Western Sahara, and I shall spend most of my speech dealing with that. However, I assure your Lordships that at no time has the United Kingdom played anything but a thoroughly active role in the United Nations Security Council's discussions on conflict resolution and prevention. The noble Viscount, Lord Waverley, mentioned that, following my right honourable friend the Prime Minister's speech in Cape Town in September, the Foreign Secretary, when he addressed the General Assembly, encouraged the international community, working with the Organisation of African Unity and the United Nations, to set up a structure of support systems running from early warning and preventive diplomacy through to humanitarian and peacekeeping deployments on the ground. I shall return to the detail of how that has been received and taken forward in a few moments.

First, I turn to the Western Sahara with regard to which I have more sympathy for the plight of the people who are suffering so greatly than perhaps the noble Earl realises. We have supported the United Nations Secretary-General's efforts, especially through the UN Mission for the Referendum in Western Sahara—that is MINURSO, to which your Lordships referred—in order to secure implementation of the settlement plan agreed by the parties on 30th August 1988. Your Lordships may say that that is a long while ago but the problem has always been achieving the acceptance of all the parties to the necessary measures to bring about that referendum. I shall update the House on that in a few moments.

There are some 300 military and police observers in the UN mission at present, but there have been very regrettable delays in implementing the plan. There have also been grave difficulties in securing the agreement of the parties to hold the referendum. In August this year, the process of identifying those who have registered to vote in the referendum was launched. We have been monitoring very carefully what has been going on since that process was launched.

Perhaps I may make two observations about the referendum. First, we attach considerable importance to the speedy resolution of all the remaining obstacles and to holding that referendum on the future of the territory as soon as possible. We have repeatedly urged all parties to co-operate in that aim. We were most disappointed that the parties have allowed the latest timetable to slip. We hope that further delays will not occur, although from some news I received just before coming into the Chamber, it seems that that may be in vain.

As one of the Security Council's Group of Friends of the Western Sahara, we have sought to facilitate the UN's preparations for the referendum. It is, therefore, of prime importance that the procedures are hastened along. Before I came into the Chamber today, I was told that the referendum will be held in 1995. However, we are now told that it may not be held until the summer for one good reason in the eyes of the UN Secretary-General, Dr. Boutros Boutros-Ghali. He is quoted as saying last Thursday that the referendum planned first for January 1992, and then later postponed to February 1995, will be organised next summer because he wants 20 new bureaux to speed up the population registration in order to end the conflict. That has much to do with the very notable anxiety about last-minute Moroccan voter applications, about which the noble Earl and other noble Lords spoke.

We are seeking to ensure that the UN's identification commission has sufficient manpower to be able to identify all those who have applied for inclusion on the voter list for the referendum, including those whose applications were only submitted by Morocco shortly before the deadline of 25th October. I believe that to be the reason for the requirement of 20 extra bureaux to be opened in addition to the two already in operation in Laayoune and in Tindouf in south-western Algeria where so many of the Western Saharan people are at present in camps. That has come about since Dr. Boutros Boutros-Ghali toured the area last month and is being done in an effort to ensure that all those who should vote are, indeed, registered to vote.

It is not just a question of solving the problems of the election. My noble friend Lord Wise asked me about the future of MINURSO, knowing that it had been considered last March by the Security Council. We believe that it should continue; but, of course, Security Council Resolution 907 said that if the referendum was not held by the end of this year, the future of MINURSO would have to be reconsidered. Since the Secretary-General visited the area, we can now see things in a new light. There is certainly no discussion at present about disbanding MINURSO, and there is the statement about the requirement of 20 new stations to help the registration for the elections. Therefore, I sincerely hope that MINURSO will continue up to the election, but what happens at that point must be a matter for the Security Council.

The noble Earl also asked me about human rights. The noble Lord, Lord Judd, made the point that there have been human rights abuses on all sides, if one may put it that way. I sometimes think that this is not a two-sided contest. We certainly raise human rights issues regularly, whether it be with the Moroccans or with others. In June this year, the Moroccan human rights Minister came to the United Kingdom as a guest of the Foreign and Commonwealth Office. My right honourable friend in another place, Mr. Hogg, and human rights organisations, such as Amnesty International, met with him. I believe that that was a valuable step forward; indeed, it was something that had never happened before. It was part of our attempt to improve human rights in that area.

We also know that it is not only human rights which are of concern: it is a fact that there have been some further unauthorised troop movements, though not normally anything as serious as was intimated by the noble Earl in terms of a cease-fire violation. Nevertheless, there is no doubt that where there is no stability—and that is what we are really talking about—there is plenty of room for troublemaking, however it occurs.

We have a situation where we are looking towards a referendum next year and where the United Nations is, under quite difficult circumstances, doing its best to help achieve that aim. I know that the noble Earl is disappointed that I have not responded to his requests to put direct help into the area, as set out in a number of letters which I have recently received from him. But there is a very good reason why that has not happened. It is because we are contributing through an already well set-up and running organisation within UNHCR which has earmarked 4 million dollars this current year for assistance to Western Saharan refugees, with a further 4 million dollars allocated for next year. We have made inquiries and they lead us to believe that there is not a need for further resources, but that there may be a need for better organisation. Certainly, the Department of Humanitarian Affairs has airlifted emergency supplies to the camps and provided money for local relief goods purchases following the tragic floods.

If there were a need for further assistance, I would, of course, look into the matter. However, I am told on reliable evidence from those who assess such matters that the current assessment is that we are giving—indeed, as we always have—our full due. We shall continue to do so and, if there is a need for more, I shall be the first to be willing to look at it. I have seen too many disasters in too many parts of the world ever to be able to turn away when there is real need. I believe that your Lordships are aware of that fact.

The debate widened very considerably, especially with the contribution made by the noble Lord, Lord Judd. It seemed to me that the noble Lord was trying, quietly, to get in on the back of the noble Earl's Unstarred Question and have that general debate that his noble friend Lady Blackstone was calling for about two weeks ago. But I now gather that the joy of that debate still awaits us. However, perhaps I may turn to the more general points that were raised by the noble Viscount, Lord Waverley, and the noble Lords, Lord Redesdale and Lord Judd. I shall deal, first, with the more general points about the United Nations as a whole.

As I said earlier, we have been playing a very full part in the United Nations, both in the Security Council and in all the General Assembly work. We have examined most carefully all the ideas that have been put to us. One of the things that I can say to the noble Lord, Lord Redesdale, without fear of any contradiction is that Her Majesty's Government have always paid their contributions to the UN on time and in full. I wish that I could say the same for other member states, because we are regularly urging others to do likewise. We have certainly never run away from those responsibilities; nor, indeed, shall we.

However, one of the things that we are careful not to do is to rush into every idea when it is promoted without having examined it very thoroughly. For a very long while I have advocated that the United Nations needs to do more in the field of conflict prevention and conflict resolution. It is for that reason that we have been looking for ways of actually operating in that mode, particularly in Africa where so many of the conflicts seem to take place these days.

The idea which has been around for a long while of the United Nations standby forces has not found support among the United Nations' member states. That may be, as the noble Lord, Lord Judd, intimated, due to the question of funding and the fact that there has not been a serious review of the finance to support the jobs within the United Nations. As yet we see no sign of that happening quickly.

One of the reasons why the idea of standby forces has not found support is that peace-keeping operations vary so greatly in type, scope, size and the training required that it has not been thought possible to train contingents literally for any eventuality.

It has been with that very much in mind that my right honourable friends have been discussing what more could be done to prevent the conflicts in Africa which the noble Viscount, Lord Waverley, and the noble Lords, Lord Redesdale and Lord Judd, described. I agree with the noble Viscount when he says that it is critical to involve the Africans in conflict prevention and resolution. Frankly, if one does not have support from the groups on the ground one does not succeed. One cannot impose troops, ideas or planning totally from outside. One can help and refine ideas alongside people of the nation concerned. It was for those very reasons that my right honourable friend the Prime Minister launched the initiative on African peace-keeping in Cape Town in September.

Why did we do that? We were looking for a way to get the international community to work with the United Nations and the Organisation of African Unity to set up a structure of support systems which would run from early warning, through preventive diplomacy and on to humanitarian peace-keeping and deployment on the ground, as I said at the beginning of my reply.

We have been exchanging information readily with fellow donor nations to see what is possible. In some part that answers the question of the noble Viscount, Lord Waverley. Our objective is a system which works effectively at three levels. The first level would be an early warning system. This would be directed at potential trouble spots in order to decide whether preventive diplomacy needs to be triggered.

The second level would be an institutional framework of preventive diplomacy which would allow the UN and the OAU to provide, together, experienced personnel, equipment and other support which would bolster the diplomatic efforts to prevent conflict breaking out.

The third level of action would be the development of the peace-keeping capabilities themselves. We envisage that being done through the establishment of peace-keeping skill centres at African staff colleges, through the creation of UN logistics centres in Africa, and some rapid mobile logistics teams which would help to maintain equipment. A great many of the problems which arise in any of those tasks relate to the need to have equipment ready to move and to use. It is so often out of date or badly maintained. The final part of that

[BARONESS CHALKER OF WALLASEY]
capability would be the creation of a UN sub-regional support centre whose staff could identify and help to remedy the logistic weaknesses which so often occur.

Were there time I could go through all the countries named by the noble Lord, Lord Judd, and talk through the logistic weaknesses, the diplomacy failures and so on. I shall not take your Lordships' time today, but I shall tell your Lordships that the British ideas have been very well received in the UN and OAU. African countries have welcomed them as a practical contribution to enhancing peace-keeping capabilities. Our ideas have also been welcomed by our European partners.

In view of that welcome we decided to hold expert level discussions on our proposals in Accra in Ghana on 14th and 15th November with the African countries, the UN and the OAU. We reached agreement there on the priority areas of early warning, preventive diplomacy and peace-keeping. We are now working further on the detail of those proposals and how best to translate them into practical action on the ground. The next step in that process will be a workshop to be held in Cairo in January.

We are moving forward with the ideas. Perhaps I may say to the noble Viscount, Lord Waverley, that those ideas have very much more backing than anything that has come from any single nation, even the one he mentioned, which might have had an idea which initially found favour in that country.

There are some tragic and preventable situations. There are others which, sadly, are less preventable because people are determined to fight and not to talk peace. That is why the type of comprehensive approach that I have just outlined, with the support of many of the neighbours of those nations which have so many problems, be it in Africa or elsewhere, is important.

I can assure your Lordships that whether it be Rwanda, Angola, Somalia, Nigeria, Ghana or Sierra Leone—and I can make a long list—we keep a watch, day by day, on each of those countries to see when and where we should intervene. There will never be any hesitation if we can do something to prevent conflict breaking out or to help resolve conflict when it has broken out. The United Kingdom will be there.

That is why I can pay a real tribute to Mozambique. Although the situation was rather touch and go towards the end of the election, I am proud to say that the British Ambassador and his staff in Mozambique worked literally day and night to help make sure that the situation was resolved satisfactorily. That is an example of both conflict resolution and conflict prevention for the future.

It is by means of that type of engagement, which we hope we shall see before long in Angola, that we shall create a greater peace in the African continent and elsewhere. But we shall do that only if we lead strongly and thoughtfully and persuade others to follow. That is exactly what we are trying to do.

House adjourned thirteen minutes before five o'clock.

Written Answers

Monday 5th December 1994

EUROPEAN UNION COUNCIL MEETINGS

Lord Brougham and Vaux asked Her Majesty's Government:

What will be the forthcoming business in the Council of the European Union.

The Minister of State, Foreign and Commonwealth Office (Baroness Chalker of Wallasey): Justice and Home Affairs and Research Councils were held on 30th November and 1st December.

The following meetings are planned:

Date	
5th December	ECOFIN, Education
6th December	Social Affairs
8th December	Internal Market
8th December	Consumer Affairs
9th December	European Council, Essen
10th December	European Council Essen
12th December	Agriculture
13th December	Agriculture
15th December	ECOFIN meeting not yet confirmed
15th December	Environment
16th December	Environment
19th December	FAC, Fisheries
20th December	FAC, Fisheries
22nd December	Health

The following subjects were discussed

30th November to 1st December: Justice and Home Affairs Council

Agenda:

—Adoption of the agenda

—Approval of the list of "A" items

—Presidency progress report on the draft convention on the establishment of Europol

—EDU/Europol staff

—Presidency report to the Council on burden-sharing with regard to the admission and residence of displaced persons. — Draft common measure on travel facilities for third country nationals (school pupils resident in a member state)

—Draft resolution on minimum guarantees for asylum procedures

—Presidency progress report to the Council on the proposal for a Council regulation laying down a uniform format for visas.

—Draft Council resolution on the further improvement in security at external borders

—Draft resolution on the admission of third country nationals to the territory of member states of the European Union for study purposes

—Draft Council resolution relating to limitations on the admission of third country nationals to the territory of the member states for the purposes of pursuing activities as self-employed persons

—1994 Budget—draft Council decision on a joint action concerning co-operation measures to be taken in the JHA sector.

—Relations with Cyprus and Malta

—Implementation of the Berlin declaration of 8 September 1994.

—Draft interim report on combating racism and xenophobia.

—Draft interim report on co-operation in the campaign against international organised crime

—Report and draft resolution on protection of the financial interests of the Communities

—Draft convention to improve extradition between the member states of the European Union

—Draft convention on jurisdiction and the enforcement of judgments in matrimonial matters (Brussels 11 convention)

—Draft convention on insolvency proceedings

—Draft report to the European Council on the implementation of the December 1993 action plan in the JHA field. —Other Business—

1st December: Research Council

Agenda:

—Adoption of 10 specific research programmes

—Council conclusions on future work of CREST

—Commission presentation of its communication on Research Co-ordination

The following subjects are likely to be discussed:

5th December ECOFIN

—White paper follow up

—Report on implementation of broad economic guidelines and multilateral surveillance

—Fraud

—Financial perspectives

—Macro economic assistance to third countries

—Taxation of savings

—Bio-fuels

—CO_2 tax

5th December: Education

—Adoption of agenda

—Adoption of the list of "A" points

—Decision establishing the Community Action Programme Socrates

—Decision establishing a European Year of Education and Training

—The quality and attractiveness of vocational education and training.

—The promotion of education and training statistics in the European Union
—Negotiations on EC/United States and EC/Canada agreements in the field of higher education and training
—Co-operation in the field of education with the associated countries of Central and Eastern Europe and with the Russian Federation.
—Education aspects of a European Union overall strategy against racism and xenophobia
—White paper on growth, competitiveness and employment

6th December: Social Affairs

—Adoption of agenda
—Adoption of the list of "A" points
—Draft directive on posted workers
—Draft directive on part-time work and fixed term employment relations and draft resolution on social security
—Commission report on employment (preparation for the Essen European Council)
—Draft decision on the Leonardo Vocational Training programme
—White paper on European social policy—political debate.—Draft resolution on social policy in the European Union.—Draft resolution on women and employment.
—Draft decision on the continuation of the handynet system.—Application of regulation 1408/71 EEC (social security for migrant workers) to posted workers—note from the Belgian delegation
—AOB

8th December: Consumer Affairs Council

—Unit pricing
—Commission Green Paper on access to justice and consumer guarantees
—Product labelling
—Distance selling

8th December: Internal Market Council

Agenda (including possible "A" points)

—Functioning of the Internal Market
—Legislative and administrative simplification
—Information procedure
—Cross-border payments
—Information society
—Data protection directive
—Legal protection of databases
—Community patents
—Pension funds
—External trade statistics (possible "A" point)
—Counterfeit goods regulation (possible)
—Mutual assistance in customs and agricultural matters (possible)
—European medicines evaluation agency fees regulation.—Food additives directive
—New foodstuffs and ingredients
—Flavourings
—Foodlabelling
—Irradiated foodstuffs
—Motor vehicle flammability (possible "A" point)
—"Multipurpose directive" on two and three-wheeled vehicles (possible "A" point for particular common position).—Marketing and use of dangerous substances: fourteenth (formerly thirteenth) amendment (false "B" point).—Measuring instrument
—Novel foods
—Flavouring
—Food labelling
—Miscellaneous food additives

9th to 10th December: European Council Essen

Agenda not available

12th to 13th December: Agriculture

—Wine regime
—GATT
—CAP simplification
—Agrimoney
—Durum wheat and oilseeds (possible)
—Aid for private storage in Norway, Finland and Austria (possible)
—Deseasonalisation premium for beef (possible)
—Sugar
—Fresh meat directive
—Mince meat directive
—BST
—Animal welfare in transport (possible)
—List of third country establishment (possible)
—Inspection fee (possible)

15th to 16th December: Environment

Agenda not available

19th to 20th December: Fisheries

—FACs and quotas
—NAFO
—French Guyana
—Annual fisheries agreement with:
    —Iceland
    —Greenland
    —Norway
    —Sweden
    —Baltic States
    —Faroes

—Annual Spanish and Portuguese control regulations—Spanish and Portugese accession review (possible)

22nd December: Health

Agenda not available

OVERSEAS STUDENTS

Lord Brougham and Vaux asked Her Majesty's Government.

How many overseas students are now studying in the United Kingdom in the higher and further education sectors compared to the numbers before the introduction of full cost fees in 1980; how many overseas students are currently benefiting from government scholarships; and how the United Kingdom's record on receiving overseas students compares to that of other countries.

Baroness Chalker of Wallasey: The numbers of overseas student studying in the United Kingdom in both the higher and further education sectors in 1979–80 was some 83,000. The number in 1992–93 was 99,700 an all-time high. In 1993–94, 21,000 students from overseas studying in the United Kingdom were benefiting from official support under a variety of British Government scholarship and award programmes. These included 3,043 students holding British Chevening Scholarships funded by the Foreign and Commonwealth Office.

According to available figures the United Kingdom is fourth in the global league table of countries receiving overseas students with 92,000, against the United States (420,000), France (136,000) and Germany (100,000).

PENGAU DAM JUDGMENT: REVIEW OF ODA ACTIVITIES

Lord Molloy asked Her Majesty's Government:

Which policy and administrative procedures they will examine in the light of the High Court judgment concerning the Pergau Dam; and to what extent.

Baroness Chalker of Wallasey: The terms of the review I advised the House of on 17th November are to examine all ODA activities that fall under Section 1 of the 1980 Overseas Development and Co-operation Act in the light of the interpretation of the Act given in the Pergau judgment by the High Court. In particular the review will consider whether any other current activities fall outside the Act as now interpreted.

BOSNIAN: ARMS EMBARGO

Whether to their knowledge, before the US unilateral defection from the UN embargo, the United States has been advising and/or training Bosnian Croat and Bosnian Muslim military.

Baroness Chalker of Wallasey: The United States Government have categorically assured us that they have not supplied military assistance or training to the Bosnian Government. They have also reiterated that they will continue to comply with the arms embargo under United Nations Security Council Resolution 713.

Lord Kennet asked Her Majesty's Government:

Whether they have any evidence of the embargo on the passing of weapons to the parties fighting in Bosnia having been breached before the United States unilateral defection from the United Nations embargo, through Croatia or by unidentified air drops, and if so have these weapons been provided, or with the connivance or the approval of, elements of the United States Administration.

Baroness Chalker of Wallasey: We are aware that there have been breaches of the United Nations arms embargo in the former Yugoslavia. The United Kingdom attaches importance to such breaches being reported to the United Nations Sanctions Committee. The United States Government have categorically assured us that they have not supplied arms to the Bosnian Government.

NATO COMMANDER, SOUTHERN EUROPE

Lord Kennet asked Her Majesty's Government:

What forces other than NATO the United States Admiral in Naples who is NATO Commander, Southern Europe has under his command in the Mediterranean area, including Albania, the Middle East and the Gulf; what collaboration there is between his two roles; and what happens when he gets conflicting orders from the United States Commander in Chief and from the NATO Council.

Baroness Chalker of Wallasey: Apart from NATO-assigned forces, the NATO commander in Naples, CINCSOUTH, also has command over all United States ships in Europe. He has delegated his command over United States ships in the Gulf to the regional commander there. He has no command over land or air forces other than those assigned to NATO.

There is no conflict between CINCSOUTH's two roles as United States and NATO commander. In order to avoid any potential conflict in the context of the NATO/WEU arms embargo enforcement operation in the Adriatic (Operation Sharp Guard), the United States President issued a directive that all United States officers in NATO command posts should give priority to NATO orders.

FORMER YUGOSLAVIA: BORDER CHANGES

Lord Kennet asked Her Majesty's Government:

Whether in their view the frontiers of Yugoslavia were varied by the "genuine consent" of all the parties concerned, as required by CSCE provisions; whether those parties included the Government of Yugoslavia; and if not why were the frontiers changed and at whose insistence.

Baroness Chalker of Wallasey: The dissolution of the former Federal Republic of Yugoslavia was not accompanied by changes in its external or internal borders. Any possible future adjustments will require agreement of all the parties.

GENERAL GALVIN'S VISIT TO YUGOSLAVIA

Lord Kennet asked Her Majesty's Government:

Whether the United States informed the Contact Group that a group of US military officers under General Galvin was to visit Yugoslavia to secure better political co-operation between Bosnian Croats and Bosnian Muslims.

Baroness Chalker of Wallasey: The United States Government informed us and other interested countries that General Galvin's visit was part of their effort to support the Bosnian Federation established by the Washington Agreement. We support this objective.

EUROPEAN COMMUNITIES ACT 1972: DESIGNATION ORDERS

Lord Skelmersdale asked Her Majesty's Government:

How many designation orders made under Section 2(2) of the European Communities Act 1972 have been revoked.

Baroness Chalker of Wallasey: None.

Lord Skelmersdale asked Her Majesty's Government:

How many designation orders have been made under section 2(2) of the European Communities Act 1972.

Baroness Chalker of Wallasey: Forty-seven.

CONGRESSIONAL HEARINGS: REQUESTS FOR RECORDS

Lord Braine of Wheatley asked Her Majesty's Government:

Whether they will seek to obtain from the United States Congress, and place in the Library of the House, a copy of the hearings held during the 95th Congress by the Senate Judiciary Committee on SJ Res 134;

Whether they will seek to obtain from the United States Congress, and place in the Library of the House, House Report 95–1405;

Whether they will seek to obtain from the United States Congress, and place in the Library of the House, a copy of the hearing held on 31 March 1981 during the 97th Congress by the Senate Labor and Human Resources Committee on Oversight of Family Planning Programs, 1981; and

Whether they will seek to obtain from the United States Congress, and place in the Library of the House, copies of the hearings Serial No 97–16; Serial No 98–52; Serial No 98–121 held by the Sub Committee on Health and the Environment of the Energy and Commerce Committee; and

Whether they will seek to obtain from the United States Congress, and place in the Library of the House, copies of the hearings held during the 97th Congress by the Senate Labor and Human Resources Sub Committee on Ageing, Family and Human Services on Oversight on Family Planning Programs under Title X of the Public Health Service Act, 1981.

Baroness Chalker of Wallasey: The British Embassy in Washington is in touch with the Library of Congress about the availability of these documents. I shall write to the noble Lord about this.

POPULATION AND DEVELOPMENT CONFERENCE: UNITED KINGDOM REPRESENTATIVES

Lord Braine of Wheatley asked Her Majesty's Government:

Whether they will publish in the *Official Report* a list of those delegates attending the International Conference on Population in Cairo who represented Great Britain and the United States.

Baroness Chalker of Wallasey: The United Kingdom Delegation's report, a copy of which has been placed in the Libraries of the House, contains details of those attending the International Conference on Population and Development from the United Kingdom. We do not have details of the delegation from the United States.

POPULATION AND DEVELOPMENT CONFERENCE: POPULATION CONTROL IN CHINA

Lord Braine of Wheatley asked Her Majesty's Government:

What discussions they had about the Chinese population control with representatives of the International Planned Parenthood Federation and United Nations Fund for Population Activities at the International Conference on Population in Cairo; and with what results.

Baroness Chalker of Wallasey: Officials met with staff from the International Planned Parenthood Federation and the United Nations Population Fund at the International Conference on Population and Development and continue to have dialogue with these two organisations. Both organisations remain committed to promoting better reproductive health care and free choice.

Lord Braine of Wheatley asked Her Majesty's Government:

Whether they will place in the Library of the House copies of reports on population control in china received by them from the International Planned Parenthood Federation and United Nations Fund for Population Activities.

Baroness Chalker of Wallasey: Copies of the United Nations Population Fund (UNFPA) 1993 Inventory of Population Projects and the International Planned Parenthood Federation (IPPF) 1994 Annual Report Supplement, together with a copy of China's National Report to the International Conference on Population and Development, have been placed in the Libraries of the House.

PREVENTION OF TERRORISM ACT EXCLUSION PROVISIONS: ECJ JURISDICTION

Lord Tebbit asked Her Majesty's Government:

The European Court of Justice has any jurisdiction in the matter of the banning of persons from the mainland of the United Kingdom under the provisions of the Prevention of Terrorism Act.

The Minister of State, Home Office (Baroness Blatch): The European Court of Justice is charged under the Treaty on European Union with the duty of ensuring that Community law is interpreted and applied correctly. The Treaty has, from the outset, provided certain rights of free movement to nationals of member states subject to limitations which may be justified on grounds, *inter alia*, of public security. Consequently the question of whether the exclusion provisions in the Prevention of Terrorism Act are compatible with Community law is one which the European Court may have jurisdiction to resolve in certain circumstances. If, for example, any person considered that their rights had been infringed by the making of an exclusion order, they could apply for judicial review of the order in the High Court. If the High Court considered it necessary to enable it to give judgement, it could seek a preliminary ruling from the European Court on the interpretation of the Treaty or of acts of the institutions of the Community. The High Court would then have to resolve the issues before it in the light of the European Court's ruling.

DANGEROUS DOGS ACT 1991: DETENTION COSTS

Lord Harris of Greenwich asked Her Majesty's Government:

What was the cost to the Receiver of the Metropolitan Police District in the last two financial years of causing dogs to be detained as a result of proceedings under the Dangerous Dogs Act 1991; and what is the estimated cost in the current financial year.

Baroness Blatch: The costs to the Receiver for the Metropolitan Police District of detaining dogs as a result of proceedings under the Dangerous Dogs Act 1991 are as follows:

	£ million
1992–93	1.3
1993–94	0.85
1994–95	[1]0.7

[1] estimated costs

COMMUNITY CHARGE RECOVERED FROM INCOME SUPPORT RECIPIENTS

Earl Russell asked Her Majesty's Government:

How many Income Support recipients in 1993–94 were subject to deductions for arrears of community charge, how much money was recovered, what was the average amount recovered per claimant, what was the cost of collecting this money, and under what head in the Appropriation Accounts these transactions are recorded.

The Minister of State, Department of Social Security (Lord Mackay of Ardbrecknish): The information is not available in the form suggested. Available information follows:

The number of Income Support recipients in 1993–94 who were subject to deductions for arrears of community charge was 533,000 (source, the *Quarterly Statistical Enquiry*. February 1994).

Statistics on the amount of money and the average amount recovered can only be obtained at disproportionate cost. However, the following table gives the average amount of deduction:

	Number with Community Charge Deduction (for arrears)	Average amount of Deduction
May 1993	438,000	2.28
August 1993	506,000	2.28
November 1993	519,000	2.28
February	533,000	2.27

Source: Income Support Annual Enquiry—May 1993, Income Support Quarterly Statistical Enquiry—August 1993, November 1993 and February 1994.

The Benefits Agency deducts standard weekly amounts from a person's Income Support. These are: £3.45, higher rate, where a joint and several liability order has been obtained by the local authority for a couple and £2.20, lower rate, where a single liability order has been obtained. The averages are different to these figures because the Community Charge debt will not necessarily be exactly divisible by the standard amount.

The cost of collecting community charge deductions from Income Support claimants is on average £14 per claimant.

These transactions are not recorded in the Appropriation Accounts as they have no consequences for the department.

DISABILITY WORKING ALLOWANCE

Earl Russell asked Her Majesty's Government:

What was the estimated expenditure on Disability Working Allowance in 1993–94, what was the actual expenditure, and what is their explanation of any discrepancy.

Lord Mackay of Ardbrecknish: The Government's planned expenditure for Disability Working Allowance was £10 million[1] in 1993-1994. The actual expenditure was £7.2 million[2]. This discrepancy is due to the fact that Disability Working Allowance is a new benefit and forecasts were inevitably tentative.

Source:
[1] Social Security Departmental Report published in March 1994.

[2]Appropriation Accounts 1993–94 (Class XIII, Vote 1 Central Government administered Social Security benefits and other payments) published in October 1994.

COMPENSATION RECOVERY SCHEME

Earl Russell asked Her Majesty's Government:

How many people are employed in the Compensation Recovery Unit of the Department of Social Security, and what are its administrative costs.

Lord Mackay of Ardbrecknish: This is a matter for Michael Bichard, the Chief Executive of the Benefits Agency. He will write to the noble Lord with such information as is available.

Letter to Earl Russell from the Chief Executive of the Benefits Agency, Mr. Michael Bichard, dated 5th December 1994:

The Secretary of State for Social Security has asked me to reply to your recent parliamentary Question asking how many people are employed in the Compensation Recovery Unit and what are its administrative costs.

The total number of people employed in the Compensation Recovery Unit at the present time is 189; this figure includes 44 part-time staff.

The administrative costs for the period 1 April 1993 to 31 March 1994 were £2.7 and for the current year, from 1 April 1994 to 31 October 1994, the costs are £1.7 million.

I hope you find this reply helpful.

COMMON AGRICULTURAL POLICY REFORM: EC REPORT

Lord Gainford asked Her Majesty's Government:

Whether they will place a copy of the European Commission's report on reform of the common agricultural Policy in the Library.

The Parliamentary Secretary, Ministry of Agriculture, Fisheries and Food (Earl Howe): This report, entitled *EC Agriculture in the 21st Century*, has now been published in the journal *European Economy* on behalf of the European Commission's Directorate-General II (Economy and Finance). Copies have been placed in the Library.

The Government welcome the Commission's decision to publish this radical look at the common agricultural policy and we shall be studying it with interest.

MILK QUOTA FRAUD: PENALTY PAYMENTS BY ITALY

Lord Tebbit asked Her Majesty's Government:

Whether the Italian Government has yet paid the penalties agreed in respect of the Italian milk quota fraud.

Earl Howe: These penalties are collected by automatic deductions from the monthly re-imbursements of CAP expenditure. Italy has paid the penalties originally imposed by the Commission in respect of 1989 and 1990. The Commission's decision in respect of the 1991 clearance of accounts was in the process of being adopted at the time of the agreement reached at the ECOFIN Council in October. Under this agreement, the financial penalties in respect of 1989 to 1991 have been increased. It has been agreed that these supplementary fines will be paid in four equal instalments from 1995 to 1998. The remainder of the financial penalty for 1991 in respect of milk quotas will be paid in 1995. The 1992 and 1993 clearance of accounts decisions have not yet been adopted, but will incorporate the financial penalties in respect of milk quota.

POLLUTION CONTROL SCHEME: FURTHER FEE CHANGE

Lord Gainford asked Her Majesty's Government:

Whether a further change is to be made to the scheme of fees and charges for integrated pollution control operated by Her Majesty's Inspectorate of Pollution.

The Minister of State, Department of the Environment (Viscount Ullswater): A minor change to the HMIP Integrated Pollution Control Fees and Charges Scheme 1994–95 is to take effect retrospectively from 1st June 1994. It introduces a provisional application fee of £0.00 for a number of processes included under IPC by the Environmental Protection (Prescribed Processes and Substances) Regulations, pending further consultation on possible amendment to those regulations.

Copies of the amendment to the scheme are being placed in the Libraries of both Houses.

ISBN 0-10-701095-X

Vol. 559
No. 11

Tuesday
6 December 1994

PARLIAMENTARY DEBATES
(HANSARD)

HOUSE OF LORDS

OFFICIAL REPORT

CONTENTS

Questions—Regent's Park: Maintenance and Development [Col. 823]
—BR Sleeper Service: Scotland-London [Col. 824]
—European Union: Environmental Legislation [Col. 826]
—Ocean Currents: Data [Col. 829]

Private International Law (Miscellaneous Provisions) Bill [H.L.]—Second Reading [Col. 830]

BBC: White Paper—Motion to Take Note [Col. 848]

Unstarred Question—South Birmingham: Hospital Services [Col. 902]

Written Answers [Col. *WA 73*]

Public Expenditure in Scotland: for Government Statement, see Official Report, Commons, 6/12/94

LONDON: HMSO
£4·20 net

Lords wishing to be supplied with these Daily Reports should give notice to this effect to the Printed Paper Office.

The bound volumes also will be sent to those Peers who similarly notify their wish to receive them.

No proofs of Daily Reports are provided. Corrections for the bound volume which Lords wish to suggest to the report of their speeches should be clearly indicated in a copy of the Daily Report, which, with the column numbers concerned shown on the front cover, should be sent to the Editor of Debates, House of Lords, within 14 days of the date of the Daily Report.

PRICES AND SUBSCRIPTION RATES

DAILY PARTS

Single copies:
Commons, £7·50; Lords £4·20

Annual subscriptions:
Commons, £1,275; Lords £615

WEEKLY HANSARD

Single copies:
Commons, £22; Lords £9·00

Annual subscriptions:
Commons, £775; Lords £310

Index—Single copies:
Commons, £6·80—published fortnightly;
Lords, £1·90—published weekly.

Annual subscriptions:
Commons, £120; Lords, £65.

LORDS CUMULATIVE INDEX obtainable on standing order only.
Details available on request.

BOUND VOLUMES OF DEBATES are issued periodically during the session.

Single copies:
Commons, £90; Lords, £68.
Standing orders will be accepted.

THE INDEX to each Bound Volume of House of Commons Debates is published separately at £9·00 and can be supplied to standing order.

WEEKLY INFORMATION BULLETIN, compiled by the House of Commons, gives details of past and forthcoming business, the work of Committees and general information on legislation, etc.
Single copies: £2·30.
Annual subscription: £88·80.

All prices are inclusive of postage.

© Parliamentary Copyright House of Lords 1994
Applications for reproduction should be made to HMSO

HMSO publications are available from:

HMSO Publications Centre
(Mail, fax and telephone orders only)
PO Box 276, London SW8 5DT
Telephone orders 0171 873 9090
General enquiries 0171 873 0011
(queueing system for both numbers in operation)
Fax orders 0171 873 8200

HMSO Bookshops
49 High Holborn, London WC1V 6HB (counter service only)
0171 873 0011 Fax 0171 831 1326
68-69 Bull Street, Birmingham B4 6AD 0121 236 9696 Fax 0121 236 9699
33 Wine Street, Bristol BS1 2BQ 0117 9264306 Fax 0117 9294515
9-21 Princess Street, Manchester M60 8AS 0161 834 7201 Fax 0161 833 0634
16 Arthur Street, Belfast BT1 4GD 01232 238451 Fax 01232 235401
71 Lothian Road, Edinburgh EH3 9AZ 0131 228 4181 Fax 0131 229 2734

The Parliamentary Bookshop
12 Bridge Street, Parliamentary Square
London SW1A 2JX
Telephone orders 0171 219 3890
General enquiries 0171 219 3890
Fax orders 0171 219 3866

HMSO's Accredited Agents
(see Yellow Pages)

and through good booksellers

Printed in England and Published by HMSO

ISBN 0 10 701195 6
ISSN 0 309-8834

House of Lords

Tuesday, 6th December 1994.

The House met at half-past two of the clock: The LORD CHANCELLOR on the Woolsack.

Prayers—Read by the Lord Bishop of Coventry.

Regent's Park: Maintenance and Development

Baroness Oppenheim-Barnes asked Her Majesty's Government:

> Whether they are satisfied with the work which has been carried out by the private companies responsible for the maintenance and development of Regent's Park.

The Parliamentary Under-Secretary of State, Department of National Heritage (Viscount Astor): My Lords, we are satisfied with the work that has been carried out by the private companies responsible for the maintenance of Regent's Park. The Royal Parks Agency was established in April 1993 to manage and police the Royal Parks. Its chief executive retains responsibility for the development of Regent's Park.

Baroness Oppenheim-Barnes: My Lords, I thank my noble friend for that reply. Is he aware that under the new management Regent's Park has been transformed? Not only are the recreational and refreshment facilities greatly improved, not only have very fine new gardens been laid out near the rose gardens, but the magnificent Avenue Gardens which are being built at present will be a tourist attraction in their own right. Is it not time that we paid tribute to the success of this policy instead of continually carping and criticising?

Viscount Astor: My Lords, I am very grateful for my noble friend's support. Regent's Park is very successful. There are 9 million visitors to the park each year, and 47 million people visit all nine Royal Parks. As my noble friend said, there have been a number of improvements, including Avenue Gardens. There are also projected improvements for the future: finishing Avenue Gardens, improvements to St. John's Lodge Gardens and the water fowl care centre.

Lord Donoughue: My Lords, will the Minister tell the House what reductions have been made in the staffing levels in the park since privatisation? Are the Government content with the levels of security which now prevail?

Viscount Astor: My Lords, the level of staff provided by the contractors is, of course, a matter for the contractors. The important issue is that they do a good job, which they are doing. The Royal Parks Agency monitors the performance of the respective contractors. As regards policing, currently 172 policemen are responsible for the Royal Parks. Twenty-five constables, three sergeants and one inspector are responsible for Regent's Park.

Lord McIntosh of Haringey: My Lords, is there any significance in the fact that in his first reply to the noble Baroness, Lady Oppenheim-Barnes, the noble Viscount repeated verbatim the wording of the Question except that he eliminated the words "and development"? In other words, he implied that the Government were not satisfied with the development work. Was that an oversight, or was it deliberate?

Viscount Astor: My Lords, I compliment the noble Lord, Lord McIntosh of Haringey, for listening so acutely to the Answer that I gave. He picked up a fine point. I was not aware of that. I stick by both my answers.

Baroness Nicol: My Lords, the Minister gave some interesting figures about the number of people who use the parks. Can he tell the House how those people are counted?

Viscount Astor: My Lords, that is indeed a very interesting question from the noble Baroness, Lady Nicol. I am not entirely sure how they are counted. The answer is that they are not counted individually, but there are estimates of how many people visit the parks. I shall look into the matter and write to the noble Baroness.

BR Sleeper Service: Scotland-London

2.40 p.m.

Lord Stodart of Leaston asked Her Majesty's Government:

> Whether they are giving any advice to the director of passenger rail franchising with regard to ensuring the continuance of the overnight sleeper service between Scotland and London.

The Parliamentary Under-Secretary of State, Department of Transport (Viscount Goschen): My Lords, the Secretary of State's objectives, instructions and guidance to the franchising director issued earlier this year made clear that for the initial letting of franchises the specifications for passenger service requirements should be based on the level of services being provided by BR immediately prior to franchising, taking into account the existence of and justification for seasonal variations in service schedules.

Lord Stodart of Leaston: My Lords, I thank my noble friend for giving me the hope that, after I have enjoyed sleepless—I beg your pardon, "sleepfull" nights on the train for the past 40 years, it looks as though the service will continue. Perhaps I may ask my noble friend whether the director has been made aware of the advice given by my noble friend Lord Younger of Prestwick (who is the chairman of Scottish Development in Industry) on the very grave effects that any diminution of the sleeper services would have on industry and tourism in Scotland? I also congratulate my noble friend

[LORD STODART OF LEASTON]
on his Statement made about a week ago that the privatisation of the railways would lead to a better service for everyone.

Viscount Goschen: My Lords, I hope that my noble friend was not right the first time with his remark about "sleeplessness". I accept that many noble Lords and many people outside the House value the sleeper services. However, they are subsidised, loss-making services and the franchising director will have a responsibility to examine that in the light of the service which is provided.

Lord Marsh: My Lords, can the Minister give an indication of the average occupancy per night of the service?

Viscount Goschen: My Lords, I believe that if one works out the figures, it comes to an average of about 64 passengers per train.

Lord Taylor of Gryfe: My Lords, is the Minister aware of the immense burden which has been placed upon the staff of British Rail as a result of bringing forward the privatisation of Railtrack? Is he aware that 14,000 separate franchise agreements have to be negotiated before the privatisation is implemented? Further, is there not a danger that essential services like the one mentioned by the noble Lord, Lord Stodart, will be overlooked in the immense burden of administration that is now being put on the shoulders of British Rail?

Viscount Goschen: My Lords, I believe that the changes are necessary and that the new franchised railway will provide great benefits in terms of service and choice to its customers. I believe that the employees of British Rail will wish to participate in the reorganisation and to produce a better service.

Lord Parry: My Lords, does the Minister have any anxiety about the welfare of passengers on overnight trains who arrive at unattended stations, often outside towns or in areas of social difficulty?

Viscount Goschen: My Lords, the noble Lord raises an interesting point. I shall look into it to see whether public awareness has been brought to the problem which he suggests exists.

Lord Pearson of Rannoch: My Lords, does my noble friend agree that the value of the sleeper services to the local social fabric in Scotland—that is, apart from the areas of industry and tourism mentioned by my noble friend Lord Stodart when he put the Question—is much greater than a simple calculation of their cost might imply? Will he further agree that that is particularly true of the West Highland line?

Viscount Goschen: My Lords, those are the very considerations which the franchising director will have to take into account when coming to his judgment.

Lord Ewing of Kirkford: My Lords, if the Minister continually refers under "franchising" to an improvement in service, if the noble Lord, Lord Stodart of Leaston, sleeps all night between London and Edinburgh, what improvement in service will he notice?

Viscount Goschen: My Lords, he might have further opportunities to sleep during the day.

Lord Carmichael of Kelvingrove: My Lords, I understand that there are now only seven sleeper services in Britain: six to Scotland and one to Penzance. I believe that the noble Lord, Lord Pearson, made an important point when he said that there was undoubtedly a fall-out to the community from the sleeper service. Will the Minister consider the possibility of "subsidiarity"—I believe that is the word—and allow ScotRail to make the decision and give it the responsibility for running the Scottish sleeper services? I think then the Minister would receive a most sympathetic hearing.

Viscount Goschen: My Lords, I can confirm to the noble Lord that the point he raised at the end of his question as regards where responsibility for the sleeper services should lie, whether it is with the West Coast main line or with ScotRail, is currently being considered by the franchising director. Of course, the franchising director will take into account the considerations of social benefits which come from services which are less than commercially used.

European Union: Environmental Legislation

2.47 p.m.

Lord Nathan asked Her Majesty's Government:

Whether they are satisfied that implementation and enforcement of European Union environmental legislation will not be adversely affected by the proposed reorganisation of Directorate General XI (Environment) whereby the responsible unit will cease to report direct to the Director General.

Lord Inglewood: My Lords, the Government's concern is to ensure that European legislation is invariably implemented on time and in full in each and every member state and that where appropriate the Commission chases and takes action against any laggards.

How the European Commission chooses to organise itself is a matter for the Commission. Her Majesty's Government have no reason to believe that any change in Directorate General XI is likely to lead to a lessening of effort on enforcement of EC environmental legislation.

Lord Nathan: My Lords, I thank the Minister for that full reply. Are the Government aware that over the past 10 years substantial and effective action has been taken to implement and enforce environmental law in the United Kingdom, as well as in other member states, when the responsible unit was under the distinguished leadership of Dr. Ludwig Krämer, reporting directly to the Directorate General? Are the Government as anxious now as they have been hitherto—and I take it from the

Minister's reply that they are—to see that the European Union environmental law is enforced, as it has been over past years?

Lord Inglewood: My Lords, as I am sure the noble Lord knows, the proper enforcement of European law has always been one of the United Kingdom's priorities. That applies equally in the specific case of environmental law. The noble Lord referred to the changes in Directorate General XI which, as I have already mentioned, are internal matters for the European Commission. Our concern is to ensure that the Commission acts as it ought to and leaves its internal arrangements to itself.

We believe that while there are problems within the European Commission about political priorities in respect of environmental law, we do not believe that the particular matter to which the noble Lord referred is necessarily a cause of it.

Lord Bruce of Donington: My Lords, is the noble Lord aware—no doubt he is—that the European Commission is so busy organising what goes on within member states that it has no time to organise itself?

Lord Inglewood: My Lords, I understand the thrust of the noble Lord's remarks, but I believe that if he compares his comments on this occasion with comments that he has made previously he will accept that the European Commission itself finds plenty of time to think up things which perhaps the noble Lord thinks are unnecessary in member states.

Lord Harmar-Nicholls: My Lords, my noble friend indicated that the power to do anything by way of implementation is in the hands of the commissioners. Is there any way that the British Government are able to convey to the British commissioners what is likely to be in the interests of this country, or do they act on their own individual responsibility as commissioners? Unless they have the sort of guidance that only a government can know it means that the point of view that ought to be of benefit to this country is not being used to the full.

Lord Inglewood: My Lords, as I am sure my noble friend knows, when the commissioners take office they take an oath of impartiality. Having said that, in the exercise of their impartial discretion it is of course the case that the British Government keep in touch with the members of the Commission who are British citizens to ensure that the British interest is not overlooked.

Lord Williams of Elvel: My Lords, does the noble Lord consider that the proposed reorganisation mentioned in the Question of the noble Lord, Lord Nathan, will improve the Commission's fairly lamentable record in publication of reports on how members of the Union are meeting EC/EU rules? For instance, the Commission is under a duty to publish regular assessments of member states' compliance with five directives on dangerous substances in water, dealing with mercury, cadmium, lindane, DDT, carbon tetrachloride; and something called penachlorophenol. Is the noble Lord aware that not one report has yet been published. What are Her Majesty's Government going to do to make sure that the Commission is less lax in its procedures?

Lord Inglewood: My Lords, I hope that the noble Lord will forgive me if I do not repeat *in extenso* the chemicals to which he referred. In the Commission's report to the Brussels summit in 1993 proposals were brought forward that the dangerous substances in water directive might be amended. We await events from the Commission in that regard.

As the noble Lord pointed out, and as I have already mentioned, there is a series of concerns about the political priority which the Commission has in respect of promoting and bringing forward environmental matters. That was identified in the report of the Institute for European Environmental Policy commissioned by this Government. I assure the noble Lord that at the forthcoming environment council this is one of the matters which the British Government will bring forward vigorously.

Lord Bridges: My Lords, will the Minister agree that we have one specific and particular interest in the efficient functioning of DGXI; namely, the supervision of the Mediterranean structural funds, which frequently are used to embark on large projects that do great environmental damage? Does the Minister further agree that in this respect we surely need a strong and effective DGXI? Will he please continue to work to ensure that the directorate is strong and forceful in this regard?

Lord Inglewood: My Lords, as I am sure the noble Lord knows and as, again, I mentioned earlier, it is one of the priorities of the Government that there is proper scrutiny of environmental legislation throughout the whole of the European Union and that it is not confined merely to the area that the noble Lord mentioned. He can rest assured that this is a matter that the Government take very seriously and on which they place priority.

Lord Pearson of Rannoch: My Lords, would my noble friend agree that any implementation and enforcement of European Union environmental legislation is less likely to be affected by any reorganisation within the Commission than by the fact that many countries in the Communities give the responsibility for environmental legislation to the local level of government rather than to the national level of government? I place Germany, Spain and Holland in that category. Is my noble friend further aware that, for instance, in the execution of the two European water directives this country has so far spent more than £9,000 million—most of it, in my view, wasted—and we are unable to find out from the Commission what any other country in the Communities has spent or what they have done about them at all?

Lord Inglewood: My Lords, as my noble friend knows, the amount of money spent on the water directives is proof positive of the commitment that this Government have to the adherence to European Community law. So far as the matter of enforcement of European legislation in member states is concerned, as is the normal procedure in the matters of the European

[LORD INGLEWOOD]
Community it is for each member state to determine what is the best way in which these decisions are taken and the enforcement procedures can be implemented. The important matter is that European Community law is not something that is *à la carte*. We cannot in the Community have legal no-go areas. What is of paramount importance is that there are proper enforcement procedures and that they are implemented universally.

Ocean Currents: Data

2.55 p.m.

Lord Campbell of Croy asked Her Majesty's Government:

> Whether they are arranging to gather information about ocean currents and winds, which may assist shipping and fisheries, from the odyssey now being made by the fleet of floating toys accidentally spilled at sea in 1992.

The Parliamentary Under-Secretary of State, Ministry of Defence (Lord Henley): My Lords, this odyssey may make for a good story, but I am afraid that it does not make for good science. I can assure my noble friend that we do not have to rely on plastic ducks for data. British oceanographers are among the best in the world, and there are already a number of proven ocean current computer models in this country. The World Ocean Circulation Experiment has its international headquarters here, and definitive data from that work will allow the models to be developed further.

Lord Campbell of Croy: My Lords, I am grateful to my noble friend for his reply. While plastic flotsam is not normally to be encouraged, is there not an opportunity to obtain useful information, already achieved by American scientists, as these durable coloured toys pass through the North Polar region and the Atlantic during the next five years? Does my noble friend agree that the traditional concern of the British public for the protection of birds is likely now to be extended to these yellow ducks as they perform this helpful service?

Lord Henley: My Lords, I am afraid that the release of various ducks—I assure my noble friend that it is not only a matter of yellow ducks but of red beavers, blue turtles and green frogs—is of very limited scientific value since, although we know the position of their release, the exact time of their arrival on the sparsely populated beaches in Alaska and the path they take is not known. Further, there are four different types of plastic bath toy—some 30,000 ducks, turtles, beavers and frogs. Since they are of different shapes and therefore have different windage and stability characteristics, again, the data is of limited use. We can obtain such data by other means.

Lord Bruce of Donington: My Lords, is it not the case that the Government are too much engaged in playing ducks and drakes in other fields?

Lord Henley: My Lords, I do not think that this is an occasion for the noble Lord, Lord Bruce, to try to score political points, but no doubt he cannot restrain himself.

Lord Harmar-Nicholls: My Lords, is my noble friend aware that today in the conference hall there was a commemoration of the need for plain English speaking? Is he further aware that I have not been able to understand one word of the exchanges on this matter?

Lord Henley: My Lords, I can only apologise to my noble friend. I thought that what I was saying was as plain as a pikestaff. I shall take my noble friend to one side afterwards and try to explain in simpler language. The rest of the House, who, I believe, are of equal intelligence to my noble friend, certainly seemed to understand what I was saying.

Baroness Strange: My Lords, would my noble friend the Minister not agree that we, as sitting ducks, might be very lucky to be struck by a flotilla of yellow ducks, beavers, frogs and so on?

Lord Henley: My Lords, I am afraid that my noble friend will have to wait a very, very long time before she sees the sitting ducks, yellow ducks, turtles, beavers or frogs on our own shores. I understand that it will take some five or 10 years for them to work their way through the polar ice. Even then, they might appear on the shores of Scotland or wherever somewhat squashed.

Private International Law (Miscellaneous Provisions) Bill [H.L.]

2.59 p.m.

The Lord Chancellor (Lord Mackay of Clashfern): My Lords, I beg to move that this Bill be now read a second time.

The Bill is drawn from three reports by the Law Commission and the Scottish Law Commission. The reports are all in the field of private international law; that is to say, the area of our law which enables our courts to deal with cases which contain a foreign element. I am sure that the implementation of the reports will be welcomed by the many noble Lords who support the valuable work that the commissions have done and are doing.

I hope that the Bill will follow the Jellicoe trail to the statute book, blazed during the last Session by the Law of Property (Miscellaneous Provisions) Act. If your Lordships give this Bill a Second Reading, I shall move that it be committed to a Special Public Bill Committee. The first use of this procedure for the Law of Property Bill was, I believe, a success. I consider the present Bill to be equally suited to consideration by such a committee because of its uncontroversial and generally technical nature.

The Bill comprises 18 clauses and one schedule and is divided into four parts. Full explanation of the current law and the proposed reforms is to be found in the three reports from which the Bill derives. Notes on clauses are also available in the Printed Paper Office. Part I implements recommendations in the report on *Foreign Money Liabilities* (Law Commission paper No. 1124) and is based on the draft clause appended to that report. This part extends only to England and Wales. It changes the law regarding the rate of interest payable on judgment debts and arbitral awards in foreign currency. At present, interest on High Court and county court judgments and arbitral awards is prescribed at a fixed rate, currently 8 per cent. This statutory rate, which is altered from time to time, reflects generally the level of interest rates currently prevailing in the United Kingdom. It does not reflect the rate appropriate to any particular foreign currency. Indeed, the statutory rate will often be entirely inappropriate to the foreign currency in question.

Clause 1 makes provision for the High Court and county courts respectively to direct that a sum awarded by a judgment given by the court which is expressed in foreign currency should carry interest at such a rate as the court thinks fit instead of at the statutory rate. Clause 3 makes analogous provision in relation to sums directed to be paid as an award by an arbitrator. Clause 4 makes various consequential amendments to certain enactments which contain provisions dealing with interest on judgment debts.

Part II and the schedule implement recommendations in the joint Law Commission and Scottish Law Commission reports on *Polygamous Marriages* (Law Commission Report No. 146 and Scottish Law Commission Report No. 96) and derive from the commissions' draft Bill. This part, which extends to England and Wales and Scotland, concerns the validity under English and Scottish law of marriages contracted by those domiciled in England and Wales or Scotland which are in fact monogamous but which have been celebrated abroad under laws that permit polygamy.

Clauses 5 and 7(1) implement the law commissions' main recommendation in this part of the Bill that persons of either sex domiciled in England and Wales or in Scotland should have the legal capacity—provided, of course, there is no other impediment—to enter into a valid marriage outside the United Kingdom which, although celebrated in a form appropriate to polygamous marriages, is not actually polygamous. All marriages validly celebrated in the United Kingdom are necessarily monogamous in character, so there is no need for this proposition to apply to marriages in the United Kingdom. Subsection (2) of Clause 5 ensures that that clause only affects the internal law of England and Wales. This means that where, under the rules of English private international law, the relevant law of another country is applied for the purpose of determining the validity of a marriage, those rules will still apply.

Clause 6 applies only to England and Wales and ensures that the reforms in Clause 5 should in general apply retrospectively. Subsection (1) extends the rule laid down in Clause 5(1) to marriages celebrated before the date on which this part of the Bill comes into force and deems it always to have applied to such marriages. This has the effect that such marriages are to be regarded as always having been valid. This effect is qualified by various exceptions and savings with the result that the rule in subsection (1) does not apply where either party to a potentially polygamous marriage has remarried or obtained an annulment and does not affect certain property and related rights, such as succession to a dignity or title of honour, which have accrued before the commencement of this part.

Clause 7(2) clarifies the effect in Scots law of a valid potentially polygamous marriage abroad which is at present an area of doubt and uncertainty. Marriages entered into abroad in polygamous form where there is in fact only one husband and wife are to be regarded as effective marriages for all purposes of the law of Scotland so long as they remain in fact monogamous. This provision brings Scots law into line with the present position under English law.

Finally, in this part, Clause 8 provides that the reforms in Part II are not to affect any rule or custom in relation to the marriage of members of the Royal Family. This is in line with the previous enactments in this general area of the law.

Part III of the Bill implements reforms proposed by the two law commissions on *Choice of Law in Tort and Delict* (Law Commission paper No. 193 and Scottish Law Commission paper No. 129) and also derives from the commissions' draft Bill. These rules relate to any action brought in a part of the United Kingdom in respect of a tort or delict which has a foreign element.

Clause 9 deals with the purpose of the choice of law rules contained in this part. That purpose is to specify the system of law, according to which the rights and liabilities of the parties must be determined, in relation to issues which the courts in this country decide are issues relating to tort or delict, as opposed, for example, to contract or some other basis of liability. This system of law is referred to in this part as "the applicable law". These rules are to take the place of the present common law rules abolished by Clause 10. Other choice of law rules which apply in particular classes of cases, such as torts committed on the high seas (which are governed by the principles of maritime law) are not affected by the Bill.

Clause 11 establishes a new general rule that, when a dispute arises in one part of the United Kingdom out of a tort or delict committed in another part of the United Kingdom or in a foreign country, the country whose law will be used to decide the dispute is that in which the events constituting the tort or delict occur. This general rule should identify the most appropriate applicable law in the majority of cases. It is likely to correspond with the reasonable expectations of the parties involved in the tort or delict. Where significant elements of the events constituting the tort or delict have occurred in different countries, the tort or delict is to be taken to have occurred in the country either where the plaintiff was

[LORD MACKAY OF CLASHFERN]
injured, or where the property was damaged, or, in other cases such as an international conspiracy to commit a tort, where the most significant elements in the sequence of events occurred.

An exception to the general rule is laid down in Clause 12 so as to displace that rule in any case in which it appears to be substantially more appropriate for the applicable law to be the law of another country. Let me emphasise the word "substantially". The exception is not intended to operate every time another applicable law might be more appropriate but only where it would be substantially so.

This seems an appropriate moment in my description of Part III to mention an exception to the rules recommended by the law commissions which the Government have decided not to implement. The law commissions proposed that where conduct constituting a tort or delict takes place in the United Kingdom the law of the relevant part of the United Kingdom should apply, irrespective of what law would apply under the new general rules. They sought to justify this exception on the ground that a person who acts in the United Kingdom should not, by the application of a foreign law, be held liable in a United Kingdom court for consequential injury, loss or damage which occurs elsewhere and would not be recoverable under our law.

The Government consider this proposal to be objectionable in that it would reintroduce the nationalistic attitude which the law commissions are otherwise seeking to obviate. Further, it might not in fact protect defendants who act in the United Kingdom. In the context of the European Economic Area plaintiffs may, under the Brussels Convention of 1968 or the Lugano Convention of 1988 on jurisdiction and enforcement of judgments in civil and commercial matters, legitimately bring their proceedings in the country where they suffered the damage instead of in this country, and the courts of the other country might well apply their own law to the case. If the plaintiff is successful, the courts in this country would be obliged under those conventions to enforce the judgment against the defendant here, notwithstanding the terms of the law commissions' proposed exception.

Clause 13 ensures that the reforms in this part do not have retrospective effect. It also saves the effect of various procedural rules, the application of the principles of public policy and certain mandatory domestic rules, which are regarded as so important that, as a matter of construction or policy, they must apply to any action before our courts, even where the issues would otherwise in principle be governed by a foreign law selected by the new choice of law rules. These are important safeguards for defendants against liabilities and remedies under foreign law that for one reason or another it would not be tolerable to enforce here.

Clause 14 removes from the Foreign Limitation Periods Act 1984 and the Foreign Limitation Periods (Northern Ireland) Order 1985 two references to the common law abolished by Clause 10.

Part IV of the Bill deals with commencement, extent and Short Title. It also, in Clause 16, modifies the Northern Ireland Act 1974 so as to facilitate the extension of the reforms in Part II to Northern Ireland.

The Bill represents a useful and uncontroversial measure of law reform which has attracted the support of the legal profession. I am grateful to the Law Commission and the Scottish Law Commission for the careful work they have put into the preparation of the reports on which the Bill is based. Accordingly, I invite noble Lords to give the Bill a Second Reading. I beg to move.

Moved, That the Bill be now read a second time.—(*The Lord Chancellor.*)

3.10 p.m.

Lord Irvine of Lairg: My Lords, we welcome all three aspects of the Bill. When the noble and learned Lord invited me to say whether or not I considered the Bill suitable for the Jellicoe procedure, I confirmed that I did. I even suggested that its then title, "Private International Law Bill" might give the wrong impression in foreign places. It might be thought that it was a comprehensive measure dealing with the whole of our private international law and therefore intended, for our country, to serve the purpose which Switzerland's Private International Law Act 1987 serves there—an Act running to a mere 200 articles and 154 pages. I suggested the title, the Private International Law (Miscellaneous Provisions) Bill. In the spirit of co-operativeness which will accompany the passage of the Bill, the noble and learned Lord was good enough to agree. From time to time I have persuaded him to accept amendments that I have moved but never before to alter the title of a Bill. This is plainly the summit of my legislative achievements thus far.

As the noble and learned Lord said, Part I will give the courts welcome flexibility in the case of foreign currency judgments to order, at their discretion, a rate of interest other than the one prescribed under the 1838 Judgments Act. As I understand it, that rate can be fixed or variable in the court's discretion and I agree with the noble and learned Lord that present rates may not reflect commercially appropriate rates in the relevant currency.

Part II ensures the validity of marriages, in fact monogamous though contracted under a law permitting polygamy. Part III abolishes the double actionability rule which provided that where a civil wrong was allegedly committed in a foreign country, it could be sued on here only if it was a civil wrong under our law and also a civil wrong under the law of the country where it was done. The new general rule that the applicable law should be the law of the country where the wrong is committed—subject to sensible qualifications where significant elements of the events constituting the wrong occur in different countries —is welcome. The Bill will bring our law into line with the laws of most other countries.

The Bill is a tribute to the work of the law commissions—of "both" commissions, as the noble and learned Lord said. At the end of September the sad fact was that of 27 Bills published by the law commissions since March 1989 only three had by then reached the statute book. I do not underestimate the difficulties in finding parliamentary time. For far too long non-controversial reports by the law commissions have been gathering dust in Whitehall. I cannot do better than quote my noble and learned friend Lord Archer of Sandwell who, in your Lordships' House on 2nd November, said:

"Between 1967 (when the Law Commission was established) and 1981, 40 Law Commission reports have been wholly or partly implemented—about half on the initiative of the government of the day and about half on the initiative of private Members in one or other of the Houses. Since 1981 only 33 have been wholly or partly implemented. Moreover, since 1989 there has been what Sir Henry Brooke"—

the present chairman of the English Law Commission—

"has described as a grade one disaster area: only one Bill has been implemented on government initiative since that time. In 1981, 13 reports were awaiting implementation. That figure had doubled to 26 by 1985. The figure now stands at 36 reports and represents the hard work of some of our most talented people—hard work which has borne no fruit of any kind".—[*Official Report*, 2/11/94; col. 874.]

I desire to take the opportunity of this Second Reading debate to state as clearly as I can the position of my party on law reform. It was the Labour Government of 1964, under its distinguished Lord Chancellor, Lord Gardiner, which set up the two law commissions. It is only possible to keep increasingly complicated and far-reaching law efficient, fair and up to date by making full and effective use of the law commissions. As Sir Henry Brooke recently observed,

"a nation which neglects the ordinary care of its laws is neglecting something which is very important to its national well-being".

The commissions have an impressive record in achieving clarification and reform of the law, but in recent years both have expressed increasing concern at government failure to implement their recommendations. Many much-needed reforms that have been fully reviewed and considered by the commissions remain unimplemented. In many cases the Government have not even troubled to give a public indication of whether they accept or reject the commissions' proposals.

The importance and momentum of law reform must be restored by enhancing the status of the commissions and putting in place arrangements for the implementation of their proposals. What is required is not merely talk about law reform, but the action that has been lacking in recent years. No government, of course, can be bound by the proposals of the commissions or undertake always to implement them. But where government disagree with those independent bodies, democracy demands that the reasons for that disagreement be stated openly and be subject to public and parliamentary scrutiny. To put law reform back with a high place on the political agenda, basic changes, as a matter of urgency, are essential.

The reports of the two commissions are usually impressive documents with proposals formulated after full consultation with all interested and informed parties. A Labour government would regard the commissions' reports as the agenda for government response and action and not as an excuse for delay through the government themselves undertaking more consultation. The important public status of the commissions should be reinforced by government accepting an obligation to respond publicly within six months of publication of any commission report, giving full reasons for non-implementation or delay in the implementation of the commissions' proposals.

Lord Harmar-Nicholls: My Lords, is not the action being called for by the noble Lord still capable of being applied through the normal parliamentary procedures? There is nothing to stop the noble Lord, for example, under the many opportunities that our procedures give, from commenting that something is being neglected or not answered.

Lord Irvine of Lairg: My Lords, as the noble Lord says, that is an opportunity which can be, and frequently is, availed of. The important point is that government should not leave the reports to gather dust unnoticed in Whitehall, without any statement as to whether they have simply failed to read them or to consider them or whether, on considered grounds, they are opposed to them for whatever reason. I am proposing a more rational approach with an obligation upon government to respond in the interests of democracy. Of course, I support, in the current state of our procedures, the suitability of the Jellicoe procedures for carrying out much needed law reform. The noble and learned Lord is well aware that that is so.

A new obligation of government to respond publicly to Law Commission reports would be important. It could be reinforced by the creation of a joint committee of both Houses of Parliament, perhaps along the lines of the Ecclesiastical Committee, with a remit to oversee government action on law reform. The committee would draw on the combined legal expertise in the other place and in this House. The Government's response to law reform reports would be monitored by the committee, and Ministers would give evidence to the committee about that response. That would be an important obligation of government.

Many law reform proposals will be controversial and will need full parliamentary debate. Many others, however, should not require that time-consuming and delaying process. One of the tasks of such a joint committee would be to indicate which recommendations, and which parts of them, are in effect technical, and which raise issues of policy and substance. Active steps should be taken to expedite the implementation of proposals that the joint committee regards as non-controversial and, fortified by the opinion of that committee, all parties in Parliament would be expected to co-operate in the rapid enactment of such proposals. That would leave more time for the full debate of law reform proposals involving issues of greater sensitivity.

There is one further consideration. Although the law commissions would be the main engine of law reform, it is not practicable, or suitable, for the law commissions to undertake all of the work themselves. In recent years too much use has been made of ad hoc committees, or of interdepartmental studies, without reference to the expertise of the law commissions. The position originally envisaged by Lord Gardiner should be

[LORD IRVINE OF LAIRG]

restored: the law commissions should once again advise government of the most suitable body to undertake any particular piece of law reform; and where law reform is contemplated by other government agencies the law commissions should give advice on procedures and approach. That should avoid duplication. It should lead to a coherent programme throughout government and ensure that all law reform work, wherever performed, is conducted to a high standard.

I have taken the opportunity to emphasise the major importance my party attaches to law reform and its conviction that it must be pushed significantly higher on the political agenda and that both law commissions must be supported and encouraged by putting the fruits of their labours, so far as possible, on the statute book. Meanwhile, we support the expeditious passage of the Bill.

3.23 p.m.

Lord Lester of Herne Hill: My Lords, the Law Commission and the Scottish Law Commission are excellent institutions, created, as the noble Lord, Lord Irvine of Lairg, has just reminded us, almost 30 years ago by Lord Chancellor Gardiner as his great innovation, supported, as I recall, by Home Secretary Jenkins. The law commissions have rightly expressed anxiety recently about the way their work has been consistently neglected by Parliament, an anxiety shared by many other people concerned with the quality of our laws. I endorse what has been said about that just now by the noble Lord, Lord Irvine of Lairg. It is therefore most welcome that the Government have introduced this Bill to give effect to three of the law commissions' reports in the field of conflict of laws. Unlike the noble Lord, Lord Irvine of Lairg, however, I must say that Part III of the Bill is highly controversial, as were some of the law commissions' own recommendations on choice of law in tort and delict. Since most noble Lords are not lawyers, I shall try to explain why in words which even I understand.

Part I of the Bill will allow an English court to order that interest on a judgment given in foreign currency is set at the rate appropriate to that currency. Until now the interest rate has been the same, no matter what currency the judgment was given in. It may come as a surprise to some noble Lords that our courts do not have this power at the moment; but they do not, and it is high time that they did. Part I of the Bill is therefore wholly sensible and entirely uncontroversial.

Part II of the Bill deals with overseas marriages in which one of the parties is domiciled in a country where polygamy is permitted. It makes a limited, sensible proposal. Just because the husband happens to be domiciled in a country where polygamy is permitted, the marriage should not be automatically invalid if the wife is domiciled in England. The present law has developed in a rather unsatisfactory way. If a man from this country wishes to marry a woman from, let us suppose, Pakistan, and goes to Pakistan for the marriage ceremony, the marriage will not be treated as polygamous, and will not be void. But if the roles are reversed, and a British woman goes to Pakistan to marry a man domiciled there, the marriage will be treated as potentially polygamous and will therefore be automatically void. It is an accident that the law has evolved in this way, but the law now discriminates between men and women in a way which is wrong in principle. Of course, if the marriage is actually polygamous, it will not be affected by the Bill. But the limited and principled measure proposed in Part II of the Bill is entirely welcome.

I regret that the same cannot be said in respect of Part III. It proposes to abolish in their entirety the carefully developed common law rules about choice of law in tort and delict cases. One of the most controversial proposals is the removal of the present rule that a plaintiff may succeed in the courts of the United Kingdom only if the conduct complained of would have amounted to a tort under our own law. The version of the Bill drafted by the law commissions did not go as far in this direction as does the present Bill and the law commissions' version provided a better balance of conflicting policy considerations. It is unfortunate that the Government have departed from the law commissions' more balanced proposals.

Some examples may help to illustrate my real concern about Part III. First, let us suppose that a complaint is made against a United Kingdom power generator that its emissions have damaged forests in Norway or that a nuclear power station has injured the livelihood of fishermen in Ireland. Let us suppose that both generators have carried out their operations in scrupulous compliance with UK common law and statute law. Under the law as it stands today, a plaintiff could not recover damages in England because the conduct would not be tortious in England or Scotland. But Clauses 10 and 11 would probably permit them to do so. At present, if proceedings are brought in Norway or Ireland, the judgment may be enforced in the United Kingdom. That is, in my opinion, a more appropriate way of dealing with the problem than to require a court in the United Kingdom simply to apply foreign law to a question like this and to displace our own statutory scheme under which the power generators have lawfully operated.

Next, let us suppose that a British newspaper or broadcaster has published truthful but damaging material about an elected politician or public officer and the publication occurs abroad as well as in this country. At present, if the plaintiff were to attempt to sue in England for libel he would fail, because it is a defence in English libel law for the publisher to prove that what he published was true. But under this Bill the plaintiff will be able to obtain damages or even an injunction in the United Kingdom if in the foreign country where the publication also took place truth would be no defence.

The same applies to the defence of qualified privilege for libel about the way in which someone has discharged, or failed to discharge, his or her public functions. That defence of qualified privilege may well be recognised as part of English common law, as it is in the United States or Australia or India, but it may not be recognised in the plaintiff's country—say, Canada, Malaysia or Singapore. The newspaper or broadcaster will not be able, under Part III of the Bill, to rely on the English defence. A foreign government or a foreign politician will be able to use a more draconian foreign libel law as a sword against the British media.

The law commissions carefully considered this problem and concluded that, where the UK is the country of origin of the defamatory statement, UK law should apply regardless of where the alleged wrong was subsequently published. The law commissions did not support this new exposure of the British media to foreign libel claims in this country which will arise if Part III of the Bill is enacted in its present form.

I believe that there is an important point of principle here. Freedom of expression and freedom of the press are vital civil rights and liberties which, as the Law Lords have also made clear in the *Spycatcher* and *Derbyshire* cases, are restricted under English law only where necessary in a democratic society in accordance with the common law and Article 10 of the European Convention on Human Rights. Surely, in this age of global communications, it would be quite wrong for the freedom of the press in this country and elsewhere to be chilled or restricted by applying in English courts the laws of foreign countries which are far more repressive of freedom of expression. I hope that your Lordships will think that there is nothing narrowly nationalistic about my saying so.

There is a third example. Suppose that an auditor acts without proper care and as a result an investor in the company suffers loss. As a matter of English law recently and clearly established by the Law Lords in the *Caparo* case, there is no liability to such a stranger for what is purely economic loss. By what if the investor lives in and loses money in a country under whose law the auditor would be liable to him? Is it right that such an investor should have a claim which would be denied to an English or a Scottish investor in exactly the same boat?

Fourthly and lastly, there are some foreign torts which sound very strange indeed to English ears, such as "insult" or "infringement of self-esteem". It would be very dangerous to require an English court to give effect to such laws which may differ very greatly from the fundamental values of English and Scots law.

I realise that some may say: if a UK court is prepared to enforce a contract governed by foreign law, why should it be reluctant to give damages for a tort under foreign law? One answer is that all contracts are agreements, and all agreements are much alike. Torts are very different, much more variable, and enshrining disparate national views as to freedoms, duties and the extent of compensation. They need more careful scrutiny than foreign contracts usually do.

Others may point out that Clause 13(3) (a) (i) allows a foreign law to be displaced if it is found to conflict with public policy. But surely it is invidious for a judge to have to find, and to say that he has found, the law of another country to be so objectionable that it offends English or Scottish public policy. Yet there is a danger that this will be more and more often what is required of our judges if the Bill is enacted in this form, and in a manner which protects our civil rights and liberties. I suggest that that is a recipe for a divisive jurisprudence —the very opposite of the aims of a fair and reasonable system for resolving conflicts of law— in which our judges are compelled to find, say, the libel law of Canada, Malaysia or Singapore to conflict with English or Scottish principles of public policy.

I should add that I do not regard Clause 12 as solving the problems to which I have referred. It is too vague to secure reference to English or Scots law in the situations to which I have referred.

I hope I shall be forgiven for having taken so long. I would like to conclude by saying this. Liability in tort raises important issues which go right to the root of civil liberty and civic responsibility. Part III of this Bill proposes making the freedoms and standards of English and Scots law largely irrelevant when the tort occurred wholly or mainly overseas. Even though this matter was examined at some length by the law commissions, it cannot be regarded as uncontroversial, and ought to be given very careful and detailed scrutiny if the new law is not to be much less satisfactory than it is today.

3.35 p.m.

Lord Wilberforce: My Lords, like both noble Lords who have just spoken, I greatly welcome the fact that this Bill takes up the reports of the Law Commission and implements its recommendations. It is therefore with considerable regret, and indeed embarrassment, that I cannot welcome Part III of the Bill. On that I go along with the noble Lord, Lord Lester, rather than with the noble Lord, Lord Irvine.

I do not see how it can possibly be said that this is a an uncontroversial part of the Bill. As the noble Lord made clear, it is intensely controversial. The Law Commission itself said in its report, quoting from the noble and learned Lord, Lord Denning, at one point, that the choice of law questions raises,

"one of the most vexed questions in the conflict of laws".

The Law Commission took a great number of opinions on it. It sent out a consultative document. It also heard a great number of witnesses, a list of whom appears in its report. It received a number of very differing views, all of which appear very fairly reflected in the Law Commission's report. These will certainly surface again. So one cannot say that this is an uncontroversial Bill within the terminology which has been used until now. Therefore, I must ask the indulgence of the House to give me the opportunity in a few moments to explain why I am opposed to this part of the Bill. The explanations slightly overlap those of the noble Lord, Lord Lester, but on rather more general grounds.

First, I take the general point that the subject of conflict of laws is essentially one which ought to be left to the judges. It has been developed by the judges over the years and, on the whole, the judges have done a very good job. There are very few cases where injustice has been seen to be done. One does not want this part of the law to be frozen into the lapidary phrases of the Parliamentary draftsmen, however well drafted they may appear to be. It is better to leave it to the judges.

Secondly, perhaps I may take this point. I suggest to your Lordships that statutory intervention in this area, or any area, is only justified if one has certain conditions fulfilled. For example, the first is where the common

[LORD WILBERFORCE]

law has given rise to injustice which it is feared may continue to exist; secondly, where the law is seen to be too complex or uncertain in its application; or, thirdly, where the reform of the law is thought to be necessary for some international reason to bring us into line with an international convention with other countries. But none of those conditions is fulfilled in the present case.

Since 1870 when this rule was enunciated in the case of *Phillips* v. *Eyre* 124 years ago, there has been only one case which has resulted in injustice. That was a Scottish case with very particular circumstances which would certainly not be applied in England or in Wales and very doubtfully followed in Scotland. Therefore, the case of injustice simply does not exist.

The law is not either uncertain or complex any more than follows from the infinite variety of cases which may have to be considered. The noble Lord, Lord Lester, gave some instances of the very great variety of cases which may happen. When one considers that there are 175 countries in the world with different nationalities, and the numbers are multiplied, one can see the number of varied cases against the hundreds of thousands of cases which may occur. You cannot cater for them all in a few phrases.

Thirdly—this is rather an interesting point—the origin of the Law Commission's report, and why it was called upon to report, was that it was hoped at that time (in the early 1980s) that there would be an international convention dealing with all sorts of obligations generally. That convention came into existence in relation to contracts. As your Lordships know, a convention was concluded and brought before this House not so many years ago. Legislation was duly and properly enacted to give effect to that international convention, but there is no such convention in relation to torts. The project for a convention has been abandoned, so there is no case whatever for saying that we need this Bill to bring us into line with some international convention.

So, in my respectful submission, the three classic reasons for legislation do not exist here. That brings me to the substance of this Bill, to Part III. Let us remember that we are talking about double action actionability. You must have actionability under the law of the place in which you are suing and under the law, if you can identify it, where the wrong took place. I now make the proposition that, as the law has been perfectly well adjusted by the judges, it is not in need of any further reform.

I shall have to explain that, I am afraid, in relation to two reported cases, but I shall do it as simply as I can. It could have been said before 1969 that the rule about double actionability was too rigid. It was stated in a very rigid form in Dicey's *Conflict of Laws* with no exceptions and no modifications. Then in 1969 we had the case of *Boys* v. *Chaplin*. That case involved two British servicemen who were serving in Malta where they had a road accident. An action to recover damages was brought in this country. The question was: could you award the damages in accordance with English law, taking account of pain and suffering, or were you limited to Maltese law, which gave only about £50?

That case came to this House and was decided by the appellate branch of the committee which decided that it was a case where one should not be limited by the rule and that a flexible approach should be applied. It was decided that British law could be applied to the issue of damages. Certainly there were a number of rather ambiguous speeches which were long and difficult to comprehend, but in the end it was decided, almost by process of Darwinian selection. One of the speeches came to be accepted generally by the textbooks and judges and can be said to be a fair description of the law so far as it went.

The Law Commission knew of the decision at the time. It referred to it in its report, stating that it was very good so far as it went but that it did not go far enough, leaving a number of points undecided. I would respect that view entirely if the situation had been left there, but it was not.

Let us see what happened in July 1994—only five months ago. The case of the *Red Sea Insurance Company Limited* v. *Bouygues SA*—I hope that I have pronounced that correctly —and 33 others was decided by the Privy Council. The case was brought in Hong Kong and related entirely to matters arising in Saudi Arabia to do with the University of Riyadh. Everything arose in Saudi Arabia, except the fact that the action was brought in Hong Kong. Action could not be brought in Hong Kong but could be brought under the law of Saudi Arabia. But the judicial committee of the Privy Council decided that it was a case in which the full and unequivocal terms of the rule could not be applied and although it was not actionable in Hong Kong, it could nevertheless be dealt with in Hong Kong under the law of Saudi Arabia.

A magnificent judgment was given by my noble and learned friend Lord Slynn—I am sorry that he is not in his place —and by four other Law Lords sitting with him—not retired Law Lords, I may say, but full-blown Law Lords. That judgment has swept away the whole of the law of the first part of *Phillips* v. *Eyre*. The common law rule has gone. The Law Lords said that there is complete liberty, where there is a proper case, to decide according to the law of the place where the tort took place. They did so in that case.

So, Clause 13 which sweeps away the common law rule, has nothing to do with the rule that is being swept away. There is a perfect opportunity for judges to decide these cases in accordance with the law of the place where the tort occurred or any other relevant place. They can decide the whole of the case in accordance with that law, not just one particular issue.

It is worth adding that the judgment referred fully to the Law Commission's report and quoted from it. It said that it was quite right to require further flexibility. It decided to give effect to that flexibility by judicial decision. In effect, therefore, the important aspects of the Law Commission's report have been carried out. It may be said that the decision is uncertain, that it does not cover every case, and that how far it does and does not go still remains to be decided. Of course, it does not cover every case. No judicial decision ever covers every case—nor is it desirable that it should—but nor does the Bill. The Bill contains all sorts of general expressions about "substantial connection" and "relevant circumstances". Obviously, such questions have to be left open. However, the decision completely frees the court from the shackles of the old rule, to sweep away which was the main purpose of the Bill.

Finally, it is worth adding quite unofficially but, I believe, firmly, that the editors of Dicey's *Conflict of Laws* are satisfied with the decision and think that the new rule can be perfectly well stated so as to give effect to it. On that point, I respectfully suggest to the Government and to the noble and learned Lord on the Woolsack that they should consider whether it is wise to proceed with Part III of this controversial Bill, which will give rise to any number of disputes, whether it reaches a Special Public Bill Committee or is dealt with on the Floor of the House. Is it wise to freeze in statutory language a result which the courts have already achieved? We do not need it for an international convention. We do not need the law further to be clarified. Admittedly, this is flexible and leaves many doors open, but the Bill rightly does that also. It leaves open many doors and refers to "significant elements" and all the "circumstances". So, why not leave these matters to the judges?

I have two short points to make in conclusion. First, it is correct that Part II deals with matters other than the direct question of double actionability. That is quite true, but on the other hand it is the double actionability point that is central, as the Law Commission said, to the whole of that suggestion. On most of the other points, the Law Commission has either left the position open or has said, "Let's leave it to the judges". Once you have dealt with the double actionability point, as I suggest the judges have, there is no real case for law reform in this area.

Secondly, assuming that there is a case for statutory intervention, the question that we must ask is: Has the Bill got it right? I do not want to argue that point now—certainly not when there are more fascinating subjects to follow—but suffice it to say that there are a number of considerably difficult points in the Bill. As the noble Lord, Lord Lester, said, this is not an easy subject. It is not uncontroversial. It is going to take a very great deal of time if we are going to sort it out. As the Law Commission said, quoting the noble and learned Lord, Lord Denning, choice of law questions raises,

"one of the most vexed questions in the conflict of laws".

Although I welcome Parts I and II of the Bill, I most earnestly suggest to the Government that it might be wiser to leave the matter where it has now been brought with the 1994 decision and to leave this to the judges rather than take up a very great deal of Committee time, as would be the case if we were to go through the Bill, to try to bring it into statutory form.

3.49 p.m.

Lord Meston: My Lords, I should like to make two preliminary points about the treatment of Bills which emanate from the law commissions. The first, which has already been touched upon, is the delay in turning them into legislation. This Bill is the product of three reports from the English Law Commission and two reports from the Scottish Law Commission. Those reports were published in 1983, 1985 and 1990. Each report was itself the result of a lengthy consultation process. The English Law Commission has justifiably commented upon the problem of delay in implementation in at least its last two annual reports.

It is characteristic of Law Commission proposals that they are researched and argued thoroughly and that they are generally uncontroversial. The reports typically come complete with draft Bills annexed to them, and when eventually introduced such Bills usually take up little parliamentary time. Thus, Law Commission Bills may not need any particular fast track or special track through Parliament but rather a faster track to the parliamentary starting gate.

The consequences of delay are various. Two consequences have struck me. First, the reports and draft Bills themselves are overtaken by other developments in the law, sometimes, but not always, small and unforeseen developments. Secondly, there is created a degree of uncertainty in the minds of the public and the legal profession who read the law commissions' proposals and assume—and indeed are entitled to assume—that change will follow within a reasonable time, and are entitled to organise themselves accordingly. Likewise, after a lengthy delay they are perhaps entitled to assume that, after all, the proposed changes will not take place. I hope that the Bill's introduction marks the beginning of an endeavour to clear up some of the backlog.

The second point is more technical. For some time of course it has been possible for the courts to look at Law Commission reports and draft Bills as an aid to statutory interpretation. It is now also possible for the courts to be referred to parliamentary debates in certain circumstances for the same purposes. With that development, the courts can focus on the reality of what Parliament intended if there is an ambiguity or obscurity apparent on the face of the Act.

However, more often than not, the lawyer who trawls through the *Hansard* reports finds that in the debates there was little or no reference or guidance to the intention behind the use of the word or phrase which concerns him or her. In the case of legislation being debated which uses the same wording as a Law Commission Bill, the absence of parliamentary comment is generally not surprising. What can be perplexing—I am speaking with experience of a case which is presently *sub judice*—is the absence of an explanation to Parliament when there are significant, or possibly significant, differences between the Law Commission's draft Bill and the Bill as introduced to Parliament.

If there are such differences, it would add to the effectiveness of the parliamentary process, as well as helping the courts in their interpretation of the enactment at a later date, if the existence of, and general nature and reason for, such differences could at some stage be mentioned, if only in the explanatory memorandum which we have as part of the printed Bills introduced into this House.

What may or may not be an example of what I am referring to is in Part I of the Bill. Paragraph 4.12 of the relevant Law Commission report and the draft Bill

[LORD MESTON]

annexed to it proposed a power to order a variable rate of interest. In the Bill today there is no such express power, and the word "rate" appears in the singular. I suspect the reason is that the Acts of 1838 and 1970 allow for a single rate only and there is no reason to treat judgment debts which are not in sterling any differently.

The noble Lord, Lord Irvine of Lairg, indicated his understanding that a variable rate could be ordered. It may therefore be that there is some other simple explanation for the difference which I am too stupid to have grasped, but it may also be that in such a situation in years to come the courts will have to speculate as to why the draftsman of the Bill, and Parliament in enacting it, departed from the words in the Law Commission Bill.

Likewise, in respect of Part II of the Bill, there are certain differences of wording. I think that I understand the reasoning behind those changes, but I may seek to probe further in Committee. In any event, the law commissions are to be congratulated on tackling the law concerning the validity of potentially polygamous marriages in the way that they have, following the difficulties thrown up by the decision of the Court of Appeal in the case of *Hussain*. Even for those who have to consider that area of law frequently, it is sometimes complex and confusing. Accordingly, the sensible proposal in the Bill to treat potentially polygamous marriages as monogamous is welcome. It is to be hoped that it will remove any disadvantages in terms of matrimonial relief, the right to remarry, rights of succession and the right to social security.

I believe that Clause 6 deals with the various particular consequences of the proposed change. I do not believe that Clause 8(1) can be read as suggesting that polygamy is an option available to the Royal Family, merely that whatever other problems the Royal Family may have to trouble them, potential polygamy is not one of them.

So far as concerns Part III of the Bill, I had thought that the proposals were uncontroversial, removing the double hurdle placed in the way of intending plaintiffs by case law both in England and Scotland. Successive works on the conflict of laws by the late Dr. Morris have cited the condemnation of the first branch of the rule in *Phillips* v. *Eyre* by Professor Lorenzen who wrote over 60 years ago:

"English law manifests an illiberal attitude which does not obtain elsewhere except in China and Japan".

Having recently read the trenchant criticism of the Law Commission's proposals in the *Law Quarterly Review* of 1991, which has been echoed by the noble and learned Lord, Lord Wilberforce, and having heard my noble friend Lord Lester on Part III of the Bill in so far as it departs from the Law Commission's Bill, I know that I am now in waters too deep for me to make any useful contribution on that aspect of the Bill beyond asking for certainty for those of us who may have to dip our toes in only occasionally.

3.57 p.m.

The Lord Chancellor: My Lords, I think that I can safely be grateful for the extent of the welcome the Bill has been given, notwithstanding the reservations expressed in respect of part of it. I am anxious to bring to the statute book, as soon as I can, those recommendations of the Law Commission and the Scottish Law Commission which appear to be generally accepted.

Before I speak about one or two matters of detail, I have to remind your Lordships that, as the noble Lord, Lord Irvine of Lairg, said, the only ultimate way of giving effect to Law Commission work is by statutory provision. It is true that the analysis of existing law which the Law Commission provides in its working papers and its final reports can of itself be useful: I have found those analyses useful from time to time while sitting judicially. But the ultimate proposal of the Law Commission is for a Bill, and therefore it is by statutory intervention only that the proposal can be given effect to.

It is a consequence of what my noble and learned friend Lord Wilberforce said, that, so far as concerns private international law at least, it would be difficult for the Law Commission to operate because it is bound to innovate ultimately—if it is to innovate effectively—by statutory means. I hope that we shall be able to have a number of these Bills. As your Lordships know, the gracious Speech indicated the promotion of law reform measures. I hope that that will occur.

One of the difficulties of law reform is that it is sometimes hard to obtain the necessary measure of agreement. In that connection, I refer to what was said by the noble Lord, Lord Irvine of Lairg. In a sense law reform embraces all changes in law. Those are proposed by the Government on the basis that they are reforms. However, here we are dealing with law reform which flows primarily from the law commissions, although from time to time other bodies may produce proposals which fall properly within that category.

I wish to comment on some of the special issues that have been mentioned, but perhaps full discussion is best left to the Committee stage. The Law Commission formulated its proposals, which are incorporated substantially in Part III of the Bill, against the background of the rule in *Phillips* v. *Eyre* and *Boys* v. *Chaplin*, as referred to by my noble and learned friend Lord Wilberforce. The latter case contains a distinguished account of the law as it then stood. The law was developed in the Privy Council in the *Red Sea Insurance* case. I believe that, technically speaking, the decisions of the Privy Council, while a persuasive authority here, are not part of the law of this country. I have come across at least one case in which the House of Lords in this jurisdiction did not follow closely a parallel case in the Privy Council in relation to the effect of duress in the criminal law.

It is fair to say that in the *Red Sea Insurance* case the Judicial Committee of the Privy Council expressed difficulty in knowing to what extent exceptions were to be permitted to the law of double actionability. Therefore, I believe that the Law Commission's proposal that that rule should be abolished is wise. I say that with all due respect to the great learning and experience in this area of my noble and learned friend Lord Wilberforce. Obviously, the matter must be discussed further and I shall reflect on all that he said.

The noble Lord, Lord Lester of Herne Hill, claimed a larger effect for the proposal of the Law Commission than it had. I understand the proposal to be that where the conduct constituting tort or delict took place in the United Kingdom the law pertaining to that part of the United Kingdom should apply. I do not believe that that proposal will in all cases have the effect that the noble Lord suggests. However, the difficulty is that if that is a good rule for England, Wales and Scotland, it is hard to see why it is not a good rule for everyone else. If that is right the whole system is undermined. The criticisms levelled at the Law Commission's proposal—that it is nationalistic in character and undermines the commission's own proposals—has a good deal of substance. As has been pointed out, there are public policy provisions and, as I indicated in my opening speech, the possibility of enforcement by reference to the convention laws of this country.

My submission to your Lordships is that these matters are technical. They involve controversy which is not party political but technical, and a good deal can be said on both sides. However, I hope that whatever is said will not be at such length as to destroy the possibility of this route for this type of reform. Those of your Lordships who are interested in having the Law Commission's reports brought forward and implemented—I know that that is true of your Lordships as a whole—will agree that the proposals of my noble friend Lord Jellicoe, which we are now using, are most important. Consistent with the proper consideration of these matters, I should not like anything to happen that would undermine the utility of that proposal for dealing with questions of this kind. I suggest that these are questions of a technical kind which are appropriate for the special committee, as I mentioned earlier. If your Lordships give the Bill a Second Reading I propose to move that it be committed to a Special Public Bill Committee. I commend the Bill to the House.

On Question, Bill read a second time.

The Lord Chancellor: My Lords, I beg to move that this Bill be committed to a Special Public Bill Committee.

Moved, That the Bill be committed to a Special Public Bill Committee.—(*The Lord Chancellor.*)

Lord Wigoder: My Lords, given the nature of the debate to which we have all listened with great interest; given the noble and learned Lord's reminders that the Jellicoe Report referred to uncontentious Law Commission Bills being suited to the new procedure; and given that the most recent view of the committee of your Lordships' House was that such a step should be taken only in relation to a few Bills of a technical nature and largely devoid of party political controversy—and I accept that the controversy that has arisen is not party political—does the noble and learned Lord believe that in the light of the major matters that have been debated on Second Reading today if we take the step proposed by him we shall be stretching the previous decisions of your Lordships' House?

The Lord Chancellor: My Lords, I think not. The nature of the controversy is of a party political kind which goes beyond the type of consideration raised here. I accept that these questions are important but they are of a technical kind and I suspect that not all Members of your Lordships' House will feel inclined fully to participate in a debate on them. I may be wrong—there may be a tremendous desire to participate in the debates—but I think not. I believe that in order to make progress this is the only way open.

I suggest that my Motion that the Bill be committed to a Special Public Bill Committee is wise. The matters can then be discussed and perhaps when the Bill returns to your Lordships' House they will have been settled. I must then consider carefully what to do in the light of my general anxiety, as far as is possible and practicable, to get reformed law on the statute book. I move the Motion in the belief that it is wise and suitable if we are to be able satisfactorily to implement proposals of this kind.

On Question, Bill committed to a Special Public Bill Committee.

BBC: White Paper

4.10 p.m.

Viscount Astor rose to move, That this House takes note of the White Paper on the future of the BBC (Cm 2621).

The noble Viscount said: My Lords, on 6th July the Government published their White Paper on the future of the BBC. In drawing up the proposals in that White Paper we have taken account of the results of a consultation exercise, following the publication of a Green Paper in November 1992. We have also had the benefit of a report on this subject by the National Heritage Select Committee in another place.

The main proposal in the White Paper is that the BBC should continue as this country's main public service broadcaster. That should remain its primary role, and it should be spelled out in its new Royal Charter.

The White Paper identifies a number of objectives for the BBC's public services. Those include providing programmes of information, education and entertainment; giving priority to the interests of the public, and being open and responsive to their views; providing diversity and choice in its services; and enriching the cultural heritage of this country through support for the arts. We have proposed that those obligations on the BBC's public services should be stated more clearly and explicitly in the BBC's new Royal Charter and Agreement.

The White Paper also proposed that the BBC should take steps to exploit the commercial opportunities represented by its experience and reputation around the world, in partnership with the private sector, and that it should develop into an international multi-media enterprise.

[VISCOUNT ASTOR]

I believe that it is fair to say that the White Paper received a good measure of support on all sides of this House, in another place, and in the country at large. The Government invited views on the White Paper by 31st October. By the end of November, some 109 members of the public and 93 organisations had sent in their comments. My right honourable friend the Secretary of State has today placed a list in the Libraries of both Houses of organisations responding to the White Paper. The vast majority of responses that we have received have welcomed the continuation of the BBC as a public service broadcaster. There has also been broad support for our proposals for the BBC's commercial activities.

There have, of course, been concerns raised about certain aspects of the White Paper. The Government welcome all the comments received and we will take those into account very carefully before reaching final decisions.

I would in particular like to thank the multi-party broadcasting group of this House, which is chaired by my noble friend Lord Caldecote, for its considered response to the White Paper, and would like to spend a little time addressing its main anxieties. Your Lordships were mainly concerned to ensure the accountability of the BBC to Parliament and to the public. The Government share those concerns, and the White Paper makes a number of proposals to achieve that.

We have proposed that there should be clearer objectives for the BBC's programmes and services and that the basic obligations on programme standards, including the obligation of due impartiality, should be stated clearly in the new Agreement between the Government and the BBC.

The BBC should publish a statement of promises to its audiences, which should include undertakings on programme standards. The BBC should also consult audiences on its services, and publish information about its performance against its objectives and promises.

I know that the multi-party group is concerned about who will ensure that the BBC meets all its obligations. The White Paper makes it clear that this is the primary responsibility of the BBC's board of governors. The board's role is not to manage the BBC, but to represent the interests of the BBC's audiences and the general public. The Government do not favour interposing a separate, outside regulatory body between the BBC and its audiences. That would undermine the close, direct links with audiences which we see as essential if the BBC is to fulfil its duties as a public service broadcaster.

The BBC's position is significantly different from other broadcasters in this country. The BBC is a public body, established solely to serve the public. It has no other object. By contrast, the commercial broadcasters are primarily motivated by the requirement to make a return for their shareholders, subject of course to their licence conditions.

The BBC's governors are appointed by Her Majesty the Queen, on the advice of the Prime Minister. They carry out the regulatory functions which in the independent sector are borne by the Independent Television Commission and the Radio Authority. If they do not fulfil their duties, they can be removed.

The noble Lord, Lord Annan, has raised an important point, in his amendment to the Motion before the House, concerning the obligation of impartiality. I can say straight away that the Government accept without reservation the noble Lord's point that the concept of impartiality is too important to be left to a reference in the annex to the BBC's current Licence and Agreement. The White Paper itself acknowledges that in agreeing with the purpose of the recommendation to that effect in the report by the Select Committee in another place.

The Government propose that the BBC should be subject to a specific obligation to observe due impartiality in dealing with controversial issues. That obligation will be expressed in the same terms as that which applies to independent broadcasters. We have considered very carefully how that should be framed, and where we should include it in order to ensure that it is effective and enforceable.

It may help the House if I briefly outline the purpose of each of the main documents which will replace the current Charter, Licence and Agreement. First, there will be a new Royal Charter. That will establish the BBC as a public corporation and will set out its constitution and give it its powers. It is, broadly speaking, an instrument of enablement.

Secondly, there will be the Agreement. As I said, that will be a binding legal contract between the Secretary of State and the BBC. It will set out the BBC's obligations and undertakings for the programmes and services which it broadcasts, and for its other activities. Those will include all the current undertakings which are currently found in the annex to the present Licence and Agreement. The annex itself will disappear. The new Agreement will therefore be, broadly, an instrument of control.

The third document which will be required will be a Licence for the BBC to transmit its television and radio signals. That is a licence dealing with technical matters only, under the Wireless Telegraphy Act and the Telecommunications Act. It will be issued on behalf of the President of the Board of Trade, as for other broadcasters. The new Licence will replace the technical parts of the current Licence and Agreement. That will allow the new Agreement to concentrate on programme obligations, rather than technical matters.

Returning to the question of impartiality, we have considered very carefully which of the governing instruments would be the right place for an obligation of this sort in order to ensure that it is effective and enforceable. We have concluded that the reference should be placed in the Agreement. That provides the most effective guarantees. It will mean that the obligation extends explicitly to every programme in each of the BBC's services.

After the recent Question in your Lordships' House, I considered very carefully the alternative approach suggested by the noble Lord, Lord Annan, of placing the reference in the Royal Charter. However, that would not provide such an effective safeguard. The Charter does not cover specific programme requirements or set controls. It is, as I said, an instrument of enablement, not of control, as is the Agreement.

We could not therefore easily frame a requirement to go into the Charter in the firm and explicit terms that we envisage putting in the Agreement. The Charter and the Agreement have equal weight in law, but do different things. In the case of the obligation on impartiality, the Agreement is the right document for such a reference.

As I said, I accept without reservation the aim of the noble Lord, Lord Annan. The Government will place a specific obligation on the BBC to observe due impartiality, and that will be included in the body of the new Agreement, which replaces the current Licence and Agreement.

On the same question, my noble friend Lord Orr-Ewing has previously raised the position regarding the role that this House will play in considering the new documents which will regulate the BBC's activities for a further 10 years. I shall try to explain the position clearly to your Lordships. The Royal Charter is issued under the Royal Prerogative. It is not, therefore, subject to the approval of either House. However, we intend that it should be debated in both Houses.

The Agreement will be a contract between the Secretary of State and the BBC. Because it deals in part with communications overseas—and only for that specific reason —it will be subject to the approval of the House of Commons, under Standing Order 55. Your Lordships' House has no equivalent standing order.

The technical Licence, setting the rules for the transmission of the BBC's radio and television signals, will be issued on behalf of the President of the Board of Trade. In common with the technical licences for all other broadcasters, there is no parliamentary process.

As I said, the Government intend, with the agreement of the usual channels, to provide your Lordships with an opportunity to debate both the Royal Charter and the Agreement before either document comes into force.

We have welcomed the responses which we have received to the White Paper and will take them carefully into account. I also look forward to hearing the views that will be expressed in your Lordships' House today. I can assure noble Lords that we shall also take those views into account. By my explanation of the Charter and the Agreement and their nature, I hope that I have satisfied the noble Lord, Lord Annan, that we have indeed taken the right course. I also hope that we have satisfied the noble Lord, Lord Donoughue, who has also tabled an amendment to the Motion—

Lord Harmar-Nicholls: My Lords, my noble friend has made it perfectly clear that the power resides in the Agreement and the Charter together. If it is felt that the Agreement has been ignored, or not dealt with correctly, but that it is in keeping with the general purpose of the Charter, which of them would have pre-eminence in any decisions that arise from that difference of view?

Viscount Astor: My Lords, I do not believe that any have pre-eminence in the way suggested by my noble friend. I do not believe that there is any conflict of interest in that way. If we had one rule of impartiality in the Charter and a separate one in the Agreement, then we could possibly find a difference between the two. But, as I said, the Charter is an enabling document which continues the establishment of the BBC as an entity; the Agreement actually applies to the specific obligations of the BBC. It is an agreement between the Secretary of State and the BBC. If the BBC does not keep to that Agreement, it is accountable to the Secretary of State.

As I said, I shall obviously listen very carefully to what your Lordships have to say. At the end of the debate I shall have the opportunity to answer any points raised. I beg to move.

Moved, That this House takes note of the White Paper on the future of the BBC (Cm 2621).—(*Viscount Astor.*)

4.23 p.m.

Lord Annan rose to move, as an amendment to the above Motion, at end to insert ("but regrets that it does not meet the recommendation in paragraph 59 of the 2nd Report of the National Heritage Committee of the House of Commons, Session 1993—94 (HC 77) that 'the principle of impartiality is too important to be confined to an Annex'; and requests Her Majesty's Government to give an assurance that this principle will be included in the Licence and Agreement of the BBC").

The noble Lord said: My Lords, I tabled the amendment because the National Heritage Select Committee in another place made the cogent criticism that impartiality was really too important a matter to be left in an annex to the Charter. I should like to say immediately that I am very satisfied by what the noble Viscount said. I cordially accept that, of course, the Agreement is the place in which impartiality should be imposed upon the BBC.

However, the amendment was designed to go a little further. It was designed to probe the ministerial mind. Ministers are very busy men and women and they cannot spend their leisure hours watching television or listening to radio. In a sense they are rather worse placed than many members of the public to judge what the broadcasters are saying. But I am sure that the noble Viscount accepts, as I hope we all do in this House, that impartiality does not mean that every programme has to be balanced and express an anodyne view. We must accept that some programmes will express a bias or at least an individual outlook.

In defending that principle the BBC says that its staff are instructed to keep a balance between conflicting views. Unfortunately, some producers interpret that principle in a somewhat cynical manner. A sizzling programme designed to cast doubts on conventional values in the most provocative way is broadcast in January. They then argue that that is balanced by transmitting the Trooping of the Colour in June.

Timing in the balance of programmes is all important. The chieftains of television and radio really must accept that if they transmit a controversial programme they must in the interests of impartiality transmit a programme, not necessarily on exactly the same topic but something as pungent, that represents the views of

[LORD ANNAN] those who found the first programme offensive. Similarly in news both sides must get a hearing on a critical news item.

The BBC should recognise that where opinions are concerned viewers and listeners are rather like Jekyll and Hyde. The noble Viscount knows me as a mild, ineffectual old fellow. But put me in front of a television screen and I am transformed into a fighting cock. If that brilliant master of words, Mr. Christopher Hichens, addresses me—he is, perhaps I should explain, the Derek Hatton among Left-wing journalists—my hackles rise. But they rise even higher when I listen to Mr. Paul Johnson, who was once an angry young man of the Left and is now an angry old man of the Right. Long may those two live to enrage me and make the adrenalin flow through my veins. But I do ask that their views should be counterbalanced within a few weeks.

There is only one exception to impartiality. When the state —I do not mean the Government—is under threat in a battle against armed terrorists or against the armed forces of another state, the BBC has a duty to remember that it is the British Broadcasting Corporation and cannot be impartial between the two sides.

Noble Lords: Hear, hear!

Lord Annan: It must of course be truthful. The BBC won an international reputation during the Second World War for trying to be so. But when our soldiers, sailors and airmen are risking their lives, broadcasters should never treat the military authorities as potential liars and on an equality with our enemies. We do not want broadcasts of the kind, "I counted them all out and I counted them all back", which suggest that our commanding officers will lie if given a chance.

Understandably enough people ask: what happens if the BBC disobeys the terms of the Agreement? Indeed, the noble Viscount, tried to address himself to that. What happens if the BBC is not impartial, and disobeys them not once but continually? In commercial broadcasting the ITA and the Radio Authority have sanctions to hand. They can fine companies or, indeed, withdraw their licence. But there is no corresponding sanction within the BBC. The governors represent the public interest but, if they fined the corporation, they would simply be penalising the public who pay the licence fee. It is absurd to imagine that any government would even dare to sack the governors *en masse* because the governors, not the Government, are responsible for seeing that the BBC obeys the law.

The governors are often attacked by the public for not insisting on impartiality or for sanctioning, extravagance and so on. And they are attacked just as ferociously by the broadcasters for interfering with their freedom.

I want to defend the governors this evening. In the 1980s the BBC got into deep political trouble over Ireland, over the Falklands and over a considerable number of other matters. The governors showed they had a sanction; they sacked the director-general. They also cleared out the top echelon of BBC policy-makers. Since then they have left Mr. Birt to improve the standard of news and current affairs output. No doubt some will say that there is still room for improvement.

There always is—perhaps the director-general would like to have a look at the "Today" programme. But in my judgment there is a substantial difference between now and 10 years ago.

Some will urge that the governors ought to be strengthened and should regard themselves as the equivalent of the board of directors of a plc. I do not myself agree with that because I think that the BBC must remain a public corporation, and the governors have to represent Scotland, Wales and Northern Ireland. Probably also someone from the Foreign Office is needed among their number. They cannot be like the board of a private limited company. But I do think that the board of management of the BBC might well invite some men and women of experience in business to join them as non-executive directors. It is there, I think, that outside advice would be particularly useful.

On impartiality, the governors and the director-general can do only so much. Impartiality depends on the heads of television and radio and the producers beneath them. Anyone who puts on controversial programmes is like a man driving along an unmarked frontier that he knows he must not cross. At some point or other he is bound to make a mistake and cross that frontier. Those who control programmes ought to work on the studio floor in rehearsal and in run through to see that that frontier is crossed as rarely as possible. Similarly, the creators of programmes must not be grindingly hostile to the controllers. They must consult right up the line to the director-general himself if necessary. And that goes for independent producers as well as for the BBC staffers.

In the 1950s when the BBC was in hot competition with ITV the creators were pushing back the frontier in the BBC. But in those days they did not regard themselves as avant-garde rebels cocking a snook at the top BBC brass. There was merry co-operation and a readiness to admit that some of the most audacious ideas went way beyond the frontier and had to be scrapped. Above all, it is important that there must never be an in-house interpretation of political events within the corporation.

I sometimes wonder whether broadcasters have read the admirable advice that the BBC gives in *Producers Guide*, chapter 3, section 5. Of course the director-general and the governors are right to back up their staff when they consider that a particular criticism is unjust. But it would impress the BBC's critics more if the BBC acknowledged that when a mistake had been made, it had been made; and if it is a gargantuan error, to state what action has been taken in regard to the offender.

More years ago than I care to remember, I wrote a sentence in the report of the Committee on the Future of Broadcasting which ran as follows:

"He who drops the clanger should carry the can".

It is because I would like occasionally to see a producer with a gloomy countenance carrying a can, that I beg to move.

Moved, as an amendment to the above Motion, at end to insert ("but regrets that it does not meet the recommendation in paragraph 59 of the 2nd Report of the National Heritage Committee of the House of Commons, Session 1993—94 (HC 77) that 'the principle of impartiality is too important to be confined to an Annex'; and requests Her Majesty's Government to give an assurance that this principle will be included in the Licence and Agreement of the BBC")—(*Lord Annan.*).

4.35 p.m.

Lord Donoughue: My Lords, I must begin by thanking the Minister for the opportunity to have this important debate and for his characteristically positive and accommodating style in opening it and especially in accepting the first amendment on impartiality. My amendment from this Bench includes that aspect and therefore we are happy, although my amendment does go much wider.

We welcome the White Paper which is commendable in a number of respects. It has been received with great relief both inside and outside Parliament. There is relief that the fanatics of privatisation have been kept at bay and that the licence fee is preserved as a source of finance, at least until 2001. It should have been for longer but we shall come to that. There is relief that the White Paper does not introduce advertising, sponsorship of programmes or a wide dependence on subscription, although a big door is opened for that with the onset of digital development. There is relief too at the continued support for the BBC World Service, surely almost the brightest jewel in the BBC's crown.

Some of the changes proposed in the White Paper such as merging the Broadcasting Standards Council with the complaints commission presumably will require primary legislation at some time—although I stand to be corrected on that—before the new Charter comes into effect. Perhaps the Minister will tell us if there are any plans for that and the Government's timetable for publishing the draft Charter and Agreement. We welcome the promise to give us an opportunity to debate that.

It is well known that the Opposition preferred an Act of Parliament to replace the Royal Charter to give greater public accountability. That was rejected by both the Select Committee report in another place and by the White Paper on the grounds of alleged greater flexibility and political independence. Personally—I speak personally here—I am content to accept the Charter approach on the grounds that it has worked reasonably well for 70 years and also based on the assumption that the needs of accountability, which we were looking for in a statute, can be met specifically in the new Agreement.

Having expressed relief that the White Paper is not as bad as had been feared in the heyday of what historians might term "late loony Thatcherism" I must, however, raise several questions about its detailed content and what it does not contain. First and most important is the White Paper's central assertion that the BBC should evolve into an international, multi-media commercial enterprise, as described by the Minister. Presumably that is based on the assumption that if that is very successful it could lead to the abolition of the licence fee. Of course, we all accept that the BBC must change and must adjust to the new technologies that are emerging. The convergence of media technologies means that the old boundaries between broadcasting, telecommunications, the printed page and other media are being eroded. The BBC must adjust to that and survive in what is now an intensely competitive industry. We welcome the efficiency savings and the commercial successes it has already achieved although one feels there are probably still too many layers of bureaucracy sitting on top of the programme makers at the sharp end.

We accept also that the BBC could do much more to exploit its great broadcasting assets, both the historic treasures in its archives and its unequalled programme making skills. But I do not accept, as the White Paper may imply, that such commercial enterprise could at some point become the BBC's main priority. What the Minister said on that was, I thought, reassuring, but it still can be interpreted as a strategic view.

I question whether the BBC can ever hope to be a major world media producer. Its best programmes seem to me to have a particularly British flavour and currently sell only to specialist markets abroad. If it tried to produce what one might call mid-Atlantic pap it could fall between two stools and compromise its domestic appeal.

I hope that I shall not be misunderstood. I am in favour of maximum commercial expansion compatible with the BBC's public service broadcasting priorities. However, we must be realistic. The present commercial revenues are still, I believe, less than £100 million. They might be doubled, trebled or quadrupled, but that would still be only a fraction of the £1.5 billion produced by the licence fee.

There is a more fundamental underlying issue about which the White Paper, like the Minister today, are encouraging. The BBC is above all a public service broadcaster. It invented public service broadcasting 70 years ago. It is still the best exponent of public service broadcasting in the world, as the Select Committee report on the BBC asserts. Maintaining that role and supremacy must be its first priority, over and above any drive to achieve commercial advantage. It must avoid the terrible traps offered by the global media market.

Therefore, striving to remain Britain's, and the world's, best public service broadcaster is a large, worthy and perfectly satisfactory corporate objective. That glittering niche offers a sound basis for the BBC's future; it is certainly better than following the siren calls of total commercialisation. The BBC has been, and can only be, built as a public service broadcaster on the foundation stone of financial stability, derived from the licence fee secured for many years ahead.

In return the BBC must deliver the public service broadcasting goods. It must be informative and educational as well as entertaining, to use the old phrase, and must satisfy the highest quality standards and standards of decency and good taste as well as impersonal performance indicators. It must produce a wide range of diverse programmes meeting the needs of minority as well as of majority groups. It must be editorially independent of all financial pressures, and should have a high percentage of programmes made in

[LORD DONOUGHUE]
the United Kingdom. For me, that is a definition of public service broadcasting; it is what the BBC must continue to do. It is not something that all of its commercial rivals seek to, or do, achieve.

Only the financial stability of the licence fee enables the BBC to perform that role in full. That is why I question in my amendment why the licence fee is only for five years. The Charter and the Agreement are extended for 10 years. In my view, so should the licence fee be. Hence the first part of my amendment and my suggestion that the commitment to public service broadcasting should be—and I sense that it may well be—explicit in the Agreement.

Given that supreme commitment to public service broadcasting and given the financial stability to support it, the BBC does not need—unlike the rest of the commercial media facing, as they do, intense competitive pressures—to descend into the sewers of contemporary tabloid journalism. The BBC has no need to experiment with so-called tabloid television, which is a cover phrase for descent into trash. It can and must avoid the trend to downmarket scheduling so apparent—and sadly increasing—elsewhere, especially in satellite but also in terrestrial television.

While the preservation of the fundamental principle of public service broadcasting is my main argument today, there are several other issues of importance which I wish to raise briefly with the Minister. While commendably attempting to confront the dramatic technological changes facing the BBC, the White Paper fails to exploit some of the opportunities which the new technological revolution offers. The first is in the area of education, and the BBC's great potential as a provider of educational services. Broadcasting is a unique educational instrument, an extra teacher in every classroom. The new interactive technology now emerging makes it much more potent, providing scope for active participation by the pupils. The opportunity must not be missed. That applies internationally. I believe that World Service Television should be encouraged to link up with the Open University and the British Council to provide British educational services to the outside world, especially to the developing third world. I believe that the commitment to expand the BBC's educational services should be explicit in the Agreement.

The related questions of the BBC's accountability, regulation and user representation also greatly concern this side of the House. The appointment and the role of the governors require further examination. Section 5 of the Charter provides that opportunity. Clearly, self-regulation has not been wholly successful. In the regulatory field we support the White Paper proposal to merge the Broadcasting Standards Council with the Broadcasting Complaints Commission. However, we wonder whether that should not go further to include the integration of the Independent Television Commission, with the remit clearly specified to provide a powerful unitary body regulating the BBC, ITV, satellite and cable television. That would be a body strong and comprehensive enough to cope with the cross-media ownership of the converging multi-media services we now see.

There is also urgent need to clarify the mushrooming structure of some 60 advisory bodies and to specify their representative, consultative and monitoring functions. Again, we probably need a single, strong institution to look after the consumer's interest.

In the arts, the BBC is the greatest single patron in Britain, spending more on the arts than the arts councils. It provides vital training for practitioners in the arts. It is unique in its scale of commissioning, especially of new drama and of new and live music. None of those would survive in a primarily commercial enterprise. We welcome the fact that that vital cultural role is highlighted in the White Paper and deduced—perhaps the Minister will confirm this—that it will be written explicitly into the Agreement as a continuing cultural obligation.

On the privatisation of the transmission service, which is contemplated although thankfully not promised in the White Paper, the Government should be aware that the Labour Party in government will oppose any privatisation of the BBC, whether as a whole, which, in my view, would be ideological vandalism, or in part, such as the transmission service or BBC Enterprises. I believe that the BBC's conclusion is that it needs its own transmission service. That was announced by the deputy director, Bob Phillis, last night.

Turning to the question of impartiality, what I have to say derives from all my previous arguments. Impartiality is intrinsic to public service broadcasting. It must be highlighted in the Charter and the Agreement. I am pleased by what the Minister said so positively and constructively on the question. However, I should like to go further and propose the inclusion of other explicit requirements, some of which I have mentioned.

Hitherto, a narrow range of obligations on quality, taste and impartiality has appeared in the annex to the Agreement as a resolution by the governors. I wish to suggest—and this may well be in line with the thinking of the Minister and the Government—that henceforward the new Agreement should contain both the comprehensive range of services which the BBC is required to provide and an extended list of the explicit conditions which the Government require from the BBC in return for granting the Licence. The Agreement should also contain the governors' resolutions to meet those conditions and obligations. So it is quite simple and logical: the Government set out requirements in the Agreement; the governors resolve that they will meet them. It is not clear to me whether the Minister, when describing the new organisation, was proposing to include in the Agreement the substance of the old annex with its valuable commitment by the governors to obey certain conditions and requirements.

I conclude by summarising our extended list of explicit conditions for inclusion in the Agreement: first, due impartiality; secondly, commitment to public service broadcasting as the BBC's supreme priority; thirdly, a commitment to universal access to BBC services, free at the point of delivery; fourthly, commitments to the highest standards of quality, taste and decency; fifthly, the expansion of educational broadcasting; sixthly, the continued patronage of the arts, including and specifying new arts; seventhly, freedom of expression; and, eighthly, the continuing coverage of parliamentary proceedings. In my view, those should be the public broadcasting service requirements of the BBC which it should give in return for the guarantee, I suggest, of a 10-year licence fee.

The challenge facing the BBC in this technological future is very daunting. It must compete with so many changing technologies. If it seriously loses market share in that competition, then it will obviously grow more difficult to justify a universal licence fee imposed on everyone. However, if it maintains its share through going downmarket it compromises its unique public service broadcasting status so making the licence fee again hard to justify.

We on this side of the House will give the BBC every support in the difficult task of reconciling those pressures, on the assumption, of course, that it will meet the standards and requirements I have set out. But we accept that it can only do so if the Government provide it with the financial stability that it deserves.

4.52 p.m.

Lord Thomson of Monifieth: My Lords, I join the noble Lord, Lord Donoughue, in thanking the Minister for the way in which he introduced the White Paper. I ought to begin with a declaration of interest, as a former chairman of the former Independent Broadcasting Authority. One of the advantages of a decade at the IBA is that it inoculated me against over-excitement at the prospect of white-hot technological revolutions. When I was invited to join the IBA in 1979 I was confronted by Ted Turner of CNN. He prophesied that a tidal wave of satellite and cable broadcasting across frontiers would wash away European terrestrial public service broadcasting and put it in the dustbin of history. We are now in 1994 and it has not happened that way, despite the growth of cable and satellite channels—a few of them good, adding to our total choice and enjoyment, but many of them full of the cheap end of American imports.

Of course, the new channels will continue to grow, but I venture a prophecy: if Parliament and governments in this country keep their nerve, if the broadcasters keep their nerve, then I believe that they will remain the heartland of British broadcasting, with the loyalty of perhaps two-thirds of the audience, well into the next century.

It is in that spirit that I give a welcome to the Government's White Paper on the BBC, albeit not an uncritical welcome. It is an infinitely wiser White Paper than the one which produced the Broadcasting Act 1990. That Act has destabilised the commercially funded half of British broadcasting and damaged the quality and character of the service it provides for its viewers. I notice that Mr. Andy Allen, the chief executive of Carlton Television, recently attacked daytime viewing for its banality. He said:

"Those who are housebound should qualify for a special allowance for watching it".

He should know.

Nor should the BBC be smug and complacent in this situation. It is not immune to the present pressures to lower standards. When I watched the launching of the National Lottery, such was the vulgarity of the programme that I wondered whether the editorial control had been handed by the BBC to Camelot, the lottery company. Gresham's law that the bad drives out the good applies to broadcasting as well as to economics. I was therefore glad to see the Government agreeing in paragraph 2.5 of the White Paper that,

"the BBC should continue to be the main public service broadcaster in the United Kingdom, and that this should remain its primary role".

I was also glad to see that the White Paper recorded the first objective in the Government's view as,

"giving priority to the interests of audiences. The BBC's services should be provided for the benefit of viewers and listeners".

That may seem almost a platitude, but it is a very important platitude.

While the commitment to keep the licence fee is welcome—at least until 2001—I totally agree with the noble Lord, Lord Donoughue, that it is a great pity that, in extending the Charter for 10 years, the Government did not decide to extend the commitment of the licence fee for the same period. For all its defects, and after all the argument and investigation of the licence fee, it remains the least bad method of funding the BBC. Currently at around 23p a day, it is a lot better value than all the competing offers from the new breed of cable and satellite broadcasters.

The licence fee also deals with the problem of maintaining BBC radio in a television age. If the licence fee were to go for television, it is hard to see how it might be maintained for radio. Since, sadly, commercial radio appears to have abandoned much of its public service role, the maintenance of BBC radio remains very important.

However, with the noble Lord, Lord Donoughue, I regret that the Government have failed in that field to respond immediately to the many proposals that were made for a single body to deal with complaints from viewers and listeners and to influence standards. Those proposals came in different forms from the Select Committee itself, from the Voice of the Listener and Viewer—of which I am a patron—from the Consumers' Association and a number of other organisations. Contrary to what the White Paper argues, I believe that such a body would strengthen rather than undermine the broadcasters and the regulators. The merger of the Broadcasting Standards Council and the Broadcasting Complaints Commission is a small step in the right direction, but I hope that the Government may have some second thoughts about the larger vision of a broadcasting consumers' council.

The two amendments on the Order Paper deal with the question of impartiality. The amendment of the noble Lord, Lord Donoughue, goes a good deal wider than that and I find myself in great agreement with its general spirit. I am glad that the Government have responded, as they have done, to the way in which impartiality should be dealt with under the new Charter and Agreement. It is right in principle that there should not be a dual standard in the legal sense between the

[LORD THOMSON OF MONIFIETH]
impartiality requirements for the independent television companies and for the BBC. As I understand it, the government proposal deals with that aspect.

I entirely agree on the general issue raised by the noble Lords, Lord Donoughue and Lord Annan. Given the special degree of influence that broadcasters have on the climate of opinion in this country, if we are to have a well-informed electorate it is vital that controversial issues should be presented fairly. I recognise that for some journalists—I had plenty of experience of this in the past—"due impartiality" is regarded as dull impartiality; crusading is much more exciting. On the other side, however, one should not let the whole issue get out of perspective. The presentation of politics in broadcasting is generally fairer than the presentation of politics in print. It is now only on television and radio—and indeed mainly on the BBC—that there is any real reporting of the proceedings in either of the two Houses of Parliament. The so-called quality press has virtually abandoned its former practice of reporting parliamentary debates.

The BBC is currently required to provide daily reports of proceedings in Parliament. There is no mention of this in the White Paper. I should be grateful for an assurance from the Minister at the end of this debate that that requirement will be included in the new agreement.

I turn now to the importance that the Government attach to what they describe as the BBC evolving into a multi-media enterprise. I share almost exactly the views of the noble Lord, Lord Donoughue, on the importance of the BBC operating as successfully as possible abroad and selling as many of its programmes abroad as it can, and also in the cautionary words that the noble Lord felt obliged to offer.

Clearly, the BBC's world radio service is one of the great achievements of Britain and is widely recognised as such round the world. For my part, I do not see why the development of a world television service from the BBC should not enjoy the same degree of public funding support from the Government as the radio service enjoys. It is important and adds value to Britain's reputation abroad.

Turning to the programme selling aspect, one has to watch this side of things rather carefully. The prime role of the BBC is to inform, educate and entertain the British public. I agree with the noble Lord, Lord Donoughue, that if the BBC becomes over-obsessed with providing material for world markets rather than attending to its domestic duties there is a risk of ending up with too much rather bland cosmopolitan programming. In any case, I believe that the market-place for British programming is sometimes greatly exaggerated. I sometimes think that the President of the Board of Trade in another place lets the excitement of that go to his head a little. Any broadcaster will tell you about the difficulties of getting a British programme, however good, from the BBC or from ITV, into prime time in the United States.

In regard to the proportions, one has to bear in mind that at present BBC sales yield under £100 million as against the licence fee running at more than £1½ billion. Against those proportions, programme sales abroad will not make a dramatic change to the British balance of payments.

There is the very real practical problem of insulating those operations in terms of sales abroad from the BBC licence revenue. Anybody with any experience of these matters in purely commercial undertakings knows how difficult cross-pricing can become. In the BBC's case, I do not believe that it has yet fully faced up to an adequate solution to the problem. It is not sufficient to rely on an internal audit in the BBC, even inviting distinguished people of the right experience to sit on the Board of Governors to chair the audit committee. That is a matter with which only the National Audit Office and the Public Accounts Committee can deal effectively.

In the old IBA—and, I understand, in the present ITC—the chief executive is the accounting officer and is responsible to the National Audit Office and the PAC. I would be interested in the Minister's comments. I can see no reason why the Director-General of the BBC should not face the same discipline and be exposed to the same openness and transparency in terms of dealing with this problem.

Finally, the future of the BBC must be seen as only part of the future of British broadcasting—important part though it is. I beg the Government, when they bring the new BBC Charter before Parliament, to bring along with it a new broadcasting Bill. I understand from the White Paper that a Bill will in any case be necessary to implement some of the proposals that are in the White Paper. It would be wise for the Government to use that opportunity and to see the future of broadcasting in this country as a comprehensive whole.

There is, for example, a need for new provisions for cross-media ownership. The Government have been grappling with this issue for some time. The rules relating to media monopoly within Britain need modernising. I do not believe that there are simple solutions, but modernisation is necessary. It is also clearly unfair that continental media within the European Union can bid to take over British television companies whereas it is impossible for a British company to take over a European one.

It is now time to insist that BSkyB conform to the rules which the terrestrial broadcasters have to follow. BSkyB has enjoyed several years of a privileged situation to enable it to get itself established. As the present flotation on the Stock Exchange shows, that has been successful. In terms, therefore, both of ownership and responsibility for making its share of original programming, BSkyB should now be ready to compete on the same playing field as the traditional British broadcasters.

There is also a need to change the provisions in the Broadcasting Act that relate to Channel 4. These provisions were designed in 1990 to provide an ITV safety net to ensure that Channel 4 was able to continue its remit for special programming even though it was now competing in the advertising market. It was never really intended that Channel 4 should begin to produce a substantial annual subsidy to the shareholders—I believe to the shareholders rather than the programme makers—of ITV.

The year of the new BBC Charter, 1996, is an opportunity to put the whole of British broadcasting on a new footing and to face the challenges of the 21st century. Despite digital technology and fibre optics, and the potentiality for hundreds of channels, I suspect that most people will finally settle for eight or 10 buttons to press in the evening; but perhaps I am getting old! As I said at the start, there is no reason why the public services of the BBC should not continue to be at the very heart of British broadcasting and still be regarded in the 21st century as the best broadcasting in the world, as they have been up to now.

5.8 p.m.

The Lord Bishop of Southwark: My Lords, I, too, am grateful for the opportunity which this debate provides to express appreciation not only of the Government's White Paper but also of the long tradition of excellence in broadcasting by the BBC. I believe I can speak for the Church of England, and also for our ecumenical partners, in expressing the conviction that the BBC should continue to serve the nation as a public service broadcaster, reflecting the nation's culture in all its breadth and richness.

Given the present period of upheaval within the BBC, with a fifth of the staff having been cut, the White Paper affords the corporation the opportunity of a period of relative calm, free from major anxieties about funding. Given also the pace of development in communications technology, it seems appropriate for the BBC's Charter to be renewed until the year 2007, by which time the broadcasting world may look very different.

My interest covers all aspects of the White Paper, but as chairman of what is euphemistically called "CRAC", the Central Religious Advisory Committee, which acts on behalf of the BBC and the ITC, I have particular concern for the role of religious broadcasting. I wish to concentrate my remarks on that subject. In doing so, I assure the House that I am not interpreting religion in a narrowly Christian sense.

It seems clear that, since the days of Lord Reith, the dramatically changed social ecology of Britain has resulted not only in deep social fragmentation but also in a pluralism which has left seriously weakened our concept of the common good. However, it would be a mistake to draw a further conclusion; namely, that religion in all its forms is being discarded and cast aside. The evidence does not seem to support such a view.

Many people still claim to be religious. In any poll which asks about the level of religious belief, the large majority will claim to believe in a supernatural being. Many parents who do not go to church still want their children to be baptised; and more than half of the marriages that take place each year are conducted in a place of worship. There is growth in the numbers of people going on religious retreats. There is parental demand for religious teaching in schools. The interest in religion and the search for the spiritual is an integral part of many people's lives, even though they may not be expressed in regular church attendance.

Television more or less consciously reflects that spiritual dimension to life. It cannot avoid it. News footage about the murder of James Bulger aired serious questions about the nature of evil, punishment and forgiveness. Documentaries, dramas, even soap operas such as "Coronation Street" and "East Enders" periodically tread in religious territory. Indeed, I believe that the broadcast media have a special responsibility. Like it or not, television in particular has enormous potential to help make or mar in our societies a sense of responsibility for each other, a sense of shared values and a sense of spiritual possibilities and meaning.

As the most reverend Primate the Archbishop of Canterbury recently remarked, religious broadcasting has a special role. It is as the trustee of that spiritual dimension, ensuring that the media's heavy responsibilities in influencing the spiritual life of the nation are exercised consciously, coherently, and for good, in both the programmes made by religious broadcasting departments themselves and other programmes too. That role is all the more essential and difficult in a society beset by the increasing fragmentation and privatisation of religion.

Bearing those matters in mind, I believe that more attention and emphasis should be given to the role of religious broadcasting within the BBC's output. If there is a moral vacuum in our society and if, for the health and wholeness of the nation, there is a desire for a shared public morality, the BBC is ideally placed to explore and express moral and ethical issues from a religious standpoint.

In the White Paper there is only one reference—on page 11—to religious programmes. But I am quite sure that that particular and somewhat passing reference picks up three very important statements contained in *Extending Choice*, the BBC's own document, in which it outlined its role in the new broadcasting age. The quotations are brief and unequivocal. First:

"The BBC should place priority on ... religious, moral and ethical programming, which maintains a prominent place in the radio and television schedules for programmes of religious worship, music and journalism, covering a wide range of faiths, portraying many aspects of religious culture, and exploring the major moral and ethical issues of our time".

Secondly:

"BBC1 should be the main national channel, delivering quality programmes to a wide audience. It should ... ensure that religious programmes retain a prominent place in the schedule".

Thirdly:

"BBC2 should be the more innovative, experimental channel, addressing different groups within the audience ... [and] ensure that programmes for special interest groups (whether religious, ethnic or community of interest) are offered when these groups are available to watch".

Noble Lords will have noted the commitment of the BBC to maintaining the place of religious programmes in the schedules. Your Lordships will also have noted the repetition of the phrase "in a prominent place in the schedules". In that connection, the BBC has kept faith. It is to be congratulated on taking the decision, for instance, to leave its "Songs of Praise" programme at its peak time slot on Sunday evening. Despite competitive scheduling on other channels, the audience figures are higher than they have been for the past six years. They

[The Lord Bishop of Southwark]
regularly reach the 7 million mark; they are watched by one in eight of the population. That is surely an indication that commercial pressures and religious programmes are not necessarily opposed.

Given the fact that for some of its other religious programmes on radio and television very considerable audiences are attracted, the BBC would, I hope, not be averse to increasing its religious output. As a lover of sport I am grateful for the full and quality coverage that sport receives on the BBC. But it is worth remembering that more people attend church, chapel, synagogue, mosque and temple than attend sporting occasions each week.

One other key factor which emerges from the quotations that I gave from *Extending Choice* concerns religious broadcasting covering a wide range of faiths and portraying many aspects of religious culture. The Central Religious Advisory Committee, which I chair, is a multi-faith committee, and rightly so. One of the key roles of religious broadcasting lies in allowing communities of different faiths to speak to one another. It is also a key aim of the Inter-Faith Network of Great Britain and Ireland, which I have the privilege to co-chair. As a former Bishop of Bradford, I know the inherent dangers of stereotyping. I know also that ignorance creates fear, which in turn produces tension and all too often intolerance. In a pluralist society the role of religious programmes must at least partly be to help people understand what others believe and how they practise those beliefs. Understanding is a key requisite for tolerance; and tolerance is a vital ingredient in a healthy society.

I thank the noble Viscount for having made this debate possible. I want to thank the BBC for the quality and spread of its religious programmes. I am not complacent; nor, I believe, is the BBC. There is room for improvement. The BBC has committed itself to that task. Along with many others, I look forward to monitoring progress and measuring delivery against commitment.

5.19 p.m.

Lord Orr-Ewing: My Lords, perhaps I may start by saying how very much we enjoyed the contribution of the right reverend Prelate. The three or four contributions that we have heard so far all made positive suggestions as to how we can go forward, not necessarily strictly in line with the White Paper. We are at liberty to make constructive suggestions because the document was described, unusually, as "a White Paper edged in green". If that means anything, it means that it is flexible; that ideas will be gathered and, where appropriate, incorporated in the final plan. I should like also to congratulate warmly the mover of the amendment. He always entertains us because he has such a light touch. The whole House is sympathetic and he gets his message across clearly and briskly.

I must pass on the apologies of my noble friend Lord Renton, who sadly underwent an operation on his eye last Friday and is therefore absent today. He was a loyal member of our group and attended every meeting. He asked me to say that, had he been here, he would have said that there is no excuse within the BBC for some of the sex and violence currently shown; that it is not appropriate to public service broadcasting. It is harming the morale of the community as a whole and it seems that powerful producers continue to compete with some of the independent elements rather than carrying out the duties of a public service lighthouse which is so appropriate to the BBC.

As the noble Lord, Lord Thomson of Monifieth, said, vast numbers of views on the White Paper were probably received. It is a question of keeping up with the reading of them, and the noble Lord mentioned one or two. On balance, our group favoured the cohesion of one complaints authority. We felt at one time, as one of the earlier Green Papers suggested, that there could well be a broadcasting council. I concede that we have probably lost that battle unless the Government decide to rethink the matter.

One task must be undertaken with regard to the ITC, the Radio Authority, Sky, Cable and so forth if they are to be in touch and complaints are to be dealt with fairly. The standard letter is too often used in replies. I was glad to see at the beginning of the year that the BBC set up its own complaints authority. I am sure that that is a move in the right direction. Peter Danneheisser is in charge of that and I have been in contact with him. However, it still means that it acts as judge and jury for itself, even if the BBC does not like that accusation being made against its administration and programmes.

When we look to the press complaints authority, we realise how difficult it is to bring a regulatory body into existence. We spent 45 years in that regard finding different chairmen and different solutions and it was not altogether successful. We wish the BBC's internal organisation well. However, it is difficult to believe that the people serving on it will not find their careers adversely affected if they are harsh on some of the headstrong leaders among the producer staff. That is just the sort of accident that happens, with people being sidelined rather than remaining in the main body of the promotions ladder. I fear that that may happen. I hope that the service of those good people will be reserved to carry out what we all hope will be to the advantage of the viewers.

The 1990 Act contained certain argumentative points. But the main thrust was to do with impartiality, taste and decency, which were to be found in Clauses 6 and 7 and in relation to the Radio Authority Clause 90. We spent 13 days in this House debating the issue. And this House is perhaps better suited to undertake such consideration than the other place, where there is less expertise than there is on these Benches. Many of us cannot see why those clauses cannot be lifted out of the Act. The BBC said that it would take cognisance— I believe that was the phrase used—of all that was contained in the Act. Perhaps we can look once again to see why those clauses should not be lifted straight out and included in the new Agreement.

Impartiality was strongly recommended, incidentally, by the House of Commons Select Committee. I wonder whether when we come to the great issues of the mixed constitution of the public service BBC it would be a good idea to have a joint Select Committee. There is a great deal of expertise and experience in this House—I think of the noble Lord who spoke earlier—which could be brought to the counsels on these issues.

It is worth looking at the results achieved by both the ITC and the Radio Authority on the question of sanctions. It is easy to say that this or that must be done. But what is the possible alternative for admonishment or even standing down a contributor who continues to disobey or disregard the rules? I have read the ITC quarterly reports since they were first published. I am sometimes surprised to find that complaints made by viewers are not upheld. I do not need to tell the House that most complaints concern Channel 4. Last week's programme on "The Word" contained a vivid description of Mr. and Mrs. Bobbitt and was pretty close to pure pornography. It was not appropriate for broadcasting into private homes.

"Spitting Image" is bad enough when it lampoons the Royal Family and particularly our Queen. But when it produced the figures showing Jesus Christ, 150 people immediately wrote in. Those complaints were only "partially upheld". But what can be more abusive to the Christian faith than to make a spitting image of Jesus Christ?

I was in touch with the authority and asked what was done about the thousands of complaints, of which only 100 or so were upheld in the past year. I will describe later the action taken by the Radio Authority. But I was told that nothing had yet been done; nobody had been fined; nobody had been stood down. I made the point that on Saturdays and Sundays there is a good deal of evidence of footballers who are shown a yellow card and warned. If they repeat their actions they are shown a red card and sent marching. Why cannot we do something like that when people continue to disobey the codes of conduct, which are very strict? I have the latest one here, but it is almost too heavy to hold up. I wonder whether any of those in control at the BBC ever read, learn and inwardly digest its contents. If they did there would not be a problem. But I fear that some of them become rather more arrogant than humble and the rules are disregarded.

"Spitting Image" was a classic example. But one example which received publicity is Granada which has been disobeying the rules of advertising codes—I believe eight times so far. At present the authority is trying to levy a £6 million fine on the channel. But that is not as bruising as some may think. Its total turnover for the year is £190 million, so it is roughly 3 per cent. That is the first action taken in the independent sector.

I asked the Radio Authority for a summary of its actions and received a fax this morning. Apparently nine stations were fined for code offences, amounts ranging from £500 to £5,000; a further five stations were fined from £800 to £1,000 for failing to record programmes. That is a little bit of a discouragement, but I wonder whether we will see any action by the ITC. I am sure it would not have happened in the noble Lord's day.

I congratulate the Government on stopping the broadcasting of Red Hot Dutch. That porn channel may be a sign of what is going to happen in the future. Perhaps we should initiate a change in the European law that satellite and cable should be licensed in the country in which the programmes are received rather than just in the country from where they are transmitted. Such a change might be universally popular in Europe and even certain people in the House of Commons might vote for it. Perhaps we could make that change. I do not believe there would be much argument about it.

I wish to make two other brief points. First, because we are not setting up a Broadcasting Council we are giving much more power to the governors. The introduction to the Directions to the Governors, signed by Duke Hussey, which I received from the BBC this morning, asks:

"How can the BBC be made more accountable to viewers and listeners while maintaining its independence?".

The governors have a part to play, but when I read this document I wondered whether they would have enough time to carry out all their responsibilities. They will have to look into cross-subsidisation as between the private sector and the public sector and it will be very difficult to unravel overheads. They will have a real problem on that score if the private sector is to be a substantial amount of the whole. The more I looked down the list of their responsibilities in the document, the more I wondered whether they would have enough time and energy to carry them out and also whether they would be suitably rewarded for all the time that they would be taking attending to the many functions for which they are now taking on responsibility.

Secondly, I should like to say a few words about the watershed. A good debate on the issue was initiated last January by the noble Earl, Lord Halsbury, and noble Lords in all parts of the House seemed to agree that the watershed should be later. In France it is 10 p.m. or 10.30 p.m., but still we make it 9 p.m. That really is unrealistic. Nine o'clock is far too soon, particularly when young people are so adept now at using video recorders. They can set them up and go to bed and watch the programme the next day. I believe that the watershed is being used as an excuse. I have seen dramas in which four-letter words are liberally used. When one asks whether that is not objectionable, the answer comes, "Well, it was after the watershed". But taste and decency and all the qualities that we are trying to encourage in this country are not allowed after 9 p.m. We are suborning the young. I believe that we should take account of the recording methods now available and strengthen the watershed. It should not be an excuse for showing sex and violence and all the other things that are leading our nation astray.

One of the biggest consumer protection associations in this field, the National Viewers and Listeners Association, which is run by Mary Whitehouse, was set up in 1966. Mary Whitehouse is now a very elderly lady but is still energetic. She wrote a book entitled *A Most Dangerous Woman*. In it she records that an order was issued by the then director-general, Hugh Greene, that,

"under peril of losing his job no employee of the BBC was to have any contact with me whatsoever".

That lasted for 11 years. Hugh Greene left the BBC three years after he made the order but it stayed there. Twenty five thousand people accepted that she could not

[LORD ORR-EWING]
be talked to. Even her letters were not allowed to be forwarded. They had to be sent to a national newspaper and then sent on.

It is extraordinary how a modest, humble lady, who was trying to work against the general swing of an extreme political slant, was sent to Coventry and was not in any way used. It is nothing new, but I hope that it has now finished. In 1981 only two people were on the list which had to be sent up for approval. One was Mary Whitehouse and the other was Enoch Powell, obviously for some past reason. I am not blaming the current BBC because I am sure that it has reconsidered the matter. However, it is very unpleasant indeed when the most powerful media influence can make sure that someone is not used on any programme. I recognise that Winston Churchill had exactly the same treatment in the 1930s. The people of the day also used their power to keep him off the air. If that had not happened we might have been better warned than we were of the rise of Hitler's militarism.

I shall finish with a quotation from the most admirable speech of the most reverend Primate the Archbishop of Canterbury in the debate on the Address. He finished with some classic words which bear repeating in this context. He said:

"The aim is not to knock as many people as possible off their pedestals and feel good about their downfall. The aim is to help all of us ... to serve the common good as well as we can".—[*Official Report*, 22/11/94; cols. 175-6.]

Those are the words of the most reverend Primate and I do not apologise for repeating them. They stand repeating. I hope that notice will be taken of them and that we shall get that message across to the broadcasters who have the power to influence for the good or for the bad.

5.35 p.m.

Lord Greenhill of Harrow: My Lords, personally I find the White Paper a somewhat disturbing document. However, I know a great deal less about this subject than I used to and mine, I think, will be regarded rather as a voice crying in the wilderness.

My attitude may well be due to my inability to anticipate and understand the full extent of the technical progress that is likely to take place sooner than we think in the broadcasting industry, nationally and internationally. Many of us have heard qualified people speak of the air being full of satellites of the Murdoch type which will be able to penetrate this country without our ability to impede them in any way. That may all be an exaggeration, and the noble Lord, Lord Thomson, was very encouraging about the situation. But there is a real possibility that some of these horrors are nearer than we really think. Others may be able to see and understand more clearly what is happening in the technical world and are content therefore to await events and just "take note" of the White Paper. The Government clearly believe that the BBC will be able to evolve into an international multi-media enterprise. I wonder whether that is true. I do not believe that the phrase "multi-media enterprise" is a very encouraging description.

It is perfectly true that the BBC has an unrivalled reputation, but it will be competing with a host of powerful competitors with great resources and very wide international experience. There is every evidence that standards of programmes, generally speaking, are declining worldwide and the BBC may well find that its virtues will be insufficient to sustain its position. I very much hope that this expectation is not ultimately found to be true.

As a governor of the BBC in the early 1970s I found the corporation a pleasantly confident organisation; financially well off, with a staff of skilled and experienced broadcasters still relying, rightly, on their wartime reputation. They faced little competition and enjoyed public support. The governors were politely treated, quietly deceived from time to time and starved of information about future programmes. I shall refrain from giving examples. Since those days the Corporation has, of course, in many ways changed for the better. The noble Lord who follows me will be able to explain what has happened. But it is still possible for laymen to pick holes in its behaviour. Impartiality is one of the key issues. I agree very much with what the noble Lords, Lord Annan and Lord Donoughue, said. The BBC has to be more honest than it has been in the past.

But if we are going to protect the BBC's position in the future, the most important thing to my mind is to change and enhance the role of the governors. They must decide the overall policies of the Corporation and ensure that the management carries them out. The chairman must exercise ultimate executive responsibility and although the governors should be non-executive their position should be virtually the same as that of the non-executive director of a public company. The present quaint arrangements must be eliminated. This, I know, has long been rejected but when the Corporation finds itself facing several powerful international rivals the Government may like to think again.

5.42 p.m.

Lord Barnett: My Lords, I suppose I should declare a past interest in that I was deputy chairman until last year. I am sorry that the noble Lord, Lord Greenhill, did not like the White Paper. I find myself therefore in the somewhat unusual position of defending the Government because I do like the White Paper. I formally welcome it, although I am bound to tell the Minister that in due course I shall mention one or two reservations.

I welcome the fact that in the White Paper the Government, as has been said, propose that the BBC should be the main public service broadcaster. I am sure that that is absolutely right and a sensible thing to have suggested. I am bound to say to my noble friend Lord Donoughue that I agree with him—and I believe I understood what he was saying—that he and I both disagreed with the Labour Party in the idea that there should have been an Act of Parliament to deal with the BBC. I believe that the Royal Charter and the Agreement which have been proposed are a much better proposition if we are to be really concerned about the independence of the BBC. That is a matter to which I wish to refer in a moment.

There has been reference to the commercial nature of the BBC; I want to say a word about that. I know that there is some anxiety about the commercial activities of the BBC, as expressed by a number of bodies outside and in this debate. Bob Phillis, the deputy director general, in a very good speech yesterday, made it clear that there would be a level playing field and that there really is no need to worry about the way the BBC proposes to carry out its commercial activities.

I believe it right to continue the establishment of the BBC with a Royal Charter. I agree with my noble friend Lord Donoughue about the period of 10 years and I wish to return to that. It is right that it should be 10 years from January 1997 and not 15 years. A great deal is going to happen in the 10 years to the year 2007. I wish I could foresee the possibilities; clearly, however, there are going to be many technological changes. It would be silly to take the matter beyond that, given that we do not know what the position will be.

I wish to say a few words on the subject of impartiality. A great deal has been said about that. I believe that my noble friend—if I may call him that—Lord Annan knows very well the enormous respect and regard I have for him even if I had not agreed with what he said, which I did. I am glad that the Minister also agreed that the word "impartiality" should appear right at the heart of the Agreement. It is made clear under Recommendation viii in an annex to the document.

As regards the period of five years or 10 years, I shall return to that in a moment. I share the concern of the noble Lord, Lord Orr-Ewing, about programmes such as "Spitting Image". I am bound to tell him that I do not normally watch it. When I did watch it in the past it was so awful that I decided not to watch it again. The noble Lord suggested that if a broadcaster had been lacking in impartiality in a programme he had produced he should perhaps be given a yellow card or two yellow cards which is the equivalent in football, as he knows, of a red card and then dismissal. I am not sure whether we should get to that level although as a strong Manchester United supporter I always regret it when one of our players gets a red card or two yellow cards or whatever. Certainly, I share the noble Lord's concern about impartiality.

My noble friend Lord Annan said that in the past the board of governors sacked a director-general. I am sure that he is aware that the current chairman and I did sack a director-general fairly shortly after we became chairman and deputy chairman. We did that with the support of the board of governors because we did not think that the director-general was doing the job as we expected. That has and can be done. We have to be very careful how we handle that particular sanction. I am sure that my noble friend Lord Annan will agree that as governors we must not be seen to be constantly breathing down the necks of programme producers; otherwise independence will go straight out of the window and I do not know what kinds of programmes we would get. In the first instance the sanction must be in the hands of the director-general and then ultimately in the hands of the board of governors, particularly those of the chairman and deputy chairman. I believe that is what the noble Lord, Lord Greenhill, was saying.

Inevitably, there is concern as regards the question of impartiality. When I was Chief Secretary to the Treasury I woke up every morning and used to think—I nearly said "My God"; I hope that the right reverend Prelate will forgive me—how on earth did that come to be the first item on the news? Why did they put it that way? I thought that they were biased. The important factor to recognise is that we are not impartial, especially those of us who were in another place. None of us is impartial; we are all biased politicians. What we see as biased, others will see as unbiased. So one man's bias is another man's wholly and absolutely perfect programme. It is important that we recognise that. The programme producers are never going to get it absolutely right.

I believe that the Minister said that the balance should be in one programme. I hope that he did not mean it because the noble Lord, Lord Annan, recognised, quite rightly, that one has to balance over a series of programmes although, as he rightly said, one must not produce something which is lacking in impartiality in January and then say that it will be put right in July or maybe August when there is a quiet session. The matter should be put right within a few weeks. It is absolutely right that that should be done.

I know for a fact that programme producers, controllers and the managing directors of programmes care very much and look very closely at this whole question. They have produced the guidelines. If producers are not abiding by them they had better watch out. Whether they get the yellow card or not is another matter, but it would certainly be frowned on if they were not carrying out their remit of producing impartial programmes. Surely it is better to do it that way. There is a very good guideline which is sent out to producers and there is a systematic review and continuing discussions about it.

That is the situation at the moment. As regards impartiality, I know that there are programmes which can never be impartial because they give the particular view of one person. By the very nature of things that cannot be unbiased. But that is part of the editorial mix. The following week another person will be giving the opposite view. That is perfectly reasonable. I am glad to see the noble Lord, Lord Orr-Ewing, nodding in agreement. It is dangerous to lay down rules that are so tight that they destroy the very independence of the BBC about which we all care.

I turn now to the question of producer choice, which has also been much criticised in many quarters. As the paragraphs in the White Paper make clear, producer choice has been abused. The new arrangements make an excellent change whereby responsibility for commissioning programmes is separated from making them. That ensures better value for money. Indeed, in its first year, there was a saving of £100 million which went straight into programmes. That has to be a good way of getting value for money.

I turn next to the question of listed events. I care a fair bit about sport and listed events bother me. I am bothered, for example, that Sky and other such channels can buy premium league football—and have done so—thus excluding public service broadcasting, apart from the BBC which has been able to get such programmes

[LORD BARNETT]
late on a Saturday night. If we are not careful and the Government do not ensure that the question of listed events is watched closely, the only way in which the public will eventually be able to see a listed event will be by subscribing to Sky or some other satellite television channel. I am sure that none of us would want to see that.

Reference has been made to World Service Radio and increasingly to World Service Television. I shall not say too much about that except to note that it has been said that World Service Radio has a good reputation all over the world and is of great benefit to the UK. It certainly is. The Select Committee said that World Service Radio provides a superb service and greatly enhances the UK's international reputation. That comment related to audibility. In fact, the World Service is not only helpful in terms of radio and television; it is helpful to our traders around the world. It is a wonderful service that people tell you about all over the world. World Service Television only began in 1991 —it is hard to believe that—and is already building a similar reputation. I believe that the competitiveness of the BBC in World Service Radio and Television does us all a great service.

I turn now to the licence fee, a point on which I have some disagreement with the Government, as does my noble friend Lord Donoughue. I am pleased that the licence fee is being proposed as the main source of funding. Paragraph 1.17 says that that will be the case for at least five years and that the position is to be reviewed before the end of 2001. Frankly, that contradicts what is said later in paragraphs 5.4 to 5.9. The Government recognise, as I did when I served in government, that although it sounds fine, democratic and fair to say that they will take from income tax, value added tax or general taxation the amount that is now provided by the licence fee, in practice it would put the BBC into the public expenditure round every single year. As one who for five years had to deal with public expenditure, I know what that would mean. I would not want to see that happen. I note that the noble Lord, Lord Boyd-Carpenter is nodding in agreement. We must ask why, if the Government believe that, they are saying that they will review the position in five years rather than 10. I simply do not understand it.

Of course, there is no disputing that the licence fee is a form of poll tax. It may be that because the Government had such misery over the poll tax they do not like the idea of continuing the licence fee beyond five years. I should be glad if the Minister could tell us that the review is only about the amount and that, in practice, they propose to continue with the licence fee for at least 10 years, and not five.

I recognise the problem that is posed by the licence fee, as would any of your Lordships who used to canvass at election time. That is especially so in sheltered accommodation where some people pay only 10p for the licence fee while others pay a lot more. I note that the noble Viscount, Lord Tonypandy, agrees. One was not well received in such circumstances, especially if one was a Minister. One had to try to find an easy explanation—and it was not easy to find one. On the other hand, I am bound to say that, much as I would have liked to find some other way of dealing with the matter, to adopt a means of funding the BBC other than by the licence fee would be to do great harm to the very independence of the BBC about which we all care.

I turn briefly to the question of the appointment of members of the board of governors. Again, I agree with the Government that to have such appointments approved by a Select Committee would once more be to bring the BBC right into the party political arena. I would be very sorry if that were to be proposed. Of course, party politics enters into the appointment of governors—although the fact that the present Government appointed me answers that argument, I suppose. I do not know, but it certainly shows a little impartiality on the part of the Government. In my seven years as deputy chairman, there was never one occasion that I can recall when party politics entered into our discussions on BBC matters. I do not know the party political views of other members of the board of governors. All that I know is that we did not have a problem with party politics.

I hope that any government would seek to be fair and balanced in making appointments to the board of governors but, after that, the board of management must be a matter for the board of governors. The board of governors should appoint the director-general, who will then advise the board of governors on the appointment of the rest of the board of management. We were very fortunate and, I believe, absolutely right as a board to appoint John Birt who has been heavily criticised and wrongly abused. I believe that he is doing an excellent job running the BBC in a way that should please all your Lordships.

Finally, perhaps I may return to the question of accountability to Parliament. Constant examination by Parliament of the details of the way in which the BBC is handling its affairs and programmes may sound like good parliamentary accountability but, as paragraph 6.41 says, it would subject the BBC to party political controversy and damage once again that crucial independence about which I have spoken.

Overall, I believe that the White Paper has got it about right. I do not have too many opportunities to congratulate the Government, so I am happy to do so today. I welcome the White Paper. The Government deserve our congratulations on introducing it.

5.57 p.m.

The Earl of Halsbury: My Lords, those responsible have concentrated ex-governors of the BBC into the middle of the list of speakers. I have to confess that I, too, am an ex-governor of the BBC—of 1960s vintage. I expect that the noble Lord, Lord Barnett, and my noble friend Lord Greenhill probably have justifiable complaints that they wasted a lot of time correcting mistakes for which in my day I was responsible.

A great deal of what is at stake depends to a certain extent upon the meaning of words. I should like to express my thanks to the noble Viscount, Lord Astor, for the temperate way in which he has addressed these problems in the correspondence that we have had from him in the unofficial all-party working group. By way of illustration, perhaps I may consider the word "impartial". You cannot be impartial as between good and evil. Somebody had a bright idea and said, "Let's coin a new term and call it 'due impartiality' and leave other people to decide what difference the word 'due' makes". That is the sort of thing that makes the amendment of the noble Lord, Lord Annan, a little difficult to agree with. When the noble Lord uses the word "impartiality" does he mean "due impartiality" or just "impartiality" stripped of any qualification? I do not know. Perusing the documents, here and there I come across a phrase which reflex action makes me search for my blue pencil immediately. It could never have been penned by somebody who understood what he was writing about. I wonder how it found its way into the documentation.

What that presupposes, of course, is some kind of hierarchical structure with a top and a bottom. Between the top and the bottom there is a process of delegation, including, possibly, the authority to delegate further. Somewhere down the lower regions of the organisation there is accountability, answerability, responsibility, and so on, to the source of authority. But when I read a combination such as "delegated responsibility" I wonder whether whoever penned those terms could possibly have been aware of what he was doing.

You can delegate authority; you cannot delegate responsibility. You cannot make someone else answerable for what you are answering for. That is the basis upon which I have been searching for the proper attitude to be taken towards the subject matter of our discussion. If one goes to any manufacturer of a product, whether it is a sewing machine or motor car, and ask him, "What do you make?", he will be able to show you a sewing machine, a motor car, a bottle of coca cola, or whatever it may be, but the product of the BBC, and all the programme companies, is variable. First, it is not the same from channel to channel; secondly, it is not the same from hour to hour; and thirdly, it is not the same from day to day of the week or from week to week of the year. It is an utter impossibility for any one person to monitor in real time the whole output of the BBC, either in advance or in retrospect. What can be done is to set up a system of monitoring. That is done for the BBC partly by the Government and partly by the BBC itself.

The answer to what should be done to those who violate the code has been much advocated by myself and the noble Lord, Lord Orr-Ewing, and has been discussed in philosophical terms by the noble Lord, Lord Barnett. For someone who disobeys a clear directive there should be a warning, followed by a final warning, followed by dismissal. That should be understood clearly, and somehow or other written into the person's contract of employment.

If we compare the structure of the BBC with the structure of an ordinary public limited company there are certain differences which are worth noting. We should ask ourselves whether they are intentional differences or whether we have merely introduced them by inattention. Of course, the establishment document of a public limited company is its memorandum and articles of association, but the shareholders elect the directors to direct the company; to settle its policies; and to approve its managerial structure. They do not issue directives to the directors telling them how to do that. Directors are supposed to be qualified to know how to do that before they ever come forward for election.

Furthermore, the directors regard their position as more or less a marriage rather than a job to be initiated at one point and dropped at another. If one joins the board of a public company it is with the belief that one is going on with it until retiring age. Of course one has to suspend one's directorship and be re-elected every three years, or whenever the company articles prescribe, but one is not put on the board for a few years with someone else put on the board to replace one. It is not like that. There is a continuing team.

The board of directors appoints its own chairman as the board's spokesman. It has complete authority from the shareholders to make that appointment. The shareholders do not appoint someone to be chairman over the heads of the other directors. In the case of the BBC, we have an appointed chairman, and that immediately derogates from the authority and responsibility of his colleagues. He becomes thereby, through the exercise of ministerial authority, or whatever it may be, *primus inter pares*. However, even he is not a permanent appointment in the sense that the chairman of a public limited company is, of course, like the other directors, subject to re-election every so often. Normally the expectation is that he will go on as chairman until he reaches retiring age, whatever the retiring age for the company may be. He then retires and takes his place at the old boys' lunch with the other former directors.

None of that applies to public corporations such as the BBC or other quangos: the chairman is appointed over the heads of his colleagues, and that puts him in an unusual position. We must ask ourselves whether that is really what we want. I go back to the analogy. The directors of a public company appoint the managers. They may recommend one or two of the senior managers to be executive directors as appointed by the shareholders. They too must come up for re-election from time to time, and if they were not re-elected by the shareholders, they would probably lose their jobs as managers.

The directors do not get down to the work of managing themselves. They see that the company has the right managerial structure. When it comes to the relationship between the governors of the BBC and the management board, they appoint the director-general, and they and the director-general may choose certain selected managers to be members of the management board. But of course they do not, and should not, interfere with the day-to-day management. They should do that through the director-general and their executive colleagues. While they cannot inspect the BBC's output on a day-to-day basis or an hour to hour basis, they can monitor it.

I remember a conversation between my father and André Citroen. My father asked him, "To what do you attribute the success of your enterprise?" André Citroen's answer was, "I have a complaints department that reports direct to me. All complaints go ultimately through my hands, after being sieved out for me". It was

[THE EARL OF HALSBURY]
to that, he said, that he attributed his success. That is what the governors of the BBC should do. They should have a monitoring system for complaints. They should then take the appropriate disciplinary action, after due warning, in respect of people who systematically disobey the rules laid down.

Whether those analogies between a public limited company and the BBC should be followed exactly and precisely, I do not know; but those are the things we should be debating. Parliament must then monitor the monitors, as it were. We are responsible for everything. So I come to the vexed question of the Charter, on the one hand, versus Act of Parliament, on the other; in other words, do the memorandum and articles of association of the BBC come from the Queen in Council, the Queen in Parliament, or from both, or from one of them?

With our usual preference for compromise, the establishment document is issued by the Queen in Council, and the Agreement is subject to approval by the Secretary of State in Parliament—the Queen in Parliament, the final authority. Whether that is a good thing or a bad thing, I do not know, but with my general distrust of words and draftsmanship and our ability to put what we mean in unambiguous writing, I am in favour of having one document issued from one ministry approved by one Parliament, as opposed to two documents where it is not necessarily obvious that words in one mean the same as words in the other and one can go on playing hide and seek indefinitely with terms of reference.

I suspect strongly that game of hide and seek with the Charter, the Licence and the Agreement is something that went on in my day and that it still goes on. That is why the board of management can do exactly as it pleases, and treat the governors, very politely, as more or less nonentities.

I want to say one thing about the corruption in the world in which we live. I received a document—I expect that the noble Viscount has it—from the National Viewers' and Listeners' Association which contained a potted version of all the pornography and violence that there has been in the broadcast media for the past six months. I was unable to circulate the document because it was embargoed until one minute past midnight this morning. However, I have placed a copy in the Library and it is available for everyone to read.

The document is absolutely shocking. The language is shocking and in that connection I must enter a disclaimer. Bad language is sometimes excused on the ground that for reasons of artistic integrity and so forth corrupt people must use corrupt language. Artistic integrity does not excuse the public display of corrupt documents. However, your Lordships should have no illusions as to where the corruption lies; it lies with us not as Members of Parliament but as human beings. The public are corrupt, we are corrupt and human beings are corrupt. We indulge our corruption at third hand, as it were, by seeing it as entertainment on broadcast media. That is why we have tolerated it so far, but we should tolerate it no further. In that spirit I shall sit down.

6.10 p.m.

Viscount Caldecote: My Lords, it is a daunting task to follow three former governors of the BBC. I well remember an incident some 70 years ago. After fiddling with a cat's whisker, I suddenly heard through the earphones, "This is 2LO. Hello children". Since then, I have had a great admiration for the BBC and therefore I am in support of the White Paper in general—in particular the decision to continue the BBC as public service broadcasting funded by a licence fee.

However, there are present drawbacks which need to be rectified when the new Charter comes into operation. Many of them stem from the lack of clarity about the responsibilities of the governors. As other noble Lords have said, clearly it is not the job of governors to manage the BBC. However, it is their job to agree the policies of the BBC and to monitor the management in carrying them out. At present, those tasks are far too remote from each other. The question is whether the governors accept full and ultimate responsibility for all the activities of the BBC, as the noble Earl, Lord Halsbury, suggested they should, or whether they see themselves principally as guardians of the public interest, acting as a regulator remote from what management does.

If it is the latter it is too much of a "judge and jury" arrangement for the BBC when criticisms are made. In limited specific cases complaints can be dealt with by the Broadcasting Standards Council and the Broadcasting Complaints Commission. Now they are to be merged but apparently will have no more power than they have at present. In my view, the Board of Governors should act in the same way as the board of any Plc. However, I entirely accept that the analogy must not be taken too far, as was said by the noble Earl, Lord Halsbury. The board should have similar obligations to obey the law and it should be answerable to a regulator, in the same way as directors of Plcs are responsible to the DTI, the independent television companies to the ITC and the trustees of charities to the Charity Commissioners.

It would be perfectly possible to make a combined BSC and BCC perform the regulatory function of ensuring that governors abide by the Charter and the Agreement. That would be preferable to setting up a second regulatory body. However, in the absence of a regulating authority, the BBC has set up its own internal complaints department. As far as it goes, that is good. It is set up to deal with criticisms not covered by the BCC or BSC but it simply emphasises that the "judge and jury" factor still exists.

I believe that there should be a regulatory body for the BBC similar to that for the ITC. It would deal with all the accusations relating to breach of the Charter and the Agreement. How else can the Agreement and the Charter be enforced, as referred to by my noble friend Lord Astor? As was pointed out by the noble Lord, Lord Annan, there are no problems with the ITC because it has full powers to revoke licences or impose financial penalties. But, clearly, that is not practicable for the BBC because such penalties would simply be passed on to the public.

That is a most difficult problem to solve. Perhaps, as has been suggested, individual producers could be penalised for consistently breaking the rules. It is possible that governors could be held to account and personally penalised, as are directors of Plcs for unlawful trading. Some solution to the problem must be found, otherwise we shall continue with the flabby disregard of the present Charter and codes of practice that lead to the kind of broadcasting so forcefully described by the noble Earl, Lord Halsbury. We must find a solution or we shall have a continuation of the present situation whether on impartiality, violence, sex, crime or children's programmes.

I have one final question. Will my noble friend Lord Astor give a categorical assurance that this House will have the opportunity to debate the Charter and the Agreement in draft form? Time can then be given for amendments to be made before publication of the final Charter and Agreement. Surely, that is the best way of enabling this House, which has so much experience in this field, fully to contribute to the continuing high quality and success of the BBC.

6.17 p.m.

Viscount Tenby: My Lords, the "ex-governors of the BBC" section has now come to a close. I thought that perhaps I should make that clear. It is right that we should have a debate on this most important, complex and sensitive subject, even though some of the "light blue" noble Lords might have wished for a happier date on which it might be held. I thank the noble Viscount the Minister for his assurances in respect of the amendment moved by my noble friend Lord Annan.

Just as beauty lies in the eye of the beholder, I am inclined to the view that partiality principally lies in the ear of the hearer. Impartiality is of importance and is greatly to be desired. But control of taste and decency and of the right of people not to have their cherished beliefs mocked or ridiculed, or of ethnic minorities not to be spoken of disparagingly, seem to me to be equally important objectives. We have heard all about impartiality; but those issues must be thought about, too.

The fact is, however, that politicians—and I hope that they will forgive me for saying this—tend to be obsessed with the subject of impartiality. As the distinguished biographer, Philip Ziegler, recently wrote:

"It can be taken for granted that every British politician believes the BBC to be prejudiced ... in favour of the other party".

How true, my Lords! I seem to recall a downward twist in the earlier relationship between the government of the noble Lord, Lord Wilson of Rievaulx, and the BBC—so nothing much changes over the years.

I further believe—and I have no statistical evidence to support the belief—that politicians tend to exaggerate the influence which radio, TV and the press have on the electorate. Incidentally, by doing so, they unconsciously diminish and patronise that very body of the people.

Having made that observation, let me say straight away that it is vital to have in place machinery to ensure that the common-sense rules of impartiality are not breached and that standards of taste and decency are not grossly offended.

The Government's statement from another place said:

"Like other broadcasters, it"—

that is, the BBC—

"will continue to have obligations to observe due impartiality on controversial issues and to ensure programmes do not encourage crime or offend against good taste, decency or public feeling".—[*Official Report*, 6/7/94; col. 1292.]

Well, Amen to that!

The objectives are certainly admirable. But with regard to "like other broadcasters", the whole point surely is that the BBC is not like other broadcasters. It handles its own affairs in isolation from the statutory framework which embraces all other broadcasters. It only has to satisfy its governors who admittedly represent the listeners and viewers but who scarcely mirror the role of non-executive directors, as we have been hearing this afternoon, in terms of a hands-on commitment. Of course, it also metes out its own justice.

Indeed, in the White Paper the Government go further and at paragraph 6.10 they envisage that the governors' main responsibility will be,

"to ensure that the BBC's programmes, services and other activities reflect the needs and interests of the public".

That may be satisfactory to ensure that the BBC does not bury Radio 4 in future or switch all listeners to FM bands; but it does not exactly send out a message to producers who are seeking to try it on that their card is numbered. After all, it is hardly the same ball game for independent broadcasters where, in extreme cases, the licence may even be removed and where financial penalties for infringement of obligations are imposed.

In a service financed by the public purse, such an outcome is clearly not possible. Very well; alternatives should be considered, and it really is important that we should not just tiptoe round this issue. We really must get down to start thinking about it properly.

Although I am doubtful whether the suggestion about the football referee's yellow and red cards or indeed a points system not unlike that in use for motoring offences, where you gradually come up until you become a "totter", would necessarily work in respect of erring directors and producers. They might be adaptable or they might not. But if they are not, then let other ways be found for I cannot seriously believe that human ingenuity cannot devise a procedure acceptable to most people which protects the freedom of artistic endeavour but which punishes those who usually abuse it—and I have to say this—for sensational or commercial reasons. That is why they do it.

I do not wish to appear unhelpful. No one could be more relieved than I at the Government's acknowledgement of and commitment to the concept of excellent public service broadcasting as exemplified by the BBC. Gone (one would hope for ever) are the flushes and fancies of the 1980s with regard to ideas such as the BBC paying for itself through advertising or appealing to the lowest common denominator in

[VISCOUNT TENBY]
programming to achieve success in the ratings war. Conversion is always to be welcomed, and I harbour a sneaking hope that like all converts, this Government, should they be in a position to be so, will in future become a stronger advocate of the merits of public service broadcasting than even the most vociferous disciple of the late Lord Reith.

As I have said, I do not wish to appear unhelpful; but I cannot for the life of me understand this preoccupation with Royal Charters. Perhaps it was a good wheeze in 1926 because it enshrined the new corporation's freedom from political control. I can understand that. But that was nearly 70 years ago and if the penny has not dropped by now that the BBC is an independent body, it never will. Why cannot the BBC be established by statute, just like all other forms of broadcasting in this country, and be not controlled by Parliament but directly answerable to it? I have the distinct feeling that that preference for Royal Charters, which, as we have heard, inevitably obscures the direct lines of responsibility, is a more cosy arrangement for the principle players involved. I believe that it serves only to obfuscate the chain of command, thereby making largely unenforceable control of the corporation's obligations.

I conclude by welcoming two proposals arising from the White Paper; first, the development of the BBC's commercial expertise in partnership with other organisations, which must be widely welcomed as must secondly be the proposed merger of the BCC and the BSC, about which we have heard so much about today. That will undoubtedly result in less confusion which arises inevitably when there is a multiplicity of bodies with disturbingly similar names and whose very existence may perversely have had the effect of deterring potential complainants who, when it came to the crunch, could not be bothered to find out which body did what.

The trouble with a debate like this is that one agrees a little bit with nearly everybody so I hope that noble Lords will forgive me if I do not refer to them by name; but I also agree with the idea of a single body in future. I would hope that the Government will look again at that.

It is right that these matters should be fully debated in this House, for what we have here are a number of noble Lords with unparalleled experience and knowledge of these matters—former governors of the BBC; chairmen of broadcasting authorities; directors of radio and TV companies; broadcasters themselves; and even the principal player in an important and admired report on the future of broadcasting. Accordingly, I would ask the Minister to ensure, via his right honourable friend in another place, that the voice of this House is heard loud and clear as the moves unfold and not—as was the case in the composition of the Select Committee, I have to say—shamefully ignored.

Put quite simply, those matters and their implications are too important to become flawed by prejudice, ignorance or hearsay.

6.27 p.m.

Lord Harmar-Nicholls: My Lords, the Minister should feel very happy about this debate. He has been given a clean bill of health as regards the White Paper and he can report back that there is almost unanimous approval of the general message which comes from the White Paper. The only exception to that for a fleeting moment, was from the noble Lord, Lord Greenhill of Harrow. He gave very wise advice with regard to future technical developments. He advised us not to take things for granted because matters which we now accept as being almost certain may proceed rather differently when these issues come to fruition.

At one stage at the very beginning of the debate I thought that we were not to have a debate at all. If one remembers the opening words of the Minister's speech, he used almost the identical words of the Motion in the name of the noble Lord, Lord Annan. Since the agreement was so complete, I thought that he was going to say, "We accept the amendment and therefore there is no need to proceed further". That was not quite what happened but it was reasonably near to it. Therefore, I believe that my noble friend should feel satisfied because what he has commended today to the House has received almost unanimous approval.

At this stage, I do not believe that we want any more inside knowledge about the BBC, the governors, the deputy chairmen and those who have been part of the actual machine itself. They have played their part and their evidence is most valuable. Of course, it ought to be taken into account, as I have no doubt it will be. I am concerned that we, as part of Parliament, should examine the effect that the BBC, under the machinery as it is set up, is likely to have on the nation. We should be the watchdogs in that respect.

I have much admiration for the right reverend Prelate. He made no bones about it. He said that, whatever minutes he had in this debate, he would use them to sell his Church. He said that he would make clear the rights that his Church has to have its beliefs and its teachings focused properly through that important media; and he did so. In my small contribution, I should like to do the same. However, I should like to do so on the basis of a parliamentary party politician.

I believe that we ought to look at what happened pre-war as compared with post-war. It really has been quite tremendous in terms of its impact on the country. Many of us were parliamentary candidates before the war and operated as such because Parliament is a parliamentary democracy based upon the party system. That is what it is and that is what it is our duty to try to operate. Before the war, Members of Parliament were the real source of influence in arriving at what was a national view on things. They were the ones who, by and large, gave the lead and that was generally accepted. However, that is not accepted today. The power of influencing thought, especially in the world of politics, no longer lies with Members of Parliament; it now lies with the BBC announcers, the people in the media and the columnists in the newspapers. They are the opinion-formers today.

Many of us were fascinated by party politics and government generally when we were very young. I recall the time when my noble friend was Deputy Speaker of the House of Commons. I remember him as a colleague back in 1932 when we were organising political schools, and so on. When I think back to those days and compare where the power and influence have moved to, it seems to me to be quite tremendous. I do not believe that it is to the good; indeed, I believe that it is very much to the bad that the influence for creating public opinion should have moved to the areas that have it today. There is nothing we can do about it. It will not go back. It is a matter of harnessing it in a way where, if it is wrong—and I believe it is in terms of the trend—it will be less wrong than it might be if we did nothing about it.

One example I can give of the contrast is that before the war I was the candidate for Nelson and Colne—little Moscow they called it—against little Sydney Silverman, who was a most adept politician. I was a parliamentary candidate at that time, not a Member of Parliament. However, people turned up when one had a meeting. Indeed, 100, 200 and sometimes thousands on the odd occasions. One was able to use one's influence as a candidate and appeal directly to the people. The influence that one had at times was not that much; but at any rate the direct contact was there. Moreover, when one made a speech it was reported by the newspapers. They did not just pick out one or two words which happened to fit in with the message that they were going to put in their editorial column that day. That applied with the local press in particular, and often with the national press.

It is not good if what I am saying is true; but I believe it to be true. In terms of standing in society, especially in the area where one is operating, my status as a parliamentary candidate then was 10-times higher than that of a Member of Parliament today in terms of public esteem. MPs have been downgraded in a way which is very dangerous indeed. At the end of the day, they are the ones who have to prepare the statutes which eventually become the law of our country. That is what happened then. Now, all the influence is exercised by the columnists and the television announcers. If one wants to influence society, one should not think in terms of becoming Prime Minister or a Member of Parliament; one should think in terms of becoming a BBC or an ITV commentator.

What can we do about the situation, if anything? I believe that the most we can hope to do is to ensure that the new communicators—the ones who in this modern age are in the position to influence public opinion, which results in the sort of government that we have—are treated in the same way. I am not arguing only from the Conservative point of view, which happens to be my belief: the same problem applies to all sides. They are as insignificant as we are in terms of exercising that great influence. But what can we do about it? The most that we can do is to try to get the new communicators—the broadcasters and the columnists —on the same level as the politicians who had this influence in the old days. Of course, our standing ought to be better; if we got theirs to the same level that would be a move somewhere.

When I first came into Parliament—and I have colleagues from those days here in the Chamber—we had no register of interests. We called each other the "honourable Member" on the basis that we were satisfied that we were honourable people. If people declared their interests before they made their speech or before they voted, which is quite correct, that was sufficient. However, that is not now the case. We have to have a register of declared interests, right down to the most minute detail. Then the new communicators pick a little bit out of that declaration, distort it and twist it in a way which makes the honourable Member concerned look as though he is a member of the corrupt brigade. That is how it works now.

I believe that that trend has had the effect of making people who make their contributions as Members of Parliament that much more careful to ensure that they do not allow their personal greed or their personal preferences to take over. Therefore, to that extent it has had a function. However, I should like to put a thought in someone's mind. It could be the mind of the BBC's complaints authority. In order to keep on the rails, why can we not have a register of interests for the new communicators, many of whom slip in as an aside some of the comments which cause the most danger? Why can we not know what is their true background? If those communicators have such power—and, make no bones about it, they have—which I argue they have taken from Members of Parliament, why can we not have something equivalent to, if not the same as, the register of declared interests for them?

It is the little aside which does most damage. "Any Questions" is one of our most prestigious programmes and some of our most estimable people act as the chairman. Great trouble is taken to ensure that the forum is properly balanced, with Government supporters, Opposition supporters, middle of the road supporters and people from industry. The chairman is supposed to be impartial and an outstanding character who can be trusted against all sorts of odds. If one or other of the people appearing on the programme seems to be making a good point which is swaying the programme, the chairman will pop in and make a few remarks as though he is one of the protagonists, but because of his position his remarks carry 10 times more weight than those of the person who made the first point.

I congratulate my noble friend on being able, after this debate, to take back to his department such unanimous approval. However, I hope he will not leave the matter there and that he will find some way of being able to control to some extent this new group of people I have mentioned who are, for the most part, represented by those who operate in the BBC. I am not talking about the governors, the deputy chairmen or the people who operate the machinery, but the people they employ, who appear on programmes and make their points from the powerful positions they hold which the BBC has given them. I support those who have suggested that there should be some way of dealing with people who find a

[LORD HARMAR-NICHOLLS]
way through the impartiality fence. Why not show them the yellow card and deny them the right to make future appearances on this prestigious, valuable platform? We need to find some way of controlling the people who have taken over the authority which once belonged to Members of Parliament in informing public opinion on political matters. I am not talking about other matters.

It is right that one should speak from one's own experience. I remember vividly that I fought a by-election in Nelson and Colne. It was impossible for a Tory to win that by-election. Six months later I was brought out of the Army again to fight a by-election in Preston against Lord Shackleton, who was the most delightful opponent to have to deal with. When it was announced that I was to be the candidate, Lord Beaverbrook, who was then the great power in the land, rang me up. He asked me whether I would fight the election, with his backing, on the basis of being the anti-American loan candidate. I had to say no. I said that I did not think I could do that because I felt that, after the cost of the war and all that that meant, the loan to prime the pump such as was envisaged in the American offer was not only desirable but vital. Lord Beaverbrook was not very pleased about that. He sent a secretary to my first public meeting to say in public what he had said in private about the desirability of my being the anti-American loan candidate. I gave the same answer in public as I had given Lord Beaverbrook over the telephone. I was an insignificant candidate who did not have a wax cat in hell's chance of winning the by-election. The majority against me in those days was 15,000 or 16,000. However, when I gave a similar answer in public to the one I had given Lord Beaverbrook in private, the whole of the opinion column in his paper said that I was a weak-kneed, vacillating Tory candidate who lacked guts.

The next day Sir Anthony Eden was due to speak for me. He said to me, "Well, your view is ours". He made a speech which more or less supported what had been done and the column in the newspaper stated, "The master is as bad as the pupil". But the column space devoted to Sir Anthony was only half that devoted to me.

I make that point to show the influence that people have who are in control of these organs—in the case I referred to, it was a leading newspaper—such as the BBC and the television companies. If we do nothing about the influence these people have and the way in which they use it, where they allow their bias and their personal views to interfere with what should be impartial leadership, we shall be in trouble.

I wish my noble friend the best of luck. He has had a good evening and he has the debate as he would like it. I think it is right that that should be the case, but I would ask him, please, to make certain that his department and, as far as he can, any who follow him are aware of the fact that everything is not rosy, easy and quite as wonderful as some people would suggest it is.

6.46 p.m.

Baroness O'Cathain: My Lords, I welcome this debate and like most previous speakers I thank the noble Viscount for making it possible because it gives us an opportunity not only to pay tribute to the BBC but also to air some concerns and, indeed, to make some suggestions.

The BBC is one of the few categories in which the United Kingdom is a world leader. It is a world leader in broadcasting and, as the noble Lord, Lord Barnett, said, the BBC World Service on radio and TV is indeed excellent. One only has to travel to experience that. The worldwide competition for the BBC tends to be banal at best and tasteless at its worst, and we really should take pride in the BBC and not knock it. I mentioned the word competition. The BBC competes both nationally and internationally for audiences and export sales, and indeed nationally for scarce financial resources.

As a country we have not yet accepted that there has to be greater public accountability in every case where public funding features. The creativity of the BBC is not an excuse for lax accountability. I hasten to say that I am not accusing the BBC of lax accountability but there is a perception, a suspicion abroad, based on evidence of, for example, TV crews "hunting in packs", that overmanning still persists. The new regime at the BBC under John Birt is to be congratulated in achieving greater management standards —producer choice being just one manifestation of this. There appear to have been strides made in achieving greater efficiency. We must be patient in demanding even more strides in these directions. Speaking from somewhat bitter experience I know that to achieve change in a creative environment is exceedingly slow.

Impartiality has featured very much tonight. I have nothing to add to that, but there are other concerns, two of which are of personal concern to me but I believe they are fairly widespread concerns and both can be tenuously linked. I refer to what I call the lowest common denominator factor and the subject of religious broadcasting.

In preparation for this debate I managed to obtain and read a copy of *Producers' Guidelines*, which refers to the objective of enabling,

"programme makers and the public alike to see the editorial and ethical principles that drive the BBC".

It is an excellent publication. It is a document of great clarity and it is easy to read.

The BBC has all sorts of responsibilities thrust upon it, some arduous and others that are almost impossible to achieve. But I believe that as a public service broadcasting organisation it has the responsibility to,

"do nothing to undermine standards of behaviour"

or, as the annex to the licence states, not to,

"offend against good taste or decency".

Both of those statements are couched in negative terms. I would prefer to be positive, and I personally should like to go further and state that the BBC should ensure that standards of behaviour are maintained or, better still, improved.

Of course I realise that I have now ventured into the quicksand of definitions of taste and decency, and that is a pretty hopeless situation. I shall try to explain my reasons by anecdote—a factual description of what occurred last Sunday evening.

Four people were in my sitting room at home. Three were watching television. The fourth, me, was struggling under a mountain of Christmas cards. I positioned myself at the far end of the room. I had no view of the television screen; there was a cabinet in front of me. However, I could hear the television. That point is relevant. The programme on the television was "Seaforth". Shortly into the programme one word appeared to be used frequently. That word was "bloody". It is a swear word. Having counted about 15 repetitions of that word I spoke to the viewers at the far end of the room. I said, "That's a bit much, isn't it?". "What is a bit much?" they replied. "The constant use of that word". They had not noticed. I was flabbergasted. I realised that while watching television one can reduce one's attention on the words and concentrate on the visual action. It is subliminal, I fear.

If the words spoken—the dialogue—had featured, say, on Radio 4, there would have been an outcry. We are subjected to lower standards on TV than on radio. Why? And why was that word so essential to the plot that it had to be repeated *ad nauseam*? I asked the viewers in my sitting room if it would have detracted from the story if the word had not been used. The answer was no.

I know the counter-argument: it is real life. It is said that people speak like that. Sadly, that may be true to a large extent. However, it is not real life. This is real life here in Parliament, and we do not use that word. It is not true of the boardrooms of our commercial companies. It is not true of the Church. It is not true of the professions—the law and medicine (at least, not universally true). Therefore, why stoop to the lowest common denominator? Speech programmes on BBC Radio 3 and 4 maintain standards and set standards in terms of little use of swear words. Why is that not true of TV?

As part of its role of public service broadcasting I suggest that the BBC should have the responsibility to try and encourage the population to desist from using swear words. Swear words cause distress and show a complete lack of respect for fellow human beings.

It is universally acknowledged that there has been a relentless and insidious deterioration in standards of behaviour and respect for others. That downward slide has led, I believe, to an unhappy and even degrading sense of malaise in so many walks of life. It is seen to be smart, chic and radical to push constantly at the existing bounds of decency. Surely the BBC can help to stop that rot rather than encourage it.

I am not so sure that programmes which offend are particularly popular. This week I have heard nobody talk about "Seaforth" but I have heard many people talk about "Martin Chuzzlewit".

My concern about the issue of the lowest common denominator and how it could be tackled is linked with my second concern —religious broadcasting. That subject was ably addressed by the right reverend Prelate, the Bishop of Southwark. Again, I know that I am on dangerous ground and will be told that we are a secular society, and so what if you have to switch on the radio at 6.25 a.m. for "Prayer for the Day", and so what if, because you have been indoctrinated by the BBC to rely on FM you are unable to find the "Daily Service" on medium wave. I know that "Songs of Praise" is popular, as we have been told. An audience of 7 million viewers is terrific. But it is difficult to find religious broadcasts on radio. In this decade of evangelism, subscribed to by all Christian Churches, very little encouragement is given by the BBC to those who wish to learn, to be informed and to draw strength from *The Bible*.

The timing of religious programmes—or is it a fact that they do not seem to be "trailed" as much as other programmes?—leads me to feel that they are accorded very low priority. Better advertised and better timed religious programmes, plus special programmes to take account of the decade of evangelism, could help to restore standards of behaviour and respect. Coupled with a reduction in bad language, that could make a big difference and enhance the public service broadcasting responsibility of the BBC.

I ask, is that Utopia? Is it achievable? Who would be responsible for effecting this? Would it be the board of governors? From what we have heard on this aspect today, I fear not.

I said at the outset that I would make some suggestions about how the BBC could be improved. I have dealt with my concerns and have given suggestions. I should like to endorse the suggestion that the organisation of the top echelons of the BBC should ensure that there is true responsibility for the product of the BBC at the highest level, as there is for any product from any commercial organisation at board level. If that is not possible at board level, I subscribe totally to the suggestion of my noble friend Lord Annan, that the board of management at the BBC be strengthened by non-executive directors. Until then, I fear that there will always be a charge of "all power and no responsibility", or, as per my noble friend Lord Annan, not enough people who drop clangers carry the can.

6.55 p.m.

Baroness Rawlings: My Lords, I welcome this opportunity to debate the White Paper. Indeed, I welcome the White Paper itself. I hope that the BBC will continue to be our major public service broadcaster, despite all the new technologies, for at least another 10 years. That is an important responsibility.

Several knowledgeable comments have been made by experienced Peers. I agree with many, especially the point concerning the role of the BBC in relation to education and the arts mentioned by the noble Lord, Lord Donoughue. I should like to make just one point.

The BBC has great influence in Britain. It has even greater influence worldwide, due entirely to the high respect in which it is held. The World Service has a worldwide audience of 130 million people a week, not only for its wireless broadcasts, but now also its highly successful television broadcasts. I wonder how many people in Britain listen regularly to foreign radio or television stations. Perhaps they do, as we did as children to "Top 20" on Radio Luxembourg.

When I visited Bulgaria at the time of its first free election after the fall of Mr. Zhivkov, so many people came to thank me—not, I hasten to add because it was me, but because I was British. Their main ray of hope

[BARONESS RAWLINGS]
for years was the possibility, often illegally, of listening to our BBC World Service. It played a vital role in their lives.

Yet back here the television that speaks to us in our own homes has an unrecognised, even disproportionate, influence on our lives and on the way we form our ideas and arguments. As my noble friend Lord Harmar-Nicholls stated so clearly—and I repeat the point because it is so important—during any national election campaign in this country today any large political meeting can no longer compete with the television screen. The BBC accordingly has an enormous responsibility.

Edmund Burke referred to the fourth estate as:

"more important than them all".

As the noble Lord, Lord Wyatt of Weeford, explained recently, he meant that through what the media wrote and said they had more influence on people's thinking than the other three estates—the Lords Spiritual, the Lords Temporal and the Commons.

A natural tension always exists between journalists working in a free and open society and the government of the nation in which they operate. It was said recently by a foreign journalist that,

"governments have the natural tendency not to reveal all the facts about their departments and operations. That tendency often clashes with the duty of the free press; to uncover and tell the people what they need to know about their government's operations".

He went on to say that,

"there should be no restrictions placed on the press when it investigates government, acting in its role as 'watchdog' or guardian of the public good".

However, investigative journalists—whether they be from the television, wireless or the written press—should always conduct themselves in accordance with professional journalistic standards when pursuing their investigations. Even in a country like Britain which is very open, where we have a great tradition of free press and free expression, any government nevertheless wants to protect itself. Our free written press and the audio visual media are vital elements in the reporting of everyday life, of the good things in our society as well as the exposure of corruption and wrongdoing.

But, in turn, my point today is that they have a duty to report responsibly and fairly. I want to thank the Minister for introducing the debate today. I welcome the Government having produced the White Paper setting out a blueprint to carry the BBC into the 21st century. I hope that they will continue the exciting new steps they have taken recently in forming a global strategic alliance with Pearson Plc. That will keep the BBC—as is the aim of the White Paper—serving the nation and competing worldwide.

7.1 p.m.

Baroness Wharton: My Lords, like many other speakers, I also welcome the White Paper on the future of the BBC. As a corporation, the BBC has played a major part in our lives. The licence fee ensures that it remains publicly funded with a firm commitment to public service broadcasting. However, the commercial advantages offered by opportunities opening up in the media market should still remain secondary to the corporation's fair and balanced public service broadcasting commitments. I sometimes wonder, I must admit, whether those principles have gone a little astray. At this point I should like to thank the Minister for his clear assurances on the matter.

I accept that there is a long-established rule of impartiality now incorporated into the BBC Licence. This should mean freedom not only from government but commercial influence. It is very important to the corporation's national and international standing.

The Broadcasting Complaints Commission and the Broadcasting Standards Council are to be merged. I hope that a stronger body will emerge from this union. Am I right in thinking that it will not have any statutory powers? By comparison, the ITC does have statutory powers. Its code on impartiality is clearly drawn up with no room for misunderstanding. The code applies to all licensees and compliance is a condition of the Licence. It is the responsibility of licensees to ensure that employees and programme makers—independent or on the staff—observe the provisions of the code. A section under the heading "Objectives" states:

"Impartiality does not mean that broadcasters have to be absolutely neutral on every controversial issue, but it should lead them to deal even-handedly with opposing points of view in the area of democratic debate. Opinion should be clearly distinguished from fact".

The BBC has undergone a substantial change to its structure in recent years and some of that change relates to training schemes. For instance, the reporter training scheme appears to have been abandoned, as have apprenticeships in engineering and technical operations. Sadly, the closure of the BBC radio and script units may mean that guidance which used to be offered to young writers has been reduced, though I now understand that a team might be transferred to the drama department.

Traditionally, the BBC has provided the seed corn for most of the entertainment industry. Practically every media person I know has either been trained by or worked at the BBC. Because of its role as a leader in industry training, it is worrying to see the BBC contracting in this department.

I am afraid I am going to take a slightly different view. I believe that the introduction of producers' choice has gone some way to undermining the stability and continuity of employment at the BBC. I gather that the input from independents has risen as high as 46 per cent. for drama and light entertainment. Just how the percentage is split between those two groups I do not know. It must be that, on average, independents could usually underbid the BBC because of differing base costs. John Birt himself has said that the BBC needs to ensure that its in-house departments are good enough to win orders but that could only come about if there was a level playing field between the two sectors.

At an all-party media group meeting, John Birt accepted that morale was at a low ebb, and that in the short term it was probably not likely to improve. However, he stressed that once the restructuring of the corporation was completed, morale would improve. He himself has also said that there are powerful arguments for the BBC to maintain its strong production base.

However, could it be that the structure of employment contracts, with their potential lack of continuity, need to be reviewed in order to preserve the BBC's greatest asset—namely, a committed, qualified and experienced workforce? Within the current climate, surely it must be difficult to retain and motivate individuals of the calibre which in the past enabled it to establish an unassailable international reputation for diversity and for excellence.

We need to make sure that the BBC, with its enduring service to public sector broadcasting, continues to prosper and build on its already considerable achievements well into the next century. I do not want to see any part of this large corporation sold off to the private sector. Once it becomes fragmented, it will gradually cease to be great.

7.6 p.m.

Lord Ashbourne: My Lords, I wish to address two issues in my brief contribution this evening: the importance of maintaining standards of taste and decency within the BBC and the particular challenges arising from increased satellite broadcasting from abroad.

I have told the House before how I believe that there is no better guide for standards in broadcasting than the inscription which appears in the foyer of Broadcasting House in Portland Square. It bears repeating:

"To Almighty God, this shrine of the arts, music and literature is dedicated by the first Governors in the year of our Lord 1931, John Reith being Director General. It is their prayer that good seed sown will produce a good harvest, that everything offensive to decency and hostile to peace will be expelled, and that the nation will incline its ear to those things which are lovely pure and of good report and thus pursue the path of wisdom and virtue".

We have sadly often had cause to feel that the BBC has departed from that path in recent years. I am glad, therefore, that this White Paper does stress in paragraph 3.13 that the BBC should pay more attention to audience concern about violence, sex and bad language.

The BBC should, for example, study seriously the latest report from the National Viewers' and Listeners' Association, showing that in 20 films screened on BBC 1 and BBC 2 between January and June this year there were 67 violent assaults. Such violence makes a profound impression on young people and surely must be one contributing factor to some of the horrific violent incidents we have seen involving young people in recent years. I should say, of course, that there was violence on other channels mentioned in the report, but this debate is mainly on the BBC.

I would favour that the proposed agreement between the Secretary of State for National Heritage and the BBC board of governors, mentioned in paragraph 6.3 of the White Paper, should spell out in simple terms what is meant by standards of "good taste and decency". Then no one would be in any doubt about what to expect from programmes.

Of course, the BBC does not operate in isolation from other broadcasters either in this country or abroad. I am not suggesting one set of rules for the BBC and one for other broadcasters. They should all operate to the same high standards on issues of taste and decency.

We caught a glimpse of what the future might hold with the broadcasting of Red Hot Dutch earlier this year, first from Holland and then from Denmark, which, thankfully, the Government stepped in to ban. I understand that the European Commission will shortly announce its proposals for a new trans-frontier broadcasting directive controlling broadcasting in Europe. I hope that Her Majesty's Government will fight hard to protect standards to avoid a repeat of the Red Hot Dutch débâcle.

In closing, I make one suggestion to the Minister. If a satellite broadcaster wishes to broadcast into a country it should have a licence in the receiving country and not just in the country from which the broadcast is made. If the new directive included such a provision, the UK could maintain standards and protect the BBC by preventing anyone from broadcasting unacceptable material into the UK. That was, of course, the point made by my noble friend Lord Orr-Ewing in his balanced and authoritative speech earlier in the debate. Is that not something which, surely, we would all support?

7.10 p.m.

Lord Elis-Thomas: My Lords, I begin by thanking the noble Viscount for enabling us to have this debate. I also welcome him back to DNH, with its major broadcasting responsibilities not only for the BBC but also for the Welsh fourth channel. I declare an interest as chair of Screen Wales, which is a media partnership agency involving BBC Wales as one of the senior partners; and also my membership of the general advisory council, which makes me responsible, among other things, for the selection process for membership of the Broadcasting Council for Wales.

I shall not, however, talk about the specifics of the structure of the BBC this evening. I want to take as my text paragraph 1.7 of the White Paper and to welcome the statement there that:

"The BBC's programmes should reflect the interests and cultural traditions of the United Kingdom as a whole. Programme-makers, presenters and performers in all parts of the United Kingdom should contribute fully to the BBC's national output, as well as to its regional and local services".

Having read my text, I want to congratulate the Government, and indeed the BBC governors and board of management, on taking the debate on broadcasting in the United Kingdom a little further than we took it in our debates in another place on previous broadcasting legislation. As a number of noble Lords emphasised, we are in the world of multi-media global culture. I make no apology for using those words. They are used generally within the industry and within culture. They present a challenge to traditional terrestrial broadcasters. They also present a challenge to traditional nation state regulators. This is where the Government are catching up with the real world. They are understanding that it is only as a public service broadcaster which is also an international media player that the BBC can survive and contribute not only to the internal cultural diversity of the UK but to broadcasting systems worldwide.

[LORD ELIS-THOMAS]

In relation to that, I would emphasise that competition in the multi-media global scene does not just emerge from the BBC centrally. It is not just BBC Enterprises or the BBC's board of management in Broadcasting House and White City which is a multi-media player. The national regions—as the BBC has always fondly called them—are also players in their own right. It is important therefore that there should be opportunities for them to play their role, not just within the network structure but also on the broader basis of the multi-media scene.

It is for those reasons that I welcome the commitment in the White Paper to the role of the BBC in the multi-media market and to looking at the BBC as an engine of economic development in the cultural field. That is just as important as the contribution that it makes to reflecting the life of the United Kingdom internally. In that sense, I do not share the concern that was expressed by some noble Lords about the role of the Department of Trade and Industry in the promotion of broadcasting (or of broadcast product) or indeed the role of the Welsh Office in the context of Wales in the development of multi-media. I warmly welcome the speech that was made on this very issue this week at a conference in Cardiff by the Secretary of State for Wales. We have an opportunity now to develop our cultural product in all parts of the UK in a way that will benefit us economically and will also benefit our cultural image. I believe that there are people world-wide who look to us to do that.

I do not share the pessimism which, again, was expressed by some noble Lords about the difficulty of programme sales in other markets. The demand for content now in our multi-media industry is so enormous that we shall be at pains to fulfil it. Therefore, there is clearly a role for the quality product of the BBC and other broadcasters in the UK in that market.

I turn now to some of the issues that arise in the way in which the White Paper is to be implemented. I share the view that was expressed by a number of noble Lords that perhaps the time has come for us to have conventional broadcasting legislation for the BBC rather than the arrangement of Charter and Agreement. I say that because, as someone who debated previous broadcasting legislation involving both the ITC (as it now is) and S4C, there seems to me to be no inherent difficulty about legislating in the normal way for broadcasting structures. I appreciate that, historically, at the time that the BBC was created there was a different relationship between the state and broadcasting. Now we are in a world of greater diversity in terms of numbers of broadcasters. It might have made more sense to go down the road of regulating for all public service broadcasting in the United Kingdom in one piece of legislation. I agree with the noble Lord on that matter. After all, it is not just the BBC that is a public service broadcaster. All our broadcasting is either publicly funded or publicly regulated in some form or other. Therefore there is a case for an organising principle in legislation which bears all those matters in common.

That is where some of the difficulties that we have arise in relation to some of the specific matters that will be in the agreement.

I turn back now to the commitments set out in the White Paper on regional product and regional programming. I refer in particular to paragraph 3.24, which reads almost as well as if it had been written by Screen Wales itself in that it talks about the importance of the variety of programme production; it says that there should be significant programme bases in Scotland, Wales and Northern Ireland and in the major English regional centres; and of course in that way incorporates part of the recommendations of the Select Committee, which emphasised that the possibility of a commitment to network production outside London might be included in the Charter.

I understand that the Minister's view is that such a statement might be included in the Agreement. I shall be very interested to have his response on that point at some later stage in our debates. I do not share the view that was expressed by some of our Scottish colleagues, and by some independent producer representatives, that there should be a quota for programme production. I believe that we are capable in the national regions of competing on a level playing field with the rest of the BBC or indeed with other independent production centres. However, we need to make sure that the playing field is level, in the sense that the resources are there and also in terms of staffing, and in financial terms to enable our media centres to develop a competitive base. For those reasons, I hope that there will be clear reference, if not in the Charter then certainly in the Agreement, to the whole question of programme bases outside regions. I understand that that may well be the Minister's view, and I look forward to hearing his response.

A related issue is the structure of the broadcasting councils, the role of governors and the role of the national councils. I welcome the statement in the White Paper about the specific role of the governors in relation to the board of management of the BBC centrally. I also welcome the fact that a similar role—to use the word in the White Paper—is envisaged for the broadcasting councils. This is significantly more than their present role. It means that they now have a role in the management, or at least in the accountability, of the BBC's operation in the national region. Controllers, will have a greater independence in relation to their budgets. (This is stated in paragraph 6.22 and in the whole range of surrounding paragraphs from paragraph 6.16 on, which I shall not quote in detail so as not to lengthen my speech inordinately). Paragraph 6.22 gives controllers a budget for programmes produced specifically for audiences in each country. We have therefore a clear devolution of the internal structure of the BBC.

My questions are: how much of this will appear in the Charter; how much will appear in the Agreement; and how is it to be policed, as it were? I appreciate that the BBC itself has taken some major steps in transferring its programming out of the metropolitan centre to other metropolitan centres or to regional centres. I appreciate also the fact that the BBC now has an English regional structure. I always believed that it was important for the English regions to be treated at least on some basis of equality with the national regions of Wales, Scotland and Northern Ireland. On all those counts therefore I welcome the level of debate which is now seen in the White Paper.

But as I said, there are a number of concerns. To what extent are we to have a clear programming policy incorporated into the objectives of BBC management? How are resources to be allocated equitably between national regions and other regions? How will we ensure that there is a sufficient level of capital investment in talent and production skills throughout the UK? How are we to ensure that the responsibility towards a regional policy is clearly stated? Is it to be in the Charter or only the Agreement? How are we to ensure that the structure for appointing the various governors and councils makes them as democratically accountable as possible? With all due respect, I do not believe that the present structure of parallel selection and nomination amounts to democratic accountability.

Having asked those questions, I end by welcoming the White Paper and the fact that there is a clear statement of the way in which public service broadcasting can be revived and made multinational in the true sense of that word, in the context of our multi-media global village and its mass culture. I believe that it is important that the whole of the UK in its cultures, regions and nations participate in that process.

7.21 p.m.

Lord Ackner: My Lords, I view my position in the list of speakers as that of a long-stop and I shall not ask your Lordships to stop long, having regard to my contribution. I propose to confine my observations to the question of impartiality.

My first point is that the BBC accept, and so inform their producers in their written guidance, that,

"the notion of impartiality lies at the heart of the BBC. No area of programming is exempt from it".

It has been said that an Irishman—maybe an Irish BBC official—when asked how he managed to be fair and just, said that he always tried very hard to be halfway between partial and impartial.

In the annex to the Licence and Agreement, which prescribes the terms and conditions of the corporation's operations, the BBC accepts as a duty,

"to ensure that programmes maintain a high general standard in all respects (and in particular in respect of content and quality), and to provide a properly balanced service which displays a wide range of subject matter [and] to treat controversial subjects with due impartiality ... both in the Corporation's news services and in the more general field of programmes dealing with matters of public policy".

That vitally important aspect of the BBC's constitutional position is clearly far too important to be confined to an annex. I am delighted to learn that that is also the view of the Government.

I should like to attempt to make a positive suggestion. I believe that the obligation to act with due impartiality needs to be spelt out, particularly having regard to the absence of any effective sanction when impartiality is not exhibited.

Noble Lords' viewing and listening habits no doubt vary considerably, but I imagine that none of your Lordships will have any difficulty in producing some clear examples of the media's failure to act fairly and justly. Let me take a recent example known to all noble Lords: the programme on your Lordships' House. It was a mocking, insulting programme, designed to ridicule and to parody the activities of the House and its important contribution to the legislative function of Parliament. Some may say that such trivia has no impact and that its lack of quality and content ensures its own almost immediate destruction. But does it? Last Friday, at a dinner in Cambridge, I met a German professor who told me that the film had been shown on Bavarian television because Bavaria has an upper House in some respects comparable with ours. He was astonished at the way in which our House had clearly been caricatured.

What is involved in the obligation to act with impartiality? I suggest that there are five features at least. First, the programmes must be properly balanced. If the programme itself does not contain its own internal balance, then, as the noble Lord, Lord Annan, said, the balancing views must be produced within a reasonable time in order that all views should be reflected in due proportion.

Secondly, a complete and detailed picture should be presented, thus avoiding any suppression or censoring of valid points on one side or another. Thirdly, questions should not be hostile, hectoring, aggressive or rude. Interruptions in the middle of a sentence should be avoided. Fourthly, the approach to contentious issues should be dispassionate. For example, the easy ride should not be allowed to one side when the other side is examined vigorously. Fifthly, the personal views of the presenters and reporters should not feature in the programme. An interview is not an occasion for the interviewer to put across his opinions and views. Its purpose is to obtain the views and opinions of the interviewee, developed and tested by questioning.

There is not the slightest novelty in any of the observations I have just made. I culled them from the guidelines produced by the BBC for its producers. I add a further proposition of my own; namely, that there should not be put in the mouth of interviewees answers which they have not given but which the interviewer hoped they would give and put into their mouths as a preamble to a long question. The experienced person will say, "One moment, I didn't say that" and then go on to deal with the question. The inexperienced person, anxious to answer the question, will overlook the fact that there has been attributed to him something that he or she did not say at all. I submit that it is essential that the elements of due impartiality are adequately recorded either in the Agreement or in some suitable exchange of letters between the Government and the BBC.

The noble Viscount observed that the obligation of due impartiality should be stated clearly. How else can it be stated? Secondly, he said that the binding legal contract is the instrument of control and added that the obligation of due impartiality should be there stated to

[LORD ACKNER]
make it effective and enforceable. However, the obligation must be adequately particularised if it is to be taken seriously. That is the purpose of my suggestions.

7.29 p.m.

Viscount Astor: My Lords, we have had a particularly interesting and wide-ranging debate in relation to the Government's proposals for the future of the BBC. The noble Viscount, Lord Tenby, said that he agreed a bit with everybody. So do I. I wish on that note I could sit down, but I should perhaps attempt to respond to some of the individual points raised by your Lordships, even though I agreed with the noble Lord, Lord Annan, when he said that Ministers are not often able to see much TV. Indeed, I shall not make my remarks too long so that I can go home this evening to watch some television.

We had wide agreement in your Lordships' House on the importance of the role of the BBC as a public service broadcaster. The noble Lord, Lord Annan, was particularly concerned with what happens if the BBC disobeys the terms of its Agreement. The Agreement is a contract between the BBC and the Secretary of State. If it contravenes the terms of the Agreement, a number of important sanctions are open to the Government. Under the Charter the Secretary of State can take steps to revoke the Charter if the terms of the Agreement are broken. I am sure the BBC would be loath to put itself in a position in which the Charter was placed in jeopardy.

The noble Lord suggested that if contraventions occurred, heads should roll. Members of the BBC staff who do not abide by the rules which stem from the Charter and the Agreement are subject to the normal disciplines of the organisation. If the governors were responsible for such contraventions, they could be removed.

It is always difficult to achieve a balance and impartiality between programmes. The noble Lord, Lord Annan, is right in saying that it is not sufficient for the BBC to say that a balance can be achieved by broadcasting an unconnected programme some months later. That does not achieve the obligation of "due impartiality over time". The BBC's *Producers' Guidelines* say,

"It is not sufficient to claim that other unconnected programmes or media will ensure that balancing views will be heard".

Those are its own guidelines in Section 3.5 to which the noble Lord referred.

The noble Lord also put forward the suggestion that the BBC's board of management should invite members of the commercial sector to act as non-executive directors. The Government have said that we will ensure that appointments are made to the board of governors to ensure that there is the necessary commercial expertise on the board. The BBC appointed senior management staff with considerable private sector experience to direct its new commercial activities. In addition, by participating in joint ventures with the private sector, the BBC will also have the benefit of the expertise of its private sector partners. However, if it wishes to appoint non-executive directors to the board of management, there is nothing to prevent it from doing so.

I welcome support from the noble Lord, Lord Donoughue, for the BBC, one of our more important institutions in this country. I am only sorry that his party feels unable to support one of the other great institutions in this country at the moment.

The noble Lord made two important points in relation to the BBC's commitment to the arts and its educational role. It is agreed that the arts are an important part of the BBC's role as a public service broadcaster. It is a major patron of the arts, spending more than £300 million a year on arts programming. The White Paper says that,

"the BBC should remain a major cultural patron of music, drama and the visual arts. It should continue to commission and broadcast new works, and to nurture creative talent".

It has undertaken to maintain its support for the arts, and that undertaking is currently contained in the annex to the Licence and Agreement. We propose that an obligation on those lines should be included in the new Agreement.

The three aims of the BBC in its programmes and services are to inform, to entertain and to educate. We propose that those three traditional aims should be stated more clearly and explicitly in the new Agreement and Charter. The White Paper says that,

"the BBC should continue to broadcast educational programmes of all kinds".

The noble Lord, Lord Donoughue, said that the Agreement should contain both a list of services and an extended list of conditions and, importantly, the governors' resolution that they will meet those requirements. The new Agreement will contain all three elements. As I said, it will be a contract between the BBC and the Secretary of State. That is an important point and I hope that it resolves the anxieties of the noble Lord, Lord Donoughue. We aim to bring forward the new Charter and Agreement to give both Houses of Parliament the opportunity to debate the documents during this parliamentary Session.

The noble Lord, Lord Donoughue, asked also whether parts of the White Paper needed legislation to be implemented. The merger of the Broadcasting Standards Council and the Broadcasting Complaints Commission will require primary legislation amending the 1990 Broadcasting Act. We hope to bring forward legislation as soon as parliamentary time allows.

The noble Lord referred also to the privatisation of transmission services and the BBC's view. The BBC is assessing the future of its transmission service. At present it has not come to any conclusion on the most effective way forward. As I said in response to a recent Question in your Lordships' House, we are considering that matter carefully ourselves.

Lord Donoughue: My Lords, I thank the Minister for giving way. Is he aware that the deputy director of the BBC last night announced that it concluded that it needed to keep the transmission service?

Viscount Astor: My Lords, I am not aware of what the deputy director of the BBC said last night. I do not believe that there is a yes or no answer on this. It is important that we put the BBC in a position where it is able to take advantage of and have the money to finance the important step into terrestrial digital television in order to be competitive in the market and in the BBC's world market.

The noble Lord, Lord Thomson of Monifieth, asked whether the new Agreement would contain an obligation to provide a daily report of Parliament. Yes: that is an important part of the BBC's obligation as a public service broadcaster and the requirement will be carried into the new Agreement.

The noble Lord made the interesting point of why world service television should not be funded from public funds in a similar way to world service radio. World service radio has a wide reach and provides news coverage and other programmes in many countries and languages. To build up that network required a large input of public funds. But world service television is different. We do not see it as replacing radio or matching its wide coverage in the near future. It is an attractive commercial product for the people around the world who value the BBC's reputation for high quality programmes and fair coverage of events. People are willing to pay for these new services, and it is right that the BBC should be able to take advantage of that interest to generate a return for the licence fee payers at home. That is why we do not propose that world service television should be paid for from public funds.

The noble Lords, Lord Donoughue and Lord Thomson of Monifieth, and my noble friend Lord Orr-Ewing were concerned about the Broadcasting Complaints Commission and the Broadcasting Standards Council. They offered the alternative of a merger with the ITC to bring forward a consumer council for broadcasting. The main responsibility for considering complaints rests properly with the broadcasters themselves and the broadcasting regulators. The BBC is subject to both the Broadcasting Standards Council and the Broadcasting Complaints Commission and their procedures. A consumer council would weaken the links that we believe should exist between the BBC and its audiences. It is essential that broadcasters stay closely in touch with public opinion and it is preferable for audiences to speak directly with broadcasters. The role of the governors is absolutely crucial in that respect.

The noble Baroness, Lady Wharton, asked whether the two merged bodies would have statutory powers. The answer is yes. The new body will continue to produce statutory codes of programme standards. All broadcasters, including the BBC, are subject to these codes. If the BSC finds that a broadcaster has failed to keep within the codes, it can require it to broadcast its findings and prevent it from repeating the offence. That will continue to be the case for the new merged body.

The noble Earl, Lord Halsbury, suggested that the BBC governors should have a complaints unit and should discipline producers who break the rules. The Government are very keen that the BBC should listen carefully to the views and complaints of its audiences. As my noble friend Lord Caldecote said, the BBC has already set up a programme complaints unit and a complaints committee to give independent consideration to serious complaints. Where the governors discover that the BBC's own rules have been breached, they will take steps to ensure that the breach does not recur and to exercise the normal desirable disciplines over its employees.

My noble friend Lord Orr-Ewing was concerned whether the BBC governors could realistically carry out the onerous responsibilities that we are putting on them. We believe that the duties we are placing on the governors are reasonable and realistic and similar to those on directors of other major organisations. The governors will have primary responsibility for all the BBC's activities and will be accountable to Parliament and the public for them. That does not mean, of course, that the governors have to have direct control over these activities. Their main duty is to ensure that the necessary framework and rules are in place to enable the BBC to meet its obligations and objectives and to ensure that the BBC employees work within that framework and those rules. That is no more onerous than the very broad responsibilities borne by boards of many major companies.

The right reverend Prelate the Bishop of Southwark, who told me that, unfortunately, he had to leave at 7.30 p.m., referred to the importance of religious programming. The BBC has committed itself in *Extending Choice* ensuring that religious programmes retain a prominent place in the schedules. We support that commitment and the BBC's wider responsibilities to serve all parts of the community. I listened with great care to the concerns expressed by the noble Baroness, Lady O'Cathain, on religious programming.

Three distinguished former governors of the BBC shared their experiences with us: the noble Lords, Lord Greenhill and Lord Barnett, and the noble Earl, Lord Halsbury. We also had the opposite view. My noble friend Lord Harmar-Nicholls, and the noble Viscount, Lord Tenby, spoke from the other end of the spectrum, from the point of view of the viewer, and referred to the effect of the BBC on this country. My noble friend Lord Harmar-Nicholls spoke while wearing what one would describe as his political hat. He explained why his career of standing in elections is over. In his speech he probably persuaded your Lordships' House why his career of standing in elections should be far from over. He made a campaigning speech which I am sure would win him any election now.

The noble Lord, Lord Barnett, outlined the role of the governors and the director general in giving guidelines to producers on programme standards, including impartiality. I very much agree with the noble Lord that the governors and the director-general have responsibility for setting the framework of standards for the BBC's programmes. The *Producers' Guidelines*, to which the noble Lord referred, provides that framework. Ultimately, it is the governors' responsibility to ensure that producers abide by the rules set out in that document.

The noble Lord, Lord Barnett, was also concerned about sport and listed events. We believe that viewers and listeners should have the best possible range of choice. Choice is being enhanced by the introduction of specialist sports channels, increasing the extent and variety of sports coverage on television services generally. The sale of rights to broadcast sporting events

[VISCOUNT ASTOR]
is one of the principal ways for sporting bodies to generate income. They generate significant income. Sporting bodies should themselves be allowed to judge the balance between the amount of income from broadcasting rights, the size of the television audience, the amount and type of broadcast coverage, and the impact on potential spectators and players and on the individual sport.

My noble friend Lord Caldecote asked whether we would debate the Charter and Agreement in draft. As I said, we shall ensure that there will be a debate. The Charter will be laid for debate in draft. The Agreement will also be capable of change if that is regarded by the Government as necessary because of what is said in debate in either place.

The noble Lord, Lord Elis-Thomas, talked about the new responsibilities of BBC Wales and how they would be spelt out in the new Charter and Agreement. The Charter will include a clearer definition of the role of the national councils. The Agreement will include an obligation on the BBC to make a reasonable proportion of its network production in Wales, Scotland and Northern Ireland. Together, the two documents will make it clear that all parts of the UK should contribute fully to the BBC's activities. The BBC's commercial activities will largely be built on the vast archive of quality programmes which the BBC holds. Those will include programmes made in Wales and other parts of the country.

The noble Lord, Lord Thomson of Monifieth, asked about an accounting officer and whether the BBC should be answerable to the Public Accounts Committee. The BBC is different from most of our public bodies. Its very establishment by means of Royal Charter helps to ensure that the BBC remains properly at arm's length from the political process. In this country we have a long tradition of ensuring that there is no undue control over broadcasters by all of us who are closely involved in the political process. That must continue. The functions of accounting officers provide a direct link of accountability to the PAC in another place. For the BBC to be put in a position of such direct accountability to Parliament could place the principle of separation in some jeopardy. The BBC reports to Parliament in laying its audited annual report and accounts before both Houses. The National Heritage Select Committee in another place can, and does, probe the activities of the BBC. I believe that these are appropriate means of holding the BBC to account.

In the second part of his Motion the noble Lord, Lord Donoughue, asks, in effect, why the licence fee should not continue for longer than five years and whether the review is only about the level of that fee. We may well conclude in five years' time that the licence fee is still the best way of paying for the BBC. That is our conclusion at the moment. We looked at the other options, as your Lordships know, and we have concluded that at present the licence fee is by far the best way of paying for the BBC. But who can tell what will happen in five years' time?

We have heard tonight of some of the changes that may happen in broadcasting. The broadcasting picture is changing very rapidly and so we cannot be sure. That is why it is important that we keep it under review, at the five-year point, before the end of the new Charter. I do not think we should prejudge this and I do not think that the Government are prejudging it. All we are saying is that we need a point to look at in five years' time in order to review the position and make sure that we are still doing the right thing.

The Government welcome the responses to the White Paper and the contributions which your Lordships have made to that process in the debate today. I can give your Lordships the assurance that the Government will consider carefully all the points made in this debate before reaching any final conclusions. I reiterate that your Lordships will have the opportunity to debate these issues again before the BBC's new Charter comes into force. It is important that I should point out that it is not only the Government who should pay careful attention to this debate but also the BBC itself—the chairman of the BBC, the governors of the BBC and the management of the BBC. I am sure that they will pay close attention to this debate. I hope that they pay particularly close attention to the speech of the noble and learned Lord, Lord Ackner.

I hope that the assurances I have given this evening will have gone all the way to satisfying the very valid point made by the noble Lord, Lord Annan. I have said that I agree entirely in principle with what he is trying to do. I hope I have explained why we believe that the Agreement is the best place to put these important elements of impartiality. I also hope that I have persuaded the noble Lord, Lord Donoughue, who has a similar intent to the noble Lord, Lord Annan. I trust that I have satisfied his concerns.

I hope that following what I have said about the review it will be felt that in no way are the Government prejudging any debate on the licence fee. To keep that option open is not a detriment but could be an advantage. It could easily be an advantage to the BBC. With that assurance I hope that the noble Lord, Lord Annan, will feel able to withdraw his amendment to my Motion.

Lord Annan: My Lords, the noble Viscount has spoken so generously that I very much hope that the House will give me leave to withdraw my amendment.

Amendment, by leave, withdrawn.

On Question, Motion agreed to.

South Birmingham: Hospital Services

7.51 p.m.

Lord Howell rose to ask Her Majesty's Government what action they propose to take to ensure that South Birmingham Health Authority provides adequate hospital services for patients.

The noble Lord said: My Lords, first, my noble friend Lady Fisher has had to go home. She has not been well recently and has had to withdraw from this debate which I am sure your Lordships will understand. Secondly, I believe I am right in saying that according to information which has reached me rather late the Minister spent a considerable amount of time in Birmingham yesterday visiting the hospitals and no doubt acquainting herself with what she believed I might say and getting the answers. Perhaps I may say how much I welcome that. It is very good—especially in the context of these hospitals—that Ministers themselves are trying to investigate and come to grips with the story as I shall unfold it. Although I am critical I want the noble Baroness to know that her visit was appreciated.

I have initiated the debate because it is no longer possible to tolerate the disastrous state of affairs governing the management of the South Birmingham hospitals. There has been financial and administrative chaos in this hospital group for many years past. Vast sums of money have been abused. At least an extra £6 million was provided to bail them out of their financial predicament, following which specific assurances were made to the Public Accounts Committee which have not been met. Now redundancies and closures are taking place on a grand scale. The essential point of this debate; namely, the health service of the good people of Birmingham is being sacrificed on the altar of financial book-keeping to which this hospital group management now gives top priority over patient care.

These are strong words, but I intend to prove every one of them. There is a long history of this matter, but I do not need to detain the House over much about it. It became so notorious that the Public Accounts Select Committee of the other place held hearings about it and issued two of the most damning reports I have ever read in 40 years' membership of Parliament. They ought to produce resignations or sackings, but no such events occurred; nor did the appropriate Ministers of the day—they are not the present Ministers—think it right to accept any responsibility.

Perhaps I may comment that every penny of public money is a Treasury and ministerial responsibility. It matters not whether it is spent by a quango or a health authority. If there is abuse, or worse, it is the ultimate responsibility of the department and the Minister. No such responsibility has been accepted in the affairs of the South Birmingham Health Authority.

In its first report issued in October last year, the Public Accounts Committee says that serious shortcomings in the management control and accountability of the regionally managed services led to a waste of at least £10 million, this at the expense of health care for sick people in the West Midlands. The PAC says that it was astonished that the privatisation of the supplies branch proceeded without the knowledge of the regional health authority. There were serious failings at all levels of management and a serious failure by members of the RHA and its then chairman.

A second hearing of the PAC took place and it reported as recently as July of this year. In the interim the RHA had provided an additional £6 million of funds to meet redundancy costs and to balance the books. The questions and answers at this second hearing on 16th February this year are the starting point for my anxieties.

My colleague, Mr. Terry Davis, Member of Parliament, took the lead. Again and again he asked for assurances that after the £6 million payment and the previous report, the financial affairs of the South Birmingham Health Authority were now in order and that it now had enough money to balance the books and to provide treatment for all who need it. He asked: is it a question of overspending or underfunding? Sir Duncan Nichol told the committee that he thought so but that he relied on the judgment of the region. Yet he was the chief executive of the National Health Service.

The same question was then directed by Mr. Davis to the chairman of the West Midland Region, Mr. Brian Baker. That revealed that an extra £11.2 million was given to the South Birmingham authority in 1992 to clear up its accumulative debt. Sir Duncan Nichol believed that the authority had now been allocated enough money year by year to meet its obligations and to ensure that there was no underfunding; so did the regional chairman.

I must now ask the House to consider the present chaos, which I shall describe, in the affairs of this group of hospitals in the light of those specific assurances. There has been a most serious and continuing deterioration of services; a serious collapse of morale affecting consultants and nursing staff; and a continual worsening of services for patients who have the right under the law—the National Health Service Act—to receive full and immediate treatment for their illnesses.

I spell out some of the factors: a daily fight to get very sick patients into an inadequate number of beds; routine cancellation of operations for seriously ill patients; no ophthalmology service now available for this large area of Birmingham; a pioneering gastro-intestinal unit has disappeared; the world-renowned burns unit is under threat. The consultants there wrote directly to the Secretary of State in September. I ask the Minister whether any action has followed their approaches to the Minister. Varicose veins patients are now shipped to Manchester for treatment which could be provided much more cheaply in Birmingham. One hundred waiting heart patients were contracted to receive treatment at the infamous Clydebank hotel, or Clydebank hospital, which has now collapsed. It is now hoped to send them to King's College Hospital in London. I shall return to that matter shortly.

There is at present a total ban on non-emergency admissions. The intensive care unit had to refuse 60 emergency patients during the year because there were no beds. The breast cancer unit was left without a consultant surgeon when he left saying:

"it is not possible to provide a top quality service under the financial restrictions".

Fracture clinics are cancelled due to the shortage of junior doctors. The consultant urologist says,

"he is ashamed of the service he can offer after having his bed complement reduced from 52 to 22".

In that department 1,000 patients have been waiting for up to two years for treatment. That is a most serious matter and one can imagine their discomfort.

In its policy document *Looking Forward* the RHA proposes to axe 1,100 beds and replace them with community care. That is in just one group of hospitals. Not only is there no money for such a programme, but

[LORD HOWELL]
the community care programme is now being asked to transfer money back to acute services to keep those acute services alive. The same policy document forecasts a reduction of between 332 and 482 beds — that is 43 per cent. of all beds—by 1997-98. In fact, the programme has been accelerated to such an extent that a 375-bed loss has already been achieved in 1994—not 1997. Staff cuts of the magnitude of 1,200 have been ordered by the region. In fact, 300 went last year, 775 this year and another 400 will go next year when the general hospital loses its acute unit.

It is my contention that the care and treatment of patients is the National Health Service's supreme duty. All financial management and book balancing are merely mechanical factors to enable patients to be treated. That is the purpose of the National Health Service, but that is not the position in that group of hospitals. The very opposite is the case.

On 11th April this year, Mr. Bryan Baker, the chairman of the West Midlands Executive, wrote to Mr. Brian Stoten, the chairman of the South Birmingham Authority and demanded a robust action plan to achieve real savings. He promised £6 million for redundancy costs and another £10 million for price support. He confirmed in his letter the 1,200 staff reductions in the acute unit and the additional 400 to be added from the general hospital. He concluded by expressing his concern that the:

"Corporate information care plan and the quarterly monitoring information have been rendered largely meaningless".

That is a disgraceful letter. It contains not one word of concern about the effect of all that on patient care and the services provided for the sick, which is the prime responsibility of those gentlemen and that authority.

The authority is now taking refuge for its policy of mass destruction in the hearings held before the Public Accounts Committee, which is why I went into detail about them earlier. In a letter to the British Medical Association dated 12th May 1994, Mr. Michael Waterland, the chief executive of the acute services unit, says that the focus of the PAC hearings was on its fiscal duty. So it was, but equally compelling were the assurances that were sought and given that funds are adequate to meet patient needs, as I have already shown.

In his letter to the BMA, Mr. Waterland says that, irrespective of quality, his hospital group has three priorities. I shall quote what he stated in his letter. He said that priority No. 1 was "income and expenditure balance"; that priority No. 2 was "income and expenditure balance"; and that priority No. 3 was "income and expenditure balance". When he made the same point to the Community Health Care Council, I understand that he added:

"patient care is a secondary consideration".

That is quite intolerable, quite contrary to the purpose of the health service and, I believe, quite contrary to the purpose of the Government. So it is, and that is the gravamen of my charge. Patient care and attention, the first duty of the health service, has been sacrificed in those hospitals on the altar of financial expediency.

Finally, I turn to the effect of all that on waiting lists and staff morale. The waiting list deterioration is quite deplorable and totally in contrast to the Government's wishes and claims about improvements. In March 1993, 218 patients had been waiting over one year. By March this year, that number had increased to 1,037. In September 1993, 20 urology patients had been waiting for more than one year. By June this year, that figure had increased to 227. In general surgery, no patients had been waiting more than a year in September 1993, but by June this year 235 patients were waiting. In ENT, the number of patients waiting for treatment for more than a year rose from 36 in September 1993 to 135 in June 1994.

I could give many examples of the suffering that that is causing very sick people. I shall content myself with just one case. Mr. Anthony Damms lives at 111 Eastfield Road, Bordesley Green. In June 1993 he suffered a heart attack and was treated at the Heartlands Hospital, from where he was referred to the Queen Elizabeth Hospital in December last year. He was told he needed bypass surgery and that that would take place in six to eight weeks' time. In April this year he was told he must wait until July or August. In August he was told it may be another 12 months. However, on 21st November—a month ago—he received a call to report for tests on 25th November with a view to being operated on on 2nd December—last week. Told to check the position on the day before—1st December—he did so only to be told not to come in as there were no beds available.

Out of the blue last Saturday morning, two days after he should have been admitted, Mr. Damms received a letter, not from the Queen Elizabeth Hospital but from the consultant he had seen 18 months ago at the Heartlands Hospital, telling him that he may still have a considerable wait and asking him whether he would consider treatment in London. His wife tells me that he also suffers very badly from arthritis and cannot walk across the road, much less travel to London

No citizen should receive such treatment. At this point I was going to ask the noble Baroness to look into the case, but such is the expedition that occurs when Members of Parliament raise matters in the House that I am glad to report that the television companies interviewing me today have informed me that Mr. Damms has now been told that he will have his operation on 29th December. Perhaps I may say how very pleased I am for Mr. Damms that we have achieved such a remarkable success, but I am bound to ask: What about the other 99 patients who have been waiting a long time and need an operation? Is somebody going to do something about them? However, we must be thankful for small mercies and on behalf of Mr. Damms and his family, I must express my appreciation.

I turn now to staff morale. It could hardly be worse. The number of consultants who have resigned is frightening. They include four consultants in haematology; one vascular surgeon; one general surgeon; and one microbiologist. Seven other consultants have taken early retirement.

In September and November last year one of the ward sisters felt it to be her duty to draw the serious situation to the attention of the directorate. Among other matters in her letter which I have seen she referred to the fact that her ward had been left with only two nurses on duty, no provision for meals or help for the manual handling of patients. Agency nurses were of poor quality. There were often no domestic services and no team cleaning. In September she wrote:

"In short, the ward is filthy. Nurses already stretched to the limit are having to clean toilets and baths. I have written to the hotel services manager to no avail. My ward has an excellent reputation. I have never known morale so low, my keen conscientious staff are looking elsewhere for other jobs where they will be valued".

Then in November the sister wrote again. She said that she had no alternative but to close the ward as patients' lives were at risk and the few remaining staff could not be expected to manage under those pressures. That shows an alarming situation which merits the most intensive investigation. Like all the facts that I have quoted, they speak for themselves. No embellishments are necessary.

Mr. Brian Edwards, the chief executive of the West Midlands NHS Executive, has kindly sent me during the past few days a copy of a letter he has written to the South Birmingham Acute Unit. I have no doubt that he has also sent a copy to the Minister in anticipation of the debate. It was obviously an attempt to anticipate what I was going to say. It expresses confidence that waiting list targets can be met and that performances will be improved. One can only hope so, but those generalised comments ignore totally the vast cuts in staff and beds that have taken place, and the vast increase in demands for admissions.

My belief is that the only way to restore confidence is to have an independent outside inquiry into the affairs of the hospital. That is not into the financial mismanagement—the PAC has done that—but into the level of patient care which is the sole purpose of the NHS.

Sir Duncan Nichol gave firm assurances that the action plan put in place to rectify the financial mismanagement in that area health authority would not damage the service. The truth is that it has not solved the financial problems, and it has damaged seriously the services provided for the public. That is why an independent inquiry is now essential to restore public confidence. If the Minister cannot grant me that request today, perhaps I may hope that she will continue to apply her mind to the hospital to ensure that the finances are put right and, what is most important, that the good people of Birmingham receive the services to which they are entitled.

8.14 p.m.

Lord Rea: My Lords, my noble friend has revealed a sad and serious catalogue of errors. It is hard to believe that a management team could have miscalculated so often, and gone against professional advice. It has been said, with some justification, that one possible beneficial effect of the Government's NHS legislation has been to remove decision-making power from the vested interests of the hospital consultants and move it to managers acting on behalf of patients and communities. But in South Birmingham that policy seems to have misfired totally.

What has happened is the equivalent of a ship dropping its pilot while it is still going through a dangerous passage, full of rocks and dangerous currents, and handing the wheel to the purser who is more skilled in financial calculation than navigation. However, even in financial terms, the Birmingham managers have managed to run the ship aground.

A further example of that, which was given to me by an orthopaedic surgeon, is the decision of the managers to ignore a carefully costed plan put forward by the clinicians concerned accepting that the famous Birmingham Accident Hospital had to be closed but proposing that the Selly Oak Hospital be the site of a new burns and trauma unit. However, that plan was rejected. The general hospital was chosen as the site for the accident and burns service which was created there at a cost of some £4 million. However, after less than two years the decision has been taken to resite the unit at Selly Oak, as originally proposed by the professional staff involved, at a cost of some £6 million.

While the bulldozers are now pulling down the old accident hospital, and patients are being treated at a new unit at Birmingham General Hospital, contractors are building yet another new unit at Selly Oak. That has meant a loss of £4 million of taxpayers' money. That is at a time when the grave shortages, redundancies and bed closures which my noble friend described are taking place. The situation has become so uncertain that, as my noble friend pointed out, a number of senior clinical staff have resigned or taken early retirement. Among those are two general surgeons, Mr. Geoffrey Oates and Mr. John Harman, who have been re-employed in a private hospital which receives patients who cannot be accommodated at the acute unit. Despite that, as my noble friend pointed out, South Birmingham has a waiting list which has been increasing steadily.

I turn now to primary care which, as the Minister knows, is my own field. One of the key features of the RHAs *Looking Forward ... Moving Ahead* strategy was the development of primary care. That involved, in particular, improving practice premises and increasing the number of nurses. But funds are needed for that, some of which were to come from the savings being made in the acute unit. However, as my noble friend pointed out, so rapid has been the run down of beds, and so great has been the disruption of services as a result, that money has had to be diverted to the private sector to contain the increasing size of the waiting list.

As a result, improvements in primary care have hardly been noticeable, except perhaps in fundholding general practices. Incidentally, in creating multi-fund administrative units of a rather luxurious nature, they seem to have no shortage of funds. Fundholders' patients are partially cushioned from the results of the administrative bungles which have been described—a further example, if one were needed, of the two-tier system that the fundholder scheme has created. Sadly that is a case of "to he that hath shall more be given", since poorer districts with the greatest health needs have the lowest proportion of GP fundholders.

[LORD REA]

In South Birmingham £500,000 has also been taken from the allocation for the psychiatric services—an area in need of more, not less funds—to buttress the acute unit in its difficulties. One answer often proffered by the Government —I have heard this from the Minister— when it is said that there has been too great an increase in the numbers of managerial staff, is that the NHS was previously undermanaged. The South Birmingham story shows, however, that far from improving services for patients these new managers have made them worse and wasted huge sums of public money in the process.

8.20 p.m.

The Parliamentary Under-Secretary of State, Department of Health (Baroness Cumberlege): My Lords, I am grateful to the noble Lord, Lord Howell, for this opportunity to debate with the select group here tonight the health services in South Birmingham. Although the Chamber is not crowded, I recognise that the subject is of enormous concern to the people of Birmingham. There has been room for misunderstanding and therefore I welcome the opportunity to go into some of the issues tonight.

As your Lordships will be aware, South Birmingham has been dogged with financial problems since its inception in 1991 when it was created out of the merger of the old Central and South Birmingham Health Authorities. I do not wish to retread old ground as to why the financial problems occurred or why it took so long for them to be rectified. As the noble Lord said, this has been thoroughly investigated by the Public Accounts Committee and was covered in detail in its 36th report, which was published last July and to which the Government responded via a Treasury Minute on 18th October 1994.

The Department of Health and West Midlands Regional Health Authority have accepted that senior managers failed to resolve the financial problems within South Birmingham Health Authority in the prescribed timescales.

New senior management teams for both the South Birmingham Acute Unit and South Birmingham Health Authority have been recruited and together they will work to resolve the immediate financial problems and ensure that the acute unit achieves a balanced income and expenditure position by October 1995. It will be announced tomorrow that John Boyak will be appointed chief executive of the acute unit and therefore both teams are fully appointed.

In parallel with these changes, new and exciting developments have also been taking place across Greater Birmingham. We should not lose sight of those. Your Lordships will appreciate that, as South Birmingham is an integral part of the city and comprises one of its two health authorities, anything that affects Birmingham as a whole has equally strong implications for health services in the South Birmingham conurbations.

Many cities throughout the country are becoming aware of the growing need to plan their health services so that they take account of today's rapidly changing demands and in doing so are in a strong position to carry them forward into the next century. As the noble Lord, Lord Rea, will know only too well, medical science and clinical practice do not stand still and we need to be aware of developments and harness them. That is good management and better quality care for patients.

Birmingham has recognised this need and accepted the challenge. On 9th December 1993 the health authorities in Greater Birmingham jointly published a discussion document called *Looking Forward*. This sets out broad proposals for reshaping health services in the city by recognising the important changes that are taking place. I assure the noble Lord, Lord Rea, that among those changes are plans to enhance and expand primary care.

I am well aware that in developing its health care services Birmingham has had many false starts. It is an enormous task and quite understandably local people have a right to be sceptical over this latest attempt. However, it was with this scepticism in mind that the Greater Birmingham purchasers ensured that *Looking Forward* was subject to as much public discussion and consultation as possible. They listened carefully to local people's views and amended the proposals to meet their concerns.

On the 1st July West Midlands RHA announced the outcome of these consultation exercises. None was formally opposed by the Birmingham Community Health Councils and this meant that the planned £100 million plus investment programme for Greater Birmingham could now begin.

In South Birmingham this involves investment of more than £70 million. It includes the planned transfer of the Children's Hospital from its present dilapidated location to a refurbished Birmingham General Hospital at a cost of more than £20 million; the development of a high quality accident and emergency service throughout the city and in particular a new £6.8 million accident and emergency department at South Birmingham Acute Unit; and the development of a new £8.5 million oncology centre for cancer sufferers at the South Birmingham Acute Unit.

During my visit to Birmingham yesterday I was told that Professor David Kerr, a leading cancer specialist of international renown based at the South Birmingham Acute Unit, has rejected the opportunity to move to a number of other leading cancer centres in this country because of the excellent facilities in South Birmingham and the encouragement and respect he has had from the management. Also planned is a new £6 million neurosciences centre, again at the acute unit; a £14 million refurbishment of Birmingham Women's Healthcare NHS Trust; a new health centre at Quinton as part of a £23 million investment in primary care across the city; and a major investment in the fabric of hospitals in South Birmingham, including £37 million on upgrading and improving facilities at Selly Oak Hospital, part of the South Birmingham Acute Unit.

Some of these initiatives are already under way and others are scheduled to take place over the next few years. In all, they represent a significant investment in local services across both the primary and secondary care sectors and all will considerably benefit the people of South Birmingham.

The noble Lords, Lord Howell and Lord Rea, drew our attention to the bed closures taking place in particular at the South Birmingham Acute Unit. As I have already pointed out, improved medical technology and clinical practice means that more patients are being treated more quickly using fewer beds. Since 1987 the average length of stay in hospitals in the West Midlands has fallen substantially. For example, in the past six years the average length of stay for general surgery has fallen from 12 to eight days and for eye surgery the fall has been from five days to three.

Day case surgery has become a more common method of treatment. In South Birmingham since 1987 the number of day cases treated has risen by 234 per cent. In the West Midlands about 40 per cent. of cases are now treated on a day case basis. The West Midlands RHA believes that a target of 60 per cent. is reasonable. This is good news for local patients. Credit must go to those who planned, built and now work in the new £640,000, 18-bed day case unit which has recently opened at Selly Oak Hospital and which will benefit the people of South Birmingham.

However, in the midst of all this investment there is a complicating factor. In the past, many health authorities have sent their patients to the South Birmingham Acute Unit for treatment. These authorities are now developing services more locally and this means that fewer patients are being referred to Birmingham. This is better for patients but means that the acute unit has had to look at the various services it provides. It has had to match the changes in demand to the income that it now receives. This is one of the key issues underlying the acute unit's current financial situation.

The noble Lord quoted from a letter from the chief executive citing the importance of having a sound financial position. Every health authority must live within its means, and there is nothing more demoralising for staff or miserable for patients than having services that are expanded one moment and cut back the next. South Birmingham has to get its house in order and regain the stability which staff and patients so badly need.

Inevitably, the review of services has had an effect on the acute unit's organisation, although actual permanent bed closures at the unit have been minimal; a total of 42 since January this year. A significant number of these have been the result of major refurbishment taking place elsewhere in South Birmingham, necessitating short-term bed closures. Unfortunately, there has also been a number of temporary closures at the acute unit because of a shortage of nurses with the required specialist skills. An example is the cardiac unit, where 10 of the 62 beds are currently closed for this reason. This matter is being addressed by the health authority, which is seeking to recruit suitable staff as soon as possible. Interestingly, the situation at the Royal Orthopaedic Hospital and Birmingham Children's Hospital is the reverse, where there has been an increase in the number of beds available over this same period.

Noble Lords have also drawn attention to the redundancies taking place. I wish to say, first, that it is always regrettable when redundancies are necessary but in this case it is essential in order to ensure that South Birmingham lives within its resources.

No significant redundancies have occurred at the Royal Orthopaedic Hospital or the Birmingham Children's Hospital; but, since the beginning of the year, 770 posts have gone at the South Birmingham Acute Unit. The vast majority have been administrative and clerical but some have been from the nursing and medical grades. Only 14 of those redundancies in total have so far been compulsory with the majority achieved through freezing of vacancies and voluntary early retirement.

Decisions on what posts should go is a matter for local managers, who must take account of local needs and the reductions in workload. It is certainly not the case that patients' lives are being put at risk because of those reductions. Posts go because the work is no longer there.

To help those whose jobs have been affected, South Birmingham Acute Unit has set up a staff commission which has been notified of some 400 nursing vacancies since June. In addition, there are plans to retrain about 60 acute nurses to work as community and practice nurses, reflecting the move towards greater care in the community.

Both noble Lords raised the question of waiting lists. The West Midlands Regional Health Authority is unique in that it has set all hospitals within the region a target of guaranteeing all patients who were on West Midlands waiting lists as at 1st July 1994 the offer of treatment by 31st March 1995—a maximum waiting time for treatment of no more than nine months. An additional £10 million region-wide has been made available to achieve that. South Birmingham is signed up to this target but to achieve it means an additional work load. I should explain to the noble Lord, Lord Rea, that that is a short-term initiative, over and above the normal workload. It will not be of a long duration once the backlog has been cleared. Therefore, it is a good idea to use other facilities in order to accommodate that increased workload.

The noble Lord mentioned the situation concerning the cancellation of operations. That is an area of great anxiety, which needs careful management. In that authority, the level of cancelled operations is high. That is partly attributable to the fact that the South Birmingham Acute Unit is heavily involved with treating emergencies and many cancelled operations are a direct result of unexpected surges in the emergency workload. That is particularly true of the cardiac services.

The noble Lord mentioned also intensive care beds. Currently in South Birmingham there are 25 intensive care beds but a further four will be opened in January 1995. Also, a new cardiac bed is due to be opened early next year. I hope that that will relieve the situation.

In his Question the noble Lord, Lord Howell, asked what action is proposed to ensure that South Birmingham provides adequate hospital services for patients. I have already outlined what is planned for the

[BARONESS CUMBERLEGE]
future, but let me also mention very briefly the excellent services already provided: the Birmingham Children's Hospital which provides first-class patient care not only to the local community, but to patients elsewhere in the UK and overseas. Their expertise includes craniofacial surgery, oncology, cochlear implants, liver programme including liver and small bowel transplants, cardiac services; the Royal Orthopaedic Hospital, a single specialty orthopaedic hospital where outcome measures compare favourably with world standards; a women's hospital providing excellent maternity facilities and gynaecological care; strong community and mental health support from the local community and mental health trusts. Perhaps the most significant is the South Birmingham Acute Unit which offers one of the widest range of specialist leading edge services in the country including: one of the largest and most extensive transplant programmes in Europe; a quick and early diagnosis facility for the early detection of cancer; a major injuries intensive care unit for burns and trauma patients; one of the top national comprehensive cardiac programmes in the country; a direct access service for GPs to the day surgery programme; the most extensive renal programme in Europe; and a urology department which was a finalist in the national Hospital Doctor of the Year Awards for this year. Add those services to the planned £70 million plus investment in services in South Birmingham over the next four years and I believe that your Lordships will agree that that shows considerable commitment to providing excellent hospital services to the people of Birmingham in the future. Sadly, therefore, I cannot accede to the noble Lord's request for an inquiry.

Lord Rea: My Lords, before the noble Baroness sits down, in her reply she said that the reason for the smaller income of the unit was that fewer patients were being referred to Birmingham for treatment and presumably for operations. How is it then that the number on the waiting list has been increasing?

Baroness Cumberlege: My Lords, I believe that I explained that it is to do with all the changes that are taking place: the need to close beds to refurbish some of the other units; and some of the moves that are taking place concerning the children's hospital and other developments.

Lord Howell: My Lords, the Minister said that she is not able to accede to my request for an inquiry; and I am sad about that. But will she assure the House that she and her ministerial colleagues will maintain a continuous interest in the affairs of those hospitals until the service provided meets the satisfaction of the Members of Parliament and the people of Birmingham?

Baroness Cumberlege: My Lords, I willingly give an undertaking to the noble Lord that we shall keep a very close eye on South Birmingham. The situation needs improvement and I shall give a personal commitment to that.

Letchworth Garden City Heritage Foundation Bill

Brought from the Commons, read a first time and referred to the Examiners.

House adjourned at twenty-four minutes before nine o'clock.

Written Answers

Tuesday 6th December 1994

COUNCIL TAX BANDING APPEALS

Baroness Jeger asked Her Majesty's Government:

How many appeals against council tax banding remain unanswered, and how many appellants have died while awaiting the outcome of appeals.

The Minister of State, Department of the Environment (Viscount Ullswater): As at the end of October, 275,231 and 19,212 initial period council tax banding appeals were outstanding in England and Wales respectively. There were 19,686 initial period appeals outstanding in Scotland at the end of September, the latest date for which figures are available. Information on the number of appellants who have died while awaiting the outcome of appeals is not collected.

WINSKILL STONES AND ORTON SCAR: LIMESTONE

Lord Norrie asked Her Majesty's Government:

Whether they will pay for the costs of revoking consents of existing permissions at Winskill Stones in the Yorkshire Dales and on Orton Scar in Cumbria to remove surface limestone pavement, which has priority status under the EC Habitats Directive.

Viscount Ullswater: Should these two areas become European sites under the EC Habitats Directive, and if it is then decided to revoke existing consents, compensation will be payable by the decision making authority under existing statutory arrangements.

LANDLORD AND TENANT CODE

Lord Gallacher asked Her Majesty's Government:

Whether the landlord and tenant code being developed by the Department of the Environment will take account of proposals for agricultural business tenancies contained in legislation now before Parliament.

Viscount Ullswater: The code is intended to address certain issues which relate to commercial property leases and which were raised in the Government's recent review. The code is being developed by the commercial property industry and it will be for them to determine its contents.

EQUAL PAY DIRECTIVE: JUDGMENT

Lord Lester of Herne Hill asked Her Majesty's Government:

Whether, and if so, when, they intend to introduce legislation correctly to transpose the EEC Equal Pay Directive 75/117/EEC into national law, in the light of the decision of the House of Lords in Equal Opportunities Commission v. Secretary of State for Employment, so that part-time workers and their employers are able to ascertain the full extent of their rights and obligations under the directive in accordance with the principle of legal certainty.

Lord Inglewood: The Government have been giving careful consideration to the House of Lords judgment and expects to announce its conclusions shortly.

ORGANOPHOSPHATE SHEEP DIPS: RESEARCH PROJECT

The Countess of Mar asked Her Majesty's Government:

Whether the research project, conducted by the Institute of Occupational Health at Birmingham University on behalf of the Health and Safety Executive, to ascertain whether chronic, low level exposure to organophosphate sheep dips causes ill-health is complete, and, if so, when the results will be published.

Lord Inglewood: The findings of the project are being analysed and the results will be submitted early next year to a scientific journal for publication.

OPERATION GRANBY: LEISHMANIASIS TESTS

The Countess of Mar asked Her Majesty's Government:

Whether they are aware of any British forces who served in Operation Granby who were bitten by sand flies whilst in the desert, and whether they have looked for, or found, leishmania infection among members of those forces who have complained of ill-health.

The Parliamentary Under-Secretary of State, Ministry of Defence (Lord Henley): The possible threat to UK personnel from sand fly bites during Operation Granby was well recognised and effective protective measures were taken. Tests for leishmaniasis are routinely performed on all personnel whose service and personnel history, symptoms and signs are suggestive of the disease. No case of leishmania has been found in British armed forces personnel who served in the Gulf.

CBDE: STUDIES AND TESTS (DEFINITIONS)

The Countess of Mar asked Her Majesty's Government:

Whether studies and tests of chemical and biological defence equipment conducted at the Chemical and Biological Defence Establishment, Porton Down, are defined as medical research, and if they are, whether the studies and tests are conducted according to Recommendation No. R(90)3 of the Committee of Ministers of Member States concerning medical research on human beings.

Lord Henley: Responsibility for the subject of this question is a matter for the Chemical and Biological Defence Establishment. The chief executive of the Chemical and Biological Defence Establishment has therefore responded to the question and his letter is given below.

Letter to the Countess of Mar from the chief executive of the Chemical and Biological Defence Establishment, Mr. Graham Pearson, dated 6th December 1994:

1. Your Parliamentary Question to Her Majesty's Government of 22 November 1994 asking whether studies and tests of chemical and biological defence equipment conducted at the Chemical and Biological Defence Establishment, Porton Down, are defined as medical research, and if they are, whether the studies and tests are conducted according to Recommendation No. R(90)3 of the Committee of Ministers of Member States concerning Medical Research on Human Beings has been passed to me to reply as Chief Executive of the Chemical and Biological Defence Establishment.

2. The role of the Chemical and Biological Defence Establishment is to ensure that the UK armed forces have effective protective measures against the threat that chemical or biological weapons may be used against them. In order to carry out this work, it is necessary to use Service volunteers to:

   a. assess the ability of Service personnel to function with new equipment and procedures,

   b. develop medical countermeasures to protect service personnel and

   c. evaluate the effects of very low and medically safe concentrations of CW agents on the ability of unprotected personnel to operate normally.

Studies and tests of chemical and biological defence equipment which do not involve volunteers are carried out as part of our research programme and are not defined as medical research.

3. Studies and tests of chemical and biological defence equipment at CBDE which involve service volunteers are only carried out where there is a clear military need and a detailed protocol has been reviewed and approved by an independent ethics committee in accordance with the guidelines laid down by the Royal College of Physicians. These guidelines define medical research as "the primary intention is to advance knowledge so that patients in general may benefit; the individual patient may or may not benefit directly." In a defence context the beneficiaries are the members of the armed forces. Consequently, studies and tests of chemical and biological defence equipment involving volunteers conducted at CBDE are regarded as being covered by the definition of medical research in the guidelines laid down by the Royal College of Physicians.

4. The principles contained in the Council of Europe Recommendation on Medical Research on Human Beings R(90)3 are encompassed within the Royal College of Physicians guidelines.

TERRITORIAL ARMY: ROLE

Lord Gainford asked Her Majesty's Government:

When they will complete their review of the Territorial Army units.

Lord Henley: We announced in July that the new role for the Territorial Army (TA) would be to act as a general reserve to the Army. It will remain an integral component of our defence forces on mobilisation, and it is intended to make a greater use of volunteers in peacetime. We have now completed our examination of the structure of the TA against this background. This process has involved wide consultation, particularly within the TA itself.

We have concluded that our operational requirement necessitates some adjustments to the current balance of arms and services within the TA. Accordingly, we intend to increase the number of sub-units in the Royal Armoured Corps from 17 to 22; in the Royal Logistic Corps from 69 to 86; in the Royal Electrical and Mechanical Engineers from 13 to 16; and in the Adjutant General's Corps from 10 to 11. We propose to reduce the number of rifle companies in the TA infantry from 109 to 87. We intend to maintain the current effective manpower strength of the Special Air Service TA, although there will be some restructuring to enable manpower to be used more flexibly and efficiently. Army Medical Services units will also be restructured to provide a more flexible capability. In all other arms and services the number of sub-units will be unaffected.

In the Infantry, we shall concentrate the support weapons platoons of the eight battalions currently so equipped into specialist, two company, fire support battalions. These fire support battalions will be available to support all infantry battalions and will, we believe, improve overall infantry training and operational effectiveness. The four battalions which will take on this role are the 5th Battalion, the Royal Green Jackets; the 3rd Battalion, the Prince of Wales' Own Regiment of Yorkshire; the 1/51st Highland Volunteers; and the 3rd Battalion, the Cheshire Regiment. The 1st and 2nd Battalions, the Wessex Regiment, will merge. The 8th Battalion, the Light Infantry, will re role as a National Defence Reconnaissance Regiment in the Royal Armoured Corps, taking over the current role of the Royal Yeomanry which will become the Army's Nuclear, Biological and Chemical Defence Regiment. The Royal Anglian TA will be reduced from three to two battalions, with elements re-roling to form a new independent transport regiment. All other new sub-units will be newly formed.

The majority of these changes will be implemented by April 1997 within an overall TA size of 59,000, as previously announced. In the months ahead we shall be considering the implications of these changes for the existing distribution of TA centres.

These plans offer the TA a structure consistent with its new role founded firmly on the operational requirement. They will, I believe, be widely welcomed in the TA.

OPERATION GRANBY PERSONNEL: HEALTH

The Countess of Mar asked Her Majesty's Government:

Whether they have any explanation for unusual illnesses suffered by the wives and pre-war children of British forces who served in Operation Granby.

Lord Henley: No requests have been received on behalf of the civilian wives or pre-war children of British forces personnel who served in the Gulf for medical assessment under our medical assessment programme for those concerned about their health as a result of Operation Grabby. Nor have we received any reports of such unusual illnesses among categories of service dependents. One United Kingdom servicewoman who served in the Gulf, and is married to a Gulf veteran, has come forward claiming that a medical condition is due to her service there, but has yet to be assessed by my department's specialist.

The Countess of Mar asked Her Majesty's Government:

Whether they have received any reports of unexplained abortions, congenital malfunctions or illnesses from British forces who served in Operation Granby of their wives, who have conceived babies the end of the Operation ended, and if not, whether they intend to conduct any research on the subject.

Lord Henley: The defence medical services have received reports of six cases which are alleged to fall into the categories mentioned, but no substantive evidence. These include one reported birth defect in a child born to the wife of a United Kingdom Gulf veteran, one miscarriage, three reports of children suffering from specified illnesses, and one reported loss of child. Five of these cases relate to potential claims which may be made against my department. We are also aware of media reports alleging an increased incidence of these health difficulties. We have no evidence to suggest that the incidence of miscarriage, genetic defects or infant morbidity among the spouses or children of United Kingdom Gulf veterans is any higher than that experienced in the general population, or that further research is required, although we shall continue to monitor developments.

The Countess of Mar asked Her Majesty's Government:

Whether they are conducting any formal surveillance on any individuals who may have been exposed to depleted uranium from anti-tank shells during Operation Granby, and if so whether any distinction is being made between those who did and those who did not receive instructions on safety precautions to be followed when handling the shells or other contaminated articles.

Lord Henley: The health of all service personnel is monitored as a matter of routine and there is no evidence of members of the British armed forces who served in the Gulf suffering from any symptoms which would call for such surveillance. None of the individuals coming forward with concerns about their health as a result of service in the Gulf who have so far been examined have displayed symptoms consistent with exposure to depleted uranium.

OPERATION GRANBY: RADIATION EXPOSURE LEVELS

The Countess of Mar asked Her Majesty's Government:

Whether any member of the members of the British forces who served in Operation Granby were issued with radiation badges when they were required to handle shells or articles contaminated with depleted uranium, and whether the level of radiation to which they were exposed is known.

Lord Henley: No radiation dosemeters were issued to personnel who handled depleted uranium ammunition during Operation Granby, but the levels of radiation to which such personnel were exposed is known from trials carried out while the ammunition was being developed. These trials showed that personnel could handle depleted uranium shot for hundreds of hours per year and remain in tanks loaded with this ammunition for thousands of hours per year before any current statutory dose limits would be exceeded.

BOSNIA: US UNMANNED AERIAL VEHICLES

Lord Kennet asked Her Majesty's Government:

Whether they still think, as stated in a letter from the Lord Henley, that the launching by the US of unmanned aerial vehicles from Croatia to "observe" events in Bosnia, is "a bilateral matter between the US and Croatian governments"; whether it is their view that these UAVs can pose no risk to NATO aircraft, including British aircraft, which are operating in the area under a UNSC resolution; and whether these aircraft are under the non-NATO command of the NATO Commander-in-Chief, Naples, and if not under whose command they are.

Lord Henley: The operation of US unmanned air vehicles from bases in Croatia is a bilateral matter between the governments concerned. The unmanned air vehicles are under US national command although their operations are carefully co-ordinated with NATO to ensure they pose no additional risk to aircraft safety.

CONFERENCE ON POPULATION AND DEVELOPMENT, CAIRO

Lord Braine of Wheatley asked Her Majesty's Government:

Whether they will place in the Library of the House the published proceedings of the International Conference on Population in Cairo.

The Minister of State, Foreign and Commonwealth Office (Baroness Chalker of Wallasey): The final version of the Cairo Programme of Action is still not available. When it is received, we will arrange for a copy to be placed in the Libraries of Parliament.

Lord Braine of Wheatley asked Her Majesty's Government:

What discussions they had with representatives of the People's Republic of China at the International Conference on Population in Cairo, and on what subjects.

Baroness Chalker of Wallasey: The United Kingdom delegation participated with Chinese and other delegations to the International Conference on Population and Development in discussions on reproductive rights and a range of other issues.

SCHOOL LIBRARY SERVICES

Lord Jenkins of Putney asked Her Majesty's Government:

Whether they have read the statement of the National Book Committee on School Library Services and what is their response.

Lord Lucas: I can assure the noble Lord that the Government has given attention to the National Book Committee's statement and welcomes the recent publication of the Department of National Heritage's report on school library services mentioned there. It is the Government's firm view that decisions about the appropriate level of expenditure on school library services, and on the purchase of books in general, are best taken at local level and not by central government. A school's governing body and its headteacher are in the best position to decide how to allocate a school's resources, taking into account their statutory responsibilities, their own priorities and the needs of their pupils.

ASYLUM APPLICATIONS

Lord Avebury asked Her Majesty's Government:

How many of the 40,000 applications for asylum which were said to be outstanding when the Asylum and Immigration Appeals Act 1993 came into force had been resolved by the latest convenient date.

The Minister of State, Home Office (Baroness Blatch): In the period 1st August 1993 to 31st October 1994, 22,050 decisions were taken on applications for asylum. Of these 4,775 decisions were made on applications which were outstanding at the time of the implementation of the Asylum and Immigration Appeals Act 1993 on 26th July 1993. In the same period, a further 2,495 of these outstanding applications were withdrawn.

LLOYD'S OF LONDON DTI SUPERVISION

Earl Alexander of Tunis asked Her Majesty's Government:

What role the Department of Trade and Industry plays in supervising the regulatory standards of Lloyd's of London.

The Minister of State, Scottish Office (Lord Fraser of Carmyllie): The principal role of Secretary of State in regulating the activities of Lloyd's of London is defined in the Insurance Companies Act 1982, (particularly sections 83 to 86 of the Act), and in the Regulations made under the Act (particularly the Insurance (Lloyd's) Regulations 1983). In addition the Department of Trade and Industry has a responsibility for the implementation by Lloyd's of relevant European Community directives.

UK-IRELAND: MILK QUOTA

Lord Tebbit asked Her Majesty's Government:

Whether they are aware of either the cross-border sale of Republic of Ireland milk quota into the United Kingdom or the sale of United Kingdom milk produced in excess of quota into the Irish Republic to avoid superlevy liabilities.

The Parliamentary Under-Secretary of State, Northern Ireland Office (Baroness Denton of Wakefield): Sale of milk quota from one member state to another is not permitted under EC law. The Government are aware of allegations that milk produced in excess of the United Kingdom milk quota is being sold into the Republic of Ireland to avoid supplementary levy liability. There is presently no evidence to confirm existence of such a trade. Any report or evidence that this is happening will be investigated.

N.I. TRIALS: DELAY REDUCTIONS

Lord Lyell asked Her Majesty's Government:

What further progress has been made to reduce delays in coming to trial in Northern Ireland.

Baroness Denton of Wakefield: The arrangements we have put in place in recent years to reduce delays are yielding clear benefits, although we must and will continue to seek further ways of attacking the problem.

My right honourable and learned friend the Secretary of State set out on 23rd November last year in reply to a question from the honourable Member for Belfast South (*Official Report*, column 19-20) the results of the first year's operation of the scheme introduced in 1992 to reduce the time defendants spent on custody awaiting trial on indictment for scheduled cases. He also announced a reduction to 11 months in the overall target set by the scheme for cases to move from first remand to arraignment, the formal start of the trial, and its extension to non-scheduled cases tried on indictment.

I can now report on the scheme's first two years of operation, up to 30th June 1994. Overall, 86 per cent. of defendants in custody awaiting trial in scheduled cases who had reached arraignment had met the overall reduced target of 11 months; and 95 per cent. of such defendants in non-scheduled cases did so. Figures for the average time taken to process scheduled cases show a substantial improvement since the introduction of the scheme. In 1991, the last full year before its introduction, average aggregated time from first remand to arraignment for defendants remanded in custody on scheduled charges was 44 weeks; in the two years ending 30th June 1994, the average for such cases in the scheme was 35 weeks, an improvement of 20 per cent. It is too early yet to present reliable comparative figures for non-scheduled cases.

I believe these results are much to the credit of the agencies who have operated the scheme, and we have decided to extend its life until at least the end of June next year.

The results do, however, also reflect the fact that there are a significant number of cases in Northern Ireland of a particularly complex nature, whose preparation is necessarily prolonged. Nevertheless I believe it is important to explore all further means by which delay may be averted. The Northern Ireland Office, in partnership with others more directly involved in the criminal justice process in Northern Ireland, is therefore investigating ways in which procedures may be further streamlined.

INCAPACITY BENEFIT: MEDICAL TEST

Earl Russell asked Her Majesty's Government:

Whether, in light of the delays in issuing copies of *The Medical Assessment for Incapacity Benefit* they will consider extending the consultation period beyond the allotted month.

The Minister of State, Department of Social Security (Lord Mackay of Ardbrecknish): Pursuant to my reply of 28th November 1994, *Official Report*, column *WA28*, I regret that the information given on the date on which regulations setting out details of the medical test were laid before Parliament was inaccurate. Regulations were laid before Parliament on Thursday 24th November 1994, not Monday 28th November, as previously stated.

ISBN 0-10-701195-

9 780107 011956

Vol. 559
No. 12

Wednesday
7 December 1994

PARLIAMENTARY DEBATES
(HANSARD)

HOUSE OF LORDS

OFFICIAL REPORT

CONTENTS

Questions—Life Prisoners: Tariff [Col. 915]
—Buses: Construction Standards [Col. 918]
—British Rail: Privatisation Expenditure [Col. 921]
—Territorial Army: Restructuring [Col. 923]

National Health Patient Accommadation Bill [H.L.]—First Reading [Col. 925]

Motion—Manufacturing Industry [Col. 925]

Statement—Bosnia [Col. 934]

Motion—Manufacturing Industry *(continued)* [Col. 944]

War Crimes (Supplementary Provisions) Bill [H.L.]—Second Reading [Col. 971]

Written Answers [Col. *WA 83*]

LONDON: HMSO
£4·20 net

Lords wishing to be supplied with these Daily Reports should give notice to this effect to the Printed Paper Office.

The bound volumes also will be sent to those Peers who similarly notify their wish to receive them.

No proofs of Daily Reports are provided. Corrections for the bound volume which Lords wish to suggest to the report of their speeches should be clearly indicated in a copy of the Daily Report, which, with the column numbers concerned shown on the front cover, should be sent to the Editor of Debates, House of Lords, within 14 days of the date of the Daily Report.

PRICES AND SUBSCRIPTION RATES

DAILY PARTS

Single copies:
Commons, £7·50; Lords £4·20

Annual subscriptions:
Commons, £1,275; Lords £615

WEEKLY HANSARD

Single copies:
Commons, £22; Lords £9·00

Annual subscriptions:
Commons, £775; Lords £310

Index—Single copies:
Commons, £6·80—published fortnightly;
Lords, £1·90—published weekly.

Annual subscriptions:
Commons, £120; Lords, £65.

LORDS CUMULATIVE INDEX obtainable on standing order only.
Details available on request.

BOUND VOLUMES OF DEBATES are issued periodically during the session.

Single copies:
Commons, £90; Lords, £68.
Standing orders will be accepted.

THE INDEX to each Bound Volume of House of Commons Debates is published separately at £9·00 and can be supplied to standing order.

WEEKLY INFORMATION BULLETIN, compiled by the House of Commons, gives details of past and forthcoming business, the work of Committees and general information on legislation, etc.
Single copies: £2·30.
Annual subscription: £88·80.

All prices are inclusive of postage.

© Parliamentary Copyright House of Lords 1994

Applications for reproduction should be made to HMSO

HMSO publications are available from:

HMSO Publications Centre
(Mail, fax and telephone orders only)
PO Box 276, London SW8 5DT
Telephone orders 0171 873 9090
General enquiries 0171 873 0011
(queueing system for both numbers in operation)
Fax orders 0171 873 8200

HMSO Bookshops
49 High Holborn, London WC1V 6HB (counter service only)
0171 873 0011 Fax 0171 831 1326
68-69 Bull Street, Birmingham B4 6AD 0121 236 9696 Fax 0121 236 9699
33 Wine Street, Bristol BS1 2BQ 0117 9264306 Fax 0117 9294515
9-21 Princess Street, Manchester M60 8AS 0161 834 7201 Fax 0161 833 0634
16 Arthur Street, Belfast BT1 4GD 01232 238451 Fax 01232 235401
71 Lothian Road, Edinburgh EH3 9AZ 0131 228 4181 Fax 0131 229 2734

The Parliamentary Bookshop
12 Bridge Street, Parliamentary Square
London SW1A 2JX
Telephone orders 0171 219 3890
General enquiries 0171 219 3890
Fax orders 0171 219 3866

HMSO's Accredited Agents
(see Yellow Pages)

and through good booksellers

Printed in England and Published by HMSO

ISBN 0 10 701295 2
ISSN 0 309-8834

House of Lords

Wednesday, 7th December 1994.

The House met at half-past two of the clock: The LORD CHANCELLOR on the Woolsack.

*Prayers—Read by
the Lord Bishop of Worcester.*

Life Prisoners: Tariff

The Earl of Longford asked Her Majesty's Government:

> What prisoners, if any, have at any time been informed that a life sentence in their case would mean life.

The Minister of State, Home Office (Baroness Blatch): My Lords, no prisoner has been so informed; but the exercise in tariff disclosure has not yet been completed. All mandatory life prisoners will have been informed of their tariff by early in the New Year.

The Earl of Longford: My Lords, the noble Baroness makes total nonsense of the remark made by the Minister on an earlier occasion. However, I am not involved in debating aspects. Is she aware that I am full of sympathy for her at the moment? I have paid repeated tributes to her as a good Christian, and here she is defending some absolutely obscene proposal that a number of people should be confined to prison and rot in prison for life.

Baroness Blatch: My Lords, I am not absolutely certain what the noble Earl means by his first remark. I think he could save his energy in being sorry for me at the moment; I am not sure that I can be defensive or over-defensive of my position. I believe that disclosure of tariffs to prisoners is a good thing.

Lord McIntosh of Haringey: My Lords, of course, the Minister's first Answer to my noble friend was, as always from her, entirely correct. She answered the Question properly. However, what she did not indicate was whether the tariffs which are now being prepared and will be announced to prisoners, as she said, by early next year will ever include the provision that a prisoner should stay for life. That is, in other words, until death, without release on licence.

Baroness Blatch: My Lords, there are some people who are serving a mandatory life sentence who are subject to life meaning life. What will happen as a result of the *Doody* judgment and the Government's commitment to honour it is that all life prisoners will be informed of the original recommendation by the judge, the recommendation by the Lord Chief Justice and the decision of the Home Secretary at the time. That information will be made available to prisoners and then the prisoner's comments, the responses to them and the historical information will be presented to my right honourable friend the Home Secretary. He will then review the tariff in the light of all that information.

The Earl of Longford: My Lords, what does the Minister mean by saying that some prisoners are subject to a decision that life means life? They have not been informed of that, so in what sense are they subject to it?

Baroness Blatch: My Lords, there are prisoners serving mandatory life sentences about whom previous Home Secretaries have said that life should be life.

The noble Earl says from a sedentary position, "Not publicly"; no, of course not publicly. What I am saying now is that in reply to a Question for Written Answer, the new procedures will be laid later today, therefore all noble Lords will be able to see what the procedures are. What is in process at the moment is that as a result of the *Doody* judgment, prisoners will be informed not only of what the tariff is but also of what the historical decisions were; what the tariff was at the time it was recommended by the judge; what the Lord Chief Justice's views were at the time; and what the recommendation and determination by the Home Secretary were at the time. In addition, the historical data will be coupled with the response of the prisoner to that information. That will be presented to the Home Secretary at the time, who will review it and either confirm the tariff or modify it.

Lord Hylton: My Lords, will the noble Baroness undertake to look again at those cases where prisoners were retrospectively affected by Sir Leon Brittan's decision that life would normally mean 20 years? Will she look with particular care at the cases of those prisoners who have been of good behaviour during their term of imprisonment?

Baroness Blatch: My Lords, we need to make a distinction here. We are talking about people serving mandatory life sentences at this moment. Those serving mandatory life sentences can ask for a review of their tariff at any time. It is up to any Home Secretary in office to consider that.

What is changing now is that that information will be made available to the prisoner with all the historical information. The Home Secretary in office will make a determination either to confirm the original tariff, with life meaning life, or to modify it in the light of a great deal of information. As to the decision about a minimum of 20 years, the present Home Secretary and his predecessors take the view that for very serious crimes of murder a minimum of 20 years is probably appropriate.

Lord Wigoder: My Lords, is there not therefore a possibility that some prisoners will be told that they will be kept in prison for the whole of their lives?

Baroness Blatch: My Lords, I am saying just that. There are prisoners whose tariff states that life should mean life as a result of previous decisions. It is possible for my right honourable friend the Home Secretary to

[BARONESS BLATCH]
confirm that or in the light of all present information—including the response of the prisoner himself to that information—to modify it.

Lord Tebbit: My Lords, will my noble friend confirm that at the time of the abolition of capital punishment it was widely suggested by the abolitionists that life imprisonment should mean life imprisonment? Have we not moved a long way since then?

Baroness Blatch: My Lords, I was not party to that debate, so I am not able to answer very specifically. I cannot respond in any pedantic way. What I can say is that the particular consideration for any Home Secretary is what is the appropriate time that would properly address retribution and deterrence. That is uppermost in the mind of the Home Secretary when he makes that determination.

Lord Ennals: My Lords, will the Minister accept, from one who was involved in the matter in 1967, that there really was no such suggestion as has been referred to by the noble Lord, Lord Tebbit?

Baroness Blatch: My Lords, of course I have to bow to the noble Lord if he was present. As a Home Office Minister, I can say that when somebody has been convicted of a very serious crime—for example, murder—which carries a mandatory sentence, there is a great deal of concern that sometimes the period served in prison does not properly address retribution and deterrence. It is up to my right honourable friend to make sure that those issues are properly addressed in determining the tariff.

Lord McIntosh of Haringey: My Lords, the Minister has given a very important and to some extent welcome announcement today that there will be an Answer to a Written Question later today. Will she communicate to her side of the usual channels what I am sure will be a universal wish on this side of the Chamber; namely, that there should be an early opportunity for a full debate on this issue as soon as the process of notifying prisoners has been completed?

Baroness Blatch: My Lords, whether there is to be a debate on this matter is very much a question for Members of this House, and of course the usual channels. I believe that there is a misunderstanding which I ought to put on record at this moment. We do not have an official policy of making these decisions public. If we are asked for this information, once the disclosure process has been gone through, then the department has an obligation to answer such questions. The prisoner will know; but we will not make public statements at the time of disclosing to the prisoner what the tariff is to be.

Lord McIntosh of Haringey: My Lords, perhaps the House will forgive me for coming back on this point; it is really a matter for information. Nobody would suggest that the details, with names, should be made public. But can we presume that the Government will wish to issue some statistical review of the announcements that have been made to prisoners?

Baroness Blatch: My Lords, I am not sure whether they are included in the statutory statistics. But certainly if that information is called for or asked for we will reply publicly.

Buses: Construction Standards

2.45 p.m.

Lord Pearson of Rannoch: asked Her Majesty's Government:

Whether they will invoke the principle of subsidiarity or otherwise secure the future of the London double-decker bus and of the British midi-bus in the current negotiations on European Community draft vehicle harmonisation directives.

The Parliamentary Under-Secretary of State, Department of Transport (Viscount Goschen): My Lords, these proposals are designed to form one of a number of directives designed to harmonise vehicle construction standards. We cannot accept this as an issue on which the doctrine of subsidiarity should apply. We shall, however, need to ensure that United Kingdom manufacturers will be able to accommodate the eventual standards, particularly in respect of double-decker buses and midi-buses.

Lord Pearson of Rannoch: My Lords, I thank my noble friend for that reply, which I fear will not bring much comfort to the British bus industry. Could I remind my noble friend that our bus industry is privatised and deregulated, unlike its European competitors, and it therefore needs to be able to respond to international and national market requirements without being fettered by red tape from Europe? In this context, is my noble friend aware that the British and Irish members of the Vehicle Working Group in Brussels are isolated from the other Community countries, so the proposed annexe to the draft directives, which seeks to alleviate the position, does not in fact meet our requirements at all? Finally, could I ask my noble friend if he is aware not only that the annexe would prevent our buses from circulating in Europe, but also that it would prevent them from being sold in the Far East, where at the moment they are doing extremely well in the interests of this country?

Viscount Goschen: My Lords, I quite agree with my noble friends that there are clear benefits from being able to operate double-decker buses and midi-buses in this country. They are popular, and we feel that they should be able to continue. We aim to ensure that the eventual standards that do come forward will take that fully into account. Progress is being made on this issue, but indeed there is a long way to go in order to convince the Commission and other European countries of the value of our position.

Lord Stoddart of Swindon: My Lords, can the noble Viscount tell the House what on earth the sort of buses we run in London and elsewhere in this country has to do with the interfering busybodies in Brussels? Is this not a case of Europe interfering in the nooks and crannies of our national life, which the Foreign Secretary said would not happen, particularly after the passing of the Maastricht Bill and the Maastricht Treaty? Will the Minister give the assurance that, if possible, any suggestion of doing away with our double-decker buses will be vetoed, or that at least the European Commission will be told that it will not be implemented?

Viscount Goschen: My Lords, I do not agree with the noble Lord at all. We aim to establish a single market for vehicles. That will be to the benefit of manufacturers. It will be to the benefit of the United Kingdom bus and coach industry. I simply do not accept that this is a matter of subsidiarity.

Noble Lords: Oh!

Lord Stoddart of Swindon: What is then?

Viscount Goschen: However, we will put forward the case very strongly to ensure that our double-decker buses and midi-buses will be able to continue to be manufactured and sold.

The Earl of Lauderdale: My Lords, why can this not be treated as a matter of subsidiarity?

Viscount Goschen: My Lords, the directive, when adopted, will be one of a number under Article 100a of the treaty designed to harmonise construction standards for motor vehicles. That will complete the single market for vehicles to the benefit of manufacturers. That is the reason why it is not an issue of subsidiarity.

Lord Monson: My Lords, does the noble Viscount agree that Continental manufacturers wanting to sell into the British market are far more handicapped by having to convert from left-hand to right-hand drive than they are by having to adapt to the characteristics of the traditional British double-decker bus, and that therefore that particular argument is a totally spurious one?

Viscount Goschen: No, my Lords, absolutely not. But I agree that there is clearly a left-hand drive/right-hand drive problem. That is obvious. We wish to see proposals which are not design restrictive, which cope with the safety requirements but are not over-prescriptive in terms of comfort and design of the interior of the vehicles, for instance.

Lord Bruce of Donington: My Lords, is the noble Viscount aware that the only reason why this duff draft directive has come about is because the French and the Germans do not have the expertise to produce a double-decker bus? Will he accept that they have no capacity to deal with it at all and are well aware that they cannot compete with us in either South America or Asia? Does he agree that that is the reason why the whole issue has arisen?

Viscount Goschen: My Lords, I agree with the noble Lord to the extent that the United Kingdom is the leader in the double-decker bus field.

Lord Cockfield: My Lords, does the Minister agree that a degree of harmonisation is absolutely essential, otherwise the Germans or the Italians, for example, would be able to block the export of buses from this country? Does he further agree that the lack of harmonisation in the case of motor vehicles was one of the grounds on which the French, Italians and others tried to obstruct the export of Nissan motor cars manufactured in this country?

Viscount Goschen: My Lords, my noble friend's question has given a clear explanation of the benefits of harmonisation in the industry.

Lord Carmichael of Kelvingrove: My Lords, I should like to emphasise that I am not by any means anti-Europe. But will he accept that such regulations and directives test the patience of the British public? So far as I remember, the one that most nearly approached this case was the directive on Arbroath smokies. Can the Minister tell the House whether we have a bus industry which is capable of meeting all the requirements of the British bus fleet? Will these directives be an excuse to allow big imports from Europe of buses from Italy, Germany and perhaps France?

Viscount Goschen: My Lords, I cannot answer the noble Lord on the matter of Arbroath smokies. But we do indeed have a very good bus industry in this country. It is well capable of producing buses to the highest specification. The important point is that we and the industry see the clear benefits of harmonisation. We are trying to achieve that without at the same time being over-prescriptive.

Lord Tebbit: My Lords, will my noble friend not simply give the assurance which would satisfy everyone in the House that under no circumstances will Her Majesty's Government allow the Germans, Italians, French, Greeks or others to cook up a set of regulations which will prevent us from manufacturing, using and exporting double-decker buses? Will he accept that, if he were to say that, he would have the support of the whole House?

Viscount Goschen: My Lords, I believe that I said very clearly that our aim in these negotiations is to produce proposals which our bus industry will be able to fit in with and that any moves which will require major design changes to our buses without taking into account safety considerations will be resisted.

Lord Peston: My Lords, will the noble Viscount accept that I find his answer very strange? Is he aware that, quite independently of whether one is for or against the Community, if ever there were a case in which a directive was not needed and competition was needed, this is it? All that is required is open competition, is it not? Why does he not agree, since I understand that that is part of the Government's policy anyway?

Viscount Goschen: My Lords, open competition is a major plank of the Government's policy. Yet we still see the very clear benefits that will come from harmonisation of this industry within the European Community.

Lord Teviot: My Lords, I can speak for the industry and the industry is supportive of the Government in

[LORD TEVIOT]
what they are doing. Are not all these questions hares in relation to the issue of double-decker buses? Contrary to what my noble friend Lord Pearson said, the industry regards this hare about double-decker buses as being a Euro-myth?

Viscount Goschen: My Lords, I agree with my noble friend that we are keeping in very close contact with the bus industry on this point and will continue to do so.

British Rail: Privatisation Expenditure

2.55 p.m.

Lord Taylor of Gryfe asked Her Majesty's Government:

What is the total expenditure incurred in consultancy, legal and accountancy fees in the privatisation of British Rail, including Railtrack, and the anticipated expenditure on franchising.

Viscount Goschen: My Lords, total expenditure on external consultancy fees for railways privatisation, including legal and accountancy fees, incurred by the Department of Transport, the Office of Passenger Rail Franchising and the Rail Regulator between 1991-92 and 1993-94 was £19 million. Consultancy costs incurred by BR and Railtrack are a matter for them, but I understand that they were in the order of £30 million up to March 1994. Total planned expenditure by the Office of Passenger Rail Franchising for 1994-95 is £7 million.

Lord Taylor of Gryfe: My Lords, will the Minister accept that I was very interested in the figures quoted? I understand from the annual accounts of British Rail that it has taken 50 per cent. of those costs and the 50 per cent. in their accounts represents £40 million. That suggests that the total amount of fees that I mentioned in my Question are in the region of £80 million. Even if we accept the Minister's figures, does he consider it a reasonable contribution to an efficient railway system when, at the same time that those substantial fees are being incurred, the investment budget of British Rail last year was reduced by 21 per cent.? The public service obligation, which is the subsidy for the day to day running of the railways, apart from investment, was also substantially reduced. Can he justify the expenditure on consultants' fees while there is a reduction in investment in new rolling stock, etcetera, which will make the railway efficient?

Viscount Goschen: My Lords, it is extremely important to put these sums in the context of the major transition that is taking place in the railway industry. It is a major privatisation and we simply do not believe that it would be good value to maintain the kind and level of specific expertise within the department for what is a short-term transition period. That is why these moneys have been spent on consultants. We see them as being good value.

Lord Marsh: My Lords, will the Minister address his mind to the extent to which British Rail, or Railtrack, will have to carry the cost of these consultancy fees— which arise wholly and solely out of government policy—in their accounts, which presumably will have a direct effect upon levels of subsidy that have nothing to do with this exercise? Alternatively, can he give the House an assurance that those very large sums in regard to either Railtrack or British Rail will not be taken into account in any way when addressing the levels of subsidy in those companies?

Viscount Goschen: My Lords, the noble Lord is right and the levels of subsidy are another issue. They will be based on the services that the franchising director will require, which will be based broadly on the existing timetable and the contracts made with the train operating companies. The consultancy fees represent the provision of very specialised services, which we do not believe exist within the department or within Railtrack, British Rail and the Office of Passenger Rail Franchising. That is why we brought them in and why we feel that they are good value.

Lord Ewing of Kirkford: My Lords, will the Minister answer a simple question? Who will pay the consultancy fees? Will it be the British taxpayer or the railway companies?

Viscount Goschen: My Lords, at the moment, of course, the taxpayer pays everything for the railways. That is the historic position. As the noble Lord knows, we are now going forward to a position where we are putting the railway companies into the private sector. Once those companies are in the private sector they will be responsible for their own costs.

Lord Clinton-Davis: My Lords, is the Minister aware that the figures he put forward seem to coincide more with Disney World than with reality? It was reliably estimated that the total costs of actual and projected expenditure in relation to privatisation, including the costs borne in the City, are nearer £1,000 million than the figure he stated. Whatever the position, does he agree with the statement made by the chairman of British Rail, Sir Bob Reid, on 4th December that the Government would have to make a long-term commitment to subsidise the railways if Railtrack is to be saleable at all? Is it right that the taxpayer should provide this life support machine for the franchisees?

Viscount Goschen: My Lords, the figure quoted by the noble Lord totally misrepresents the situation. He was talking about the total cost of privatisation, which is by no means the same as the total cost of consultancies. The larger figure includes the smaller, but I dispute vigorously his assessment of the larger figure. It is grossly overstated. The noble Lord then asked a supplementary question which had nothing to do with the consultation cost. We stated that we will provide a subsidy to the railway industry, as long as it is needed, to provide the services required by the franchising director.

Lord Clinton-Davis: My Lords, if the Minister disputes my figure, what is his view of the total cost of privatisation?

Viscount Goschen: My Lords, British Rail estimates that it has incurred reorganisation costs of £102 million up to March 1994 and that includes £30 million consultancy costs.

Territorial Army: Restructuring

3.1 p.m.

Lord Richard asked Her Majesty's Government:

Whether, as part of the proposed restructuring of the Territorial Army, the two TA battalions of the Parachute Regiment are to have an endorsed role as reserves in support of 5 Airborne Brigade; and whether they are to retain their support weapons.

The Parliamentary Under-Secretary of State, Ministry of Defence (Lord Henley): My Lords, as we announced yesterday, the support weapons platoons of TA infantry battalions will be concentrated in four fire support battalions. The two TA battalions of the Parachute Regiment will restructure on a three rifle company basis without support weapons. On mobilisation, both battalions will be available to meet NATO or national requirements; in other circumstances they will, like the rest of the TA, serve as a general reserve to the Army. This may involve the battalions or parts of them augmenting the Regular Army on operations either in support of 5 Airborne Brigade or other formations, or independently.

Lord Richard: My Lords, I am obliged to the Minister for that Answer. I do not have a direct interest in this matter since I am not a member of the TA. I have never jumped out of an aeroplane either with or without a parachute. But this is a matter which was brought to my attention and is causing anxiety, particularly in those two battalions.

Can the Minister give us a specific statement this afternoon that the role of those two TA battalions is to act as reserves in support of the 5 Airborne Brigade? If he can say that, he will quell a great deal of anxiety. If that is not their role, presumably they have some role other than that of teaching men to jump out of aeroplanes with parachutes on, and perhaps he can tell us what that is.

Lord Henley: My Lords, I suspected that the noble Lord would not have an interest to declare. I thought it unlikely that he jumped out of aeroplanes either now or in the past. My first Answer gave the noble Lord the assurance he wanted. I was trying to make clear that those battalions do not have a specific endorsed role in support of 5 Airborne Brigade. If 5 Airborne Brigade needed reinforcement, it may come from those battalions or it may come from others. But, like other TA infantry battalions, they continue to have an important role in the restructured TA as part of the general reserve for the Armed Forces.

I understand that the changes can cause some anxiety. We looked at other alternatives, possibly re roling one battalion of the TA paras as a fire support battalion. But that would cause even greater anxiety because it would reduce the number of parachute trained soldiers in that the establishment of a support battalion would be 336 as opposed to 519 for an ordinary battalion.

Lord Mason of Barnsley: My Lords, the Minister said in a written reply in the *Official Report* that,

"The 8th Battalion, the Light Infantry, will re role as a National Defence Reconnaissance Regiment in the Royal Armoured Corps, taking over the current role of the Royal Yeomanry which will become the Army's Nuclear, Biological and Chemical Defence Regiment".—[*Official Report*, 6/12/94; col. WA 76.]

Though I accept that the 8th Battalion, the Yorkshire Light Infantry, is to be given a new role, can I take it that its members will be able to maintain their present cap badges and titles?

Lord Henley: My Lords, I can give that confirmation to the noble Lord. They will be able to retain their cap badge and title.

Viscount Ridley: My Lords, is the Minister aware that the great majority of the Territorial Army will welcome yesterday's statement about its future, not least as an end to a long period of uncertainty? Is he further aware that what is needed now is a long period of stability to implement these sensible changes?

Lord Henley: My Lords, I am grateful for the noble Viscount's comments. I agree that the vast majority of the TA is happy with the changes. It is obviously difficult, when announcing a restructuring of this sort, to avoid any disturbance whatever. We tried to avoid any excessive disturbance. As I said, some units will find their role changed but I hope that the vast majority of units will be happy without their existing role or in the new role to which they have been assigned.

Lord Gisborough: My Lords, can my noble friend say why the recce role, which is essentially that of the cavalry, was given to an infantry regiment rather than to one of the cavalry regiments?

Lord Henley: My Lords, in the restructuring we were reducing the number of infantry units and increasing other corps. To retain the loyalties and cap badges that have been built up it was necessary to restructure on that basis.

Lord Molloy: My Lords, bearing in mind the magnificent history of Britain's Territorial Army, particularly in times of need, can the Minister say that there will be no serious change in relation to our Territorial Army without a debate in this House?

Lord Henley: My Lords, if a debate is necessary I am sure that the usual channels will note what the noble Lord said. I shall be more than happy to debate the role and future of the TA on some future occasion.

Business

3.6 p.m.

Lord Strathclyde: My Lords, at a convenient moment after 3.30 p.m. my noble friend Lady Chalker of Wallasey will, with the leave of the House, repeat a Statement that is to be made in another place on the situation in Bosnia.

National Health Patient Accommodation Bill [H.L.]

3.7 p.m.

Lord Stoddart of Swindon: My Lords, I beg to introduce a Bill to provide a right to single sex accommodation for National Health Service patients. I beg to move that this Bill be now read a first time.

Moved, That the Bill be now read a first time.—(*Lord Stoddart of Swindon.*)

On Question, Bill read a first time, and to be printed.

Manufacturing Industry

3.8 p.m.

Lord Trefgarne rose To call attention to the importance of increased output from United Kingdom manufacturing industry, with particular reference to the contribution made by small and medium sized enterprises; and to move for Papers.

The noble Lord said: My Lords, in rising to move the Motion standing in my name on the Order Paper, perhaps I may start by quoting from the Government's White Paper on competitiveness published in May 1994. At that time they said:

"A competitive manufacturing sector is essential for our long term prosperity. The share of manufacturing in total output has fallen over time in the UK and in other major economies. But manufacturing is a major employer and its output, more than any other sector, is tested on international markets".

Let me emphasise that if our manufacturing companies are to compete successfully there is an urgent need for improved efficiency in the areas of manufacturing production, marketing and sales. At its simplest that is ensuring that we have the right product at the right price available in the right markets. In order to achieve those aims there is a vital need for sound and stable financial policies, leading to investment in plant, people, the infrastructure and, above all, education and training.

One area where government support is of importance is in the promotion and support of exports, both in European and world markets. Thus the work of ECGD in long and medium-term credit guarantees is of continuing and vital importance. Shorter term facilities are now provided by the privatised NCM company which appears to be going pretty well. But even in that market a continuing element of Government involvement continues to be essential, if only in relation to political risk.

Turning to the position of our companies within the European Union and hence the single European market, I warmly applaud the position taken by Her Majesty's Government, not least in their rejection of the social chapter of the Maastricht Treaty which I believe would lead to reduced employment opportunities in the United Kingdom and greater difficulty for employers in other ways also. I should mention in parenthesis at this stage that I am the Honorary President of the Mechanical and Metal Trades Confederation and I know that my views are almost universally shared by METCOM members.

Within the broad scope of manufacturing, I should like to draw your Lordships' attention to the significant role played by small and medium-sized enterprises. These firms are defined as employing fewer than 500 people and are generally known as SMEs. It may come as a surprise to learn that more than half of all people employed in the United Kingdom work for such companies. Many of these firms employ only one or two people and empirical evidence gathered from research carried out at Warwick University suggests that such tiny organisations tend to stay small. But, of course, just one more employee for all of them would make a huge difference to our unemployment figures. The Smaller Firms Council of the CBI has estimated that there are some 100,000 firms employing between 20 and 500 people. Of those, 25,000 have been identified as expecting to grow substantially. These surely are the companies which need help and support.

What are the characteristics of these companies and what kind of support do they need? First, there must be motivational and entrepreneurial drive by the owners and the key managers. This must come from within the business itself. Without it nothing can be achieved.

Secondly, there must be a carefully planned product policy which requires both R&D and market research which is often beyond the resources of smaller companies. It has to be said that these smaller companies sometimes eschew this approach to business and, rather than focusing on becoming winners and leaders in their chosen field, become diffused in their efforts and end up "Jack-of-all-trades and master of none"! Clearly, that is wholly undesirable. One of the very important services provided over recent years by the DTI has been the availability of consultancy services, especially to smaller companies, for the purposes to which I have referred. I believe that these arrangements have made a most valuable contribution to improving the competitiveness of companies in this sector, and I hope that they will continue.

Thirdly, there is a need for professional marketing and selling of the product and, again, small companies often lack real experience and training in these areas. This is a matter on which consultants can no doubt offer some guidance, but perhaps more importantly— particularly in overseas markets—is the selection of appropriate agents in the countries concerned. Here I wish to applaud the work of our missions overseas which are able to identify suitable local partners and bring them together with British exporters. I should perhaps remind your Lordships at this point that much of the work of small companies is very often as sub-contractors to larger enterprises, so the fact that I am, on this occasion, focusing on the needs of the smaller companies should not blind us to the important consideration that their health is equally dependent upon that of their larger cousins. So much, if not all, of the encouragement I seek for SMEs should apply equally to the larger enterprises.

Fourthly, finance is the lifeblood of any business and is especially vital as small and medium-sized companies strive to grow, especially when operating in the export field. I am not sure that the range of sources of finance available to SMEs is adequate—too many rely almost solely on their bank—but let us discuss that on another occasion.

Perhaps the most important area in which the Government can assist in the creation, growth and continued health of smaller companies is in the reduction of bureaucracy and regulation. Here I must applaud the various initiatives which have emerged recently from the DTI from the personal spur, we understand, of the President of the Board of Trade himself. There is still a long way to go, not least in containing the plethora of directives, rules and regulations which emerge from Brussels—we had a flavour of that at Question Time—but I urge my right honourable friend to redouble his efforts in this area. It is, in my view, the single most important aspect of government oversight of business generally and small businesses in particular.

I now turn to the vital area of training and education. I quote my right honourable friend the Prime Minister who, in the introduction to the White Paper to which I referred, said:

"I believe we must give our young people the highest standards of education and training. These skills will be the key to our future".

Perhaps I should say, in parenthesis again, that I have recently been appointed chairman of the Engineering Training Authority, so clearly I must take the Prime Minister's words closely to heart.

To compete effectively in international markets, the United Kingdom must address the immediate issue of skills training. In the longer term, we need to examine how our education system must develop to bring about greater levels of achievement. Compared with our main international competitors, the United Kingdom is consistently shown to be well behind in this area. This is the case in all levels of skills but especially for the intermediate levels—those traditionally described as craft, technician and supervisory skills.

Recent research carried out by the Engineering Training Authority shows that an encouraging 80 per cent. of engineering sites with 500 or more employees are implementing the new national vocational qualifications. Equally promising is the significant interest employers expressed in using NVQs at the higher levels—the very levels appropriate to the crucial intermediate skills, to which I have referred. But there is some evidence that smaller companies are not in the vanguard of these welcome developments. I hope that they will be in the future.

Investors in People is an important mechanism for employers to develop workforce skills and competence as an integrated part of the organisation's business plan. The importance of this initiative was underlined in the White Paper, to which I referred, and rightly so. There is, however, a risk that smaller companies may tend to dismiss these ideas as irrelevant to their needs. I do not agree. No company is too small to benefit from the proper management of its human resources, and *Investors in People* helps them to do just that.

The Government's firm commitment to modern apprenticeships is to be applauded. Prototype schemes are currently running in 17 sectors, the largest of those being engineering manufacturing. The Employment Department has pledged further major funds over the next three years to support launches in other sectors. Let us hope that they do not fall foul of whatever changes my right honourable friend the Chancellor of the Exchequer may announce tomorrow, following his "little local difficulty" in the other place last night.

Modern apprenticeships are an excellent means of giving quality training, providing young people with a foundation on which to develop a career or a route to higher education. Whatever the chosen path, modern apprenticeships, with their educational and core skills components, offer a sound basis for life-long learning which is so necessary in helping young people to adapt to change and cope flexibly with varying demands.

In an industry which has seen the number of trainees fall by about a third in fewer than three years, this initiative is an excellent opportunity to reverse this trend and to raise our intermediate skills levels to international standards.

Turning now to education, as distinct from training, the United Kingdom's failure to rank high in the industry league can, in part, be attributed to a comparatively poor output from our nation's schools. A study showed that in 1991, only 27 per cent. of 16 year-olds in the United Kingdom achieved GCSE grades A to C in the national language, maths and science, compared with 62 per cent. in Germany and 66 per cent. in France. United Kingdom pupils achieving two A-levels or equivalent numbered only 28 per cent. compared with 68 per cent. and 48 per cent. in the same countries. This country's highly selective approach to education, together with its emphasis on academic study, serve the minority well, no doubt, but the majority poorly. A fundamental cultural change is needed to bring about the acceptance of vocational courses. This change is crucially important if the manufacturing industry is not to lose out.

My Motion calls attention to the importance of increased output from all sectors of UK manufacturing industry including, in particular, smaller companies. But this vitally important increased output depends crucially upon our companies increasing their efficiency and hence their competitiveness if they are to compete not only here at home but more widely across Europe and the world. We have made enormous strides in the right direction in recent years as our economic recovery now demonstrates. But there is still much to be done. I believe that the main thrust of government policy is in the right direction and I commend the enthusiasm and drive of Ministers in this regard. But in the end our

[LORD TREFGARNE]
future depends not upon Ministers, regardless of their political complexion, but on the companies themselves. My Lords, I beg to move for Papers.

3.20 p.m.

Lord Haskel: My Lords, I start by apologising to the House for the fact that I may have to leave before the end of this debate in view of the delay that will arise from the Statement which is to be made. I shall read the Minister's response and the last few contributions in *Hansard* with great interest.

I am most grateful to the noble Lord, Lord Trefgarne, for moving this Motion because in it he states precisely the objective of the Department of Trade and Industry. It is to increase the output from United Kingdom manufacturing industry while maintaining and expanding the wealth of every citizen. The short answer is to produce more world-class products in the United Kingdom and for the small and medium-sized enterprises to become suppliers to those companies producing them, if they are not end-producers themselves.

We must start from the point of view that international comparisons indicate that there is plenty of under-performance by our manufacturing sector, particularly among the small and medium-sized enterprises, and we must catch up. How are we to achieve that objective?

Much research shows that most manufacturing small and medium-sized enterprises are single product companies often supplying niche markets. Their future is often tied to the life cycle of their product, or to where the economy is in the economic cycle. When their product becomes obsolete, or the market moves on, everything depends on the owner or manager. Does he or she have the ability, the money, the vision or the wish to move on also?

Again, research has shown that the small and medium-sized enterprise will progress if at this stage it is a supplier to a world-class manufacturer, or to a major original equipment manufacturer or to an important retailer. The close association with such a company will have forced the small and medium-sized enterprise to progress. Their customers will have forced the company to introduce new technology, new best practice, to innovate and to become competitive. These relationships are extremely important. We have all read about retailers and manufacturers cutting back on the number of their suppliers. They do this to concentrate on improving the performance of their suppliers. The hope is that these suppliers become world class and continue to be world class. This culture of buying by developing relationships and not purely on price is becoming more important in UK manufacturing. Not only in the private sector but also large public-sector purchasers, such as the Post Office and the National Health Service, are playing an important role in this.

Of course, the customers of small and medium-sized enterprises can be in the United Kingdom, in Europe or anywhere in the world. In manufacturing it is developing these relationships which is important, and if we wish to increase the output from the United Kingdom manufacturers it is up to the DTI to encourage this activity. Perhaps the Minister will tell us what plans his department has to speed up this work.

If one believes in that scenario, as I do, a number of things follow. First, it is long term. The main element for a successful long-term strategy of this kind is for government to get away from the stop-go roller coaster economy that we have experienced during my business life. I hear what the Government say about the current positive economic outlook, but many believe that nothing fundamental has changed and that we are at the start of a period of go after a long period of stop. Perhaps that is why the current levels of investment are disappointingly low.

A second principle that follows from my scenario concerns the people working in manufacturing. My experience is rather different to that of the noble Lord, Lord Trefgarne. To create a prosperous manufacturing sector we must move away from the casualisation of the workforce. A modern manufacturing economy demands more training, skill, versatility, commitment, education, and initiative from its workforce. But you do not achieve that by punishing people with fewer social benefits than their colleagues in the rest of Europe and by casualising the labour market.

Thirdly, the relationship between government and industry changes. Most successful manufacturing nations have governments which have developed a partnership with industry to the overall benefit of the nation as a whole. This partnership provides investment in the infrastructure necessary for manufacturing to be competitive. Between 1980 and 1990 the Japanese Government invested 5.1 per cent. of their gross domestic product and their growth rate was 3.8 per cent. We invested 1.9 per cent. of our gross domestic product and our growth rate was only 1.7 per cent. I leave your Lordships to draw the conclusions.

Another element of this partnership is that government should welcome the desire of purchasers to improve their suppliers rather than to continually shop around for alternative sources. Even though this leads to customers and suppliers becoming interdependent, it is nevertheless the task of government to encourage a vigorous competition policy. At present they are failing to do this.

Part of this partnership is also for government to discourage unrealistically high expectations from returns on investment and to deter short-termism in investment in manufacturing industry. I was pleased to see in the *Financial Times* of 5th December that the investigation into why UK companies need to pay higher dividends than companies elsewhere is being reinstated after it was cancelled earlier this year because the noble Lord, Lord Hanson, wrote to the Financial Secretary to the Treasury and accused him of acting like a socialist.

A word about inward investment. This is a welcome addition to our weak manufacturing base. It has brought jobs, new technology, and raised standards, but it is not an alternative and it is expensive in grants. Remember that the employment created is dependent on continued support from overseas investors. If we become too dependent on overseas investors, then our own ability to create manufacturing businesses will decrease.

In 1993, £9.5 billion was invested in Britain by overseas companies, but UK companies invested £17.2 billion overseas. UK manufacturing needs investment. Perhaps the Minister can say how we can redress this balance.

There are thus many elements in increasing the output of UK manufacturing and the balance is changing all the time. It is essential to get the balance right. If we improve training and fall down on quality, then all we will do is end up with a better educated army of unemployed. I welcome the research being carried out by the Warwick Business School and the Federation for Manufacturing Industry in this area.

Growth in UK manufacturing depends on our ability to produce world-class products. We will do it by the methods I have outlined which we on these Benches call "an active modern industrial policy". We do not seek intervention for intervention's sake. We see it as a means of working in partnership with manufacturing to make the market economy really dynamic.

3.29 p.m.

Lord Weatherill: My Lords, we are all indebted to the noble Lord, Lord Trefgarne, for initiating a debate on the very important subject of the contribution that is made by small and medium-sized businesses. I am pleased to return to the subject of my maiden speech not only in this House but also, incidentally, in another place many years ago when I spoke about the youth employment service. It is a plain fact that important though big businesses are in the manufacturing sector, it is to small firms and, in particular, new businesses that we must look to provide the jobs of the future and at the same time to make a vitally important contribution to solving many of our country's social problems which arise undoubtedly from unemployment.

I seek to intervene today on behalf of new businesses. I trust that I am qualified to do so from personal experience. I was apprenticed to the business that had been started by my father way back in 1912. I was not apprenticed in 1912, although some people may think so! My father had led the last successful strike of tailors. He was crippled and unemployed. I regularly go round schools these days talking about the good old days; but they were not so good if you were poor and had very little education. As my father was unemployable, he therefore had to set up on his own account. We still have the bicycle with a small wheel at the front and a bigger wheel at the back on which he used to cycle out to take the orders and then cycle back and deliver the clothes when he had made them. I entered a business which started in South Ascot and which, I am proud to say, is now in Savile Row. It is not a big business, but it employs a considerable number of people, and two-thirds of our turnover is in overseas markets.

Self-employment offers a way out of unemployment, particularly for those who are made redundant, and especially for young people for whom the inability to find a job breeds a cycle of alienation which is a threat to the quality of life in our country. No organisation knows more about those problems than the Prince's Youth Business Trust, of which I am proud to be a trustee. The trust started through the personal initiative of His Royal Highness the Prince of Wales and can claim to be the biggest—the No. 1—youth start-up organisation in the country. If a Japanese company comes to our country and creates 1,000 jobs, we lay a red carpet half way down the M.1 to congratulate it, yet the Prince's Youth Business Trust has established 24,000 new businesses since its inception, with 3,000 being created in the past year. Of those new businesses, 40 per cent. were started by females; 15 per cent. by the ethnic minority communities; 5 per cent. by the disabled; and a number were begun by former young offenders. It is a remarkable success story which should be better known, more widely appreciated and more positively supported.

The trust provides "soft" loans, small grants and post-start-up advice to those between the ages of 18 and 29, who the banks will not consider. However, no one is given money without being assigned a business adviser. That has ensured that two-thirds of the new businesses started in the past three years are still trading today. That is a much higher success rate than any of the banks can claim. Those who assist as business advisers do so voluntarily. They are all experienced people. Some are retired, but others are still working as managers in large firms and successful businesses.

The average net cost of taking someone off the unemployment register and putting him or her to work in this way is £2,500 per annum. That is far far less than the cost of a year of unemployment. The trust is able to be so successful and cost-effective because a high proportion of its staff are seconded from the private sector, and because some 6,000 people give their time voluntarily to support its work. One of them is the noble Lord, Lord Mason of Barnsley, who has been chairman of the South Yorkshire Board of the Prince's Youth Business Trust since its inception. He is one of 38 such chairmen throughout the United Kingdom. It must be true that the Prince's Youth Business Trust is the largest free consultancy service in the world.

I am also patron of Croydon Business Ventures, an enterprise agency in my former constituency of Croydon, North-East. Some 13 years ago, shortly after I was chosen as Speaker of another place, I attempted to attend a party on the ground floor of the House of Commons. I was dragged into a room by the honourable Member for Bow and Poplar who, pulling me in, said, "I am very anxious to introduce you all to our new Speaker, Sir Jasper More". I said, "I suppose that I ought to know your name". The name of that organisation was the Tower Hamlets Enterprise Agency. I went to visit it and resolved that we would have such an agency in my constituency. I wrote a letter to 12 friends saying, "Please send me £1,000", and giving a telephone number. All of them rang me up, asking why I wanted the money. I said, "To finance your future competitors". We have been in business now for 10 years, during which time we have established 1,170 new businesses and provided, we estimate, 5,300 new jobs in Croydon. Despite difficult times, three-quarters of those businesses have survived. We estimate that Croydon Business Ventures generates £100 million turnover per year. Some of those businesses, which started from

[LORD WEATHERILL]

scratch, have grown into quite big firms. The average turnover is £76,000, and 37 per cent. of the firms have a turnover of between £100,000 and £500,000.

It is good that the Minister who is responsible for small firms is a Member of your Lordships' House because I should like to address a number of concerns directly to the noble Earl, Lord Ferrers, who is to reply to the debate. First, both the Prince's Youth Business Trust and Croydon Business Ventures, like other enterprise agencies, are concerned about the business start-up scheme, which was previously known as the enterprise allowance. The latter seemed a good phrase and it is a pity that it has been dropped. Many small enterprises have depended on that allowance to help them through the crucial start-up phase. I hope that the noble Earl will be able to reassure the House that that crucially important allowance will not be neutered, let alone done away with.

A further worry is the trend to focus TEC and the Business Links support on firms with between 20 and 200 employees. Few firms start with 20 employees, and to reduce support from the very small enterprises and new businesses that have been nurtured by the PYBT and the enterprise agencies is to cut off at source one of the key features of healthy industrial and commercial birth. I must tell the Minister that there is considerable concern that local enterprise agencies, which as I have sought to prove have been highly successful in helping to establish new businesses, may themselves not survive if, as seems possible, TECs and Business Links put a lower priority on the future of small enterprises. For many small businesses, the loss of the business start-up scheme would be a major blow; but the loss of the associated start-up training would, if anything, be worse leading inevitably to a higher rate of business failure. I hope therefore that the Minister will intervene on their behalf to ensure that those important sources of funding are not cut off.

Napoleon never did say that we were a nation of shopkeepers. What he did say was that we were a nation of merchant adventurers. Britain's prosperity in the past, and also in the future, is, and will be, dependent upon trade, and in particular upon a healthy manufacturing base. We must not be simply a nation of shopkeepers selling other people's goods. Of course, as other noble Lords have said, big businesses, as major employers, must be the concern of the Government; but employment in that sector has declined steadily since 1980, while employment in small and medium-sized enterprises has grown steadily.

The figures have been quoted already; but it is worth repeating them: firms with fewer than 10 employees comprise 90 per cent. of all enterprises and contribute 25 per cent. to our GDP. It therefore seems inevitable that we must look to small firms to provide jobs for the future, and in doing so, that sector will be making a vital contribution towards the solution of social consequences—the social consequences of unemployment which besides costing millions of pounds a year is a source of deep frustration which is potentially a threat to the life of us all in this country.

Bosnia

3.40 p.m.

The Minister of State, Foreign and Commonwealth Office (Baroness Chalker of Wallasey): My Lords, with the leave of the House, I shall now repeat a Statement on Bosnia which is being made in another place by my right honourable friend the Foreign Secretary. The Statement is as follows:

"The situation on the ground deteriorated over the last month. Around the Bihac pocket, Bosnian Government forces launched an attack but were then forced back by the Bosnian Serbs. The Bosnian Serbs, with support from Croatian Serb forces and rebel Bosnian Moslems, have taken the fighting into the United Nations safe area. The contravention of Security Council resolutions led the commanders of the UN force and NATO to call for and carry out air strikes to deter attacks against the safe area.

"The fighting has also intensified in central Bosnia with Bosnian Government forces making gains against the Bosnian Serbs. In the safe areas of Sarajevo, Gorazde and Srebrenica the civilian populations and the UN contingents are short of supplies as convoys have been held up. Over 400 UN troops had their movements limited by the Bosnian Serbs. Some were effectively held hostage.

"That was the situation which faced the ministerial meeting of the Contact Group on 2nd December. The Contact Group countries—Britain, France, Germany, Russia and the United States—united in calling for an immediate ceasefire in the Bihac pocket, including the withdrawal of Bosnian Serb and Croatian Serb forces from the safe area. We also called for talks to begin on a comprehensive agreement to cease hostilities throughout Bosnia. The Contact Group supported UNPROFOR's mission and demanded immediate freedom of movement for UNPROFOR and for humanitarian supplies throughout the country. Only once these steps have been taken and the Bosnian Serbs have accepted the Contact Group plan as the basis for a settlement can negotiations continue.

"The Contact Group reaffirmed the plan adopted last July. Under this plan the integrity of Bosnia-Hercegovina would be preserved. The Bosnian Serbs would hold 49 per cent. of the territory, the Bosnian Federation of Croats and Moslems 51 per cent. We reiterated that the territorial proposal—that is, the map of the 51 per cent. and 49 per cent.—can be adjusted by mutual agreement between the parties. Constitutional arrangements agreeable to the parties will also need to be drawn up which preserve the integrity of Bosnia-Hercegovina and allow equitable and balanced arrangements for the Bosnian-Croat Federation and the Bosnian-Serb entity. The Contact Group agreed that its officials would help the parties reach a settlement on these issues. We did not discuss the lifting of the arms embargo or any change in the arrangements for the use of NATO airpower in support of the UN.

"The purpose of the Contact Group meeting was to help relaunch the political process following agreement, which we hope will come soon, on a ceasefire.

"To carry this forward, I travelled to Belgrade with my French colleague, M. Juppé, for talks with President Milosevic. Mr. Milosevic welcomed the clarifications we were able to provide. He said that they would help him to put again to the Bosnian Serb Assembly the case for accepting the peace plan. The next day over 20 members—more than a quarter of the Bosnian Serb Assembly—saw Mr. Milosevic in Belgrade. They issued a statement saying that in the light of the clarifications made to the Contact Group plan, the Pale Assembly should consider accepting it and entering negotiations on the map and the constitution to reach a final settlement. This is an encouraging step forward, but not enough. The Bosnian Serb leadership has yet to accept the plan.

"At the summit of the Conference on Security and Co-operation in Europe, which my right honourable friend the Prime Minister and I attended in Budapest on 5th and 6th December, I met President Izetbegovic of Bosnia, President Tudjman of Croatia and the Secretaries-General of the United Nations and NATO.

"The three presidents—Milosevic, Izetbegovic and Tudjman —all support the Contact Group plan for Bosnia and the continued presence of the UN force. They are all willing in principle to agree to a ceasefire throughout Bosnia, as are the Bosnian Serbs, though there remains a disagreement over its duration. We hope that the UN special representative, Mr. Akashi, will be able to make progress on a ceasefire this week.

"The British Government want the UN force to be able to continue its mission and the British contingent to continue to play a major part. But we must be clear about its role. It is not there to impose solutions on unwilling parties. It cannot fight on one side. It does not defend one army's territory against the attacks of another. It is there to support the impressive aid effort, much of it British, delivered by ODA teams, to buttress ceasefires where they exist and, within its limitations, to underpin the safe areas and exclusion zones designated by the United Nations and NATO.

"Withdrawal would be a difficult operation in itself. The consequences for the civilians whom the force are there to protect would be severe. But UNPROFOR can only continue its mission if it can do so without unacceptable risk and if it can continue to fulfil its mandate. As with all military operations, planning is in hand to cover a variety of eventualities, including withdrawal. These are constantly updated. The Government are not considering unilateral withdrawal of the British contingent. We are working with our partners in NATO and the United Nations.

"The Government's preferred way forward is clear: first, a ceasefire in the Bihac safe area and throughout Bosnia; secondly, agreement on the free movement of UNPROFOR and for aid convoys; thirdly, resumption of urgent negotiations for a peace settlement on the basis of the Contact Group plan; and, fourthly, once agreement has been reached, withdrawal by the Bosnian Serbs from the land they hold to the new lines agreed.

"Before I end, I should also record welcome progress between the Croatian Government and the Croatian Serbs. Last week they signed an economic agreement which provides for the resumption of oil, water and electricity links between the Serb held areas of Croatia and the rest of the country and for re-opening the highway between Zagreb and Belgrade. I pay tribute to the months of patient and persistent diplomacy by the noble Lord, Lord Owen, and Mr. Stoltenberg which was needed to achieve this. I hope the agreement can be implemented soon. It improves the prospects for negotiations leading to a lasting political settlement in Croatia and for normalisation of ties between Croatia and Serbia."

My Lords, that concludes the Statement.

Baroness Blackstone: My Lords, I am grateful to the Minister for repeating the Statement. I welcome the progress that has been made in negotiating at least a modicum of agreement between the Croatian Government and the Croatian Serbs. I share with the Minister our gratitude to the noble Lord, Lord Owen, and Mr. Stoltenberg for their work in achieving that. I also welcome the decision to maintain British troops as part of the UN forces in Bosnia. While lives continue to be saved and while humanitarian aid is provided as a direct result of the presence of UN troops in Bosnia, we on this side of the House hope that members of the British Armed Forces will continue to be part of that presence.

There has been in the press a great deal of loose talk about the withdrawal of our troops without sufficient consideration of the effects on the Bosnian civilian community. Many more lives would be at risk if UN troops, among whom British troops play such a crucial part, were to be withdrawn. We also accept, as the Statement makes absolutely clear, that the role of British troops is not to fight on one side or the other or to defend one army's territory against another. We agree that, provided that their future safety is not seriously threatened, they are there to monitor the cease-fire and to ensure that UN resolutions on the exclusion areas and the safe havens are implemented. However, what has happened in Bihac during the past couple of weeks has shown only too clearly that, as we predicted, the safe haven policy has not worked and it is still not working.

Will the Minister tell the House how the United Nations and NATO intend to ensure that what happened in Bihac during the past two or three weeks is not repeated elsewhere in the near future? Will she also tell the House what steps will be taken to stop other Bosnian Serbs taking more UN troops hostage? Surely it is totally unacceptable that Bosnian Serbs, with the support of rebel Bosnian Moslems and Croatian Serbs, should have mounted an attack on one of the designated safe havens. That attack had considerable success and led to 400 United Nations troops being denied basic supplies and the ability to move freely.

[BARONESS BLACKSTONE]

It is not clear what political steps are being taken to deal with that in the ongoing negotiations with the Bosnian Serbs. Does the Minister agree that in such circumstances it is entirely wrong to make concessions to the Bosnian Serbs? In offering an association between the Bosnian Serbs and the state of Serbia, is not the international community making just such a concession? Moreover, will not this concession jeopardise the long-term independence of Bosnia and the future of the Bosnian Moslem community.

The Statement indicates that at the recent meeting of the Contact Group there was no discussion on the lifting of the arms embargo. Will the Minister confirm that there are to be no further changes to the current position on the arms embargo? Does she agree that to provide American, British or French arms to the Bosnian Moslems at this delicate stage will serve only to inflame the military situation and to damage progress towards a political settlement?

The Statement strikes a note of optimism about the Contact Group's planned basis for a settlement which is difficult to share. The Minister has given no assessment of the chances of the Bosnian Serb leadership accepting it after the Minister's right honourable friend the Foreign Secretary and the French Minister for Foreign Affairs visited Belgrade. Perhaps she is now able to give such an assessment.

I wish to pay tribute again to the brave and courageous role played by our troops in Bosnia. As I said earlier, they have saved many lives. We hope that the international community will be more successful in obtaining the political settlement which will allow the troops to return home safely as soon as possible.

Lord Thomson of Monifieth: My Lords, I join the noble Baroness, Lady Blackstone, in thanking the Minister for repeating the Statement. I, too, pay tribute to the noble Lord, Lord Owen, and Mr. Stoltenberg for the patient efforts that they have made on the Croatian Serbian front. Useful progress has been made and we hope that that will contribute to a wider settlement.

The Statement is one of some gravity. The situation has deteriorated and the implications of a further deterioration are serious indeed. Against that background, we wish to pay tribute to the patience and persistence of the Foreign Secretary and his efforts to try to arrest that deterioration. Clearly, the first step is to try to bring about a cease-fire in the Bihac area. We would be grateful for any further information that the Minister can give us on that matter.

I echo the words of the noble Baroness, Lady Blackstone, that what happened in Bihac was an ominous event as regards the possibility of the same deterioration taking place in other safe havens. We would all like to know what steps the Government believe can be taken by the Contact Group, the NATO forces and the United Nations to try to prevent that possibility. It is unacceptable that 400 United Nations soldiers should, in effect, be turned into hostages.

Finally, we welcome the statement that the Government are not contemplating any unilateral withdrawal of the British contribution to the United Nations contingent and that they are dealing with the problems collectively with our colleagues and allies. At the same time, all our thoughts are with the British Armed Forces and civilian aid workers in Bosnia. They are doing fine work in terms of humanitarian aid in alleviating suffering. I too pay tribute to the role that they are undertaking in Bosnia, but we need every possible reassurance that their safety and security is paramount in the mind of Her Majesty's Government.

Baroness Chalker of Wallasey: My Lords, I thank the noble Baroness, Lady Blackstone, and the noble Lord, Lord Thomson of Monifieth, for the tributes that they paid not only to the noble Lord, Lord Owen, and Mr. Stoltenberg but also to my right honourable friend the Foreign Secretary. I assure your Lordships that the British Government—and, I believe, the French Government, too—will not cease in their efforts to stop the extension of the terrible situation that we have seen in Bihac. We will use every means at our disposal to stop its spread.

Of course, the spread can best be stopped by the agreement that President Milosevic is seeking with some members of the Bosnian Serb Parliament. I mentioned in the Statement that more than 20 members had issued a statement and we believe that there may be more. There is a total of 83 members of that Bosnian Serb Parliament in Pale. The majority would have to be convinced to achieve acceptance of that plan. That is quite clearly what everyone hopes will happen because only when there has been an acceptance of the Contact Group plan can we begin to see the beginning of real progress.

The noble Baroness said that safe havens are not working. She knows that if you do not give support to the implementation of safe havens it is very difficult for the safe areas to work in the way that was first envisaged. Although Britain has more than played her part as one of the main force contributors among the 39,000 or so troops who are there, there are countries which have not played a role in UNPROFOR. From what I have seen on the ground, I am firmly convinced that you can make safe havens really safe only when you have people on the ground so to do.

The noble Baroness asked how we could prevent the Bihac tragedy being repeated elsewhere and how we could stop Bosnian Serbs taking servicemen and, indeed, others hostage while making no concessions. A very active role is being played not only by Mr. Akashi who secured the release of 160 troops last week, 60 of whom were British, but also work is going on to secure the release of the other 350 UNPROFOR troops from France, Russia, the Ukraine and Canada and the UNMOs who are being held to ransom. That can be done only through patient negotiation and not through concessions because they would indeed jeopardise the future.

I assure your Lordships that there are no changes with regard to lifting the arms embargo. Although it was not discussed at the meeting none of the members of the Contact Group, with the exception of certain members of Congress in the United States, is envisaging a lifting of the embargo. I believe that that is absolutely right because putting more arms into an already febrile situation would do nothing to help the people of Bosnia.

I close by thanking the noble Lord, Lord Thomson of Monifieth, for the tribute that he paid to the aid workers. There are many from non-governmental organisations as well as our own ODA personnel who are there on the ground. If they cannot get into one area, they will deliver to another area. They are keeping men, women and children alive and giving them some hope for the future. Without UNPROFOR and without the aid workers, that simply could not have happened.

4.2 p.m.

The Earl of Lauderdale: My Lords, perhaps I may ask my noble friend about the assembly at Pale. She gave us the interesting information that some 20 out of 83 members went to Belgrade and issued a statement. Do we know when the assembly will meet and when it will reach a decision? Do we know whether the Russians are actively helping to encourage those members of the assembly to agree to peace?

In addition, will the Minister say something about the unhappy plight, which we read about, of the Bangladeshi troops. Apparently they have one rifle to five men and are shivering in an unfamiliar climate.

Baroness Chalker of Wallasey: My Lords, I thank my noble friend for his questions. The answer to his first question is that I cannot give him any more detail about when the discussion will take place in Pale. We believe that the Russians are helping but I am not privy to exactly how that is being done, so cannot pass on that information to my noble friend.

My noble friend asked about the 1,400 brave Bangladeshi troops. They are in the Bihac pocket. I am glad to say that a convoy of rations and fuel arrived for them on 4th December. They are doing a very valuable job under the most difficult conditions. There are a number of problems for them in the area but we are quite determined that they, as well as the ordinary people in Bihac who are suffering too, should have supplies. I assure my noble friend that we shall play a full role in helping to ensure that they are so supplied.

Lord Taylor of Gryfe: My Lords, one of the most helpful aspects of the Statement and the recent developments in Yugoslavia has been the role of Mr. Milosevic. He has supported and endorsed the Contact Group's plan, despite the hostility of many of his fellow Serbs. As a result of that, there has been some relaxation of the severe sanctions—the opening of the airport and the resumption of cultural activities, including football matches, is now permitted. However, most pressing of all is the need for medical supplies. I was recently in Belgrade and I visited hospitals in which doctors had to make a decision on which child to save because they had supplies for only one. Will the Minister give me an assurance—and it would be a useful gesture in the light of the role of Mr. Milosevic—that the question of sanctions as applied to medical supplies might be reviewed?

Baroness Chalker of Wallasey: My Lords, we have made it clear that medical supplies are certainly to be sent and they are not caught by the sanctions provisions. It is true that doctors have to make difficult decisions in any country where there is war and conflict. But there is no way in which we stand in the way of medical supplies. Medical supplies are indeed going into Belgrade and some are travelling on from Belgrade with the convoys into some of the areas to the east of Bosnia-Hercegovina where there is much need.

Lord Harmar-Nicholls: My Lords, is my noble friend aware that we all hope that the present proposals referred to in the Statement will bring about a satisfactory result? But is there not some risk in stating categorically that British troops should not be removed, because uncertainty with regard to the possibility of that happening may have played some part in creating an atmosphere among people who at present are intransigent on meeting any reasonable request?

Baroness Chalker of Wallasey: My Lords, I thank my noble friend for allowing me to make clear once again, as I did in repeating the Statement, that British troops, or indeed UNPROFOR as a whole, can continue their mission only if they can do so without unacceptable risk and if they continue to fulfil their mandate. That is why we have made contingency plans for a withdrawal, if that had to happen. We hope sincerely that it will not because the troops are carrying out a most valuable role. But we have never said that we shall not withdraw them if they faced an unacceptable risk or if they could not continue to fulfil their mandate.

Lord Mackie of Benshie: My Lords, is it not true that the whole treatment of this crisis has been an absolute disgrace to Western Europe and to the countries of the United Nations? Is it not a fact that the Serbs have played up Western Europe and NATO in the most disgraceful manner and that we have retreated from saying that no territory conquered by force would be held but are now proposing to let the Serbs get away with the vast majority of their conquests?

Is it not a fact that we have threatened force with overwhelming air power at our disposal but failed to use it? Is not what is happening today similar to what happened to the League of Nations? The UN resolve and the political will of the governments of Europe is at such a low ebb that we shall probably go on to further disasters because potential aggressors in their own territory will know that the governments of Western Europe will never use force to stop them?

Baroness Chalker of Wallasey: My Lords, the mandate does not entitle UNPROFOR or NATO to use force to stop one party against another. The mandate is absolutely clear. I believe that the noble Lord was most unfair in what he said. It is very easy to be an armchair critic of this highly complicated situation. It is not simple because one is not even talking—for example, in the Bihac pocket—of Bosnian Serbs fighting Bosnian Moslems; one is talking of a third group, a breakaway group, and of the complexities of the Serbs in Krajina. Indeed, the situation is continually changing. That does not make it easy to carry through the mandate in the first place.

[BARONESS CHALKER OF WALLASEY]

Secondly, in no way have the Contact Group or the allies been giving in to the Serbs in the way implied by the noble Lord. There simply is no alternative to the Contact Group plan. That is why the role that Mr. Milosevic has begun to play is so important. I can say that we are certainly encouraged by the statement from the Bosnian Serb Assembly delegation supporting the Contact Group plan. It remains to be seen whether that view will be acceptable in Pale and acceptable to a larger number of the Bosnian Serb Assembly. However, that does not alter the fact that the Bosnian Serb leadership knows that it cannot return to normality until the war ends. That is why we are working so hard for a peace settlement.

I should point out to the noble Lord that anyone who had read the detail of the discussions which my right honourable friend the Foreign Secretary and Alain Juppé, and others, have had over the past five days, could not put the questions that he has just put to me.

Lord Ennals: My Lords, will the Minister accept my great satisfaction that she dealt as firmly as she did with what I thought was the grossly oversimplified interpretation of the situation presented by the noble Lord, Lord Mackie of Benshie? Looking especially at the role of the UN, with which I obviously have a particular interest as an officer of the United Nations Association, perhaps I may say how glad I am that the Minister referred to the task carried out by Mr. Akashi who has absolutely, and with persistence, sought to find a way through a very complicated situation.

Bearing in mind the Minister's words about the possibility of imposing solutions on unwilling partners—a statement which seems to me to be absolutely accurate—can she confirm that the UN is not there in order to fight a war but to do what it can mainly by humanitarian means? Will the Minister condemn some of the statements made in the newspapers, which rather reflect what the noble Lord, Lord Mackie of Benshie, said, suggesting that, somehow or other, it showed a failure of an organisation; namely, the United Nations or, for that matter, NATO? Such organisations simply cannot force people to do what they are not willing to do.

As regards the treatment of the Bangladeshi forces of UNPROFOR, will the Minister openly condemn the quite appalling behaviour of the Bosnian Serbs in treating them as hostages when, under very difficult circumstances, they have been acting in the name and in the duty of the United Nations?

Baroness Chalker of Wallasey: My Lords, it is quite right that the noble Lord, Lord Ennals, should also pay tribute to Mr. Akashi who has a nearly impossible task. He has been at the forefront of seeking the release of those troops detained by the Bosnian Serb army. As I said, his intervention on behalf of Dutch and British troops has already been successful. We hope that he will very soon be successful in securing the release of others.

Of course we unequivocally condemn the holding of all military personnel or civilians by the Bosnian Serbs. That goes back to the situation nearly two years ago when we went in to try to help. There is absolutely no question that the Bangladeshi battalion has carried out a very valuable job. Indeed, those troops have worked under very difficult conditions in an area of former Yugoslavia, which is very difficult to police because of its sheer terrain. But in addition, I should stress that all that is the art of the possible. That is why the work that is carried out on the ground, whether by the commander of UNPROFOR, General Sir Michael Rose, or by Mr. Akashi, needs to be viewed with great care.

There are far too many armchair critics in this country who think that they know best. As for some of the attacks in the media and by certain other people on General Sir Michael Rose, I have been appalled by what I have read. It is so far from the truth that it defies reason. Perhaps I may join the noble Lord, Lord Ennals, and repeat something that I said in a debate in the House on Monday. Where people are determined to go on fighting, it is very difficult to stop them until there is a break in that determination. What we hope we are seeing in the Bosnian Serb Assembly is a willingness to bring the fighting to an end and let the negotiation and the peace process really begin again.

Lord Monson: My Lords, in her reply to the noble Earl, Lord Lauderdale, the Minister expressed the belief that Russia was being helpful. However, does the noble Baroness agree that the Russian veto of a recent resolution condemning Bosnian-Serb aggression is an ominous sign? Does it not appear to indicate that Russia is now taking a blatantly partisan approach to the conflict and that it is effectively condoning Bosnian-Serb aggression?

Baroness Chalker of Wallasey: My Lords, it is very easy to believe that the use of the veto by the Russians indicates such a mood. One fact that is quite clear is that the Russians are asking for much earlier consultation about events and about planning. We have taken that very much on board. I told my noble friend that, while we believe the Russians were being helpful in some ways, I could not go into the detail of how they were acting.

Baroness Strange: My Lords, can my noble friend the Minister tell us whether supplies have been getting through to the troops in Sarajevo? Perhaps I may also reiterate what has been said by noble Lords on all sides of the House; namely, how very proud and grateful we are of our British forces in the United Nations. While we are going about our normal business at this time of the year, buying turkeys and tangerines, we are thinking a great deal about those who are not able to do so.

Baroness Chalker of Wallasey: My Lords, supplies do get through, but we had to suspend the airlift into Sarajevo on 21st November because neither party would guarantee the security of the aircraft. That remains the case today. I hope that we shall be able to secure guarantees from the parties; indeed, UNPROFOR and UNHCR are seeking to do so at this very moment. The United Kingdom provides some 20 per cent. of the airlift capacity into Sarajevo. UK aircraft run by my department and the Royal Air Force remain committed to the operation. We are at least in a situation at present where there are some supplies available. While the critical state of supplies varies from area to area, we believe that we shall get further resupply for the population across the country. The most urgent area is probably Sebrenica. However, our troops are not in danger at the moment.

Lord Hylton: My Lords, will the Government find a suitable opportunity to remind the Russians that the Croatians and the Bosnian Moslems are just as much Slavs as their Serb cousins and that a substantial proportion even of the Bosnian Serbs are opposed to Mr. Karadzic?

Baroness Chalker of Wallasey: My Lords, I can assure the noble Lord, Lord Hylton, that that point has already been made. My right honourable friend the Foreign Secretary was able to spend quite a long while talking directly to Mr. Kozyrev and not one of those points was left out of the discussion.

Lord Whaddon: My Lords, the noble Baroness has rightly paid tribute to the constructive part played recently by President Milosevic. Perhaps I may also pay tribute to the balanced and delicate way that the Minister has acted in this most tricky situation. However, is it not most important that Britain should be seen to keep the spirit as well as the letter of any agreements that we make? Further, is the Minister aware that when the easing of flights to Belgrade was agreed in September by the United Nations, flights between Belgrade and Frankfurt, Zurich, Amsterdam and Paris were started within 10 days but that the flights from Belgrade to London have still not been restored, or certainly had not been a week ago? This is due to difficulties arising from a whole series of technical objections, such as the fact that the Serbs were not allowed to pay for their landing fees at London Airport. Can the Minister help to overcome those technical objections so that we are seen to be keeping the spirit as well as the letter of agreements?

Baroness Chalker of Wallasey: My Lords, I thank the noble Lord, Lord Whaddon, for his kind comments. I agree with him that the spirit as well as the letter of our intention should be kept. I will look into what he said about landing fees at Heathrow, but I am not aware of the problem as he outlined it to your Lordships. I shall write to him.

Lord Craig of Radley: My Lords, the noble Baroness said that we would use every means at our disposal in dealing with problems such as have happened recently in Bihac. Could she tell us whether General Rose is content with the level of forces which he has at his disposal and, if he is not, whether Her Majesty's Government would consider sending additional forces?

Baroness Chalker of Wallasey: My Lords, I have not for some time personally spoken to General Sir Michael Rose, but I believe that he considers that they can do a good job with the forces they have. If he had need for further forces I am sure that he would have asked my right honourable friend the Secretary of State for Defence who has been in the area recently. I am sure that he would ask my right honourable friend Mr. Hogg and myself when we are there in the weeks to come.

Lord McNair: My Lords, may I ask the Minister for a reassurance that the more helpful attitude by Mr. Milosevic towards the plan put forward by the five nation Contact Group will not win him any concessions on the stance that the British Government are taking on the situation in Kosovo?

Baroness Chalker of Wallasey: My Lords, I can give the noble Lord that assurance.

Lord Mackie of Benshie: My Lords, may I ask one more question? Does the noble Baroness consider that Mr. Milosevic's helpful attitude is due to his good nature or the effects of the blockade on his country?

Baroness Chalker of Wallasey: My Lords, I am quite sure that any sane man when deprived of resources starts to take notice and that is exactly why Britain was among the first to believe that we should have sanctions against Serbia, but we wait to see whether that is fully successful. However, I have said that medical supplies are a different matter from that of supplies which are caught by the sanctions.

Manufacturing Industry

4.22 p.m.

Debate resumed.

Lord Skelmersdale: My Lords, it seems to me that the time has come to move on. I am most grateful to my noble friend Lord Trefgarne for giving me the opportunity to speak on a subject that I have slept with for over 20 years now. Being a director of a micro family business is something that constantly engages your thoughts, even if, like myself, you no longer run it on a daily basis.

So far we have heard of the best in the small and medium-sized business sector, but I would like just briefly to paint a rather different picture. My picture is of a small, cluttered, sometimes smoke-filled room with a desk, two telephones ringing loudly, a filing cabinet, an in-tray, a pending tray, a boiling kettle, two shelves and a man with tears rolling down his face. He sits at the desk answering one telephone with one hand, picking up stamps with the other and sticking them on envelopes in front of the overflowing in-tray. With one foot he is trying to turn off the kettle, with the other he is trying, unsuccessfully, to shut an overstuffed filing cabinet. The pending tray overflows on to the floor. On the wall behind him are the two shelves. On the bottom one are four box files. The first is marked "Tax", the second "VAT", the third "Invoices" and the fourth "Receipts". On the shelf above are four bowler hats marked "Development Manager", "Marketing Manager", "Finance Director" and "Personnel Manager", and last but not least a white helmet marked "Safety".

This cartoon, which still hangs in the office at home, shows the very model of an embryonic small businessman, and something that small businessmen try very hard to get out of at the earliest opportunity.

[LORD SKELMERSDALE]
Governments and civil servants, it seems, often forget what it is like out there in what we sometimes refer to as the real world. That causes them to pile on the regulations, change the rate of VAT overnight; in a word, doing things without warning. They give the impression that businessmen and women are well-educated and well-organised from the time they get up in the morning till they sink, overtired, under the duvet at night. Life is not like that. From the smile on his face I anticipate that the noble Lord, Lord Weatherill, for one, will acknowledge and understand exactly what I am talking about.

Over the years I have identified four types of small business, which the noble Lord, Lord Haskel, touched on, one of which has, I believe, all but disappeared. When I was doing my vocational education in horticulture it was still quite common for there to be businesses that were designed to make a tax loss in order to mop up excess profits made in another trade or profession. Then there is the hobby business designed to break even financially but most definitely not to pay tax. There is the business which sets out from the beginning to make money, to pay fair taxes and to grow into what my noble friend's Motion calls a "medium sized" business, and eventually a corporation. The Body Shop for example would fit this description. I believe that the conglomerate chaired by my noble friend Lord Hanson also fits that description, although obviously over a very much longer timescale. Then—this is something we sometimes forget—there are the charities in which many of your Lordships are involved in one way or another. Arguably they could be said to be slightly different but there is more than one that I could think of running an obvious business which covenants its profits back to the parent charity.

Yet we are sometimes given the impression that the DTI believes that it is invariable that from little acorns mighty oaks do grow. In that well-worn phrase from the musical, "It ain't necessarily so". Horticulturally speaking, it is comparatively few acorns that grow at all. They must be given the right conditions either in the nursery, where their chances are better—or they should be if it is a decently run nursery—or in the wild. As oily seeds they must not dry out before putting down their first root.

In fact that is not a bad analogy. Experience has taught us that of those small businesses that fail, a high proportion fail in the first year. Another dangerous time is that of expansion when the embryonic businessman delegates one or more of the hats I spoke about earlier, or when, later, he tries to execute a major expansion plan. It is small wonder that there are not many Hansons or Roddicks about.

I think that the department would do well to ponder upon this, and my right honourable friend the Chancellor too. I believe that over the past 10 years or so they have become better at this and realise that they can make life easier for business. What small and medium-sized business needs is well known. The noble Lord, Lord Haskel, summed it up in two words—economic stability. They need low real interest rates so that they can afford to reinvest; a planned pay-back time that the banks do not suddenly change; a steady rate of inflation, preferably a low one, so that their customers are not put off by sudden swings in prices; the minimum of regulation; easily accessible information; low taxes and achievable training as my noble friend Lord Trefgarne pointed out. They also need a constant rate of VAT. Twice now I have had a catalogue just despatched to my customers when the VAT rate changed. The hidden cost of chasing up small amounts of extra money is high and one must make a difficult assessment as to whether the business can or should bear the rise in VAT from its profits. I only hope that my right honourable friend the Chancellor will not try to recoup his missing billion pounds by a small but general hike in value added tax. I am prepared to bet that if that is the case, the rate of first year failures will increase.

That said, the Government have much to be proud of: the introduction of the single market has done wonders for exports at little cost to business; the introduction of one-stop shops which save time and effort for a busy person; the reduction of corporation tax from 42 to 25 per cent., so pegging it to the basic rate of income tax; keeping VAT stable; managing to reduce interest rates to affordable levels; and, most important of all, a low rate of inflation. I believe that when the figures come out for new businesses in 1994-95 we shall see an upturn in start-ups and a drop in failures. We all have high hopes for deregulation. I look forward to the first fruits of this policy after Christmas.

The corollary of deregulation is, of course, more regulation. Small businesses are great employers of part-time labour, sometimes throughout the year and sometimes on a seasonal basis. Many of those employees are women who are prepared to work for a lower income than men to top up the general pool of the family income. Some are semi-retired men who have taken early retirement—those whom the noble Lord, Lord Desai, might call potentially economically semi-active. Those workers represent a major part of the workforce of this country. The party opposite sneers that they are not real jobs. But they are very real for the people holding them and for the businesses who employ those workers. However, the Opposition seem to wish to damage that sector of the employment market by introducing not only a minimum wage but the social chapter, giving those workers the same rights as full-time employees. I can think of no policy more damaging to small businesses and their employees.

That brings me to charities. There are 170,000 charities registered with the charity commissioners, employing 482,000 people. That represents 2 per cent. of the total workforce, 8 per cent. more than the motor industry employs today and as many as the combined water and energy industries employ. Of the top 500 fund-raising charities, 200 are in the medical field supporting the salaries of well over 500 people in British universities. The House will be as amazed as I was to learn that the 21 cancer charities provide £120 million for research. That amounts to 70 per cent. of the total spent on cancer research in this country. If that is not a business activity, I do not know what is.

Over and above that, we increasingly expect charities to take on work in social services and in environmental protection, and government and quangos pay them to do so. More and more of that work is by contract. It makes for enormous pressures on the charities' income because the overheads cannot normally be allocated. According to the Charities Aid Foundation, the top 200 fund-raising charities raised their income by 4 per cent. in 1992 and increased their expenditure by the same amount. The second 200 charities show a different picture: a drop of 9 per cent. in income matched by an 8 per cent. drop in expenditure. From that we can see that the smaller charities are being squeezed. Why, my Lords? I believe that, as with any other small business, charities suffer from the problems of employing part-time female labour. Increases in maternity leave and the reduction in statutory maternity pay have hit them hard. So, too, would compulsory occupational pension schemes if they were introduced.

However, I wish to congratulate the Government on two fronts; for making covenant forms both shorter and easier, and for the introduction of gift aid. Alas, the figures show that only 10 per cent. of donations are made tax effectively. However, it is as much for the charities themselves as for the Government to increase that figure. What is in the Government's hands is the ability to do something about the £350 million a year which charities pay in VAT. The amount is worked out by a very complicated formula. Essentially, it means that the charities can only claim back the input tax in the ratio provided by the proportion of VAT attracting income to their total income. In other words, if 20 per cent. of their income arises from contracts or subscriptions, or a mixture of both, and the remainder from donations, charities can claim back only 20 per cent. of the tax they have paid out. The charities tax reform group has been told by Customs and Excise that there is no technical reason why that cannot be changed. It seems that the political will is lacking.

My conclusion is that with that one exception the problems of charities are identical with the problems besetting small businesses. The Government should recognise the great value that small businesses bring to this country, whether or not in the charitable sector. I believe that the Government recognise that, but they could do more in the ways already proposed and, I am sure, still to be suggested in the debate. Above all, they should always bend over backwards not to kill the goose that just sometimes lays the golden egg.

4.35 p.m.

Lord Desai: My Lords, we are grateful to the noble Lord, Lord Trefgarne, for giving us the opportunity for this debate. Like the noble Lord, Lord Weatherill, I made my maiden speech on this very question about three years ago. I shall confine my attention to the first part of the Motion—the importance of increased output from the United Kingdom manufacturing industry.

I do not know much about actual business. I am an economist and economists have a fond relationship with the real world: they know about it but do not want to be anywhere near it if they can help it. I wish my life to be comfortable. After what the noble Lord, Lord Skelmersdale, said, I am glad that I am not in the real world; I am in academia. It is hard work in the real world.

I wish to talk about the general state of manufacturing industry. My points are not made in a partisan spirit. Manufacturing industry is an important part of the economy. But increasingly there is a contrast between the ability of the manufacturing sector to generate wealth and its ability to generate jobs. Increasingly, because productivity increases have had to be rather fast in this competitive world, manufacturing industry can generate wealth but cannot always generate jobs at the rate it once did.

Virtually everything that I say arises from *Economic Trends*. It is an excellent publication; I recommend everyone to study it. Since 1970 production industries—manufacturing and other aspects such as North Sea oil—have grown but more slowly than any other sector of the British economy. Since 1970 there has been growth of approximately a third, from 73 to 98 in index number form. The recession has meant that we have not caught up with the previous peak in output in 1989. But there has been growth in manufacturing industry.

By the same token we have to be aware that as employers of people manufacturing industry has shrunk quite remarkably. In 1970 about 8 million people were employed. About 4 million people are now employed. That means that while output has grown by about a third, employment has declined by about a half. Of course, the balance lies in increased productivity.

When considering productivity, one achievement has been noticeable—a good rate of productivity growth in manufacturing industry. I believe that increasingly that will be so. Another good feature is that since 1980 productivity growth has been very rapid. We had slow productivity growth in the 1970s and good, rapid productivity growth in the 1980s. That means that productivity growth has to be kept up. We cannot look benignly to the manufacturing sector to provide us with jobs. We have to be sure that manufacturing industry stays competitive and generates wealth, especially manufacturing exports which are absolutely vital for the national economy.

I have to point out a disturbing trend. The rate of investment in our manufacturing industry is no longer as high as it was. With proper allowance for inflation, in real terms investment in our manufacturing industry is lower today than it was in 1970. I have to admit that it reached a peak in 1989 when about £15 billion was invested. Today the figure is only about £11 billion, compared with £13 billion in 1970.

We should approach the problem of manufacturing investment much more seriously. We may differ across party lines as to methods but encouraging manufacturing investment is urgent and central for our economic future. Whether we do that by inviting foreign investment or by encouraging domestic investment, or whether it takes place in small or large firms, are matters of choice. Indeed, I believe that one should do everything across the board.

Encouraging manufacturing investment in every way we can is central to the problem of British manufacturing industry. Our outward growth is slowed

[LORD DESAI]
to the extent that our manufacturing investment is not rapid. Of course, by the same token, we get more out of our investment than other countries. We are very efficient at getting more out of the pound than others. That has to be said. However, it is true that we are not investing enough. It is a matter of diverting resources from other uses—consumption, government spending or whatever it is—to manufacturing investment. Perhaps on another occasion we should debate the best ways of encouraging manufacturing investment in the British economy.

What I think is happening, not just in the UK but throughout the world in the modern context of the global economy, is that countries who wish to survive as manufacturing nations must continue innovating at a rapid rate. They must put a great deal of money into research and development. They must move along the product front because the products we used to make can be made much more cheaply and better elsewhere in the world. We shall not be able to resist the tide of free trade. It is a delusion to think that we could. I would not even advocate it.

We live in a climate of growing free trade; we face global competition. Unless we invest a lot of money in manufacturing industry, unless we research and develop new products rapidly, we shall fall behind. It is a matter of vital national policy that we concentrate on quality output in manufacturing industry. Through debates like this we can draw the attention of our policy makers to the matter. Therefore, I am doubly grateful to the noble Lord, Lord Trefgarne, for having introduced this subject.

4.43 p.m.

The Viscount of Oxfuird: My Lords, there are few in your Lordships' House who are so eminently qualified as my noble friend Lord Trefgarne to speak on this subject, an area in which he made such a significant contribution in his days as a Minister of State at the Department of Trade and Industry. He is still so much involved with manufacturing industry by virtue of his presidency of the Mechanical and Metal Trades Confederation, METCOM, which numbers many small and medium-sized enterprises within its membership.

It has been obvious from the contributions from all parts of the House this afternoon that there are few of us who have not grieved at the decline of some sectors of the United Kingdom's manufacturing infrastructure over the past decades or alternatively have been heartened by the reversal of that trend in recent years. That reversal has been seriously spearheaded by our small and medium-sized enterprises—the SMEs.

There is growing evidence—and it has been highlighted by a number of noble Lords already—that we have turned the corner. In the three months to September 1994, manufacturing productivity was up 6 per cent. on the previous year, a level of growth not seen since the mid-1980s, but against a backdrop of the lowest inflation for generations. Manufactured exports are at record levels, having grown by 80 per cent. since 1981 and by over 10 per cent. in the past year.

However, encouraging as these statistics are, they are frankly not good enough. In the British manufacturing company with which I was so closely involved for many years, the introduction of the principles of total quality management became one of the prime philosophies. That experience taught me that constant vigilance was needed for continuous improvement. No enterprise or institution, of whatever size, should forget this constant requirement for continuous improvement. Those who do will in the end decline and perish.

So what factors do we need to study and address in looking for greater improvements in output within our manufacturing enterprises? It was, as some noble Lords may recall, Rudyard Kipling who referred to the,

"Dear hearts across the seas".

Perhaps I could, first of all, recall the thinking of some of the industrial leaders from beyond our shores. I think, first, of some points I made in a debate back in 1988 proposed by my noble friend Lord Joseph, recorded in the *Official Report* of 4th May, vol. 496, col. 620. I spoke of the research of the learned American, Professor Birch of the Massachusetts Institute of Technology and of his emphasis on the importance of training our manufacturing workforce in the new technologies. He also emphasised how important the small business was in reducing unemployment. This business is by nature dynamic; it has young entrepreneurs and a very high percentage effect on the unemployment figures.

However, it is equally important to consider the training of people. How heartening it is that we are beginning to see the fruits of some of the investments that the Government have made in this field since that time.

I confess that I have also been somewhat influenced by the works of the American writer, Tom Peters, and I was reading one of his books this weekend, *Thriving on Chaos*. In it, he contrasts the American penchant for what he describes as "giantism" with the Japanese passion for smallness. He argues that part of the Japanese economic miracle since the Second World War can be explained by their exploitation of the "smaller is better" strategy. He quotes from the book: *Smaller is better: Japan's Mastery of the Miniature* by the Korean writer O-Young Lee who emphasises the "smaller is better" philosophy. He argues that this is a major factor in explaining the reasons for Japan's economic success since the Second World War.

He is thinking in part, of course, of the success that the miniaturisation of consumer electronic products has brought to the Japanese electronics industry, but he also highlights that the small business sector in Japan is more vital than that in the West and that even the largest Japanese corporations are less vertically integrated and count upon a network of smaller subcontractors for a significant part of their innovation. This helps to foster their commitment to continuous improvement.

This theme is taken up most positively in the recent White Paper to which some noble Lords have already referred, *Competitiveness—Helping Business to Win*.

The White Paper emphasises that to become more competitive companies need to change the climate within their organisations to stimulate innovation, to train their people, to invest in new technology, to take advantage of external skills and knowhow and to use, adapt and develop novel processes.

It is often in these very areas that our small and medium-sized enterprises tend to be more responsive and faster on their feet. That is why a significant and growing proportion of total employment, not just in the United Kingdom but in most of the developed economies of the world, is in small and medium-sized enterprises.

The White Paper on competitiveness highlights the need to improve the effectiveness of our financial institutions in supplying funds to SMEs. It seems that there is an over-reliance in the United Kingdom on the part of small firms on the use of overdraft facilities to provide the funding to sustain growth. In the United Kingdom, overdrafts account for 56 per cent. of small firms debt, compared with 14 per cent. in Germany. It seems that there is a need for both the banks and the SMEs to place greater emphasis on longer term finance.

It is encouraging that the Chancellor took heed of that need in last week's Budget in his plan to create venture capital trusts (VCTs). These are investment trusts which will be owned by individual shareholders and which will attract generous tax relief. They are designed to encourage investors to put their money into equity for small businesses. The trusts will be able to make investments up to £1 million in companies whose net assets cannot exceed £10 million. As an inducement, investors will be able to claim tax relief at 20 per cent. on the investment and to defer capital gains tax that is due on other asset sales if the proceeds are invested in such a trust. Profits and dividends from the trusts will be tax free.

There were also measures to shelter the small and medium-sized enterprises from some of the more onerous requirements of government regulation until they are strong enough to cope with them. The proposal to extend the number of businesses which can pay their PAYE and national insurance contributions quarterly rather than monthly will help an estimated 100,000 employers. The gradual rise in the VAT threshold to £46,000 will also help, as will the proposal to move to annual simplified VAT accounting for small businesses.

I spoke of a Korean observation earlier which asserted confidently with respect to Japanese economic success that "smaller is better". Let me be extremely careful to make it clear that I do not believe that smallness should be an end in itself. Smallness is at its best when it acts as a precursor for growth—a fact that was excellently illustrated by the *Financial Times* a couple of years ago when it changed the name of its regular "Small Businesses Column" to the "Growing Businesses Column".

A very real example of what I am trying to say is provided by the common agricultural policy of the European Community. The CAP insulates European farmers from market forces and encourages uneconomic farmers to stay in business. Most British farms would still fall within the DTI's definition of small and medium-sized enterprises; but the size of farms in the United Kingdom tends to be larger than elsewhere in the Community. They are hindered from exploiting their competitive advantage by the millstone of the CAP.

Smallness is not an advantage in itself if it encourages the Luddite forces of reactionism to resist change and shun improvement. The farming community in parts of our European Union should take note, and the Government should continue to press for further reforms of the CAP and seek further reductions in support prices.

Our British farms are successful medium-sized enterprises and might well be described in the phrase that was immortalised by William Cowper in the late 18th century in his *Tirocinium*,

"Tenants of life's middle state,
Securely plac'd between the small and the great".

I conclude on a note of optimism. Our debate this afternoon has emphasised the need for improved manufacturing output and has given us all a number of valuable indicators of the direction that we should take. The outlook is improving. About 226,000 new businesses were started in the first half of 1994, an increase of 10 per cent. over the first half of 1993. The DTI's Business Link initiative is beginning to provide a most effective support network for our businesses, particularly our small and medium-sized enterprises. With hard work and a commitment to continuous improvement, I believe that we can succeed.

4.54 p.m.

The Earl of Kintore: My Lords, I also thank the noble Lord, Lord Trefgarne, for introducing this important debate. I should like to address a few points about small and medium-sized businesses which not only do not increase their output but actually cease trading, not because they are making the wrong product at the wrong price but because their internal financial procedures are poor or even non-existent.

I must immediately declare an interest as president of the International Association of Bookkeepers. The association, founded over 20 years ago, offers a professional qualification in manual bookkeeping. It also offers diploma courses in computerised bookkeeping, small business financial management and payroll administration. I am delighted to learn that my noble friend Lord Weatherill still has the office bike. I hope that the noble Lord also has good internal financial procedures, as many small and medium-sized companies do. But, sadly, far too many businesses are going into liquidation. Many will have gone under from lack of financial control. Very basic mistakes are made, such as failing to send out invoices; taking too long to chase up moneys that are owing; and taking too much cash out of the business too early.

I believe that some companies really do still put all their paperwork into a box and present the box to their accountants at the end of the year. Apart from considerable expense, it means—unless the accountants work considerably more sharply than many whom I know—that the financial state of the business will not be known for 10 to 12 months after the year end, and vital information that the chairman's Rolls costs more to run per month than the company is making may not be available until it is too late. The Inland Revenue and

[The Earl of Kintore]

Customs and Excise—and, I imagine, the banks—feel rather unloved over this period as they do not receive the returns that are required. I know that the Inland Revenue starts with blue-coloured demands, and then, round about Easter, the demands change to a rather fetching shade of red. I imagine that, red being the final colour, once it is ignored the game is up. It probably comes as no surprise that, in desperation, both the Inland Revenue and Customs and Excise institute insolvency proceedings.

I was pleased to read in the Budget snapshot, HMT1, published on 29th November, that there are to be consultations on the reform of the insolvency law to help firms in difficulty and to help avoid wasteful liquidations. But surely problems must be identified at a much earlier stage. I therefore welcome the Government's initiative which appears on page 2 of the Budget Day press release, HMT5, under the heading, "To Widen Small Firms' Access to External Finance". I quote:

> "Representatives of small business and others will shortly be consulted on the development of a financial management certificate. The aim would be to devise a certificate that provided a clear signal of a firm's financial competence, thus providing an additional incentive for firms to improve and implement their financial management skills".

I appreciate that the Government are to consult, but I should like to ask the noble Earl the Minister two questions, of which I have tried to give him prior notification. The first is: can he give any more details about the financial management certificate than appeared in the press release? Secondly: can he say whom the "others" who are to be consulted are likely to be?

5 p.m.

Viscount Caldecote: My Lords, in the welter of discussion on the economy—inflation, interest rates, PSBR, competitiveness, productivity and a stable currency to encourage growth in the GDP—I believe that, important though they are, we are in danger of failing to see the wood for the trees. We need to remember that the ultimate objective of all economic policy is to give everyone the opportunity to lead a full and satisfying life. Unemployment is a major obstacle to achieving that. So I very much welcome the subject of today's debate, so ably introduced by my noble friend Lord Trefgarne, with its emphasis on increased output and on SMEs (small and medium-sized enterprises), both of which create jobs.

Everywhere, increased output is largely dependent on investment. Recent OECD and IMF data show the connection clearly in the figures averaged over the past 30 years—which may account for the slight difference from the figures given by the noble Lord, Lord Haskel. The United Kingdom's GDP growth averaged $2\frac{1}{4}$ per cent. per annum. With fixed investment at 18 per cent. of GDP, we were at the bottom of the league, compared with Japanese growth of 6 per cent. and investment of over 30 per cent. of GDP. Other competitors were between those two limits. Nevertheless, the UK has made huge improvements in productivity and competitiveness, particularly over the past 15 years. But others have improved, too.

The figures quoted earlier are for fixed investment. Of equal importance—as the noble Lord, Lord Desai, so clearly said—is investment in innovation in competitive products which will sell all over the world. For price is not the only factor which affects sales. Quality and value for money are just as relevant. Switzerland is a good example. The products that they make are usually very expensive but of the highest quality, and they have a very good record in the export field.

Those considerations apply to every company, from the biggest to the smallest. Among them are many world-class companies which make a full contribution to output growth. But there are too few of them. There are many reasons for inadequate investment—for example, short termism; bias of taxation in favour of earnings distribution rather than investment, which means that more of the earnings are used in consumption rather than being reinvested in the company for innovation and the like; and a lack of confidence in demand in the future and in a stable value for sterling.

We have often discussed this topic in this Chamber. I shall not go into the issues today because there is not the time. They have been well covered in the past. I should like to emphasise the enormous progress that has been made under this Government in creating the right climate for investment. But the fact is that, overall, industry has not taken full advantage of it. So there is much more to do.

SMEs can make a major contribution. Many of them—probably the great majority—are owner-managed. That gives them greater flexibility to react to market conditions and invest for the future. There is no short-termism there. Just as important is that investment in SMEs is almost always investment for expansion of both output and employment, whereas in larger companies the objective of investment is frequently to produce the same output with fewer people employed.

What then are the main obstacles to even greater growth in the sector? They are, I believe, largely financial. Adequate cash flow is vital to the success of SMEs or even their existence. In that connection I hope that the Government, the CBI and others will continue to press for measures to deal with the great problem of late payment of bills to small companies. It is a very important issue which must be dealt with.

Also, funding for smaller companies is a major problem. I regret that the Budget did little to help SMEs by, for instance, granting 100 per cent. capital allowances for the purchase of plant and equipment up to a limit, say, of £250,000, as was widely recommended. Similar allowances to encourage investment in innovation should also receive high priority. But much more can be done by the financial institutions and industry itself, without waiting for government action. There is genuine difficulty in raising relatively small amounts of risk capital. Owing to the setting up and administration charges, no venture capitalist will consider investing less than £250,000 and more often less than £1 million. There is a major problem for fledgling SMEs and it is important to find a solution.

The noble Lord, Lord Weatherill, mentioned the Prince's Youth Business Trust, of which I once had the privilege of being a trustee. That is an example of how the problem is overcome at the lowest level of investment—probably under £5,000, unless it has changed very much since my day. The administration costs, advice given and so on are either undertaken by voluntary workers or paid for by money subscribed on a charitable basis. Perhaps for larger companies—those that are dealt with through the Prince's Youth Business Trust—there could be a fund contributed to by banks and other big financial institutions which would facilitate smaller investments to SMEs by contributing to the administrative costs. Thereby, they would benefit from the resulting growth in the longer term future.

But, as has been said, many SMEs depend heavily on overdraft and other forms of bank lending. That makes them very vulnerable to a recession, when cash flow comes under pressure. Banks should be more flexible and not too greedy in providing fixed term loans. That gives great confidence to a smaller company that the overdraft facility or other type of loan will not be withdrawn at a difficult moment. Above all, it should be made absolutely clear by bank managers at the start of negotiations when dealing with SMEs whether they are acting as principals with power to make a binding agreement or simply as messengers making recommendations to some higher authority.

A few years ago I was chairman of a very small company. At a difficult time, we thought that we had made a satisfactory and firm agreement with the bank manager with whom we had dealt for several years, only to find some three weeks later that a higher authority had vetoed the agreement. That was certainly a factor in the ultimate collapse of the company.

Lastly, I should like to see more SMEs prepared to fund their growth by selling, say, 20 per cent. of their equity, as an alternative to more bank loan finance of whatever kind. It is better to own 80 per cent. of a successful company than 100 per cent. of a failure. I hope that investors, especially those taking advantage of investment through the new venture capital trusts, which my noble friend Lord Oxfuird mentioned, will make a real contribution to solving the problem and will not be too greedy in the terms of the agreements that they make with SMEs.

I emphasise again that much has already been achieved in the past 15 years in encouraging enterprise and investment. But we must always remember that our competitors too are improving all the time. We have to get and remain ahead of them. Greater investment is essential to achieve that.

5.10 p.m.

Lord Cochrane of Cults: My Lords, I start by thanking my noble friend Lord Trefgarne for introducing this subject today. It is right, as said by others, that he plays an important part in the engineering training organisations. I should mention also that he is a non-executive director of an interesting SME which has perhaps become more large than small, as I shall relate in a moment. I refer to Siebe, a company with a history extending back 170 years. It was founded by an Austrian artillery man by the name of Augustus Siebe who came to this country in 1816. In due time he invented, among other things, a better method for making screws—a vital engineering component—but is now predominantly remembered for the invention of the first serviceable and durable method of working underwater, the traditional hard-hat diver as it later became known.

Siebe is an interesting company. For a long time, it remained quite small, describing its activities as those of submarine engineers. It remained with the descendants of Siebe for a long time and came to the market in the 1950s. I should perhaps declare an interest. I have been a shareholder fairly continuously ever since. The vicissitudes of school fees and so forth perhaps led me to reduce my shareholding; otherwise I might not feel quite so poor as I sometimes do.

Siebe is now an immense company. It has a huge turnover. The profits published today are a great improvement. It is not particularly highly geared. That has all taken place due to a change of ethos in the company and the arrival of determined and skilful managers on the board of directors. At one stage it looked as though they had slightly overdone it but in fact they got it exactly right. The results we see today illustrate how growth is possible if it is well aimed and well controlled. The traditional manufacturer is often described as a maker of "widgets". I gather that that word is now obsolete because widgets are those things which cause beer to shoot out of tins. While useful that is not quite what was originally intended.

As the last Back Bench speaker I do not want to bore your Lordships with a multitude of figures or anything else. But I shall make one or two points and reiterate what was said earlier, particularly by my noble friend Lord Caldecote, on the role of banks. In this country small businesses rely immensely—as I know personally—on bank finance. Banks get cold feet at intervals. I mentioned that the other day in another context. A bank manager was overplaying his hand; he received a rude answer from me; eventually he lost the account and lost a good many other people's accounts too. That merely shows that not all bank managers are wise. We know that, but there was a chap determined that a certain class of business within his branch was unacceptable.

The role of the banks must be continually supportive. They must support us from the word go. In order to do that they need information. In order to give them the information, as my noble friend Lord Caldecote said, we need a decent financial system. That is of prime importance. Again, it tells us whether or not we are actually making money. There was a famous case many years ago of Crittall Engineering which could not get stuff out of the factory quick enough. Yet, mysteriously, it never seemed to have more money in the bank. It was during the period of Nye Bevan's housing boom. The company made steel windows. Unfortunately, it was receiving five shillings a window less than the cost of making them; so gradually it went down and down.

[LORD COCHRANE OF CULTS]

I saw something similar in my father's time with his mineral supply business. When my brother and I picked it up after his death we discovered that we were popping a 10 shilling note into every lorry-load of stuff we sold. Nobody realised that. Therefore, if one can persuade the banks to be more supportive on a continuing basis they will lose less money, feel less endangered and will not ultimately find themselves in the situation which was put to me by an experienced bank manager who said, "It is all very well having security of this factory and that factory, but they are worthless when the whole industrial estate is empty."

Another role which could be played by the banks in relation to companies is to put in a part-time, non-executive director who acts as liaison. He can say, "I do not think that that is a good idea; perhaps we should go this way rather than that way". That happened to my grandfather. The Royal Bank put him as signatory and director into a privately-owned coal company many years ago. Following the death of the head of that family, the coal company was discovered to be immensely in debt. I believe the personal guarantee of the executors was well over £7 million at the turn of the century. Through the energy of the next generation and possibly the wise guidance given by my grandfather and the bank, they all lived happily ever after, although they did have to mine under the castle gardens. I am sure that the noble Lord, Lord Ezra, appreciates the risks of mining, especially when one already has a huge bank overdraft.

I shall not continue except to say that in relation to part-time expertise in finance—picking up a point made by the noble Earl, Lord Kintore—there are plenty of retired executives with good financial experience who could be obtained to attend one day a week to keep control of a company's finances. That is particularly important when it is at the dangerous stage when, the idea having taken off, capacity needs to be expanded. The question is: more money is needed but how will it be obtained?

In a recent speech the Chancellor of the Exchequer eased the climate. But if those running small businesses think more carefully about the financial implications of what they are doing, they are more likely to prosper in the way we all want.

5.17 p.m.

Lord Ezra: My Lords, although there have been a number of debates in this House on manufacturing in recent years, the noble Lord, Lord Trefgarne, was right to introduce this debate today. Manufacturing remains a vital ingredient in the future economic development of the country. That is shown by the large number of important reports recently published on the subject. They include the Government's White Paper on competitiveness, the European Commission's White Paper on growth, competitiveness and employment, the House of Commons Trade and Industry Committee report on the competitiveness of the UK manufacturing industry, the CBI series of reports issued by the National Manufacturing Council and the report by UNICEE (the European equivalent of the CBI) on making Europe more competitive. All those centred on the vital role of manufacturing.

I have participated in most of the debates on manufacturing in this House over the past 10 years. I believe that the most significant development has been the changing attitude of the Government. In the 1980s the Government's attitude was that manufacturing represented only one element in the economy and it did not really matter how wealth was created so long as that was achieved. As we moved into the 1990s, however, the Government have increasingly recognised the importance of manufacturing, and they are right to do so. Fifty per cent. of consumer spending and 70 per cent. of exports of goods and related services are accounted for by manufacturing. In spite of the diminution in the industrial base, to which the noble Lord, Lord Desai, referred, there are still 4 million people employed in manufacturing with at least as many more supplying supporting services. There is therefore little doubt that manufacturing remains a crucial element in the economy.

The Government repeatedly draw our attention, and I am sure will do so again today, to the various positive signs in the economy, such as improved growth, better exports and reduced inflation. It is perfectly true that those developments have taken place. However, the impression created by the repetition of these positive developments is one of complacency. That is regrettable.

While the present indicators may be positive, the underlying trends are not. As the CBI and others have shown, we are still lagging some 20 per cent. to 40 per cent. in average levels of productivity below our principal competitors, even though there has been a narrowing of the gap in recent times. Our investment in manufacturing and related activities has been sluggish to say the least and leads to capacity restraints even at an early stage of economic recovery, such as we are beginning to witness at the present time. We have noticeably lower levels of skills than our main competitors. The noble Lord, Lord Trefgarne, and others referred to that. Finally, our inadequate capacity shows up in terms of a major trade deficit in manufactured goods, which is still running at the level of £10 billion a year, in spite of recent improvements in export performance. It is to these long-term problems, particularly the role of the smaller firms in overcoming them, that we should be addressing ourselves.

If we were asked to encapsulate in a very few words the major weakness which has developed in the British economy for several years past, I believe the answer must be lack of adequate investment, both of a physical nature and in people. Let us look for a moment at physical investment in the public sector, which is very necessary to create the conditions under which private enterprise can thrive. In spite of repeated pleas that the last thing that should be cut is investment in capital projects which are intended to provide an improved infrastructure, this seems to be the first thing the Government turn to when they wish to reduce the public sector borrowing requirement. I am afraid that we saw evidence of that in the recent Budget, when expenditure on transport infrastructure was cut from £10.8 billion to £8.8 billion. The main argument for doing that, according to the Chancellor, was that the private finance initiative would close the gap. All I can say is that that is by no means certain. In the meantime, industry, and in particular manufacturing industry, will go on suffering from continued congestion and delays.

Much reference has been made to the inadequacy of investment in manufacturing industry, a point made by the noble Lord, Lord Desai, the noble Viscount, Lord Caldecote, and others. One of the reasons for this inadequacy has been the uncertainty about demand caused by macro-economic volatility. We have just lived through a classic example of this, with the major stimulus to consumption in the late 1980s leading to overheating and then a massive cutback. It is no wonder, with these memories of not so long ago, that manufacturers are cautious about moving ahead too fast with investment and are insisting on high rates of return, to which the CBI, the Governor of the Bank and others have recently drawn attention, in spite of the current low level of inflation. I believe that there is a major role for the Government at the present time to try to put this right.

Of course the Government must continue to take the necessary measures—we saw one of them today—to keep inflation under control. But in addition—this is what is lacking so far—they must take complementary measures to stimulate investment. In this connection, I share with the noble Viscount, Lord Caldecote, the regret that the Government did not follow the advice of the CBI, the Engineering Employers Federation and many others in introducing fiscal measures in the recent Budget to stimulate investment. One of the measures proposed, as the noble Viscount pointed out, was for a 100 per cent. capital allowance on the first £200,000 of investment in any one year. That would have been particularly helpful to small firms.

As many other speakers have emphasised in the debate today, small firms play a crucial role in the economy. Within manufacturing industry almost a third of employment and a quarter of output are accounted for by such firms. Access to finance and the cost of finance are crucial elements in their success. In addition to capital allowances directed at small firms, to which I have referred, there is a strong case for considering an investment bank on lines which have existed for many years in France and Germany, and which are now being looked at in many quarters, to offer debt finance to small firms on terms which are at the very least no worse than those obtainable by larger firms. To get bank money these days small firms have to pay 3, 4, 5 or 6 per cent. above bank rate, whereas a large firm, with all its connections and its ability to go anywhere in the world to raise its money, can usually achieve a rate of between 1 and 2 per cent. That is a big impediment to the small firm.

What is required is a long-term strategy for stimulating investment in essential public infrastructure and in manufacturing to offset the uncertainties which have been created by past policies. No one can be certain that those policies will be avoided in the future. The upturn through which we are now going is being seen in many other countries. As we noted in the recent debate on the economy, while we have done very well in containing inflation, some of our neighbours have done even better, such as France which has inflation at only 1.6 per cent.

There is a need, agreed on all sides, in addition to a stimulus to investment, for greater resources and efforts to be devoted to training. Differences in skill levels are a significant factor contributing to the UK's lower productivity compared with its main trading partners. The noble Lord, Lord Trefgarne, referred to that point in his opening speech and the noble Lord, Lord Weatherill, gave us good examples of voluntary efforts to try to deal with this matter. More than 60 per cent. of the UK's manufacturing labourforce have no vocational qualifications compared with 50 per cent. in France, 40 per cent. in Holland and 25 per cent. in Germany. The gap is most pronounced in people with intermediate skills. This is therefore the area where the greatest efforts need to be made.

The Government repeatedly state that the economy is set on a virtuous path of sustained growth with minimum inflation. Well, that has yet to be proved. The recovery in Britain has been mirrored elsewhere. The test will come when a cyclical downturn sets in. In such circumstances, will the British economy suffer less than it has in the past? If manufacturing is to thrive in spite of future possible cyclical recession, the Government will need to set a framework within which there is a consistent macro-economic policy, a point made by many noble Lords. A major impetus on a continuing basis must be given to investment in physical assets in the public and private sectors and to the development of the necessary skills to make the best use of those assets.

5.29 p.m.

Lord Peston: My Lords, the noble Lord, Lord Trefgarne, introduced this important debate in an interesting and effective way. Indeed, he was no help to me because most of what he said made perfectly good sense and I agreed with him, which does not make for much of a debate. Happily, he will soon know that there are at least one or two things with which I disagree with him and that, at least, might enable me to add a certain amount of life to what would otherwise be an extremely boring progression of, "Yes, he said that and I agree with him".

Certainly, all of us now agree about the importance of manufacturing and there is no argument there. There is no argument about the importance of small and medium-sized firms. In that regard one should not forget that every year large numbers of firms start up but, regretfully, within about three years most of them have gone. I was extremely interested in the intervention of the noble Lord, Lord Weatherill. He referred to an institutional arrangement which not only helped firms to start but to survive. I believe that he is aware, as all noble Lords are, that going into business as a small firm is highly risky. As I say, the odds are overwhelmingly that the firm will not be there for very long. It is very hard to start a surviving business. I believe that the noble Lord, Lord Skelmersdale, also pointed that out.

[LORD PESTON]

In a way, of course, that is the basis of a free market economy. Essentially, entrepreneurship is risk taking. If it were a stone cold certainty it would not be entrepreneurship. Risks are taken and some firms survive and some do not. What is important is to create an environment in which it is easier to survive, particularly if one has products which consumers want. Again, we have to remind ourselves that the ultimate test is: Are you producing goods and services which can meet the test of the market? Are you producing things which people want? I hope we all agree—I have said this several times—that firms do not exist for their own sake but in order ultimately to meet demand.

In that regard we have to ask ourselves this question: What is it that the small and medium-sized firm wants? Again, I believe that we all agree that what they want is a stable economic environment. They want an environment in which markets are growing, but what they do not particularly want is a highly fluctuating economy. Given that when this Government first came into power they intended to produce a serious change in economic policy-making, the puzzle is that the economy has fluctuated just as much under this Government as it ever did before. I say it is a puzzle because I thought that perhaps some of the things they were doing might lead to more stability, but they have not.

The manufacturing sector in particular has shown wild swings. Manufacturing output did fall between 1989 to 1992. It has only just risen, almost this very month, to its previous peak. That means that over the whole of the period there has been no growth, although over the longer period there has been growth. Manufacturing investment has not yet got back to its previous peak. We all agree about the importance of investment, as the noble Viscount, Lord Caldecote, emphasised. We have to ask: What is conducive to investment? My own judgment of what is most conducive to investment is that the market should be there when one has the new capital equipment. It is a commonplace to say that it takes time to get the new equipment in. What one does not want is to bring it in during the good times and to find that it is fully operational when the market has gone. That is why economic stability and growth are so tremendously important.

I said that I would introduce an occasional remark of a controversial kind. I certainly do not believe that what the Chancellor of the Exchequer did today in raising the bank rate is remotely of any help to small businesses. We may have a chance to discuss that, I am told, tomorrow, but since I may not be speaking tomorrow I must say that raising the bank rate today makes no economic sense to me whatever. I say to noble Lords opposite that it does not make any political sense to behave in such a panicky way either, but that is for them to reflect on.

I turn to the whole question of finance which other noble Lords have mentioned. I am with them all the way. What a small business wants is a helpful financial environment, but in particular it wants help on a rainy day. To offer a small business funds when times are good is not bad, but what it really wants is that when things are going wrong help will be available from the financial institutions, which we all agree are, for the most part, the banks. Help is wanted at that time. It does not seem to me that within recent years the banking system has been as helpful to business as it might have been and as I hope it will become again.

In fact, the noble Lord, Lord Trefgarne, said—and I nearly decided to agree with him on the point—that we should discuss this matter on another day. I am not sure when the next day is to be so I thought that I should at least mention the importance of financial arrangements and liquidity to small businesses. I agree with the point made by the noble Lord, Lord Ezra, about interest rates. There must be some loading of interest rates because small business is riskier than big business, but the difference does not seem to me to be justified by market forces. We should consider changed institutional arrangements that might help us.

I believe that there is no difference between us as regards education and vocational training. We simply have to do more, but what we do has to be more effective. One of the matters which concerns me is that there are far too many courses which are not very good. I am delighted that the noble Lord, Lord Trefgarne, has been appointed chairman of the engineering training board. I am sure he will ensure that from now on training is effective and produces the kind of people we want. I am not saying that if I were chairman I could not do the job better. That may well happen within the not too distant future.

There is another point as regards finance which we should bear in mind. The small businessman wants to engage in his business. He or she wants to make the goods or provide the services. Very often finance is not of great interest and the small businessman does not want to get involved. That is why such businesses need a sympathetic financial environment. That is why in the old days the bank manager was a help. He coaxed them along and would say, "Do it this way and it will work out, while you do what you know how to do". As I say, I believe that the problem today is that the sympathetic bank manager has gone. I cannot remember the last time I had an opportunity to see a bank manager. I see either a computer screen or a person who is clearly not a manager with any authority.

I found the contribution of the noble Earl, Lord Kintore, absolutely fascinating. I did not know that there was an international body concerned with bookkeepers, so I have learned something definite today. I have a very sophisticated computer package which I am supposed to use in order to manage my finances. But my experience is that you cannot beat the old box in which you put all the papers. It is the only system I have ever come across which does not fail. All the stuff is in the box and when the time comes you can work through it. I am as much a modernist in these areas as anybody and I am a great believer in optimal information flows, and all that. I keep a box and I always put every piece of paper in it. If any noble Lord wants to know how to run his finances my advice is, first, to get a box and, secondly, put every piece of paper in it and never throw anything away. That is the secret of first-class financial management.

One topic which arose in the debate was our old friend deregulation. Of course one wants to create an environment in which small firms are not over-regulated so that they can get on with what they want to do. The noble Lord, Lord Trefgarne, made a point which is not exactly apposite. He referred to the plethora of directions from Brussels. As I pointed out several times during the passage of the deregulation Bill, we cannot do anything about Brussels. The Brussels directives cannot be overcome via the deregulation procedure. Noble Lords may not like it, but that, I am afraid, is the world in which we now live. The way to deal with directives from Brussels is to try to stop them at source before they get here, as we discussed at Question Time today in relation to buses. So we do not disagree on certain aspects of deregulation, but I do not think that we should be too optimistic.

Reference has been made to the social chapter and the minimum wage. The noble Lord, Lord Skelmersdale, mentioned the latter. I suppose that we just have to disagree on that. A minimum wage policy raises the average cost per employee, but it lowers the marginal cost of an employee. Putting on my old teaching hat, perhaps I may say that what matters is the marginal cost, not the average cost. If I had a blackboard I could demonstrate as part of elementary economic theory that a minimum wage may just as likely be employment-creating as employment-destroying. Therefore, one needs to look at the evidence. And looking at the evidence—without boasting I think that I can say that I have read all of it—the evidence does not tell us one way or the other. There are studies showing that a minimum wage can lose jobs and other studies, interestingly enough, showing that such a policy can create jobs. Therefore, I am a bit puzzled by the strength of some noble Lords' opposition to a minimum wage. To put it at its mildest, which is all that I want to do today, the point is arguable.

I am also puzzled by the attitude that is sometimes taken even now towards the social chapter. I refer particularly to the attitude of the Confederation of British Industry. I know that I shall offend one or two noble Lords by saying this, but I do not expect rationality and good sense from the Institute of Directors. However, although the CBI tends mostly to support the party of noble Lords opposite, it occasionally gives the impression that it is interested in serious argument. Therefore, I simply do not understand why the CBI fails to see that the social chapter is part of good industrial relations which, if appropriately applied, will raise productivity and lower costs.

I reiterate the main point, which we have argued before. There is no possibility of this country being able to compete with, say, the Pacific Rim countries on low wages. There is no way in which we can ever get our wages low enough to become competitive with such countries. Therefore, returning to a point on which we agree, we need high levels of skills, flexibility, worker co-operation and excellent management. I believe that the social chapter provides the economic environment for that. Old-fashioned distant management, which simply wants to give orders to a poorly paid, supine labour force, cannot deliver the hyper-efficiency that we need. Low wages are like devaluation; they are the easy way out for a management that cannot do its job properly. That is not what we want.

In conclusion, I am extremely pleased that at long last we are having a meeting of minds in this area. When I first became a Member of your Lordships' House, noble Lords opposite could see little or no role for government except perhaps to deal with inflation, and my noble friends and I seemed to be saying that every problem was to be solved by government intervention. As today's debate shows, we have now moved closer together. Noble Lords opposite now see a more positive role for government—they have said so today —and I hope that I have made it clear on this occasion and others that we recognise the limits of government intervention. That does not mean that we agree—I hasten to add, in case any of your Lordships end up in a state of shock—but it does mean that we can argue more constructively and rationally on economic and industrial subjects. I hope that we continue to do that.

5.43 p.m.

The Minister of State, Department of Trade and Industry (Earl Ferrers): My Lords, we have had a most interesting debate, initiated by my noble friend Lord Trefgarne. I should like to repeat what others have said and thank my noble friend for having given the House the opportunity of discussing the important subject of manufacturing industry.

A thriving manufacturing industry means a healthy small firms sector. There are nearly 3 million firms in the country, and 96 per cent. of them employ fewer than 20 people. Therefore, a thriving manufacturing industry implies, and is dependent on, a thriving small firms sector.

I agree with my noble friend Lord Skelmersdale that small firms are important. My noble friend also referred to charities which are important too. He raised some specific points about charities which I should like to look into before writing to him. I am unable to give him an answer immediately on what is obviously an important matter.

The Motion brings together the two strands that are at the very heart of the Government's industrial policy. I refer to the small firms sector and the need for a thriving manufacturing sector. I would want to leave your Lordships in no doubt as to the Government's commitment to a strong and vibrant manufacturing sector. Manufacturing has traditionally been the way by which a country can increase its growth, whether it is a third world country or a developed country. After decades of decline, the 1980s saw a significant improvement in the competitiveness of our own manufacturing industries.

Since 1981 manufacturing output in the UK has risen by 25 per cent.; productivity has risen by over 75 per cent.; and exports are up by well over 80 per cent. That is a good performance, particularly when we bear in mind that it has taken place over a period when we have witnessed a world recession of almost unparalleled severity. But this strong performance is continuing.

[EARL FERRERS]
Manufacturing output is 5 per cent. higher now than it was a year ago—and that is the strongest growth since 1989.

I know that in making these remarks I shall upset the noble Lord, Lord Ezra. He says that the fact that we always mention the good points shows that we are complacent. I do not think that that is the case. I make no apology for mentioning the good points. I believe that as a country all too often we denigrate ourselves and mention only the bad points. Yet when we do well and say so, the noble Lord, Lord Ezra, says, "You're complacent". The noble Lord's speech was, as always, fascinating. But it was also a bit depressing. The noble Lord said, "We'll have to wait and see what happens to firms when we have the next economic cyclical downturn". That reminded me of the lovely song that Stanley Holloway used to sing, "Oh my word, you do look ill". That almost encapsulates the otherwise fascinating speech of the noble Lord, Lord Ezra.

Manufacturing is important, but so also is the service sector. The two are vital. It is not a matter of trading one off against the other. We need both to be competitive. What is more, they need each other. The Government also recognise the true value of small firms. Many of your Lordships have referred to their importance. They are a vital source of new ideas and new products. They also provide services and, very importantly, new jobs. They stimulate competition and they help individuals to realise their personal ambitions. That is no bad thing. From among their ranks some of the great names of tomorrow will emerge.

Small businesses are built up by hard work, by dedication, and, very often, by personal sacrifice. I welcome this opportunity to applaud the success of those who are involved in small businesses and to assure your Lordships that the Government are determined to see that their well being continues.

Taken as a whole, the role of the small firms sector in creating jobs has been particularly impressive. It is worth reminding ourselves that in just two years, between 1989 and 1991, firms with fewer than 20 employees created an additional 350,000 jobs. When one looks at the number of extra jobs created and the number of small firms that have started up, it is interesting to note that six out of 10 were initiated by people with no prior business experience. I do not think that that is something to be ashamed of; I think we can take great pride in the fact that there is an entrepreneurial spirit in our people and a determination to try to do their bit for their families and their country.

Taken as a whole, the role of the small firm sector in creating jobs has been particularly impressive. The number of business start-ups remains buoyant at about 400,000 a year. There is every indication that firms of that nature will remain a crucial and vital source of new jobs. Small firms have a powerful influence on the economy. They are at the forefront of economic recovery. We have only to look at the survey of smaller manufacturing firms carried out in the summer by the CBI in conjunction with Panell Kerr Forster. It shows that output and new orders, particularly export orders, have increased strongly. No less importantly, but rather less tangibly, the survey shows an increase in business optimism, in employment, and in export confidence. I hope that that will encourage the noble Lord, Lord Ezra.

There is further evidence of the prospects for small manufacturing firms. The last *Quarterly Survey of Small Businesses in Britain* undertaken by the NatWest and the Small Business Research Trust shows that throughout 1994 manufacturing was one of the most optimistic sectors in terms of expected sales and that it remains the single most optimistic sector for growth in employment. Those are encouraging facts.

The objective of the Government's policies for all businesses, small and large, can be summed up in one word. I make no apology for using it. That word is "competitiveness". Competitiveness means having what it takes to obtain business in world markets against the competition of others. It is the only way to guarantee our future prosperity. It does not necessarily mean producing the cheapest item, although cheapness is of course important. It means providing the best value for money; it means producing goods of the right type, at the right time and in the right place; and it means creating confidence in the purchaser. People will often buy something which is not the cheapest, merely because they have confidence in the product and, in particular, in the manufacturer.

Markets are increasingly global rather than national. The pace of change is accelerating. It is not slowing down. When I was a young man I went to Singapore. The journey took four weeks. I went there two months ago; it took 13 hours. Everyone said what a terribly long journey it was. But, of course, it is not. It is, relatively speaking, around the corner. So are all the other places in that part of the world. There are tremendous opportunities there for us. But there are threats too. I agree only marginally with the noble Lord, Lord Peston, when he says that countries in the Far East are producing goods at a rate we cannot possibly match. To some extent, that is true. However, I was surprised to be told the other day that women's wages in Korea are higher than those in Northern Ireland. That was as much a surprise to me as I dare say it is to the noble Lord.

Lord Peston: It is indeed.

Earl Ferrers: What all this means is that our companies are operating in an increasingly competitive world, especially with the emergence of the fast-growing nations of the Far East and the new markets in eastern Europe. Those changes bring tremendous opportunities but they also bring threats. Improving competitiveness is essential; it is fundamentally down to individual companies and their managers to achieve it.

I agree with my noble friend Lord Caldecote that governments have to set the conditions. On the whole he felt that industry had not made the best use of them in the past. He said that much has been done, and he is right. Much has been done. But it is also, as he said, being done by our competitors too. We cannot stop the search for increasing competitiveness. That is something which will go on and on.

Earlier this year the Government published a White Paper. It was not a DTI White Paper. It was a White Paper which articulated, for the first time, policies across all government departments which have a bearing on the competitiveness of industry. It is, I suppose, the first time that any government have said, as a matter of policy, that before they bring forward any legislation they must first ask the question, "How will this affect the competitiveness of industry?".

Enhancing competitiveness is not something one can achieve by turning a knob, issuing a diktat, or passing a law. Competitiveness is a culture of continuous improvement. Everyone has to play his part in that, including smaller companies. They have a crucial role to play.

New regulations are framed with small businesses in mind. We require that all legislative proposals brought before Parliament, which impact on business, must have an assessment of their compliance costs. That must include a small business test to show how the regulation will impact on small businesses. My noble friend Lord Skelmersdale said that he wanted the climate to be right. He wanted low inflation, low interest rates, more deregulation, and less tax. I agree. In some ways he asks for Utopia. We have already done a great deal. The policies the Government have been pursuing have resulted in inflation running at its lowest level now for over a quarter of a century; interest rates being brought down to their lowest level for 17 years; and unemployment dropping by 400,000 since the beginning of 1993. That means that more people are employed.

An essential ingredient in getting the climate right, particularly for smaller enterprises, is to minimise the burden of bureaucracy. Industry cannot get on with its job of producing and selling if it is perpetually strapped around with red tape. Deregulation is an essential part of the Government's strategy for improving competitiveness. Our aim is not just to strike out regulations which are unnecessarily burdensome on industry but to ensure that regulation which is necessary is thought out properly and soundly and properly based. The new powers available to us under the Deregulation and Contracting Out Act are a major advance in the deregulation campaign.

My noble friend Lord Trefgarne was right when he said that industry must become more efficient. I agree. It must. Much of it is, but a great deal of it has a long way to go. My noble friend was also right to applaud the fact that we are not part of the social chapter. The noble Lord, Lord Peston, said that he could not see that being out of the social chapter could be good for staff relationships. The noble Lord looks worried. I am paraphrasing what he said. He looks less worried now, so perhaps I have it right. I can tell him why it is good for staff relationships. It means that other people invest in this country. Forty per cent. of investment from Japan into the EU comes to this country; 43 per cent. of all investment from America into the EU comes to this country. Why does it come to this country? It is because we have a better climate; our labour costs are more competitive than those of other countries. That produces good jobs, and that is good labour relations.

Lord Peston: My Lords, perhaps I may interrupt the Minister. Will he say why so much of British capital is invested in the rest of the EU where they do have the social chapter? The argument should work both ways, but it does not. We invest enormously over there where the social chapter is in operation and will continue. It is more complicated than the Minister suggests.

Earl Ferrers: My Lords, I should not try to make things too complicated. The answer to that question is simple. British firms invest their money where they find it attractive and important to do so. That does not rely only on the social chapter. It may well be that in order to supply what they want to supply in France and Germany they find that they have to have their own firms in those countries. It is not as simple as the noble Lord, Lord Peston, makes out either.

My noble friends Lord Skelmersdale and Lord Oxfuird, and the noble Lords, Lord Haskel and Lord Weatherill, referred to small and medium-sized enterprises. They were right in what they said. My noble friend Lord Skelmersdale said that some businesses stay small and have only one or two employees. The businesses with one or two people do not get bigger because they do not want to or they cannot. Often those who run such firms are the ones producing and selling the goods; keeping the books; going to the bank manager; doing everything. They want advice. That is why we have set up the Business Link system. It will enable people to have business advisers who will be friends and who will ask, "Can we help you over this?". The man may say, "Yes, this is the trouble that I have", and be told, "Yes, I have seen someone else down the road and he has got out of it this way". The business advisers will be able to help such people. Business Link will include advisers on design and export promotion. It is an essential part of what the Government are trying to achieve, referred to by several noble Lords as a partnership between government and industry. I agree with my noble friend that the future depends not on Ministers but on companies themselves.

The noble Lord, Lord Haskel, said that it was inward investment in a weak manufacturing industry. The noble Lord, Lord Preston, made a similar point. The noble Lord, Lord Haskel, said that we have £9.2 billion of inward investment and £17.2 billion of investment outside this country. That is good both ways. Traditionally, Britain has been an investor in the outside world, which is good for this country and good for business. Often companies, for the reason that I gave to the noble Lord, Lord Desai, have to locate themselves in other countries in order to carry out their business. Equally, it is good for other countries to invest in this country. That stimulates work, business and employment and often it stimulates other companies in this country to supply the new companies with products.

The noble Lord, Lord Desai, gave his views on these matters. I agree with his comments on investment from abroad. He said that he was an economist and he did not want to go anywhere near the real world. I understand

[EARL FERRERS]
that feeling but say to him that sometimes those who are in the real world say that they do not want to go anywhere near an economist. They certainly do not want to go anywhere near three economists because they will receive four answers, which is not particularly helpful.

We had a lovely speech from the noble Lord, Lord Weatherill. I was intrigued to hear that his father led a strike of tailors. I did not realise that but I am sure that it must have been in a good cause. Whatever the cause, it is good to learn that his small family firm has prospered and that it now exports two-thirds of its product. Perhaps I may say, without being too platitudinous, that the noble Lord's father would have been as proud of his son as he was of his business.

The noble Lord, Lord Weatherill, reminded us that Napoleon did not say that we were a nation of shopkeepers but that we were a nation of merchants and adventurers. He regaled us with a story about his family; perhaps I may say that my family also played a part by being adventurers. One member went abroad and taught the Persians how to use gunpowder. I am not sure whether that was a good form of trading but he was so successful that he returned as the Persian Ambassador to the Court of St. James's. That was a glittering career.

The noble Lord mentioned the Prince's Youth Business Trust. It is an important trust and has undertaken remarkable work, as I have been lucky enough to be told. He was also concerned about the Croydon Business Venture which resulted in his writing to 12 people asking them for £1,000 each and getting it. I am glad that he did not write to me.

A certain amount of money has been available for business start-up. The noble Lord was fearful that that will not be specifically available in the future because it forms a part of the single regeneration budget. I know that the fragmentation of start-up support has been the cause of anxiety in a number of organisations, in particular the local enterprise agency network. I realise too that there may be some short-term difficulties. Real opportunities exist in the longer term for local partners to bid for the funds that will be available through the single regeneration budget. In looking to the future, we consider that local enterprise agencies will be important partners in the Business Link. I hope that the individual enterprise agencies will work closely with their local Business Link partnerships. Businesses are starting up effectively and I hope that that will continue.

A number of noble Lords referred to the financial arrangements. My noble friend Lord Trefgarne referred to finance for industry, as did my noble friends Lord Oxfuird, Lord Caldecote and Lord Cochrane of Cults. The noble Lord, Lord Ezra, said that businesses fail too and the noble Lord, Lord Peston, said that banks have not always been helpful. In some respects, people have found that to be the case. However, a recession scythes through everything. Both banks and small businesses are vulnerable but I agree with the noble Lord, Lord Peston, that within prudent guidelines there should be a relatively long-term commitment. If that can be done by medium-term loans that the banks are prepared to make that would be good.

Small businesses are reliant on short-term finance and overdrafts. The Government encourage small firms to consider alternative forms of finance. Informal investment by the Business Angels is one of them. There is access to the right kind of finance at the right time. That is vital if businesses are to succeed and prosper. It is true that banks are likely to remain the main providers of finance for small businesses. Currently they are providing approximately £40 billion to small firms, mainly as loans and overdrafts. It is vital that there should be a relationship of trust and mutual understanding between the banks and small businesses. There is also in existence the small firms loan guarantee scheme. That was changed last year; the maximum loan was increased from £100,000 to £250,000 to firms which have been trading for two years or more and for some firms the guarantee level was increased from 75 per cent. to 85 per cent. There has been a reduction in premium for all firms.

The noble Lord, Lord Ezra, referred to the commercial investment bank. In some parts of government there is not too much enthusiasm for that but my department is to undertake a review of the issue in order to establish whether small firms and enterprises in the United Kingdom are disadvantaged and what role the banks should play. I should have liked to have referred to many other issues but time runs out. Perhaps I may write to noble Lords.

The noble Lord, Lord Desai, referred to manufacturing investment. Business investment is estimated to have risen by 1.25 per cent. in the year to the third quarter. The Treasury forecasts this to rise to 2 per cent. for the year as a whole and to 10.75 per cent. for 1995. Manufacturing investment accounts for about one-fifth of the total business investment and is expected to increase strongly next year. The CBI has forecast a growth of more than 11 per cent. Those are encouraging facts.

I return to the point made by my noble friend Lord Trefgarne at the end of his speech. On the whole, government's contribution to industry can best be made by supporting and helping businesses but as far as possible by getting out of their hair. We can help by providing information and advice, by making available specific schemes and special initiatives and by providing all kinds of statistics. But it is not the Government who create wealth; it is individuals and the businesses. That is what we want to encourage.

It is always tempting to think that the past was easier than the present. That is nonsense. Many years ago my noble friend Lord Waldegrave said something that I have never forgotten. He said, "Always remember that there is a better opportunity tomorrow". So there is. We are leading Europe out of recession. There are stacks of opportunities and it is our business, whether as government playing their part or businessmen playing their part, to grab those opportunities and to make the best of them that we can.

6.10 p.m.

Lord Trefgarne: My Lords, at this stage in the evening, with an important debate to follow, it is not for me to do more than thank every noble Lord who has taken part in the debate. The speeches were uniformly interesting and informative and I am grateful to each and every noble Lord.

I am particularly grateful to my noble friend Lord Ferrers for replying to the debate today. I know that being here today has caused difficulties for him with regard to commitments in his diary and therefore I am doubly grateful to him. With that, I beg leave to withdraw the Motion.

Motion for Papers, by leave, withdrawn.

War Crimes (Supplementary Provisions) Bill [H.L.]

6.11 p.m.

Lord Campbell of Alloway: My Lords, I beg to move that this Bill be now read a second time.

The purpose of the Bill is to afford a fair administration of justice in the context of the War Crimes Act in two distinct ways which are not mutually dependent, so each requires separate consideration. The Bill does not amend any provisions of the Act and to some extent, Clause 1 reflects the sense of urgency as regards implementation of the Act, as appears from the *Official Reports* to have been the understanding of another place.

If this Bill is given a Second Reading and reaches another place, there would be a long period of time before it could ever receive Royal Assent during which investigations could be ended. A decision could be made as to whether to charge or exclude on the available evidence. Only on the passing of the Act would the limitation provisions of Clause 1 bite. Proceedings instituted before that date would not be affected in any way.

Clause 2 imports from Scotland a pre-trial appellate procedure on which I took advice from the noble and learned Lords, Lord Jauncey of Tullichettle and Lord Morton of Shuna. That is with regard to applications to quash the indictment on grounds of delay. The reason for its introduction is to avoid abortive trials which should not have taken place, because in England those trials must take place as there is no appellate jurisdiction until after conviction.

The Bill has the support of many noble and learned Lords to whom I have spoken informally, including the noble and learned Lord the Lord Chief Justice, who are not able to attend. The right reverend Prelate the Bishop of St. Albans, whose annual meeting is taking place at this very moment, has written to say that he wishes well for these laudable efforts on an important moral and legal issue.

Let it be said at the outset with respect to the memory of millions who suffered, and some of whom are still suffering, that it is proven beyond doubt that mass murders were perpetrated—a policy of extermination— by the Third German Reich to the everlasting shame of all mankind. But since the War Crimes Act received Royal Assent on 9th May 1991, no charges have been made. And even today, it is not known whether and indeed, if so, when the continuing investigations may end or whether any charges will be made. Already one-third of the suspects interrogated have died.

When the War Crimes Bill was before another place, there was an air of urgency, of resolve, to implement the recommendations of Part I of the Hetherington-Chalmers Report on the basis of the evidence of 301 case files and other material in Part II of that report which was not disclosed in either House. But another place was permitted to labour under a crucial misunderstanding, a crucial misapprehension, which was repeated in your Lordships' House by my noble friend Lord Waddington, that on that evidence, which the noble Lord said that he had read, those trials were warranted and so would ensue with dispatch.

There was no sufficient evidence on which to charge anyone. Another place, in good faith, had to take for granted the supposed quality and cogency of that evidence in Part II to avoid prejudicing a fair trial in impending proceedings, and did so. Even today, there is no sufficient evidence on which to charge anyone and as yet, the Crown Prosecution Service has not even decided whether to seek the consent of Mr. Attorney to institute proceedings in any single case.

It was never envisaged by another place that a delay of that order could possibly arise; that 15 of the 301 people who have been under investigation since 1988 would still be under investigation today; that new investigations would have been initiated as late as March this year; that by today, a decision as to whether or not to prosecute would not have been taken in all cases; and that by now, those trials would not have been either instituted or concluded.

Indeed, on the contrary, it was common ground among all Members of both Houses that if those trials were to ensue, they must be fair trials in accordance with our concepts of justice. Each year of delay infects the prospects of a fair trial as prejudicial to the defence: especially so where the alleged conduct took place so very long ago and the crucial issue is one of identity.

Clause 1 proposes a time limit on the institution of proceedings. Why so? That is because the Crown Prosecution Service, having received substantive reports from the police on which charges could not be laid, remitted the matter to the police for further investigation. Both my noble friend Lord Ferrers and my noble and learned friend the Lord Chancellor have informed your Lordships' House that the end of those investigations cannot be predicted. It is also because in Scotland, all were excluded from prosecution before 27th June 1994 in exactly the same circumstances in which the Crown Prosecution Service remitted the matter to the police for further investigation. A disparate regime for exclusion on either side of the Border, operating under the same statute, all but beggars belief.

Your Lordships may well think that the only fair and just approach was that adopted by the noble and learned Lord the Lord Advocate, which was explained in a Written Answer on 11th July of this year. It read:

"After extensive enquiries in the United Kingdom and overseas, Crown Counsel decided that there was not sufficient available evidence for a criminal prosecution in any of the cases".—[*Official Report*, 11/7/94; col. WA 93.]

[LORD CAMPBELL OF ALLOWAY]

The book was closed in Scotland by the noble and learned Lord the Lord Advocate on that basis before 27th July, yet the Crown Prosecution Service continues investigations on the same basis, the end of which, the Government take the view, cannot be predicted.

The purpose of Clause 2 is to remove the disparity of procedure in an act of general application and to introduce in England and Wales and in Northern Ireland the appellate procedure as it existed for many years in Scotland. The justification is to avoid a long, complex and costly trial with unusually emotive overtones conducted so long after the event which should not have taken place, and to avoid the "backlash" factor to which the right reverend Prelate the Bishop of St. Albans referred on Second Reading of the Bill. In all those cases, it is inevitable that an application will be made to the court to quash the indictment on grounds of delay, as being prejudicial to a fair trial.

As to the present position and the attitude of government, noble Lords will be grateful to my noble friend the Minister for what she said on 28th November this year (at col. 473 of *Hansard*). There are now 24 men who have been candidates for prosecution since before 27th June 1994. As I have mentioned, 15 of them have been under investigation since 1988; three since July 1991; and the rest since February, April and December 1993 and January and March 1994 respectively. Of the 369 suspects investigated, 233 have been excluded and 112 have died.

What is the attitude of government? Parliament has had its say. There is no limitation period for murder at common law, so none will be introduced. The continuance of those investigations, whatever delay may be involved, is entirely a matter for the Crown Prosecution Service and must be left to the CPS. It is a matter for the courts to decide whether to quash the indictment on grounds of delay as from 1st September 1939 up to and including the date of trial, or on grounds of abuse of process.

As to Parliament having had its say, having read the *Official Reports*, perhaps I may say with great respect to my noble friend Lord Tonypandy and to my noble friend the Minister that, on any objective analysis, Parliament has not had its say on either of the procedural matters, the subject of this Bill, which were neither envisaged nor discussed in either House.

There is of course no period of limitation at common law; we know that. But the common law was introduced by a statute with retrospective effect as from 1st September 1939 over persons who owed no allegiance and to whom the common law did not apply. It was a unique and wholly exceptional assumption of retroactive extra-territorial jurisdiction which may no longer be questioned. But your Lordships may well think that some form of control, some form of limitation, is called for in those exceptional circumstances where investigations continue, the end of which cannot be predicted.

Investigations to gather up evidence against a set of octogenarians, some 50 or 60 years after the alleged event, has little to do with my personal concept of the fair administration of justice.

As regards leaving matters to the Crown Prosecution Service, perhaps enough has been said about the disparate regime operating either side of the Border and about the continuance of the unpredictable delay under the aegis of the CPS which the Government are apparently prepared to countenance. This is not the occasion upon which to consider the judgment, efficiency or competence of the CPS, either generally or in context with this affair in which, perhaps, it may speak for itself. But if the Government are prepared to leave the matter in the hands of the Crown Prosecution Service without any control over continuing delay, then surely a case is made out for some limitation on the institution of proceedings.

Moved, That the Bill be now read a second time.—(*Lord Campbell of Alloway*.)

6.26 p.m.

Lord Merlyn-Rees: My Lords, I should, first, declare an interest in the matter of war crimes as chairman for many years of the all-party group on war crimes. I am glad to say that we played a part in getting the Hetherington-Chalmers Report published. We also played some part, along with my colleagues in another place, in getting an overwhelming vote in favour of the War Crimes Bill when it appeared before that place. It is my view that if today's Bill were to get to the other place—although I do not believe that it will—it would be overwhelmingly defeated.

I have been two years in your Lordships' House and I am second to none in my appreciation of the role of this place as a revising Chamber. Very often the quality of debates here is far better than those in another place. The purpose of the Bill now before us is to overturn the Act which was passed overwhelmingly in the other place; indeed, it would nullify it. I should like to argue the case for leaving things as they are.

Even if the effect of the Bill were not to nullify the Act, as came out in the discussion that we had during Question Time recently it is not the role of Home Office Ministers to interfere in any way with the police through their War Crimes Unit. The police are independent. The glory of the police—sometimes it is not so; indeed, it never used to happen in Northern Ireland where the police were the creatures of the state—is that they are independent when they are investigating crimes. The Home Office is quite clear on that fact. There have been one or two occasions in recent years when I believed, with no knowledge perhaps, that there had been an overstepping of the mark in that respect. The independence of the Crown Prosecution Service and of the War Crimes Unit is, I believe, most important.

However, that is not to say that one cannot ask questions. Nevertheless, it is not the job of the Home Office to hasten progress and ask, "What are you doing about this?", or say, "Drop that, and do something else". It must be a matter for the independence of the police. I was going to crack a joke, but this is the wrong place for doing so.

As regards my own role as Home Secretary, I often used to reflect on the fact that Winston Churchill said, "Never make a lawyer a Home Secretary." I believe that he had in mind Sir John Simon. The obverse of that remark, of course, is that it does not mean that if you are not a lawyer you would be a good Home Secretary. I believe that sometimes judgment has to take over from the detail of the matter—it can be left to other people.

There is no need for me to rehearse the facts that led to the Act of Parliament, and its antecedents in the Hetherington-Chalmers Report. The report came to a conclusion which I mentioned during the first reading of the Act in another place. I shall not quote the whole thing again, just the following sentences:

"The cases we have investigated disclose horrific instances of mass murders, and we do not consider that the lapse of time since the offences were committed, or the age of the offenders, provide sufficient reason for taking no action in such cases. We therefore recommend that some action should be taken in each case in which the evidence is adequate".—[*Official Report*, Commons, 12/12/89; col. 886.]

I shall return to that point. When I quoted those sentences in another place Mr. Edward Heath interrupted me and asked if I would read on. He was being helpful. I said that I would willingly do so and continued, at col. 886:

"In paragraph 9.18 we describe possible courses of action. We do not recommend deprivation of citizenship and deportation".

That would have constituted another way of dealing with this matter. The noble and learned Lord, Lord Hailsham, discussed this matter in this place. The people we are talking about had entered this country too easily at the time of a Labour Government, which I supported as an ex-serviceman. I had been active in the Labour Party as a kid before the war. People entered this country from Italy —a country I know well—and from Austria too easily. That situation was badly handled. People were not checked. One course of action is not to accuse these people of war crimes but to say that they did not tell the truth when they filled in the forms at the time they entered this country as cheap labour in 1945 and 1946. The young men of South Wales and Yorkshire did not work in the pits at that time because of all the cheap labour entering the country. Many of those people who entered this country wanted a job and I do not blame them for that. Many of them played an important role in the areas to which they moved, but they did not tell the truth about their situation when they entered the country.

The Hetherington-Chalmers Report referred to English and Scots law. I believe this matter has already been mentioned tonight. The report stated that neither English nor Scots law have imposed time limits in the prosecution of indictable crime. The War Crimes Unit has taken its time over this matter. The noble and learned Lord, Lord Scarman, the noble Lord, Lord Jenkins of Hillhead, the Cardinal of Westminster and I have formed ourselves into a committee which has sought new legislation to deal with miscarriages of justice. We have dealt with the case of the Guildford Four and that of the Maguires. I have not checked my papers but I believe that when I was Home Secretary I sent the Maguire case back to the Appeal Court. I was given a dusty answer and told not to waste the court's time. The Maguires are now out and so are the Guildford Four.

I am the last person to want miscarriages of justice to occur. There must be a cloud over parts of the judiciary and the police, otherwise the Government would not be about to introduce legislation to deal with miscarriages of justice. As interested as I am in war crimes, I do not wish to see miscarriages of justice. I would not care if no one who was investigated was charged if the evidence does not stand up. That is the glory of our system. I am not seeking to catch people for alleged crimes because of what I witnessed at an impressionable period in my life.

As regards miscarriages of justice, I understand that a body, separate from the Court of Appeal, and separate from the Home Office, is to be set up to deal with this. However, I believe, the Court of Appeal will be involved. I am not worried about delay. What is important is that this work must be carefully carried out.

I wish to say a few words about the nature of these war crimes. I am an oldish man now but sometimes when one is inside this place one feels younger than when one is outside it. As an old man I sometimes talk with my young sons. They ask me about Dresden. I was proud to serve at Dresden. But I also talk to my sons about the rocket attacks on London and on Lewisham. A ceremony was held in Lewisham recently to mark the anniversary of a rocket attack. However, those events are not war crimes according to the definition of the law.

I have just revisited—as I do every year—war graves in those parts of the world in which I served. I visited Sicily to see the graves of the 51st Highlanders and the 50th Northumbrians. Some of my friends are buried there. My father died as a result of the First World War; he was gassed. I have taken my children to see the war graves of north eastern France. What a society there was at that time, but millions of Germans, French, British and other nationalities died in the First World War and no wonder in the inter-war years the cream of manhood had disappeared.

I regard those events as war crimes in the non-legal sense. However, the war crimes we are discussing are of a different nature. They were committed away from the front. The Hetherington-Chalmers Report describes various crimes. It describes how people were lined up in front of a trench and shot so that they would fall into the trench. What happened at Dresden was terrible, as were the rocket attacks on London, the bombing of Rotterdam and the heavy bombing of the German cities. But the crimes we are talking about must not be forgotten. I shall return to that matter in a moment.

I served in the Air Force but I also spent some time working with Army personnel. Recently I returned to the south of France. When I served in that area I was astonished to discover that the German soldiers who wore Iron Crosses came from eastern Europe. I had been fed the idea that Europe was waiting to be liberated and that most of the people in Europe were waiting to be liberated by us and were not on the side of the Germans. I did not find that to be true. They had fought willingly for the Germans. I found that was the case in Yugoslavia and as regards the troops who were streaming from the Hungarian front. I understand, although I do not know

[LORD MERLYN-REES]
about this, that there were similar soldiers —not soldiers of fortune, but working with the Germans—in pockets on the second front.

It was those people from eastern Europe who found their way into this country. That is why we should examine how they entered this country rather than actual war crimes. Some of those people committed heinous crimes.

In the past few years I have talked to Jewish friends who were in concentration camps. My friends told me that the personnel in those camps, who came from the Baltic states and parts of eastern Europe, were worse than the Germans. They tried to outdo the Germans in their behaviour. Only some of those crimes will be able to be proven. I do not want revenge. I have fought against capital punishment. I do not wish those people to be hung if they are found guilty. All I want is for the world to face up to what has happened.

We need to face up to what is happening in Yugoslavia now. The Government have embarked on a scheme with the UN to establish war crimes tribunals, and then trials, in Yugoslavia. Therefore, that process will happen again there. However, I should have thought it would be extremely difficult to obtain evidence. I believe it is a mistake to hurry things up. I have no knowledge of how many cases have been considered. Let the matter be dealt with but at least let it be known that we in the Parliament in this country have stood up and declared that war crimes are evil. Let us not be sidetracked from that.

I saw Barbie's Lyons. I saw Lyons airfield bombed to smithereens. The light bombers—or the posh name for them, the tactical bombers—bombed the airfield. The French kids cheered and they were shot. I saw their legs sticking through the earth. That is a war crime and it is that sort of war crime—not the events that occurred in battle in north eastern France that I describe to my sons—that was perpetrated, mainly on members of the Jewish faith in eastern Europe, that we need to consider. The other House, in which I was proud to play a part, stood clearly for dealing with such war crimes. We should not renege on that. Let us see what happens.

6.40 p.m.

Lord Mayhew: My Lords, supporters of war crimes trials are fortunate indeed to have as their leader, and chairman, someone who speaks not only in a most agreeable and persuasive manner but who was also a Home Secretary—and a much better Home Secretary than Sir John Simon whom he mentioned.

I confess that I had hoped that the experience that we have had since the passage of the Act might have modified the enthusiasm of the noble Lord, Lord Merlyn-Rees, for pursuing the war crimes trials. I think, for instance, of the experience of other countries. I recall that during those debates the noble Lord and others urged us to follow the example of Canada, Australia and Israel. Experience since confirms all the worst fears of those who opposed the Act at that time. All the trials were disasters, especially the one in Israel, which illustrated in the most dramatic way how right those noble and learned Lords were who said that it is impossible to identify people after all this time.

The trial of Demjanjuk was a show trial. It was televised. Schoolchildren were bused in. I recall seeing on the television, on the BBC news, the eye witnesses advancing on the accused, Demjanjuk, saying, with complete sincerity and conviction, "That's the man, how could I possibly mistake him?" The Israeli judiciary, and everyone, now knows that those witnesses were wrong. On that occasion it did not stop Demjanjuk being sentenced—to death, as I recall. But it was a tremendous warning of how such war crimes trials can go wrong and it fulfils all the forebodings that we had at the time. I had hoped that that might have modified the attitude of the noble Lord, Lord Merlyn-Rees.

Other events have occurred since the Act was passed. We have had a revelation of the amount of money and the substantial quantity of skilled servicemen who have been devoted not to anti-drug or anti-terrorist activities in the United Kingdom but to searching out in remote parts of Eastern Europe people who might have committed war crimes. Those people were not even British at the time.

Since the Act, there has been the passage of time itself. The noble Lord, Lord Merlyn-Rees, said—I believe I quote him—"I am not worried about delay". But we ought to be greatly worried about delay. Let us consider the Hetherington report which was the basis upon which the Government took up the cause, framed the Act, and pushed it through. The report stated,

"Given the age of the suspects and witnesses any proposed legislation should be introduced and brought into force as quickly as possible".

That was stated five and a half years ago. In describing their investigations in Eastern Europe, the authors of the report stated:

"The greatest difficulty we encountered was simply the age of the suspects and witnesses".

That was their finding, six and a half years ago.

The offences were committed more than 50 years ago. The noble Lord states that he is not worried by the delay. But, of course, that is not the end of the delay. Justice will be further delayed. Let us assume for a moment that the Crown Prosecution Service puts a case to the Attorney-General and the Attorney-General judges in favour of the prosecution. That might occur within a month or weeks. But what then, my Lords? The defence starts to build its case. It will have to go to Eastern Europe, with translators and interpreters. It will have to examine records and archives. It will have to start a desperate, almost certainly futile, search for defence witnesses. I should have thought it likely that all possible defence witnesses will either be untraceable or dead.

Eventually the trial may begin. The Act contains some unprecedented aspects, especially in relation to retrospection. Therefore there will be an enormous number of points of procedure during the trial. The trial will drag on for a long time. When the verdict is eventually reached, how old will the accused be? If he had a rather senior post when his alleged crime was committed, he will at that time be in his nineties. If he were a smaller fry, he will be in his eighties. That is too old. It is far too long since the offence was committed. People's memories are wholly unreliable. Defence witnesses cannot be found. Such a prosecution is wrong.

Those of us who as soldiers took part in the liberation of Europe were brought very close indeed in the concentration camps to the horrors of which the noble Lord spoke. However, despite the appalling nature and seriousness of the charges, the passage of time has made it, in my view, not only unfair but actually indecent to bring charges under the Act.

Perhaps I may say a word about the attitude of the Government. In this House Ministers have not attempted recently to defend the Act or its purposes. Their constant cry has been, "It's on the statute book. The Commons passed it. Therefore we have to carry it out". I believe that that is a little disingenuous. After all, it was the Government who started it. The author of the report, Sir Thomas Hetherington, was asked at a meeting here, "Seeing that the Government ended war crimes trials with the support of all parties in 1948, what has caused this sudden recurrence of a demand for war crimes trials?" He put as one of the major factors the visit to Israel of the then Prime Minister, the noble Baroness, Lady Thatcher. It was perfectly legitimate. I do not complain. However, the fact is that the Government took the initiative in producing the Bill. They passed the Bill; they supported it in both Houses. They are now relentlessly seeking to implement it. The Government cannot avoid responsibility. They cannot simply say, "The House of Commons passed it and we are carrying out what is on the statute book".

Furthermore, the Bill before us now is not on the statute book. We are in a new situation as a result of the passage of time and the Government are perfectly free if they wish to support the Bill. Nothing that the House of Commons has done should stand in their way if they wish to do so. All that the Government have done meanwhile is to devote a lot of money and much badly needed trained security personnel to investigate atrocities committed more than 50 years ago in remote parts of Eastern Europe by people who were not then British. It is hard to imagine a more perverse sense of priorities than that.

6.49 p.m.

Lord Jakobovits: My Lords, this is the third time that we are debating the subject of war crimes. Looking through the list of speakers today, it appears to me that those who are taking part have previously expressed their opinions—or at least the great majority of them. It appears from the speeches made so far that the opinions have not changed, nor is it likely that they will because these are matters of deep conviction. I wonder therefore why the debate has been introduced and why efforts are now being made in the supplementary provisions to undo what Parliament has decided by an overwhelming overall majority on two previous occasions.

The noble Lord, Lord Mayhew, cited the experience of Israel as an example of the dangers involved in bringing such prosecutions. I think that it proves the opposite. It proves that despite the legislation, the courts are still powerful enough to discern the truth, or at least to question allegations if they cannot be absolutely proved. Therefore, in that case, as in so many other cases, the law has not been changed. None of the countries changed its legislation; all that was done was to apply the rigours of the law to ensure that there should be no miscarriage of justice.

But let me come to a more fundamental point. Even though I too have spoken in the two previous debates and can offer little originality in my contribution to the renewed discussion, I wish to add a couple of questions. Is it really suggested that the millions of victims are any less dead now than they were 50 years ago or, for that matter, than they were a couple of years ago when Parliament overwhelmingly passed certain legislation? Is our debt to those who have been exterminated with such fearful and unprecedented horrors any less now than it was then?

That leads me to perhaps a more topical question. As this current year is about to conclude and we usher in the new year 1995, the world will observe the 50th anniversary of the liberation of Auschwitz and Majdanek, of Dachau and of Belsen, when we first discovered the horrors that had occurred. This commemoration will be marked throughout the world. There will be gatherings in which the world will be reminded of what took place and what the rest of the world tolerated at the time. In Europe in particular, occupied as it was, there will be countless efforts made to recall, remind and remember. Shall we in this country—because by the grace of God we were spared occupation by the Nazis—be the only or nearly the only European country that will move in the opposite direction? Instead of recalling and perpetuating what happened, shall we expunge it and say that because a number of years have passed we are no longer interested in the execution of justice? It would be inconceivable that we should be the odd man out in this impending year of the 50th anniversary by giving a signal that we care less than others who suffered so much more than we did in this country.

I believe that here I can apply the final verse of the Book of Ecclesiastes the Preacher, written, as our tradition has it, by the wisest of all men. He said:

"This is the end of the matter; all has been heard. Fear God and observe His commandments, for this is the whole duty of man".

None of the commandments is more sacred than the one in the fifth Book of Moses:

"Justice, justice shall you pursue".

Justice needs to be pursued, and not only done when it comes our way.

I hope that even if we never find a single criminal whose guilt can be proved by all the rigid tests that we apply—and rightly—at least our statute books will record that we will for ever remember the ultimate in injustice and in cruelty that has been perpetrated and will wish to count ourselves during the coming year among those who will remember, will recall and will warn future generations that mankind will never again tolerate that fearful slight, not just on human rights but on human life by the million.

[LORD JAKOBOVITS]

I believe that by sending out this message from this venerated House to our country and to the rest of the world we shall be counted among those who have not failed in the fulfilment of the law—to ensure that justice will be pursued even if it cannot always be done.

6.56 p.m.

Lord Campbell of Croy: My Lords, my contribution in the debate is aimed at helping to find the answer to the question: what was it that put the United Kingdom in a thoroughly unsatisfactory situation in 1989? There had been no way of dealing with any alleged war criminals from World War II who were resident in the United Kingdom. Any new legislation in 1989 would be for events nearly 50 years earlier, with all the difficulties of obtaining clear evidence and certain identification.

The situation arose because in 1948 nothing was done to ensure that there would be legislation in the United Kingdom to deal with any war criminals who had entered this country in disguise. It is important to recognise this crucial omission. The Nuremberg tribunal was established by the victorious allies after World War II. It tried Hitler's accomplices—Goering and Hess, plus military and other leaders who had perpetrated horrors. These were the ringleaders. They and some others who were prominently suspected of war crimes were tried by that tribunal.

Some who should have been tried had escaped and were later found in South America and elsewhere, long after 1948. Others were never found. After three years, the Nuremberg tribunal was brought to an end. It was never intended to have a long life. The big fish had been dealt with. Lesser suspects had been tried in courts in the British and other zones of Germany and these were the smaller fry.

This process was handed over by the British in our zone to the newly formed German courts in the newly democratic West Germany, which continued to try cases over the next 40 years. Other countries in continental Europe also retained the means to try alleged war crimes from World War II. Britain was a notable exception. It was presumed that no war criminal would have found a place in our society here. This was an idle assumption because large numbers of refugees from areas such as the Baltic States, the Ukraine and other parts of Europe entered Britain in the late 1940s with very little screening. It was not difficult for a war criminal who was not widely or easily recognisable to conceal himself among those refugees. With false papers, he was then safe.

Until the War Crimes Act 1991, there was no way in which an accused in this country could be brought to trial in the United Kingdom for a war crime committed in World War II. In 1957 it was made possible for prosecutions to be brought in the UK, but not for war crimes that had taken place before that year. The legislation was not retrospective to World War II. The noble Lord, Lord Merlyn-Rees, recalled cases in the late 1940s when refugees came to this country from south and central Europe. I remember similar events in the late 1940s—I worked in the Foreign Office from 1946 to 1949, dealing with Eastern Europe. The alleged war criminals involving our department were Yugoslavs in the United Kingdom, some of whom were sent back to Yugoslavia for trial. But the refugees who had come in from the Baltic States and the Ukraine had been behind the German and Russian front and very little was known about their background. In brief, anyone who thought in 1948 that all war criminals had been brought to trial deluded himself. Any deliberate amnesty then or calling a halt to the process in this country had the effect of a reprieve for the war criminal who had so far escaped arrest by means of disguise and deceit. Trials continued in other countries into the 1950s and later.

In my opinion, the 1991 Act was many years too late. Although the Statute of Limitations does not apply to murder, firm evidence and indisputable identification is very difficult to collect after 50 years. I take an illustration in Scotland. Recently, in a Scottish court, an individual was found to be a war criminal after he had brought a defamation case and after investigation in the Baltic States. However, no prosecutions are to be initiated in Scotland under the 1991 Act because sufficient hard evidence is not available. That is an anomalous and very unsatisfactory situation. Of course the individual should not have brought the defamation case. He must have thought that he was even safer than he was.

The noble Lord, Lord Mayhew, for whom I have the highest regard and for whom I worked in those days when I was a Foreign Office official and he was a Parliamentary Secretary at the Foreign Office, rightly recorded that the Nuremberg tribunal and the trials in the British zone were brought to an end in 1948 with general support. Unfortunately, there was a gap in UK legislation for any person in this country who might be suspected or accused. In the late 1940s I was sending notes to the noble Lord from the Official Box up there because the Commons was sitting in this Chamber after the bombing of the other place. I also sent notes to Mr. Ernest Bevin and Mr. Hector McNeil. The noble Lord, Lord Mayhew, took more notice of my notes, of course, then than he would now.

I shall end by recounting a personal experience. Leading elements of the Scottish division in which I was serving, with our accompanying armoured units, discovered Belsen. That was on 15th April 1945, exactly two weeks before I was wounded and disabled. The concentration camp happened to be on our line of advance. Many of our officers and men had witnessed horror and carnage in the previous 11 months, but they felt a sense of outrage at what they found. There had been rumours that such camps existed but this was the first one to be discovered in the West. Here was the awful proof. The press arrived as we were moving on towards the Elbe, and in the following days newspapers were full of accounts and photographs. Belsen had no gas chambers but its victims were left to expire miserably from starvation and disease. We were several months too late to save Anne Frank.

7.5 p.m.

Lord Houghton of Sowerby: My Lords, I shall be brief; at present late hours are not good for me, and I do not think that I ought to take up the time of the House if I cannot stay to the end of the debate. I apologise.

However, I wish to register my position. I am in support of the noble Lord who introduced the Bill. I am fully in support of everything that was just said by the noble Lord, Lord Campbell of Croy, and also the remarks of the noble Lord, Lord Mayhew, who spoke before him. Therefore a good deal of what I might say would be to underline what they said. But perhaps I may just offer the following advice.

The whole of this debate in favour of the course upon which we are now set ignores the fact that we have a jury system. The three countries which have joined in the compact to carry out these prosecutions for war crimes and which have our judicial system have found that their first case has been their last and nothing but frustration and social discontent has followed. We are on a course that we shall regret if we pursue it. It is far too late. Our system of judicial treatment is much more exacting and fastidious than most. When we hear about evidence that is adequate, we probably do not take into account that members of the jury have to be convinced that the evidence they hear is fully corroborated and is the basis upon which they can reach a verdict without reasonable doubt. That is a very severe test to apply to their judgment.

It is not convictions that we have to worry about—it is acquittals. Acquittals are the disaster. Other countries do not have the "fitness to plead" rules that we have. In Canada the accused was so ill during the nine months of his trial that he was able to be in the dock only for limited times on doctor's orders. At other times he appeared wilting and listless and paid no attention to the proceedings. I hope that we can avert a repetition of the social discontent and racial disharmony which follows acquittals in these cases.

Those who press for retribution through the trial of war crimes are after what they conceive to be justice and which is in fact punishment. When they do not bring about the punishment, they cannot be satisfied with the system; and they cannot be content that justice has been done.

I hope that circumstances will allow us to come out of this with honour and dignity. Next year we shall commemorate the 50th year after the ending of the war. No trials relating to events that took place over 50 years previously can possibly succeed under our system. Let us think of what the Canadian case imposed on all concerned. The noble Lord, Lord Shaughnessy, can tell your Lordships a great deal more about that case than I can. The jury listened to evidence for six months. Six months! Let us think of that jury then taking three months to consider their verdict: they came to a unanimous conclusion which led to acquittal. Then the balloon went up. It was very sad and it is still sad. They have not had another.

In Australia, the question arose of fitness to plead, when the accused in the first case shot himself in the chest and rendered himself incapable of going to trial. The question arose as to how long one waited for the accused to be fit to plead before going ahead. We do not realise what we are in for. I hope that wiser counsels will prevail. Let us get the emotion out of the issue now. It is a practical matter.

In Canada, 43 witnesses from eastern Europe had to be kept in Toronto for nine months while the case proceeded. There were six months of listening to testimony, with translations; the examination of witnesses had to be translated. How can that be a practical basis for a trial? In the Canadian case the defending counsel offered no defence and called no witnesses on the ground that he had no facilities for getting witnesses. The prosecution had all the opportunity and time that they cared to take to find witnesses; but the defence had no similar facilities in order to find evidence to the contrary. Let us pay attention to what noble Lords are saying in that direction.

7.11 p.m.

Lord Lester of Herne Hill: My Lords, unlike other noble Lords who have already spoken or who will speak in this debate, I was not a Member of your Lordships' House during the turbulent and painful passage of the War Crimes Bill. Therefore I may be the only Member of the House to speak on this subject for the first time. However, I have carefully read the remarkable, protracted and sometimes emotive debates. Like most noble Lords, I wish that the Bill had never been introduced, though I do not hold that view for the reasons given by many of its harshest critics.

I do not believe that the rule of law was violated by the coming into force of the War Crimes Act 1991. It gave jurisdiction to our courts to try offences of murder or manslaughter committed as war crimes in Germany or German-occupied territory during the Second World War. It did not change the law retrospectively to make someone liable to prosecution and punishment for an act which, when he did it, he had no reason to believe was a criminal act.

The cold-blooded and sadistic crimes covered by the Act were individual crimes of mass murder, as the noble Lord, Lord Merlyn-Rees, so forcefully reminded us. They flagrantly violated the laws and customs of war as well as of peace. What was done by the perpetrators was criminal according to the general principles of law recognised by all civilised nations, including pre-war Germany.

The 1991 Act removed immunity from prosecution for those war criminals who were not British citizens during the Holocaust and its bestial atrocities. But it did not take them by surprise as to the criminality of their horrific acts. The Act was therefore fully in accordance with the international human rights codes.

Nor do I believe that the fact that the Labour Government decided in 1948, with Sir Winston Churchill's support, not to proceed with war crimes trials in the British-occupied zone, in any way precluded Parliament from passing that Act giving jurisdiction to

[LORD LESTER OF HERNE HILL]
our courts. As the noble Lord, Lord Campbell of Croy, rightly observed, what was done in the late 1940s was and remains controversial. It has been powerfully criticised by writers such as Mr. Tom Bower, in his disturbing and dispiriting book *Blind Eye to Murder*. But what was done by the British Government (rather than Parliament) in that bleak Cold War era did not in any way decide that Nazi war criminals could obtain a safe and permanent haven from justice in this country by deceiving the Home Office and obtaining British citizenship.

Nor do I consider that the Act has authorised, still less required, unfair criminal trials. It did not create some newfangled procedure for Soviet-style or McCarthyite show trials. Rather, it included the public interest safeguard (in Section 1(3)) for the accused that cases can only come to trial with the consent of the Attorney General or, in Scotland, the Lord Advocate. That is an important safeguard in preventing miscarriages of justice. So is the even more vital safeguard of the independent judiciary in securing a fair trial by jury in accordance with the presumption of innocence, the rights of the accused and the stringent standards to which the noble Lord, Lord Houghton of Sowerby, referred.

The strongest argument made during the debates against the Bill was that it was futile because a fair trial would be very difficult to achieve for a man in his seventies, a half century after the alleged crime was committed. Such a trial would be unlikely to succeed and would be a daunting undertaking for the judge and jury as well as for the prosecution and defence.

I agree with that powerful objection. But another and more troubling reason for wishing that the Bill had never been introduced is that the controversy about its passage stirred that very light sleeper, antisemitism. It did so without contributing in a positive way to public education about the evil banalities of the Nazi atrocities and the lessons still to be learnt, especially at a time when ethnic and religious hatred and antisemitism again stalk across Europe.

In my view, the Bill and its passage revived terrible memories and nightmares. At times there seemed almost to be more concern in some quarters for septuagenarian war criminals than for the traumatic memories and feelings of the survivors who escaped them. Supporters of the Bill were accused, insensitively and unfairly, of harbouring feelings of revenge and retribution rather than the quality of mercy.

That was an exorbitant price to pay for enacting a statute that at best could not result in more than a handful of successful prosecutions. That is why I was firmly opposed to the original Bill and would have voted against it. But —I emphasise—that is past history.

So strong was the opposition in this House, led by the noble Lords, Lord Campbell of Alloway and Lord Houghton of Sowerby, and my noble friend Lord Mayhew, all of whom have spoken this evening, that the Government were compelled to invoke the Parliament Act to secure the Bill's passage. Those noble Lords should be content with their victory in forcing the Government to invoke the Parliament Act to give effect to the will of the democratically elected other place. It is regrettable that now, instead of leaving matters to take their course, they seek to stultify the Act altogether by preventing proceedings from being brought in the future and by empowering the Court of Appeal (Criminal Division) to stifle any pending prosecution at its birth. That is a wholly unnecessary power because paragraphs 6 and 11 of the Schedule to the 1991 Act give the Crown Court a specific power to dismiss a charge and quash an indictment if it appears to the judge that the evidence would not be sufficient for a jury properly to convict.

I am sorry to say that this Bill reopens the wounds inflicted during the passage of the 1991 Act three years ago. It seeks to override the Act just when police investigations are concluding and the responsible public authorities are deciding whether or not it is in the public interest to bring a prosecution against suspected war criminals.

Surely we should respect the will of Parliament, as expressed in the 1991 Act, and leave it to the prosecuting authorities, the law officers and the courts to decide whether anyone should now face trial. If the noble Lord presses his Bill further we will send a message to the world that this House is so concerned with the well-being of a handful of suspected war criminals living here that the House is prepared to attempt to take power away from those entrusted by Parliament with the task of reviewing the evidence, so painstakingly obtained, and from those entrusted by Parliament with deciding whether a prosecution is or is not in the public interest. That would suggest a curious scale of values and priorities. It would also imply, without any rational basis, that we in this House lack confidence in the prosecuting authorities and the law officers, and ultimately in our independent courts including the Lord Chief Justice, to pursue justice or not to pursue justice according to the law of the land. That is why I devoutly hope that the noble Lord, Lord Campbell of Alloway, will not proceed further with his unnecessary, divisive and untimely Bill.

7.20 p.m.

Lord Bridge of Harwich: My Lords, I have always thought that by far the gravest objection to the jurisdiction which the War Crimes Act conferred on the English courts was the near impossibility that anyone tried in the exercise of that jurisdiction could be guaranteed a fair trial. It was a near impossibility at the time when the Act went on the statute book. As the years pass the prospect of a fair trial becomes more and more remote.

The noble Lord, Lord Merlyn-Rees, spoke of miscarriages of justice. He spoke of the judiciary being under a cloud, which implies that he thinks those miscarriages were due to judicial incompetence. I hope he is wrong. I do not believe they were. I believe that the miscarriages of justice were due to the fallibility of the criminal justice system. Any criminal justice system must be fallible and regrettably will always remain so. I do not know how it can be made infallible. But however those miscarriages of justice occurred, they vividly brought home to us that an English jury, on apparently credible evidence, trying someone for a crime committed in recent times and in the familiar social environment of this country, can still be shown to have been wrong and to have caused a miscarriage of justice. To ask an English jury to try an old man of my generation for one of the gravest crimes in the calendar on the basis of evidence presumably given by witnesses of similar advanced age about events which occurred in eastern Europe in circumstances of great social upheaval is surely to invite a miscarriage of justice.

Before the Bill can reach the statute book, if ever it does, more than 50 years will have passed since the latest date when any of the crimes to which the 1991 Act is directed were committed, and that is a long enough limitation period for any crime, however serious. That is why I support the principle of Clause 1 of the Bill.

That said, of course I recognise the sincerity and understand the depth of feeling of those who take the view that the crimes to which the 1991 Act was directed were of such enormity that the attempt to bring the perpetrators to justice is one which can never properly be abandoned. They must presumably proceed on the basis that, even after so long a time, a fair trial is still theoretically possible. In one of the debates on the Bill which became the 1991 Act the noble Lord, Lord Mishcon, by virtue of a vivid exercise of his fertile imagination, gave an example of how such a case may arise. He envisaged my noble friend Lord Campbell of Alloway walking along Piccadilly and recognising someone with a peculiar scar on his face as being a guard at Colditz who had subsequently murdered a prisoner. When one imagines a case of that kind it is theoretically possible that there may still be a fair trial; but the theory is a remote one.

Even the most passionate advocate of continued prosecution must recognise that whether or not there can be a fair trial in a specific case must depend on the nature of the issues and the character of the evidence involved. When the Bill which became the 1991 Act was before the House for the second time, I urged the House, having opposed a Second Reading when it was before the House on the first occasion, to give it a Second Reading in the hope that the procedures involved could be amended and improved. But the House was not persuaded with the inevitable result that, under the Parliament Act, the Bill immediately received Royal Assent without amendment. If this Bill proceeds there will be an opportunity to enhance the procedure in ways I believe are necessary.

The 1991 Act does not spell out in terms that despite its retrospective character in one sense it is still open to the courts to exercise their jurisdiction to stay a prosecution on the grounds that the defence would be substantially prejudiced by delay or that delay would make a fair trial impossible. I understand the Government's position always to have been that the courts will have that power and now that they can look at *Hansard* perhaps that will cure the ambiguity. But in principle it is wrong that a statute should remain ambiguous on the basis that *Hansard* will cure the ambiguity. I hope that if this Bill proceeds it will be possible in Committee to introduce a suitable provision making it perfectly clear that the courts have that unfettered discretion.

When it comes to the exercise of the discretion, had the Bill in 1991 received a Second Reading, I was minded to table an amendment on the lines of the provision in Clause 2 of this Bill. To my mind there should be an appeal either way. An application to stay a prosecution on the ground of prejudice by delay comes before the single trial judge and, as the law stands at the moment, there is no appeal from his decision. In the special circumstances of a war crimes prosecution—so long as they can and do continue—it seems to me entirely right that the onerous responsibility of deciding on an application whether, in the circumstances of a specific case, there is such prejudice that the prosecution should be stayed or whether there cannot be a fair trial should not rest on the shoulders of a single judge. Any such decision is bound to be highly controversial and it is only right that the last word and the responsibility for taking the decision should rest on the shoulders of three judges in the Court of Appeal.

7.29 p.m.

Lord Beloff: My Lords, few noble Lords would disagree with me were I to say that Lords *Hansard* does not have a very wide circulation in the Balkans. But it might be the case that someone who had perpetrated crimes of equal horror, if not on the same scale, as those alleged against the people we are discussing might come across our debates and say, "Well, it's all right chaps. I have only to get to England and I will find a group of British aristocrats and lawyers who have devoted themselves to preventing the prosecution of war criminals". War crimes, as we now know—though not on the scale of those that have been alluded to by the noble Lord, Lord Merlyn-Rees—are a feature of our world, and although we cannot prevent them, it is not for us, by indulging them, to make them more likely.

People have talked about the changes that have occurred in the past few years since 1988, when the current movement which led to the 1991 Act began, in the circumstances of some of the individuals involved. But more important are the changes that have occurred in the countries where these crimes were perpetrated. In 1988 those countries were still part of the Soviet bloc. It was obviously very difficult for our investigators to be sure of receiving the co-operation of the local police and legal authorities which they would require in order to amass the evidence that they were looking for. Circumstances in those countries have changed. We now have governments which are eager to do what they can to enlist the support and sympathy of the West. That makes it possible—I am not in the confidence of those who are in charge of the investigations—that it will not simply be a question of whether one old man can identify another. There may well be written records which were certainly not available five or six years ago and, as we know, our outlook on the Soviet Union itself—these crimes occurred not in Russia but in places which were then part of the Soviet Union—has changed enormously. For instance, the Katyn massacre was long maintained to be a crime of the Germans but has now turned out not to be so. It therefore seems that we are

[LORD BELOFF]
entitled to look at whether or not this is a suitable thing to do in the light of the legislation which is on our statute book.

It is curious, because the argument has been exploded so often, that the noble Lord, Lord Mayhew, continues to insist that the agreement to cease war crimes trials in the British zone of occupation in Germany is binding on the British Parliament in relation to crimes which were not committed by Germans, nor in that territory. The decision, which was a perfectly understandable one, to end those war crimes trials was, as the noble Lord, Lord Campbell of Croy, reminded us, a part of handing over criminal jurisdiction to the burgeoning democratic courts of the new German federal republic. Indeed, to their credit, the German federal government have been from time to time prosecuting, and are still prosecuting, war crimes, where the criminals have been identified. Though they may have a different system of courts and prosecution, as is true of other continental countries, no one has so far suggested that there have been miscarriages of justice there or in the war crimes trials that have taken place in France. In other words, this is a matter which deeply affects Europe and ourselves. As the noble Lord, Lord Jakobovits, said, for many of us it is a matter of conscience.

I agree with the noble Lord, Lord Lester of Herne Hill, that there are problems in raising the issue of the motive of these appalling crimes. On the issue of anti-semitism, I am sure that it has had its effect, in the debates both in this country and in Canada and Australia, on the attitude to these crimes, but that surely is not something which we should take into account. It was wrong to massacre Jews in eastern Europe because they were Jews, just as it is wrong to massacre people in Bosnia because they are Moslems. The identity of the victims is not the important point. The important point is the motive and the conduct of the crimes.

Therefore, I can see no reason why we should, as this Bill would demand of us, suddenly intervene politically in a process which is proceeding, albeit slowly. No doubt the delays will limit the number of prosecutions and possibly the number of convictions. But I feel that it would be sending a signal to every neo-Nazi in Europe if the House of Lords was thought to be in any way acting so as to condone crimes which, as I say, have been repeated but never on the scale of those with which we are dealing.

7.35 p.m.

Lord Shaughnessy: My Lords, to support this Bill, sponsored by the noble Lord, Lord Campbell of Alloway, is not to condone in any way the hideous, almost unbelievable, atrocities that happened in Europe in the course of World War 2. The noble Lords, Lord Mayhew and Lord Campbell of Croy, had a similar experience to mine at the end of the conflict in 1945 and witnessed the liberation—at least the freeing—of the concentration camps in north west Europe. That horrifying experience will be ingrained in the minds of many other noble Lords—it certainly is in mine—and therefore the question of even contemplating the mitigation of such crimes is not a factor so far as I am concerned. I do not view this Bill in a technical sense as many other noble Lords have, but as an attempt to limit the whole process which was inaugurated with the War Crimes Act 1991. The biggest problem is the passage of time and the possibility of a fair trial after 50-odd years which have passed since any of these crimes may or may not have been committed.

There is no use repeating the problems of age, identification and the possibility of finding reliable witnesses either for the prosecution or the defence. That has all been discussed before. But if the process continues, the problem becomes bigger. Each month and year that passes the difficulties which face mounting a fair trial are increased.

The noble Lord, Lord Houghton of Sowerby, in what might have been considered as a trailer for my speech, referred to the experience under the Canadian War Crimes Act. I shall refer only to a couple of instances in order to give examples. The first prosecution was against a man called Imre Finta. As a constable under the Nazi regime, he was accused of sending a number of people to their deaths in a concentration camp. He was apprehended. I am not sure whether he was actually indicted, but after his arrest under the Canadian War Crimes Act, it was about two years before he came to trial. The whole process of assembling evidence and whatever else which had to transpire, took that long. He came to trial and in May 1990, shortly before the War Crimes Bill was debated for the first time in your Lordships' House, he was acquitted. Because of a technicality, the Crown in Canada was granted the right to appeal to a higher court. That process had gone on since May 1990. In March of this year the case reached the Supreme Court of Canada, which denied the appeal and at last Finta was discharged.

That is a very long time for a man who is now 82 years old, who has lost his business, his house, and who is now in reduced circumstances, to go through such a process. I raise this point because if that kind of thing were repeated under the War Crimes Act which we are now discussing—it probably would not because I believe that an acquittal cannot be appealed under the British criminal system—it would be a very severe curtailment of human rights and compares to the dreadful experience which people experienced under the Nazis during the war with whom we are concerned in this exercise.

No other prosecutions have been mounted under the Act in Canada. One man was charged but the proceedings were stayed because of his ill-health. He was 83 years of age. Three other prosecutions were mounted and in two of the cases they were stayed because a witness became ill and unfit to attend the trial although, if there is a recovery, the trial can be started again. In another prosecution the key witness died. In a further prosecution an application was made to take evidence in the former Soviet Union, but that was refused by the trial judge. There has been no success in any of these trials in Canada. I shall not dwell on that any more.

As some noble Lords may know, in Australia an investigation under the Special Investigation Unit of the Attorney-General's department has been set up to go into the whole question of their war crimes legislation. In its final report, which took four years to prepare and which cost 40 million Australian dollars, the conclusion was that the unit found that 16 members of the Belgrade special police unit were allegedly responsible for the arrest and torture of thousands of Nazi opponents, including 856 inmates who migrated to Australia. On the evidence gathered, the SIU found it insufficient to sustain charges even though investigators believed that suspects were likely or highly likely to have committed war crimes. The report states that the others were too old or infirm to go to trial. That is the Australian experience.

I do not wish to detain your Lordships much longer. If retribution has to be made, we have to think of some other method. The experience of other jurisdictions would indicate that proceeding as Parliament has decreed with this legislation, which I accept, may not be successful. We have had no prosecutions mounted so far although we have been told that there are a number of possibilities. I believe that it was Bacon who said,

"Revenge is a kind of wild justice, which the more man's nature runs to, the more ought the law to weed it out".

I have no proposals about how we should proceed. As I said, I think the Bill gives some hope that we can at least limit the continuing unpleasant legal situation that exists today. The noble Lord, Lord Jakobovits, quoted the Old Testament. The doctrine that is proposed in Exodus of,

"Eye for eye, tooth for tooth",

has little relevance in this context. If we proceed under the existing War Crimes Act without limitation, we shall be doing an injustice to a hapless group of suspects, probably toothless and failing in eyesight.

7.51 p.m.

Lord Archer of Sandwell: My Lords, like my noble friend Lord Merlyn-Rees, I have to declare an interest as an officer of the All-Party Group on War Crimes, and like the noble Lord, Lord Lester, I am speaking on this subject in your Lordships' House for the first time.

A number of threads have run through the debate. The first touches on the constitutional implications of the Bill. The effect of Clause 1 would be to disapply the War Crimes Act in respect of future prosecutions. Since we know as a fact that no prosecutions have been initiated under the Act—indeed, as I understand it, that was the very reason that the noble Lord, Lord Campbell, was induced to introduce the Bill—it would follow that, in effect, it would repeal the 1991 Act—

Lord Campbell of Alloway: My Lords—

Lord Archer of Sandwell: My Lords, if the noble Lord will forgive me for one moment, I believe that I can anticipate his point. If not, I shall certainly give way to him. The noble Lord asked us to remember that if the Bill is given a Second Reading and makes its way in due course onto the statute book, there will be a period of time—a window, as it were—in which the authorities can act. I understand that that was the reason that the noble Lord sought to intervene. I understand the noble Lord's desire that no time should be lost, but I am bound to say that I doubt whether it is conducive to justice to compel those concerned to initiate a prosecution by a specific cut-off point, to clear their desks by a specific stroke of the clock. I would be very concerned if that were the effect of what we have done.

Whatever the merits of the 1991 Act, it is on the statute book and it would be curious to seek to repeal it three years later, particularly in view of the overwhelming majority that it received in another place, unless there had been some material and unpredictable change of circumstance since it was passed. So I listened with great care to what the noble Lord said about how the situation had changed. The answer appears to be that when the Act was passed no one knew that by the end of 1994 no proceedings would have been initiated. I believe that there are two answers to that.

First, it was obvious then that investigations would take some time. Their very nature would involve some time-consuming inquiries and no one would have the authority to undertake them in the first place until the Act was on the statute book. Certainly, as the noble Lord, Lord Beloff, pointed out, the way in which the political situation would change was not then wholly predictable. That may have made some difference. However, no one then wanted to see prosecutions being initiated without proper consideration.

Secondly, it was clear in 1991 that even if some prosecutions had been initiated, not every prosecution would have been initiated within three years. Inevitably, some cases would still be outstanding in December 1994, and if it was then considered right to make provision which would necessarily have that effect, it now seems strange that it was not envisaged that prosecutions might run into 1995.

I turn now to the question of whether it is right to impose a time limit on any category of criminal prosecution. That proposal has never found favour in this country. There is something repugnant in the suggestion that if a criminal can by subterfuge or dissimulation contrive to remain undetected for a sufficient period of time, that should earn him exemption from paying the penalty for his crimes. That is an unattractive proposition when applied to any offence. It becomes less enticing with the seriousness of the offence. When it is sought to apply it to some of the most horrifying offences in history, it surely has few attractions. It was considered by the authors of the Hetherington-Chalmers Report, who rejected it on at least two grounds. First, in paragraph 9.19, they pointed out that it is not applied in the criminal law of this country. We would have to make specific provision for a specific category of case. They pointed out the recent example of a domestic murder that was committed 27 years before the trial. Secondly, in paragraphs 5.41 and 5.45, they pointed out that the United Nations, expressing the consensus of the civilised world, had agreed in 1968 on the Convention of the Non-applicability of Statutory Limits to War Crimes and Crimes against Humanity. In 1974 the Council of Europe took the same view in a similar convention. The Bill would fly in the face of that consensus.

What is not in dispute in this debate—it has been clear from virtually every contribution—is that in each case the court should be assiduous to ensure that no injustice arises from any delay and if, in consequence,

[LORD ARCHER OF SANDWELL]

there are no convictions, so be it. Where there is a doubt, clearly the benefit of the doubt should be accorded to the defendant. That is what the noble Lord appears to contemplate in Clause 2.

Whether there is a doubt depends on the facts of each individual case. As the noble and learned Lord, Lord Bridge, reminded us, it depends partly on the question at issue. In some cases, there may be an issue as to identity. Clearly, the court should have in mind that for any of us, alas, appearances change with the years. I am still surprised at how, encountering people I knew in my youth and have not seen for many years, I am frequently able to recognise them. I am sometimes flattered to discover that they recognise me. Of course, the judge should consider with the greatest care the guidance that was given in the case of *Turnbull* and warn the jury accordingly. Of course, a jury may be wrong. In considering any category of offence, the only way to ensure that a jury is never wrong is never to allow a jury to convict anyone. I have a great respect for British jurists and I am not unduly troubled on that score.

Something may turn on a witness's opportunity for recognising the defendant and on any reason that he may have had for paying particular regard to him. I once heard someone who had spent time in a concentration camp say, "If someone is peering into your face and you know that he has absolute power of life and death over you, you are not likely to forget his face".

However, not all war crimes' cases turn on the issue of identification. In many cases the defendant admits that he is the person in question; what he disputes are the acts imputed to him. Then the question may turn, as one of your Lordships indicated, on the authenticity of documentary evidence. We have good reason to know how meticulously the Nazis made and retained records even of their vilest crimes and how when they fell into the hands of Communist regimes, they were obsessively concerned to preserve them. The American courts have subjected such documents to the most scrupulous examination and have found them to be reliable. Of course, each case must turn on the issues and the nature of the evidence. No one would recommend any lapse in the usual standards.

This country undertook the exercise because there was a campaign by certain national groups in this country on behalf of those who had reason to anticipate that they might be accused of war crimes. It was a campaign to resist any extradition or deportation of those who might be accused. It was said in response to that campaign that, instead of returning them, the British Government proposed that they should be tried in this country. It would be curious indeed if, having rejected the other alternative, we then withdrew from this one. That would isolate us from the whole community of nations where the question has arisen, and it would occasion great hurt to the families of the victims.

My noble friend Lord Merlyn-Rees has already quoted what was said by the authors of the Hetherington-Chalmers Report on the point of whether crimes so monstrous should ever be forgotten. Perhaps I may quote something else of which they reminded us.

It was a quotation issued by President Roosevelt, Marshal Stalin and Mr. Churchill at the Moscow Declaration in 1943. They said:

"Let those who have hitherto not imbrued their hands with innocent blood beware lest they join the ranks of the guilty, for most assuredly the three Allied Powers will pursue them to the uttermost ends of the earth and will deliver them to their accusers in order that justice may be done".

That was said before many of the crimes were committed. I hope that we will not now resile from that obligation.

8.1 p.m.

Baroness Elles: My Lords, it is just about five years since the main debates on the Hetherington-Chalmers Report took place in this House and another place. They were sombre and impressive debates. Whatever view Members of either House took, and whichever way they voted, I think that it can be said, without any fear of contradiction, that every vote was cast while conscious of the great devastation and evil that was committed, and was in no way either for or against the Bill, or could be taken as condoning any of the acts that were committed and that we had debated.

I should like at this stage to welcome the presence of the noble Lord, Lord Lester of Herne Hill, and the noble and learned Lord, Lord Archer of Sandwell, who have joined in these debates, because they have contributed great legal knowledge. I should add modestly that I, too, am speaking for the first time, but do not pretend to add to the great legal knowledge which they are contributing to the debate. I did not speak previously because there were so many distinguished noble and learned Lords speaking in the debate of December 1989. It was not because I was not a Member of the House, and perhaps I should explain that.

It is evident that there will be many more Members of your Lordships' House, as compared with Members of another place, who will have had personal knowledge and experience of the effects of the appalling and evil deeds that were committed and about which we have been thinking tonight. We have had several examples of that. I insist on saying, as some people have said before, that old men forget. The issues through which we lived are never to be forgotten. I was a young WAAF officer at Bletchley during the war in the sector dealing with the German airforce. Of course I am still subject to the Official Secret Acts, but I can say that there were things that passed my desk which I shall never forget.

I went to Crete after the war and saw columns of names of people from the age of six to 76 who were killed by the occupying forces in retaliation. Those, again, are matters that remain indelibly on one's mind. There is no question of forgetting what happened. That is why I put the argument that the War Crimes Act which was passed—I accept that it was passed through the functioning of the Parliament Act—was a piece of legislation which was not necessary to remind us and the world at large of the atrocities and evils that were committed so long ago.

I have a cousin who at the time was a young medical student at the Middlesex Hospital. He, with about 100 others, volunteered to help the Army Medical Corp in

Germany to deal with health and other related problems. He found himself at Belsen having to clear up some of the appalling situations there. I see that my noble friend Lord Campbell of Croy is not in his place. I should like to tell him that those young medical students had to decide who was fit enough to be kept alive. Those for whom they did not have enough medicines they had to leave to die. Those are things which a young medical student does not forget. Of course the situation at Belsen was one of the most appalling.

To return to the Bill, I should like to support it. It limits the time within which these prosecutions can take place, but the memory of the acts and the record of horror —I repeat this—is not eliminated. My noble friend Lord Campbell of Alloway has argued fully and cogently for such a limitation to be imposed for these particular cases, and he has dealt with the legal and moral issues. I believe that I am right in saying, in reply to what my noble friend Lord Beloff said in a very moving speech, that no one would now be able to evade prosecution by coming to this country because of the Geneva Conventions Act 1957. So even if people in the Balkans were to read *Hansard*, we need not worry that they would be able to escape to this country to avoid prosecution.

Having dealt with those issues, and with so many other noble Lords having dealt with vital and crucial issues, I wish to deal with two or three practical matters. I believe that it is accepted that all the Scottish cases have been dealt with and withdrawn. According to the Answer given by my noble friend Lady Blatch in this House on 28th November, I understand that 233 of the total of 369 cases have been investigated fully and that the CPS has decided that they will not be proceeded with. Secondly, 15 of the 34 remaining cases are still to be investigated and nine are with the CPS. I have given my noble friend the Minister notice of this question: Has there been any common factor in the investigative reports of the 223 cases which have led the CPS to advise against prosecution and which would be likely or certain to apply to the remaining 24 cases? That is important when we consider the effects of the Bill. I ask that also because I noticed in her reply that there are three cases into which the investigations started only this year. That would be relevant to whether the proposed statute of limitation would apply to those cases and which might result in a prosecution.

My second point relates to costs. I realise that this is a delicate subject and that people may think that we should not be talking about finance when we are discussing the tragedies and evils that have been committed, but it is relevant to today. The cases, in which there has not been one prosecution, have cost over £5 million so far. Those of us who sometimes come into contact with the Metropolitan Police, as opposed to the Metropolitan Police War Crimes Unit, and who are so impressed with the valuable work that they do when dealing with crime on the streets and in people's houses know that they are short of financial resources. Is it therefore justifiable to spend that kind of money on these special cases in which most noble Lords have led me to believe that even one prosecution is unlikely.

Could not that £5 million be better spent by the police authorities in dealing with today's crimes and seeking to protect present and future victims of crime?

The CPS is heavily burdened in reading through the vast number of documents which result from the investigations. They have led it to advise the Attorney General that there should not be any prosecutions. Is it right that that service which is so often criticised—I must confess that I, too, have criticised it from time to time—for failing to be efficient and occasionally failing to be at court, should be burdened by this extra large and important task when the results are again going to be negative.

No one condones the acts that were committed. Nobody who lived during that period will ever forget them. I do not believe that anyone who hears the debates in your Lordships' House, or anywhere else, or who reads a newspaper will ever forget them. However, I believe that the funds and the people who are being made available to deal with the cases should be diverted to deal with today's problems and not left to deal with those of 50 years ago.

8.10 p.m.

Earl Attlee: My Lords, I echo the noble Baroness's final comments about the horror of these crimes. However, I am perhaps one of the youngest Members of your Lordships' House and I believe that we must bear in mind that the majority of any jury may be in the same position. They will not have been alive when these offences were supposed to have been committed.

Difficult moral and ethical questions are posed. I read the Second Reading debates of the original War Crimes Act in *Hansard*. I found them interesting but the content was heavy. The arguments against the War Crimes Act appeared to be stronger.

I have also listened to many Starred Questions in your Lordships' House and have been dismayed at the reluctance of the various Ministers to give an indication of the age of the youngest suspect. That cannot conceivably be due to a poor brief; it must be possible to anticipate such a simple and obvious question. Clearly, many suspects will be too old or too feeble to plead. Will the Minister say how old the youngest suspect is?

I support the noble Lord's Bill because I do not believe that anyone will be convicted or even prosecuted under the Act. I do not rely upon my own judgment but that of your Lordships' House when debating the original Bill.

8.12 p.m.

Lord Dacre of Glanton: My Lords, after the debates on the War Crimes Bill in 1991 I read in the press about those Peers who believed that time carried away guilt. I do not believe that anyone here today holds that view. We all agree that the crimes to which we are referring should be neither forgiven nor forgotten. They are unexampled in modern history and it is most important that we should remember them. Our generation will never forget them because they passed through our consciousness. But we want them to be remembered by later generations. If we are to achieve that we need an

[Lord Dacre of Glanton]
emphatic gesture. Several noble Lords have spoken as though these trials will be that gesture. I do not believe that. I believe that the trials will send an indistinct message. Perhaps they will never take place; as we know, none has taken place yet. Time is passing and perhaps none will take place.

I believe that a true history is the proper means of recording these horrible events. The true history is being constructed, I may say, to a large extent by the Germans themselves. When I say that the crimes should never be forgiven I refer to the authors of them and not their descendants who are guiltless in that respect. I should like the real record of this awful period to be in a correct and accurate history and not in muddled trials leading nowhere.

There are enemies of a true history. We all know about the historical revisionists in France, in America and in this country. There were none in Germany but perhaps the situation has changed. Such people wish to argue that these crimes did not take place. There are also well-meaning people who, through failure to understand their true nature and to distinguish between extermination camps and concentration camps, sometimes play into their hands. I wish to ensure that the historical record is clear and emphatic and that it is passed on to the next generation. I do not believe that the lesson will be conveyed by trials if, in fact, they ever take place.

The noble Lord, Lord Mayhew, has made many of the comments I intended to make. I take the liberty of emphasising one point. We heard about the trials which foundered in America, Canada and Australia. But the classic case is that of Ivan Demjenjuk. He was identified as Ivan the Terrible of Treblinka. Inquiries into the case began in 1975. The process dragged on. He was denaturalised in America in 1981 and after a further five years he was extradited to Israel. Two years after that he was sentenced to death. Three years later, in 1991, new evidence was produced which totally destroyed the case that had been based on the evidence of 13 Israeli witnesses. They saw him not on a television screen but face to face in Israel. They all swore, allegedly independently, that he was the man whom they knew. What is the use of people saying that if one has once looked into the eyes of an extermination camp guard or torturer one will recognise him wherever one sees him? Here were 13 Israeli subjects who had looked into the face of Ivan the Terrible in Treblinka and said that they recognised him. In fact, they had "recognised" a man who had never been in Treblinka in his life.

I do not believe that there will be any effective trial. By the time the evidence has been collected, the defence has had time to prepare its cases and the trials have been mounted, all such people will be dead. What will be gained? I do not believe that justice or even the monumental record which people want will be achieved. What will be left will be a fuzzy impression and, to a great extent, acquittal, as was said by the noble Lord, Lord Houghton of Sowerby.

The monument that I should like this generation to leave to the next generation, in order to show how thin is the crust of civilisation and how easily, if the rule of law, accepted morality and international order are allowed to lapse, the beast in man can emerge, will not result from the kind of justice that well-meaning people are seeking through trials which will not be effective. The trials may achieve condemnation but they will not leave an effective impression on the next generation. That is what really matters. We need to make an emphatic gesture which will last and make an impression. We do not want a muddle such as will emerge from the trials which are envisaged.

Noble Lords have referred to previous debates in this House and the other place and have said that Parliament voted by an overwhelming majority in favour of the Bill. The noble Lord, Lord Jakobovits, said that, as did other noble Lords. But this House is part of Parliament and this House voted the other way by a substantial majority. Therefore, Parliament did not vote in favour of it by a substantial majority. The House of Commons did but that is only half of Parliament, whatever the respective powers conferred by the constitution. We know that votes in the other place are subject to more discipline and are less independent than they are in this House. That is the message I should like to leave. I support the Bill of my noble friend Lord Campbell of Alloway.

8.20 p.m.

Lady Saltoun of Abernethy: My Lords, like other noble Lords, I have never questioned the heinousness of the crimes, the perpetrators of which the War Crimes Bill was designed to bring to trial. I have never questioned that they took place because on the morning after the press got into Belsen, I saw the newspapers before my parents could hide them from me.

Having said that, I support the Bill. There is very little that I can add to what the noble Lords, Lord Campbell of Alloway, Lord Mayhew, Lord Houghton of Sowerby, Lord Dacre of Glanton, Lord Shaughnessy and the noble and learned Lord, Lord Bridge of Harwich, have said. I support it because I believe that it is very doubtful, after the passage of so much time, whether it is possible for any of the suspects to receive a fair trial.

If we had a statute of limitation in this country we should not be discussing this matter now. I do not know why we do not have that. It may be because Article 4 of the Magna Carta says that justice should not be prolonged, meaning postponed. Since we disregard that, perhaps we should consider introducing a statute of limitation in this country for murder cases. Meanwhile, Clause 1 would provide such a statute in this particular context.

Clause 2 introduces one of the most sensible and practical procedures of the Scottish judicial system in the context of prosecutions under the War Crimes Act. I wonder whether those procedures could not be adopted usefully in England as a general rule.

8.23 p.m.

Lord Cochrane of Cults: My Lords, I am grateful to my noble friend Lord Campbell of Alloway for introducing this Bill. It seeks to rectify a situation which he has described in detail, all the problems which it engenders, and the injustices that it may cause. It is doubtless causing anxiety among many people who, as matters stand at present, are innocent and elderly. I do not know whether or not they are innocent but I do know that when I first spoke in your Lordships' House in April 1991 I found it a terrifying experience. I spoke on this subject for the first time in your Lordships' House after the noble and learned Lord, Lord Shawcross. The House was packed, unlike now, and I did not know whether I should be able to cope with a problem of this complexity in the presence of so many experts.

But with the passage of years—and how the years have gone by—the difficulties which I tried to address then about ensuring a fair trial have not diminished. The problem remains intractable and I can see no solution.

In replying to my noble friend on 28th November, my noble friend Lady Blatch said, quite correctly, that there is no limit on the time which needs to elapse before a charge of homicide or murder can be laid. As I see it, that is perfectly true. But what was not said was that it derives from common law and I believe that common law never assumed that anybody would try to lay a charge some 55 years or thereabouts after the events are alleged to have taken place. There is no doubt that a great many of those crimes did take place. But the passage of time is a great impediment.

Perhaps I may remind my noble friend Lady Blatch of another circumstance for which the law made no provision—the opening of shops on a Sunday in Scotland. That was never considered necessary but, with the passage of time, shops opened in Scotland. It was not provided for earlier because it was deemed to be unthinkable. I believe that the same applies to the laying of charges of murder or homicide after very many years. That is why I do not find that particular argument very convincing.

On the last occasion on which this matter was debated, my noble and learned friend Lord Hailsham of Saint Marylebone said that he knew of no case where a charge of murder had been preferred after 27 years. Earlier today I had an opportunity to speak to the noble and learned Lord, who confirmed that as far as he knew—with the qualification that he had not researched it in detail but nobody had complained in the interval— 27 years still remained a fair answer.

We are a long way from 1st September 1939. Unlike the noble Lord to whom I was speaking at dinner, on 1st September 1939 I was 12 years, 11 months and one week old. I can remember it. But because of that distance of time there are problems of identification: whether the chap was there, if it happened, and whether he did it.

That was brought to my mind the other day at a dinner given for the former pupils of the prep school which I attended. The first year that was truly represented was 1935 and there were four of us. I had not seen three of them since 1939, as far as I can tell within the limits of evidence and recollection. I did not recognise them and, indeed, I hardly recognised their names until they added a few supporting details. One of the four I had seen once. It is an awfully long time ago. Okay, we were young then and we have matured. If people want to know how I have matured, they can look at my picture in *Dod's*, which was taken in 1957. It is the best one that I have. Again, a chap may confess and say, "Yes, of course I did it", but has he gone dotty, has it been screwed out of him, or does he want to get his name in the *Sun*? I do not know.

On the day to which I alluded earlier noble and learned Lords remarked, as they have again this evening, on the retrospective enlargement of the jurisdiction. Is that right? I do not think that it is. If we count back, we are now some 55 years from September 1939. Let us go back, those of us who were alive then. I made this argument in my maiden speech and it attracted a modest degree of approbation and I hope that I shall be equally favoured tonight. We can perhaps go back to 1884, the year after my father was born. I looked it up and saw that, in February of that year, General Gordon was sent to the Sudan. In November the Mahdi occupied Omdurman. The annual Army Act was passed which set the billeting allowance for an ordinary soldier at tuppence halfpenny.

I am now convinced, as other noble Lords and other noble and learned Lords have said, that it is time to leave the problem alone. All that can be said has been said. For my part, I believe that it is now time to leave this awful affair for judgment by a greater power than ourselves, as we in time will face in death.

8.30 p.m.

Lord Hylton: My Lords, the noble Lord, Lord Mayhew, and the noble Lord, Lord Dacre of Glanton, both referred to the case of Mr. John Demjanjuk. It so happened that I found myself in January 1992 having breakfast in a hotel in Jerusalem with his American defence counsel. At that time, Mr. Demjanjuk had been convicted in a show trial in Israel of being, as has been mentioned, Ivan the Terrible, a Nazi concentration camp guard in the Ukraine. I am glad to say that that man was later cleared on appeal in Israel. It turned out to have been a case of mistaken identity.

I also happen to have been in contact with members of the groups known as the Birmingham Six, the Guildford Four and the Ulster Defence Regiment Four. The first two cases were heard before juries in England, while the third case was heard before a judge alone in Northern Ireland. All three of them were severe, serious cases of miscarriage of justice. They just go to show that, even in the most esteemed systems of justice, things can go wrong. Indeed, they can even go wrong when the cases are recent and are being tried relatively soon after the events in question.

In my view, there should be a worldwide period of limitation on the prosecution of serious crimes, including murder and genocide. I would suggest a period of 30 years. After all, that is the equivalent of one whole generation. To adopt such a period would be to follow the good precedent set by Belgium.

I trust that the Bill will receive a Second Reading. I support it at the same time as supporting the prosecution of recent war criminals for offences committed in such countries as Croatia and Bosnia. As a layman, I support

[LORD HYLTON]
the noble Lord, Lord Campbell of Alloway, because I cannot see how anyone in the circumstances that we are discussing can get a fair trial after 50 years.

8.33 p.m.

Lord Gridley: My Lords, I have not come to your Lordships' House today to be critical of the Government's actions in pursuing those who, in their opinion, were responsible for war crimes. However, I hope to be constructive and I am critical of the delay that has occurred in that operation. Looking back over that period, it seems to me that, basically, the Second World War was about preserving territorial boundaries, the preservation of people when under attack and the preservation of the freedom of those who were suffering in that respect. We also went to war 65 years ago to rid the world of Hitler's Germany and the brutal power wielded by his secret police over the European territories invaded, conquered and occupied by the Germans.

I speak with an interest in the matter because as an hereditary Peer one Christmas I was looked after by Tenno Heika the Emperor of Japan when I was interned in Changi Goal. He sent us some of his excellent brandy. Unfortunately some of us were suffering from sores due to malnutrition, so it was handed to our doctors to use to treat us.

In tonight's debate we have not considered whether it would be normal for people who are active, or those who are rather slow in pursuing obtaining evidence, to bring a suitable case against people in Scotland or Britain which would be evidence of past action during the war.

Also of relevance is the fact that one must realise that the secret police operated in Hitler's Germany. His so-called method of government was to use secret police in his own territory. When he occupied the territories of northern Europe, he brought those individuals with him. The peoples of occupied Europe suffered from the action taken by him in those territories, which lasted for six years until we had our victory.

When victory came I was amazed to find that those in occupation had used that kind of government in a country. Many people were in dire disorganisation; they were accusing one another of giving evidence against each other. Indeed, there existed grave disorganisation generally.

It seems to me that the only way we can get some evidence—that is, if it is obtainable and reliable after 50 years—would be from those who had suffered. That is where the evidence would be. It would be extremely difficult to get it.

I am not privy to what is going on in Scotland or to the difficulty that people are finding there. However, generally it is very unwise or very unusual for the British to be slow in bringing charges against such people after a lapse of many years. I do not think that they would stand for it. I do not believe that it is acceptable in any court of law in Britain to delay such an action against a person who has to be tried. The evidence must be brought against that person. Then he is either cleared and goes free, or he is sentenced for what he has done.

I wrote a great deal about what I was going to say. However, I have tried to meet the spirit of what has been said this evening. Some of the speeches have been quite brilliant. I do not feel capable of arguing the matter from the legal aspect. I can simply speak from my experience of those things about which I have felt so strongly since I have been back in this country. I see the wonderful things that are done or that people try to do and how we carry out our affairs generally—except, of course, what happens in the press. It is a fact that this is a fair place to be.

I remember when the victory came, I went outside and Mountbatten was there in all the glory of his naval uniform. A great load left my mind. There is nothing more terrible than to be defeated, to lose one's freedom and not to know what on earth will happen to get one out of the situation. How different at a time of victory! I am eternally grateful for the way in which we were rescued and for the action that this great country took in bringing that about. I only hope that the debate this evening, which I think and hope will be useful to the Government, will enable them to make things move faster than they are at present.

I praise my noble friend Lord Campbell of Alloway for having brought this matter to our attention again. I warmly support what he has said. I think that we must make some effort to take a decision on this matter and either convict people of crimes which they have committed or let them go free. That is the way that Britain carries out its affairs. I warmly hope, with all my heart, that we will adopt that course.

8.40 p.m.

Lord Belhaven and Stenton: My Lords, in supporting my noble friend Lord Campbell of Alloway, I should like first to say, as other noble Lords have said, that I have no wish to detract in any way from the wickedness of the crimes which we are discussing. I wish that the perpetrators had been caught quite a long time ago; but as many noble Lords have said, "caught" is the relevant word here.

In the 16th century I believe that it was a custom occasionally to dig up corpses and to try them. I suggest that if we keep this up much longer that is what we may have to do in this country. But, seriously, I ask how many more years will have to pass before we bury this matter and take more note of what is happening now in many parts of the world. However, if we must go back 50, 60 or 70 years we will find that Germany was not the only European country to practise mass terrorism. Lenin is quoted—at a period before the events in Germany—as having said,

"Do you imagine that the victory can be ours without the most extreme revolutionary terror"?

Terror there was. And after Lenin, it got worse and worse.

It is astonishing to me, and perhaps to other noble Lords, that in the course of these investigations we are discussing —I apologise if I am wrong—the help of the KGB was enlisted. The KGB, as your Lordships well know, is exactly the same organisation as the NKVD, Cheka, OGPU and many other acronyms, but it is one still-existing organisation. I have to say that one might as well, had things turned out otherwise, have enlisted the help of the Gestapo in the investigation of Soviet crimes.

The Hetherington Report gives a brief account of the activities of the NKVD in 1939-40 in the Baltic states and eastern Poland. The full horror of these activities stretches the imagination of those of us who have lived under civilised regimes. I would tell your Lordships in this context that my Polish mother-in-law, having seen her father and many others murdered by the NKVD, fled to the German occupied area of Poland as she thought it was safer than the Russian occupied area. It was not exactly a good area to go to but it was the best thing she could find. That gives one an idea of what it was like in the Soviet occupied area.

My point is this: at that time, crimes were committed by the German and Soviet authorities which beggar belief. Every day nowadays in the Ukraine and other areas of the former Soviet Union more evidence of atrocious Soviet crimes is coming to light. The mass graves at Katyn of Polish soldiers are by no means unique, and evidence of mass murder is being dug up everywhere. Yet no one has suggested that ex-members of the NKVD should be investigated. Some may be living here but not a finger has been lifted against them. Their crimes were as bad or worse as those of others, but they were on the winning side. Soviet judges actually sat on the Nuremberg tribunal. Perhaps they knew something about war crimes.

We would do far better to pay more attention to what is happening in the world today. On Monday the noble Earl, Lord Winchilsea, asked an Unstarred Question on Moroccan atrocities in the Western Sahara. This year appalling atrocities continue to be committed by countries most of which are members of the United Nations. There is Tibet, Rwanda, Bosnia and East Timor to mention but a few. There is a long list. It is nearly 50 years ago since the Gestapo and SS committed their last crimes. The perpetrators are old and almost impossible to identify. I believe we ought now to leave the judgment to Almighty God.

8.45 p.m.

Lord McIntosh of Haringey: My Lords, as in all debates on Private Members' Bills I should make it clear that the Opposition does not have a collective view and that I speak for myself personally.

What is curious about this debate is that although noble Lords have come to very different conclusions, they are really not in disagreement about the fundamental facts behind the issue. No one disagrees with our recognition of the horror of war crimes, particularly not the noble Lord, Lord Belhaven and Stenton, who wishes to extend the discussion beyond German war crimes. He is quite right to do that; but we are talking about German war crimes, and no one believes that the horror of those crimes should go unrecognised in any way.

I do not believe that anyone is departing from the principle that crimes of this sort should, if possible, in principle be pursued indefinitely, and from the principle that there should be no statute of limitations for crimes of this kind. If convictions can be achieved, the law should make that possible. That is why I believe that the War Crimes Act 1991 was thought to be unwise by a number of people—I am not talking about this House—but it was not thought to be wrong in principle. It was not thought to be wrong in principle to pursue war crimes. At the same time, I sense, even among those who support the War Crimes Act with most conviction, that they feel there will not be any convictions arising from it. That is certainly my view. I believe we are embarking on this exercise because we believe it is right to do so and not because we think that anyone will be convicted, and certainly not from any view that it is desirable to put someone aged 80 in prison for a period of, in theory, 25 years, or whatever length the life sentence may be in their case. Therefore we are not looking at the results; we are looking at the principle behind pursuing war crimes indefinitely.

I have to say that in those circumstances, with those options, I opt for pursuing the principle that we do not impose a statute of limitations on war crimes which we would not impose on any other crime. I support the view that the War Crimes Act 1991, however imprudent it may be in judicial terms, ought not to be overturned. Let us be clear that the Bill of the noble Lord, Lord Campbell of Alloway, would overturn the War Crimes Act. If it were carried, there would be no War Crimes Act.

I now turn to my final argument for disagreeing personally with this Bill, and for wishing that Clause 1, certainly, should not succeed. I have no legal expertise to enable me to assess the virtues of Clause 2 of the Bill. My final argument is as it was when I voted for the War Crimes Bill in 1991, and in the previous Session. This Bill was carried by an overwhelming majority on a free vote in the elected Chamber and I do not think it would be right for us to seek to overturn it now by a Private Member's Bill.

8.49 p.m.

Baroness Blatch: My Lords, my noble friend Lord Campbell will know from the Answer I gave to his Question on 28th November 1994 (at col. 473 of *Hansard*) that his Bill raises a most important point; indeed a fundamental question of principle. The title of the Bill explains that a purpose of the proposed legislation is to place a time bar on the institution of proceedings under the War Crimes Act 1991. The 1991 Act, as noble Lords will recall from the lengthy and detailed debates in Parliament during the passage of that legislation, is about acts of murder, manslaughter, or, in Scotland, culpable homicide which were committed as war crimes in Europe during the Second World War. Such offences are of the gravest kind it is possible to imagine. That, as the noble Lord, Lord McIntosh, said, is agreed all over the House, whatever side of the debate noble Lords are on. We do not have a time bar in the United Kingdom on bringing charges for murder, manslaughter or culpable homicide and that applies

[BARONESS BLATCH]
irrespective of the circumstances in which such acts are committed. Clearly, therefore, the proposal in the Bill now before us—that, in effect, an exception should be made for such acts committed as violations of the laws and customs of war—requires more than usually careful attention.

Before I go to the detail of the Bill, I do not think that it will come amiss if I remind noble Lords briefly of the background to the War Crimes Act and of the Government's policy on war crimes in relation to the Act. Just over five years ago, the Report of the War Crimes Inquiry (Cm 744) was presented to Parliament. That inquiry was conducted by Sir Thomas Hetherington and Mr. William Chalmers at the request of my right honourable friend the then Home Secretary. The inquiry had been appointed following allegations that persons now living in the United Kingdom committed war crimes during the Second World War. The inquiry was asked, among other things, to obtain and examine relevant material relating to the allegations and to consider, in the light of the likely probative value in court proceedings of the relevant documentary material and the evidence of potential witnesses, whether the law of the United Kingdom should be amended in order to make it possible to prosecute such persons for war crimes.

The inquiry recommended that our courts should indeed be given jurisdiction over such crimes and that consideration should be given to the investigation of a number of cases and to possible prosecutions. The report of the inquiry was published in June 1989 and recommended action as soon as possible. Soon after, in March 1990, the Government introduced into Parliament the War Crimes Bill, now the War Crimes Act.

The Bill proposed, in line with the recommendations of the inquiry, that our courts should be given jurisdiction over murder, manslaughter and culpable homicide committed as violations of the laws and customs of war during the Second World War in Germany or German-held territory by people who are now British citizens or resident in the United Kingdom, the Channel Islands or the Isle of Man.

The Act makes clear that such people may include those who were not British at the material time. I emphasise this because our courts already had jurisdiction over murder, manslaughter and culpable homicide committed abroad by British nationals, by virtue of Section 9 of the Offences Against the Person Act 1861 and Section 6(1) of the Criminal Procedure (Scotland) Act 1975, which was a consolidating statute incorporating the corresponding provision in Section 29 of the Criminal Justice (Scotland) Act 1949. Indeed, our courts already had jurisdiction over grave breaches of the 1949 Geneva Conventions, including wilful killing and torture, wherever in the world the offence was committed and whatever the nationality of the offender, by virtue of the Geneva Conventions Act 1957. But that Act did not apply to grave breaches committed before its enactment.

I should also emphasise that the War Crimes Act did not create any new offences. Violations of the laws and customs of war have long been criminal according to the general principles of law recognised by this country and all other members of the community of civilised nations. What the Act did was to make it possible to proceed against people who, at the time of the alleged war crimes, did not have British nationality and who would, therefore, have escaped liability for prosecution before the Act came into force.

The Bill was approved in another place on a free vote by a large majority—to be precise, by 273 votes to 60. Noble Lords will recall that the Bill was then denied a Second Reading in this House, in June 1990, by 207 votes to 74. The Government then reintroduced the Bill in identical form in another place in March 1991, where it was again approved on a free vote, and again by a large majority—by 254 votes to 88. It was subsequently denied once more a Second Reading by noble Lords, in April 1991, by 131 votes to 109. The Bill was enacted in May 1991 through operation of the Parliament Acts 1911 and 1949.

These details of the passage of the Act make clear that the legislation aroused strong feelings and passions—all of which have been illustrated again today. But the War Crimes Act is now law. The police and the prosecuting authorities do, therefore, have a clear remit and clear responsibilities to investigate and prosecute, as appropriate, where there is information that people now living in the United Kingdom committed war crimes in Europe during World War II. The Government stand fully behind the principle of the Act. The Government's declared policy is that those who committed most terrible crimes in Nazi-occupied Europe during the Second World War should not be able to use the privilege of residence in the United Kingdom to escape justice.

I should make clear that the Hetherington-Chalmers Inquiry was just that—an inquiry. It was not a criminal investigation. Investigations with a view to possible prosecutions were not necessarily appropriate or possible until the Act came into force. It came into effect on Royal Assent in May 1991. Investigations began later that month and it was understandable that the police and the prosecuting authorities should have wanted to proceed without delay. They had a formidable task ahead of them. The report of the Hetherington-Chalmers Inquiry included recommendations that investigations be undertaken in no less than 124 cases known to the inquiry team and, both before and after the coming into force of the Act, further information was received. The Government accordingly ensured that the police were resourced to undertake the necessary investigations. These were thought likely to take some time, not only because inquiries had in some cases to be made far away in unfamiliar territory, such as in parts of the former Soviet Union, but also because the events to be investigated took place a long time ago. But there was a clear expectation when the Act came into effect that information that war crimes had been committed should be acted on. As I said in response to my noble friend's Question on 28th November, there is no statutory time bar for laying charges of murder, manslaughter or culpable homicide in the United Kingdom and this applies no less where such acts are committed as war crimes.

Since May 1991, the Metropolitan Police War Crimes Unit has investigated 369 cases in England and Wales. Of these, a further 112 people who were investigated are now dead. Further to my Answer last week to my noble friend Lord Campbell of Alloway, I understand that 23 people are now being investigated, of whom nine are being considered for prosecution by the Crown Prosecution Service. That leaves 234 cases which have been dropped.

There are no investigations at present in Scotland or Northern Ireland. I cannot, of course, say what decisions will be taken regarding prosecutions or when decisions will be reached. Such matters are for the independent consideration of the Director of Public Prosecutions and the Attorney-General. But the figures clearly show that substantial progress has been made with the investigations.

It is against that background that I turn to the detail of the Bill put forward by my noble friend, Lord Campbell of Alloway. The Bill has two substantive clauses. The first clause provides that no prosecutions shall be instituted for offences in relation to the War Crimes Act 1991 with effect from the coming into force of the Bill, if enacted. Such a provision, if it were passed into law, would render the War Crimes Act ineffective. The clause would be tantamount to repeal of the 1991 Act and would, therefore, mean that people who did not have British nationality at the material time would again be immune from prosecution.

Parliament did not intend at the time the War Crimes Act was enacted that the police and prosecuting authorities should have a prescribed period of time in which to undertake investigations into war crimes and bring charges as appropriate. That point was well made by the noble and learned Lord, Lord Archer. The police and prosecuting authorities were enabled to see their work through to a conclusion, and, as I said, they have already made substantial progress.

But in the context of Clause 1, I must return again to the point of principle to which I have already alluded. I question whether Parliament would ever wish seriously to contemplate a time bar on institution of proceedings for such serious offences as murder, manslaughter and culpable homicide. To do so would be viewed with the utmost concern and alarm. Clause 1 of the Bill does not, of course, propose introduction of a time bar for such acts generally but is nonetheless dangerous in that its effect would be to make an exception for people who did not have British nationality and committed uniquely horrible acts against humanity in Nazi-occupied Europe.

Clause 2 of my noble friend's Bill would confer jurisdiction on the Criminal Division of the Court of Appeal to consider appeals against refusals by the Crown Court to dismiss charges, on grounds of delay or abuse of process, by persons indicted for crimes by virtue of the War Crimes Act 1991. The function of the Criminal Division of the Court of Appeal is to hear appeals against convictions after trial. It is not to determine questions of jurisdiction during trial. That is not to say that where a person has been indicted, whether or not on charges in relation to the 1991 Act, he cannot challenge the indictment. He can, by applying for the proceedings to be stayed on the ground of abuse of process, including delay. If such an application were refused, there would be the opportunity to seek judicial review of that decision in the High Court. Like Clause 1, therefore, Clause 2 proposes that in war crimes matters we depart from general criminal law and procedure. Both clauses, therefore, if enacted, would set precedents whose effects would be far-reaching.

My noble friend Lord Campbell said that he aimed, through Clause 2, to put England and Wales on a par with Scotland. But I have to say to him that the different legal systems make such comparisons rather misleading. In particular, Scotland does not have the same system of judicial review as we have in this country.

I think I can fairly say that this Bill is not necessary to remove any possible injustice which might be thought to arise from operation of the War Crimes Act 1991. A prosecution will not be brought on a bare prima facie case. Rather, the test will be whether there is a realistic prospect of conviction. Furthermore, proceedings by virtue of the War Crimes Act may be instituted in this country only with the consent of the Attorney-General. If proceedings are instituted, then, as I explained, the Crown Court has inherent jurisdiction to stay those proceedings on grounds of abuse of process, including delay. But we have to think also of the enormity of war crimes and of those who suffered at the hands of the perpetrators of such crimes. The passage of time and the difficulties in investigating these crimes do not diminish the wrong that was done nor the need, now that the 1991 Act has been enacted, to investigate the evidence as in any other case of murder or manslaughter.

My noble friend Lord Dacre challenged claims that Parliament had agreed. Each time I mentioned the War Crimes Act I referred to it as having been passed by Parliament. It is, of course, true that the House of Commons voted overwhelmingly for it, as I said. But the Parliament Act is a proper part of our process. It was invoked and was accepted, and that ought to be an end to it. I believe that technically one can state that Parliament has had its say.

The question was also asked: could not the money be better spent or put to better use? I have to refer to the overwhelming commitment by the House of Commons and the invoking of the Parliament Act, including the provision of the necessary money for the war crimes legislation. The question of costs in bringing criminal procedures has to be weighed against the gravity of the offences alleged. There can be few, if any, graver allegations than those being dealt with under the War Crimes Act.

The protracted and complicated nature of the inquiry was known to Parliament when the Act was passed. It was also recognised that officers would have to visit scenes of crimes and witnesses in many different countries. It was known that it would be expensive and all matters were reflected in the budget that was set at that time. The same considerations apply to the Crown Prosecution Service which, of course, is the responsibility of my right honourable friend the Attorney-General.

[BARONESS BLATCH]

The noble Earl, Lord Attlee asked whether I could tell him the age of the youngest person under investigation. I am afraid that I am not able to give him that information but I shall write to him if it should become available to me.

My noble friend Lady Elles asked whether there was any common reason for decisions not to prosecute. There are no common reasons for decisions not to prosecute which can be identified. In some cases, there was a lack of credible eye-witness evidence of the alleged crimes; in others, no allegation of murder or manslaughter was made. In some cases, death has intervened. Each case currently under investigation will be considered on its merits.

This is a Private Member's Bill and the Government would not therefore propose to vote against it. But, as I have explained, the provisions of the Bill would have profound implications which the Government do not feel able to accept.

Lord Bridge of Harwich: My Lords, before the noble Baroness sits down, may I ask her one question on a matter of procedure? If I heard her rightly, she said that a decision of a trial judge in a Crown Court is subject to judicial review. My understanding is that that was the law, as pronounced by the divisional court, until the recent decision of your Lordships' House in its judicial capacity to which I was a party and in which we overruled that decision. Unless our decision has in turn been departed from, the present law, as I understand it, is that a decision on an application to stay a prosecution on the grounds of delay or abuse of process is not open to judicial review in the Crown Court. It was for that reason that I gave such wholehearted support to my noble friend's Clause 2, so that the ultimate responsibility for such a decision should rest with three judges and not with one.

Baroness Blatch: My Lords, I am incredibly diffident about taking on the noble and learned Lord, Lord Bridge, on the matter. My understanding is that the judicial review process applied. I shall, of course, write to the noble and learned Lord and make my reply available to the House when I have taken proper technical advice on the matter.

9.7 p.m.

Lord Campbell of Alloway: My Lords, this has been a good-natured, balanced debate on a very serious subject. At this hour of night I believe all noble Lords would agree that it is appropriate that I should thank all those who spoke for and against Clause 1—even the noble Lord, Lord Lester of Herne Hill, who perhaps when he reads the *Official Report* tomorrow may think that he went a bit over the top.

My heart bleeds for my noble friend the Minister, because the Home Office did not do its homework properly on Clause 2. Anyway, she could not have answered many of the arguments in my speech because obviously her brief was written before the speech was made.

All that having been said, we come to the point that there has been a balanced debate on Clause 1, and nobody has spoken against Clause 2. The two are not mutually dependent. They require separate consideration. I commend this Bill to the House.

On Question, Bill read a second time and committed to a Committee of the Whole House.

> House adjourned at nine minutes past nine o'clock.

Written Answers

Wednesday 7th December 1994

OVERSEAS AID TARGET

Lord Redesdale asked Her Majesty's Government:

Whether, in view of the United Kingdom's increasing commitments to the European Union aid budget and in the light of the freeze in the United Kingdom aid budget for the next three years in real terms, they continue to support the United Nations target of 0.7 per cent. of GNP for overseas aid; and, if so, when they will set a timetable to achieve that target.

The Minister of State, Foreign and Commonwealth Office (Baroness Chalker of Wallasey): We have agreed to reach the UN aid/GNP target as soon as possible, but are not prepared to set a timetable for reaching it. The increased funding for the aid programme announced by my right honourable friend the Chancellor of the Exchequer on 29 November demonstrates our commitment to a substantial aid budget.

NORTHERN IRAQ: POVERTY RELIEF

Lord Avebury asked Her Majesty's Government:

What action they have taken on the findings in the report *Targeting Basic Assistance in Northern Iraq; Findings from a Household Expenditure Survey,* which they commissioned, and in particular on the fall in living standards suffered by the population as a whole, and the chronic energy deficiency shown by 12 per cent. of the female population.

Baroness Chalker of Wallasey: We received the report in September. Since then we have agreed to provide £365,000 to Save the Children Fund for a further village rehabilitation project, which includes special measures for assisting female-headed households, and for a pilot income-generation project for very poor urban households, many of which are headed by women. We have distributed the report widely to other aid agencies, in particular the UN agencies, who have welcomed it as a basis for targeting food aid and other assistance.

KENYA: ASYLUM APPLICATIONS

Lord Avebury asked Her Majesty's Government:

Whether, during his conversation with President Moi of Kenya on 15 November, the Prime Minister raised the increase in the number of applications for asylum from citizens of Kenya, and the reasons why this has occurred.

Baroness Chalker of Wallasey: My right honourable friend the Prime Minister did not raise this matter with President Moi during his conversation with him on 15 November.

HUMAN RIGHTS TREATIES: DUTY OF COMPLIANCE

Lord Lester of Herne Hill asked Her Majesty's Government:

Whether they consider that Ministers and civil servants, in discharging their public functions, have a duty to comply with the European Convention on Human Rights and the International Covenant on Civil and Political Rights.

Baroness Chalker of Wallasey: International treaties are binding on states and not on individuals. The United Kingdom is party to both treaties and it must comply with its obligations under them. In so far as acts of Ministers and civil servants in the discharge of their public functions constitute acts which engage the responsibility of the United Kingdom, they must comply with the terms of the treaties.

NUCLEAR WEAPONS: INTERNATIONAL LAW

Lord Jenkins of Putney asked Her Majesty's Government:

Whether the use or threatened use or possession and deployment of nuclear weapons is illegal under international law.

Baroness Chalker of Wallasey: Many states have accepted international obligations not to possess nuclear weapons (for example, by becoming non-nuclear-weapon states parties to the non-proliferation treaty). Otherwise there is no general prohibition of the possession of nuclear weapons. Whether the use or the threatened use of nuclear weapons was unlawful in any individual case would depend on the particular circumstances of that case.

ZAIRE: REFUGEE CAMPS

Lord Judd asked Her Majesty's Government:

What action they have taken to support the proposal by the Secretary-General of the United Nations on 21 November last that "a United Nations peacekeeping operation, set up in accordance with normal procedures, to establish security progressively in the camps, area by area, over a period of time" should be urgently mobilised to deal with the deteriorating security situation in the refugee camps in Zaire.

Baroness Chalker of Wallasey: The President of the United Nations Security Council issued a statement on 30 November in response to the Secretary-General's report on the situation in the refugee camps in Zaire and the proposals put forward in that report. We fully support that statement, copies of which have been placed in the Libraries of the House.

PERGAU DAM: REPAYMENT OF FUNDING

Lord Judd asked Her Majesty's Government:

What steps they are taking to restore the funds so far expended on the Pergau Dam in Malaysia to the Overseas Aid Programme.

Baroness Chalker of Wallasey: I refer the noble Lord to the reply I gave the noble Lord, Lord Molloy, on 28 November at cols. WA 26–27.

ILLICIT DRUGS: CONTROL MEASURES

Lord Gainford asked Her Majesty's Government:

What contribution they are making to the development of international co-operation against illicit drug production and trafficking.

Baroness Chalker of Wallasey: The Government's consultative paper *Tackling Drugs Together*, launched on 19 October, demonstrates the Government's firm commitment to tackling the menace of illicit drugs both at home and abroad.

In his reply of 24 November to my honourable friend the Member for Swindon, my right honourable friend the Home Secretary set out the action the Government is taking to improve the effectiveness of international co-operation against drug traffickers. The Foreign and Commonwealth Office is actively involved in supporting these activities.

In this context, we have raised the profile and priority of drugs in our bilateral contacts with other countries, taking advantage of ministerial contacts where this would be useful and through our diplomatic missions abroad.

At the multilateral level, my right honourable friend the Foreign Secretary stressed at the United Nations General Assembly on 28 September that "the international community needs to give full support to the UN International Drugs Control Programme (UNDCP), which has responsibility for leading the global effort in this field. The UN is the best resource for tackling this global menace". We are providing an extra £1.2 million to fund UNDCP projects. This will bring total United Kingdom assistance to other governments (including through UNDCP) to £8 million in this financial year.

The United Kingdom, as Chairman of the group of UNDCP major donors, will continue to encourage others to increase their contributions to UNDCP. We are moreover actively encouraging the international financial and development institutions to give higher priority to drugs and crime in their country programmes.

We also play a prominent role in other international meetings—for example, in the Dublin Group of donors, which seeks to develop a dialogue with governments of producer and transit countries on drugs issues. We are also encouraging the EU to be more active in combatting drug trafficking, particularly in areas of intergovernmental co-operation. We have, for example, been at the forefront of efforts to associate countries of central and eastern Europe with EU work on drugs and organised crime; and we have taken a leading part in EU efforts to develop co-operation with other neighbouring countries in the Mehgreb and Levant. We are furthermore encouraging the Commonwealth to give the issue of drugs and crime a higher political priority.

SYRIAN ARMS PURCHASES: POLICY

Lord Gainford asked Her Majesty's Government:

What is their policy with regard to arms sales to Syria.

Baroness Chalker of Wallasey: The EU arms embargo on Syria was lifted on 28 November. All applications for the sale of arms will be considered on a case-by-case basis in the light of the international guidelines to which we are committed. These include whether a proposed transfer would be likely to increase tension in the region or contribute to regional instability.

EU DEVELOPMENT COUNCIL, 25 NOVEMBER

Lord Gainford asked Her Majesty's Government:

What matters were discussed at the European Union Development Council in Brussels on 25 November.

Baroness Chalker of Wallasey: I represented the United Kingdom at the Council. There was extensive discussion of the situation in Rwanda. an action programme totalling 67 mecu (c£52 million) was endorsed and the importance of national reconciliation underlined. Further progress was made on co-ordination between Community and member state aid programmes, notably through agreement on joint guidelines on food security and education. There were also useful exchanges of view on the state of play on the mid term review of the Lomé Convention, future assistance to South Africa and evaluation.

A.2/M.2: LIGHTING

Lord Northbourne asked Her Majesty's Government:

Whether they are proposing to provide streetlighting for the whole, or part of the A.2/M.2 trunk route, and whether they have undertaken an economic assessment to justify the cost on grounds of increased safety; and

Whether they undertook an environmental impact before introducing streetlighting on the A.2/M.2 trunk route, and what environmental bodies, if any, they consulted.

The Parliamentary Under-Secretary of State, Department of Transport (Viscount Goschen): These are operational matters for the Highways Agency. I have asked the Chief Executive, Mr. Lawrie Haynes, to write to the noble Lord.

Letter to Lord Northbourne from the Chief Executive of the Highways Agency, Mr. L. Haynes, dated 6 December 1994:

Viscount Goschen has asked me to write to you in reply to your recent parliamentary Questions about street lighting on the A.2/M.2 trunk route.

The Highways Agency's contractors are currently installing lighting on a 7-mile (11 km) length of the A.2 from its junction with the A.296 almost to the M.2 (Junction 1). With the completion of the work—

hopefully by Christmas—the A.2 will be lit to modern standards over a continuous length of 14 miles (22 kms) starting from the boundary of the London Borough of Bexley at the River Gray. A 200-metre section close to the M.2 (J1) will remain unlit for the time being, but lighting proposals for this will form part of the planned future widening of the M.2 between Junctions 1 and 4. The Agency has no plans at the present time to implement further lighting schemes on this route.

The present lighting scheme is justified economically on the basis of a projected 30 per cent. reduction in the night-time accident record. The scheme, which complies fully with the latest Department of Transport design standards, involves the installation of lighting columns providing a 15-metre mounting height for lanterns of 'flat glass' construction using high pressure sodium lamp sources. This type of equipment minimises lighting spillage beyond the highway and is considered to be the most environmentally friendly currently available.

Although it is not our practice to carry out full environmental assessments in respect for road safety schemes on existing unaltered road, we are careful to ensure that any adverse effects are kept to an absolute minimum. This applies particularly in environmentally sensitive urban areas. The department's publication *Road Lighting and the Environment* sets out the policy on this. The A.2 lighting scheme was discussed with members of the Landscape Advisory Committee, who made special day and night-time inspections of the lit and unlit sections of the road. Their recommendations were incorporated into the design. A full environmental assessment has been carried out in respect of the M.2 widening scheme.

LIFE SENTENCE PRISONERS: REVIEW ARRANGEMENTS

Lord Gainford asked Her Majesty's Government:

What changes have been made in the review procedures in cases of persons sentenced to life imprisonment.

The Minister of State, Home Office (Baroness Blatch): Two of my right honourable friend's predecessors as Secretary of State, the right honourable Sir Leon Brittan and my right honourable friend the member for Witney, made statements in 1983 and 1987, respectively, about the review arrangements for life sentence prisoners. Under those arrangements, the first review by the Parole Board takes place three years before the expiry of the period thought necessary to satisfy the requirements of retribution and deterrence (commonly referred to as "the tariff"). However, no life sentence prisoner is detained for more than 17 years without a Parole Board review of his or her case, even where the period in question exceeds 20 years. The Secretary of State also reviews the case of every life sentence prisoner who has been detained for 10 years.

From now on all life sentence prisoners will have a Parole Board review three years before the expiry of their tariff. Since all prisoners will now know the length of their tariff and also the date of this review, we consider that the automatic review at the 17-year point no longer serves any useful purpose. The 17-year review will therefore be discontinued, save in respect of those existing prisoners for whom such a review has already been fixed.

This means that the review three years before the expiry of the tariff will be the first review for all prisoners. The setting of a review at this point is intended to allow sufficient time for preparing the release of those life sentence prisoners who may be considered an acceptable risk. This is subject, in the case of mandatory life prisoners, to the question of the public acceptability of early release.

In recent years, successive Secretaries of State have recognised that, for the majority of life sentence prisoners, a period in open prison conditions is generally vital in terms of testing the prisoner's suitability for release and in preparing him or her for a successful return to the community. It is, therefore, now normally the practice to require the prisoner to spend some time in open conditions before release and to arrange a further review while the prisoner is in an open prison for a formal assessment of his or her progress. We intend to continue with this practice and the first Parole Board review will therefore normally serve the purpose of assessing the prisoner for open conditions.

The purpose of the 10-year ministerial review is to consider whether there are any grounds for bringing forward the date of the first review by the Parole Board. This review is now redundant as far as discretionary life sentence prisoners are concerned, since their cases are dealt with in accordance with the arrangements introduced by Part II of the Criminal Justice Act 1991. However, the 10-year ministerial review will continue to take place for mandatory life sentence prisoners.

In addition we have decided that for those life sentence prisoners for whom it is decided that the requirements of retribution and deterrence can be satisfied only by their remaining in prison for the whole of their life, there will in future be an additional ministerial review when the prisoner has been in custody for 25 years. The purpose of this review will be solely to consider whether the whole life tariff should be converted to a tariff of a determinate period. The review will be confined to the considerations of retribution and deterrence. Where appropriate, further ministerial reviews will normally take place at five-yearly intervals thereafter. Existing prisoners who fall into this category and who have already served 25 years or more in custody will not be disadvantaged. Their cases will be reviewed by Ministers as soon as is practicable and after any representations they may wish to make.

As my right honourable friend announced in reply to a Question by the right honourable Member for Burton (Sir Ivan Lawrence) on 27 July 1993, successive Secretaries of State have been, and continue to be, willing to consider any written representations by life sentence prisoners about their tariff.

They will also continue to be afforded the opportunity to submit such written representations at the beginning of the sentence and before we have formed a view as to the appropriate period in question.

HUMAN RIGHTS COMMITTEE: 4TH PERIODIC REPORT

Lord Lester of Herne Hill asked Her Majesty's Government:

Whether the 4th Periodic Report to the Human Rights Committee under Article 40 to the International Covenant on Civil and Political Rights will be subject to parliamentary debate, and if not, why not.

Baroness Blatch: We have no plans for such a debate.

Lord Lester of Herne Hill asked Her Majesty's Government:

Whether they will make their 4th Periodic Report to the Human Rights Committee under Article 40 to the International Covenant on Civil and Political Rights widely available to members of the public, and if so how.

Baroness Blatch: The report is already freely available from the Home Office publications unit, and in the British Library and the other legal deposit libraries.

SALMON REPORT RECOMMENDATIONS: IMPLEMENTATION

Lord Harris of Greenwich asked Her Majesty's Government:

Which recommendations of the Salmon Commission on standards in public life have been implemented and which have not.

Baroness Blatch: Of the 29 recommendations identified as requiring action by central and local government, 19 are known to have been implemented, fully or in part, although not necessarily in direct response to the Salmon report. They are recommendations 4, 6, 8, 11–14, 16–21, 24–25, 27 and 33–35. Recommendations 1–3, 7, 9 and 10 have not been implemented. Information about the status of recommendations 31, 32 and 26 is not yet available. The organisation which was the subject of recommendation 26 has now been abolished. Of the remaining nine recommendations, six required no action and three were addressed to national political parties. I shall write to the noble Lord with further details of implementation, or the reasons for not implementing the recommendations, as soon as the information is complete.

GENERAL GOVERNMENT BORROWING REQUIREMENT: ESTIMATES

Lord Barnett asked Her Majesty's Government:

What is their latest estimate of the general government borrowing requirement for the next three financial years; and what are the main reasons why this differs from the public sector borrowing requirement.

The Parliamentary Under-Secretary of State, Ministry of Defence (Lord Henley): The latest estimates of the general government borrowing requirement (GGBR) for the next three years were published in table 4.1 of the *Financial Statement and Budget Report 1995–96* and are given in the table below. The difference between the public sector borrowing requirement (PSBR) and the GGBR is accounted for by public corporations market and overseas borrowing (PCMOB), which has been a repayment of debt for the past 3 years and is projected to continue as such.

£ billion	GGBR	PCMOB	PSBR
1995–96	23.1	–1.6	21.5
1996–97	15	–2	13
1997–98	7	–2	5

UNIDENTIFIED FLYING OBJECTS: SIGHTINGS RECORDS

Lord Mason of Barnsley asked Her Majesty's Government:

To what extent official records are kept of sightings of unidentified flying objects, especially those sightings that may have a bearing on the air defence of this country; whether units of the Ministry of Defence, especially RAF units, have standing instructions to report sightings of unusual flying objects; whether reports are logged; and whether these can now be made public.

Lord Henley: My department evaluates reports of unexplained aerial phenomena solely in order to establish whether they may have any defence significance. Reports are received from a wide range of sources, including the police and general public, as well as the RAF, which in the context of its air defence responsibilities has standing instructions to report all sightings of unexplained aerial phenomena. Reports are placed on departmental files in the normal way and are therefore subject to the Public Records Act; several files on this subject are available for viewing at the Public Record Office.

NAIAD AND CAM: TRIGGERS

The Countess of Mar asked Her Majesty's Government:

Whether NAIAD (Nerve Agent Immobilised Enzyme Alarm and Detector) alarms and CAM (Computer-Aided Measurement and Control) monitors are commonly triggered by compounds emitted by jet engines.

Lord Henley: NAIAD (Nerve Agent Immobilised Enzyme Alarm and Detector) and CAM (Chemical Agent Monitor) are designed to be used in conditions where they would not normally be in close proximity to jet engines. Nevertheless NAIAD was extensively evaluated against a wide range of aircraft engine effluent during its acceptance testing for military use. Out of 18 aircraft types, in only one case was alarm condition attained. In the case of CAM, although aircraft turbine exhaust does not produce a response, field experience suggests that this could happen if the instrument was contaminated with JP4 fuel. It follows that although neither CAM nor NAIAD are commonly triggered by compounds emitted from jet engines, circumstances might arise in which this could happen.

OPERATION GRANBY: PYRIDOSTIGMINE BROMIDE

The Countess of Mar asked Her Majesty's Government:

Whether the issue of pyridostigmine bromide to British forces who served in Operation Granby was on a named patient basis in view of the fact that a product licence was not obtained until 11th August 1993 (*The London Gazette, 27th August 1993*), and if not, upon what basis was the normal procedure for prescription of unlicensed medicines suspended.

Lord Henley: Pyridostigmine bromide, when given as a nerve agent pretreatment, as in Operation Granby, is not given as a medicinal product in accordance with normal procedures for prescribing medicines. Pyridostigmine bromide is taken by service personnel when a threat of chemical warfare exists. It was not issued on a named patient basis.

OPERATION GRANBY: VACCINES

The Countess of Mar asked Her Majesty's Government:

Whether, in view of the fact that the plaque vaccine administered to British forces who served in Operation was not licensed in the UK at the time, it was administered on a named patient basis, and if not, upon what basis was the normal procedure for prescription of unlicensed medicines suspended.

Lord Henley: Details of the specific medical countermeasures employed by British forces against the potential biological warfare threat during Operation Granby remain classified. All vaccines administered to British forces during Operation Granby were offered on the basis of voluntary informed consent. Any vaccines without a UK product licence were licensed in their country of origin, fully tested in the UK and cleared for use.

OPERATION GRANBY: ALLEGED CHEMICAL INCIDENT

The Countess of Mar asked Her Majesty's Government:

To what chemicals the two RVD (Residual Vapour Detector) tests gave positive responses following the triggering of the NAIAD (Nerve Agent Immobilised Enzyme Alarm and Detector) alarms on the night of 20th–21st January 1991 during Operation Granby.

Lord Henley: My department has no record of an incident taking place on the night of 20–21 January 1991 during Operation Granby. There are, however, records of an incident on 19 January 1991 in the Al Jubayl area when CAM (Chemical Agent Monitor) and RVD (Residual Vapour Detector) indicated the presence of blister agent (Mustard). NAIAD (Nerve Agent Immobilised Enzyme Alarm and Detector) did not respond, thus ruling out the presence of nerve agent.

An immediate follow up by Explosive Ordnance Device (EOD) and chemical reconnaissance teams failed to find any evidence for chemical attack which, had it taken place, would have included ground contamination (blister is a persistent agent) and weapon debris.

The identity of the compounds which caused CAM and RVD to respond on 19 January 1991 is therefore not known. Clearly it was not nerve agent since NAIAD did not alarm; neither was it blister since there was no ground contamination. It was assessed that the most likely cause of this incident was a damaged coalition aircraft jettisoning JP4 fuel which is consistent with reports of air activity at the time.

AIR TRAINING CORPS: SQUADRON AND GLIDING SCHOOLS

Lord Trefgarne asked Her Majesty's Government:

What is the present number of squadrons and voluntary gliding schools within the Air Training Corps and whether the numbers are set to change.

Lord Henley: At present, there is a ceiling of 920 Air Training Corps squadrons in the United Kingdom, which is fully committed. Overseas there are seven of a possible 10 squadrons. The ceiling of United Kingdom Squadrons is under review by the Air Officer Commanding Air Cadets. There are 27 volunteer gliding schools operational from an establishment of 30. All of these are based in the United Kingdom. There are no current plans for any change.

OPERATION GRANBY: VACCINE AND MEDICATION RECORDS

The Countess of Mar asked Her Majesty's Government:

Whether a complete record of all vaccines and medication administered to British forces who served in Operation Granby was entered on their medical records, and whether these records, are available to their military or civilian general medical practitioners.

Lord Henley: Standard peacetime procedures involve records of vaccines and prescribed medication being kept on every individual's service medical documents. Under operational conditions individual service medical records are not held locally for logistic reasons, and a field medical documentation system is invoked. During Operation Granby vaccinations or prescribed medications were entered on a nominal roll for later transfer to individual records. Given the rapid repatriation and demobilisation of personnel at the end of the conflict, it is likely that some individual medical records were not fully annotated. Service medical records are the property of the department, but can be made available to service medical officers or civilian general practitioners on request.

INDIVIDUAL RIGHTS OF ACCESS TO HEALTH AND SAFETY INFORMATION: LEGISLATION

Lord Lestor of Herne Hill asked Her Majesty's Government:

Whether they intend, during this parliamentary session, to introduce legislation creating individual rights of access to health and safety information and to personal information.

The Parliamentary Secretary, Ministry of Agriculture, Fisheries and Food (Earl Howe): The Government remain committed to legislation on these subjects at the earliest convenient opportunity.

NEXT STEPS INITIATIVE

Lord Colnbrook asked Her Majesty's Government:
What is the progress of the Next Steps initiative.

Earl Howe: The Government today published the fifth *Next Steps Review*—Cm 2750. It brings together information on the 102 agencies within Government, and the executive organisations of HM Customs and Excise and the Inland Revenue, which now constitute 62 per cent. of the Civil Service. Within central government, agencies are delivering the Citizen's Charter commitment to improved customer service and value for money. The review highlights how under the charter, agencies focus on the needs of the users of their services and gives examples of what individual agencies have achieved. Thirty Charter Marks have been awarded to agencies in the first three years of the competition, reflecting the commitment of agency chief executives and their staff to high standards of customer service.

The review reports the targets set for agencies and their performance against them in 1993–94 and lists key targets for 1994–95. In 1993–94 agencies met around 80 per cent. of their key targets, compared with 77 per cent. last year. Most targets have also become progressively more demand year on year.

The Government's aim is that every public service should be provided in the most appropriate and cost-effective way. All the executive functions of the Civil Service are therefore being examined against the following tests: whether they need to continue to be performed at all; whether they need to remain the responsibility of Government; where the Government does need to remain responsible for an activity, does the Government have to carry out the task or can it buy in from outside providers; and whether they should become the responsibility of an agency within Government. The review reports further progress in this work.

Once established, agencies are subject to periodic review, now normally after five years of operation. To ensure that the widest possible range of views are taken into account, both the initial examination of an activity and these reviews are publicly announced, including through the *Next Steps Review*. The review also demonstrates many ways in which agencies are entering into partnership with the private sector, for example, by contracting out existing work to the private sector under a partnership arrangement or through joint ventures.

Over the last six years, the Next Steps initiative has fundamentally altered the way in which the Civil Service is managed. It is a key part of the programme of change outlined in the White Paper *The Civil Service: Continuity and Change*. The White Paper also proposed extending throughout the Civil Service many of the principles of Next Steps, including maximum clarity about objectives and targets, delegation of management responsibility and a clear focus on outputs and outcomes. The aim is a flexible and cost-effective Civil Service well-equipped to provide support for Ministers on policy matters and in the management of public services which meet the needs of their users.

ORGANOPHOSPHORUS: POISONING INCIDENTS

The Countess of Mar asked Her Majesty's Government:

How many reports of suspected adverse reactions to organophosphate pesticides were recorded by the Health and Safety Executive for each of the 10 years.

Lord Inglewood: The number of poisoning incidents involving organophosphorus pesticides investigated by the Health and Safety Executive (HSE) for each of the last 10 years is set out in the following table. The table does not show proven cases of adverse reactions to organophosphorus pesticides, but merely those reported to, and investigated by, HSE.

Poisoning incidents involving organophosphorus pesticides investigated by HSE

Year	Number of Incidents	Number of People Involved
1984	30	54
1985	21	25
1986	9	12
1987	17	51[1]
1988	13	19
1989–90	24	35
1990–91	29	45
1991–92	21	127[2]
1992–93	13	16
1993–94	16	27

[1] 32 in one incident (laboratory fumigation)
[2] 100 in one incident (pesticide store fire)

RESPITE CARE: FUNDING

Lord Holme of Cheltenham asked Her Majesty's Government:

Whether the rules on the use of grants from the Housing Corporation by housing associations are intended to deny the provision of respite care when such care is available.

The Minister of State, Department of the Environment (Viscount Ullswater): The funding of respite care is not the responsibility of the Housing Corporation. This is a matter for social service authorities and it is for them to decide the best way of meeting individual needs. The Government has provided an extra £20 million in community care funding for respite and home care services this year, rising to £30 million next year.

PRIVY COUNCIL OATH

Lord Tebbit asked Her Majesty's Government:

Whether the solemn declaration made by Commissioners of the European Community that they will perform their duties in "complete independence in the general interest of the Communities" is compatible with the oath sworn by those admitted to the Privy Council that they "will bear faith and allegiance to Her Majesty and defend all her jurisdictions, pre-eminences and authorities, against all foreign princes, persons, prelates, states or potentates".

The Lord Privy Seal (Viscount Cranborne): Yes.

CSCE SUMMIT MEETINGS 5th–6th DECEMBER

Lord Colnbrook asked Her Majesty's Government:

What was the outcome of the conference on Security and Co-operation in Europe Summit in Budapest.

Viscount Cranborne: The Prime Minister represented the United Kingdom at the Summit meeting of the Conference on Security and Co-operation in Europe in Budapest on 5th—6th December, accompanied by the Foreign Secretary.

The meeting adopted the Budapest Summit Declaration; and separate declarations on the 50th Anniversary of the termination of World War II, and on Baltic issues. It is also adopted 10 decisions on different aspects of the CSCE's work.

These decisions embraced strengthening the CSCE; regional issues; further development of the capabilities of the CSCE in conflict prevention and crisis management; code of conduct on politico-military aspects of security; further tasks of the CSCE forum for security co-operation; principles governing non-proliferation; a common and comprehensive security model for Europe for the 21st century; the human dimension; the economic dimension; and the mediterranean.

Copies of all of these documents will be placed in the Library.

The CSCE is no longer just a conference. Its role has widened since the end of the Cold War. Under the Budapest decision on strengthening the CSCE, its title will change from 1st January 1995 to the Organisation for Security and Co-operation in Europe (OSCE). This change of title has been accompanied by some structural changes which are set out in the relevant decision.

Among its other decisions, the Summit:

—initiated planning for a CSCE-led peace-keeping operation in Nagorno-Karabakh. Deployment of a multinational CSCE peace-keeping force will depend on progress towards a political settlement, on United Nations Security Council backing, and on the requisite military preparation;

—adopted measures to strengthen the CSCE in its central role of conflict prevention;

—reinforced (as a result of a British initiative) the CSCE's arrangements for dealing with the problem of minorities and other human rights questions;

—set out standards for the democratic control of armed forces, in a new code of conduct;

—added to military confidence building measures, including provisions for the exchange of information on all conventional forces.

At a separate ceremony in Budapest on 5th December, Ukraine acceded to the non-proliferation treaty. On behalf of the United Kingdom, the Prime Minister extended to Belarus, Kazakhstan and Ukraine the nuclear security assurances which we have give in the past to other non-nuclear weapon states. Presidents Clinton and Yeltsin extended the same assurances on behalf of the United States of America and the Russian Federation.

In the margins of the conference, the Prime Minister had discussions with many of the CSCE heads of government, including the presidents of the Czech Republic, Georgia, Russia, Ukraine and the United States; the German Federal Chancellor; and the Prime Ministers of Hungary, Norway and Turkey.

The future development of the North Atlantic Alliance was one of the subjects mentioned in many speeches to the conference, and also during bilateral meetings. It was a point of particular concern to the Russian delegation. The Prime Minister explained to President Yeltsin that the United Kingdom's aim, which was widely supported by our partners in NATO and the European Union, was to extend to the East the prosperity and stability which members of the European Union and NATO now enjoy. That was why both organisations were developing their links with the countries of central and eastern Europe. NATO had commissioned a study of the principles of enlargement, but had taken no decisions yet on which countries might join the organisation or when. It was very important for NATO to build up its relationship with Russia, and we therefore hoped that the Russian Government would soon sign its agreement with NATO on the partnership for peace programme. It was common ground that there should be no new dividing line across Europe.

The dominant political issue at the Summit was the conflict in Bosnia. CSCE decisions are adopted by consensus, and because of differences of view between certain participants a draft declaration on Bosnia was not adopted. However, the chairman of the conference spoke for many delegations in issuing, in his personal capacity, a call on all warring parties in Bosnia, and particularly in Bihac, to end the fighting, declare a ceasefire and allow free access of humanitarian assistance throughout Bosnia.

DISCRIMINATION CONVENTION

Lord Lester of Herne Hill asked Her Majesty's Government:

Further to their Answer of 1st November 1994 (HL column *WA 59*), whether they will amend the nationality rules for the Armed Forces and Civil Service by eliminating distinctions, exclusions or preferences on the basis of race, colour or national extraction (as distinct from nationality or residence) so as to enable the United Kingdom to ratify the International Labour Organisation Discrimination (Employment and Occupation) Convention 1958; and, if not, why not;

Further to their Answer of 1st November 1994 (HL col. *WA 59*), whether they consider that it is appropriate or necessary to maintain rules for the Armed Forces and Civil Service which make distinctions, exclusions or preferences, on grounds forbidden by the International Labour Organisation Discrimination (Employment and Occupation) Convention 1958, namely on the basis of race, colour or national extraction (as distinct from nationality or residence) "to ensure the close identification of the personnel concerned with the United Kingdom"; and

Further to their Answer of 1st November 1994 (HL col. *WA 59*), whether they consider that the needs of the United Kingdom are different from the needs of the 118 States parties to the International Labour Organisation Discrimination (Employment and Occupation) Convention 1958, in making it appropriate and necessary to maintain rules for the Armed Forces and Civil Service which make distinctions, exclusions or preferences, on grounds forbidden by the Convention, namely on the basis of race, colour or national extraction (as distinct from nationality or residence); and, if so, how.

Viscount Cranborne: The Race Relations Act 1976 preserves the validity of nationality rules governing eligibility for employment in the service of the Crown. The special rules relating to national extraction (as distinct from nationality or residence) governing employment in the Civil Service apply only to posts in the Cabinet Office, the Ministry of Defence and the Foreign and Commonwealth Office. The extent to which those rules could be relaxed is the subject of a review which is being co-ordinated by the Minister for the Civil Service. Similar rules govern eligibility for service in the armed Forces and these will be reviewed by the Secretary of State for Defence in the light of the outcome of the current review in relation to civilian employment in the Ministry of Defence.

ISBN 0-10-701295-2

Vol. 559
No. 13

Thursday
8 December 1994

PARLIAMENTARY DEBATES
(HANSARD)

HOUSE OF LORDS

OFFICIAL REPORT

CONTENTS

Questions—Chemical Weapons Convention: Consultation Document [Col. 1011]
　　—Cot Deaths [Col. 1013]
　　—Iraq: Sanctions [Col. 1015]
　　—Defence Cuts [Col. 1017]

Statement—Financial Statement [Col. 1019]

Statement—Christmas Recess [Col. 1019]

Visas and Border Controls: EEC Report—Motion to Take Note [Col. 1033]

Defence Research Agency: Select Committee Report—Motion to Take Note [Col. 1060]

Written Answers [Col. *WA 99*]

LONDON: HMSO
£4·20 net

Lords wishing to be supplied with these Daily Reports should give notice to this effect to the Printed Paper Office.

The bound volumes also will be sent to those Peers who similarly notify their wish to receive them.

No proofs of Daily Reports are provided. Corrections for the bound volume which Lords wish to suggest to the report of their speeches should be clearly indicated in a copy of the Daily Report, which, with the column numbers concerned shown on the front cover, should be sent to the Editor of Debates, House of Lords, within 14 days of the date of the Daily Report.

PRICES AND SUBSCRIPTION RATES

DAILY PARTS

Single copies:
Commons, £7·50; Lords £4·20

Annual subscriptions:
Commons, £1,275; Lords £615

WEEKLY HANSARD

Single copies:
Commons, £22; Lords £9·00

Annual subscriptions:
Commons, £775; Lords £310

Index—Single copies:
Commons, £6·80—published fortnightly;
Lords, £1·90—published weekly.

Annual subscriptions:
Commons, £120; Lords, £65.

LORDS CUMULATIVE INDEX obtainable on standing order only.
Details available on request.

BOUND VOLUMES OF DEBATES are issued periodically during the session.

Single copies:
Commons, £90; Lords, £68.
Standing orders will be accepted.

THE INDEX to each Bound Volume of House of Commons Debates is published separately at £9·00 and can be supplied to standing order.

WEEKLY INFORMATION BULLETIN, compiled by the House of Commons, gives details of past and forthcoming business, the work of Committees and general information on legislation, etc.
Single copies: £2·30.
Annual subscription: £88·80.

All prices are inclusive of postage.

© Parliamentary Copyright House of Lords 1994
Applications for reproduction should be made to HMSO

HMSO publications are available from:

HMSO Publications Centre
(Mail, fax and telephone orders only)
PO Box 276, London SW8 5DT
Telephone orders 0171 873 9090
General enquiries 0171 873 0011
(queueing system for both numbers in operation)
Fax orders 0171 873 8200

HMSO Bookshops
49 High Holborn, London WC1V 6HB (counter service only)
0171 873 0011 Fax 0171 831 1326
68-69 Bull Street, Birmingham B4 6AD 0121 236 9696 Fax 0121 236 9699
33 Wine Street, Bristol BS1 2BQ 0117 9264306 Fax 0117 9294515
9-21 Princess Street, Manchester M60 8AS 0161 834 7201 Fax 0161 833 0634
16 Arthur Street, Belfast BT1 4GD 01232 238451 Fax 01232 235401
71 Lothian Road, Edinburgh EH3 9AZ 0131 228 4181 Fax 0131 229 2734

The Parliamentary Bookshop
12 Bridge Street, Parliamentary Square
London SW1A 2JX
Telephone orders 0171 219 3890
General enquiries 0171 219 3890
Fax orders 0171 219 3866

HMSO's Accredited Agents
(see Yellow Pages)

and through good booksellers

Printed in England and Published by HMSO

ISBN 0 10 701395 9
ISSN 0 309-8834

House of Lords

Thursday, 8th December 1994.

The House met at three of the clock: The LORD CHANCELLOR on the Woolsack.

Prayers—Read by the Lord Bishop of Coventry.

Chemical Weapons Convention: Consultation Document

Lord Mayhew asked Her Majesty's Government:

When they propose to introduce legislation to ratify the Chemical Weapons Convention.

The Minister of State, Department of Trade and Industry (Earl Ferrers): My Lords, legislation to enable the United Kingdom to ratify the Chemical Weapons Convention will be introduced as soon as parliamentary time and other government legislative priorities permit. My right honourable friend the President of the Board of Trade announced today in a Written Answer that the Department of Trade and Industry will issue a discussion document early in the New Year to canvass the views of industry on the implementation of the Chemical Weapons Convention in the United Kingdom.

Lord Mayhew: My Lords, will the noble Earl agree that this country has done more than any other to bring about this admirable convention; and that 16 countries have now ratified but Britain has not? What is the reason for this delay? Presumably, it is a matter of a short Bill; both Opposition parties have made it clear that they will give it a fair wind; and it cannot be claimed that the legislative programme is overcrowded with important measures. What is the reason for this?

Earl Ferrers: My Lords, I agree with the noble Lord on a number of points: first, the United Kingdom has indeed played a major part over a period of 20 years in getting this convention agreed to, and Britain has signed it. The noble Lord said that 16 states had ratified. In fact, the number is 17. But he will also understand, I am sure, that when the convention comes into operation it will have quite an effect on industry. It is necessary to discuss with industry the best way of setting about this. I can assure the noble Lord that the legislation will be introduced as soon as it can be.

Lord Ennals: My Lords, can the Minister clarify one point? He said that there is to be a discussion paper. Will that paper be published before legislation, or will deal with how the measure will be implemented? Will he accept from me that there are many of us who feel that Britain ought to ratify this measure at the earliest possible moment and that, for the reasons already given by the noble Lord, Lord Mayhew, we ought to be taking the lead. Is there not a danger with a discussion paper that there will be a long delay before there is legislation?

Earl Ferrers: My Lords, I hope that there will not be a long delay before the legislation is brought forward. The noble Lord will be only too well aware of the pressures that are experienced by any government in respect of legislative timetables. I have given the assurance that we will introduce this measure as soon as is reasonable.

The consultation document will contain the outline of our proposals for the implementation of the Chemical Weapons Convention and it will seek the views of industry. It will cover issues that are important to industry such as declarations; the way in which industries will be inspected; and respecting commercial confidences.

Lord Jenkins of Putney: My Lords, does the Minister agree that it is in the nature of things that when legislation affects industry there are bound to be people who are opposed to it? As it has long been the Government's policy that this legislation should be put into effect, would it not be much more encouraging and satisfactory for the Government to complete their legislative programme, put this legislation through and then discuss it afterwards? They are often ready to do that on other occasions; why not do it now?

Earl Ferrers: My Lords, that is a most extraordinary suggestion from the noble Lord. He will recall that periodically the Government are blamed for not taking account of people's views before they introduce legislation. We are doing the sensible thing and taking account of people's views.

The Lord Bishop of Coventry: My Lords, can the noble Earl inform the House of steps that are being taken by Her Majesty's Government to achieve full international application of effective intrusive inspection and verification measures with regard to chemical and biological weapons?

Earl Ferrers: My Lords, I think I can give an assurance to the right reverend Prelate that the inspection and verification of the way in which countries operate is an essential part of the convention. It will first come into operation 180 days after 65 countries have ratified. The chemicals in which Britain is interested are not those in Schedule 1, which will come into operation immediately, but those listed in Schedule 2 which will be banned when the schedule comes into force three years later. Ensuring that countries behave fairly and properly is an essential part of the convention.

Lord Mackie of Benshie: My Lords, will the Minister tell the House what he meant by "consulting industry"? Does he mean that industry in this country is heavily involved in the export of chemical weapons or with the manufacture for the home market of chemical weapons?

Earl Ferrers: My Lords, as the noble Lord will know, there are certain chemical weapons which are deeply offensive. The constituent part of those weapons can also be a chemical which is used by industry. One example is phosgene, which as a gas is very offensive, but which is used perfectly correctly in the plastics industry. We want to make sure that industry is not

[EARL FERRERS]
affected adversely in relation to the activities that it is perfectly legitimate for it to undertake, but that it does not sell or use such materials for weaponry purposes.

Lord Kennet: My Lords, the noble Earl said that there must be time for consultation with industry, which is very comprehensible. But should we take it that among the 16 or 17 countries which have ratified there are not also industrial powers?

Earl Ferrers: My Lords, I can only answer for Her Majesty's Government. I do not know what happens in the countries which have ratified. They have their own methods of ratification and doubtless some of them have their own methods of consultation.

The Countess of Mar: My Lords, does the noble Earl recall that I asked a similar Question early in the summer? Is it not the case that, if we do not ratify the convention by next month, there could be some very harmful implications for British industry?

Earl Ferrers: My Lords, I am aware that the noble Countess asked a similar Question. I am not aware that if we do not ratify within a month there will be serious implications, for the reason that the chemicals that are in Schedule 1, as I explained earlier, are the ones which operate immediately the convention comes into force. We have no industries which use those Schedule 1 chemicals for weaponry purposes. Therefore, they will not be affected. Our industry is concerned in the main with Schedule 2 chemicals, which operate three years later.

Lord Williams of Elvel: My Lords, the Minister said that the Government wish to canvass industry's views to find out which industries, if any, are adversely affected—I hope that I quote his words accurately. If industry (whatever "industry" may be) comes back to the Government and says, "We are all adversely affected", do the Government intend to drop the ratification proposal?

Earl Ferrers: My Lords, if I may say so, that is also a very curious question from the noble Lord. I said that the Government intend to ratify, and they will ratify. What I said that we intend to do is to discuss with industry the methods by which the implementation will take place. There is nothing sinister and nothing wrong about that.

Cot Deaths

3.14 p.m.

Lord Ashley of Stoke asked Her Majesty's Government:

> What further steps they are taking to avoid child cot deaths.

The Parliamentary Under-Secretary of State, Department of Health (Baroness Cumberlege): My Lords, responding on the 18th November to media speculation about the causes of cot death, the Chief Medical Officer issued a statement which reiterated the earlier advice given to health professionals and parents during the Back to Sleep campaign. On 30th November he announced the composition of an expert group which has been formed to steer further work on cot deaths by the department.

Lord Ashley of Stoke: My Lords, is the Minister aware that most people will welcome the Government's decision to set up that group to look again at the question of whether toxic gases from cot mattresses can in fact contribute to child death? Is she further aware that the anxieties of many parents would be allayed if they could have a specific undertaking that that committee would look into the levels of antimony in human tissues, especially as the original committee failed to do so adequately?

Baroness Cumberlege: My Lords, the original committee made a very thorough investigation. Its findings were that there was no causal link between the antimony found in cot mattresses and those babies who suffered sudden infant death syndrome. The terms of reference of the new group are to review the findings of the Turner Report—the report to which I referred—in 1991 and to see whether there are any subsequent data on the hypothesis linking antimony with unexplained deaths in infants. It is to advise the Chief Medical Officer on what further studies should be undertaken to investigate postulated causal relationships between chemicals and cot deaths. I hope that that covers the point.

Lord Molloy: My Lords, when Dr. Calman, the Government's Chief Medical Officer, has called together the new group of experts—I believe that the Government made the correct decision and that it will be a great satisfaction to many people—and it has reported, will that report be submitted for examination in the House?

Baroness Cumberlege: Yes, my Lords.

Baroness Jay of Paddington: My Lords, will the noble Baroness accept that there are many worried parents who probably need immediate counselling and advice on this subject? We welcome some of the terms of reference of the new committee of investigation; but is the Minister aware that the Royal College of Nursing has set up a helpline on this subject which has already received many hundreds of telephone calls? What other action will the Government take to support that kind of proposal, which offers practical help to worried parents at the very moment when they need it?

Baroness Cumberlege: My Lords, I am sure the noble Baroness knows that we have a very sophisticated system with health visitors and midwives advising young parents on the care of their babies. We have also issued posters to be displayed in GP surgeries and leaflets on this matter. I should like to commend the Royal College of Nursing on their helpline. It has received 3,000 calls and the Foundation for the Study of Infant Deaths had 4,000 calls. It was a great pity that that particular programme caused so much anxiety and unrest among young parents.

Lord Ashley of Stoke: My Lords, will the noble Baroness forgive me if I challenge an assertion that she made in her Answer? She said that the previous committee conducted a thorough investigation, and that means a comprehensive investigation. I am stating that that committee did not investigate thoroughly the antimony levels in human tissues. That is the issue before us today. That is what we want the expert group to inspect. Will the Minister therefore consider that specific request? It is very important to the outcome of the whole investigation, to the parents and to other people.

Baroness Cumberlege: My Lords, the new expert group will do a very thorough job. It will take into account all the points made in the two television programmes. The original group looked into the hypothesis that toxic gases evolved from chemicals in cot mattresses and cot mattress covers, and therefore could have been the cause of sudden infant death syndrome. However, this group will do an even more thorough job.

Iraq: Sanctions

3.20 p.m.

Lord Archer of Weston-Super-Mare asked Her Majesty's Government:

> Whether they remain unwilling to lift sanctions on Iraq until they are convinced that Saddam Hussein will respect the rights of the Kurds.

The Minister of State, Foreign and Commonwealth Office (Baroness Chalker of Wallasey): My Lords, yes. The United Nations has repeatedly made clear to the Iraqi regime that there can be no question of relaxing sanctions until they comply fully with the relevant UN Security Council resolutions.

Lord Archer of Weston-Super-Mare: My Lords, while thanking the Minister for that reply, is it her opinion that things have improved for the Kurds in the north of Iraq in the past year or is Saddam Hussein still ignoring Resolutions 688 and 712?

Baroness Chalker of Wallasey: No, my Lords. Things have not improved. In his latest report the UN Special Rapporteur commented that there had been no improvement in Iraq's human rights record. Indeed, the situation has deteriorated even further during the past year. But we are all mindful of what needs to be done and are working to try to ensure that it is done.

Lord Ennals: My Lords, several times the Minister expressed concern for the Kurds and confirmed again just now that their situation in northern Iraq is getting worse rather than better. Is it not possible to negotiate some arrangement whereby the Kurds are not doubly disadvantaged by the sanctions? What attempts have the Foreign Office made to seek some sort of exemption for people who are clearly suffering?

Baroness Chalker of Wallasey: My Lords, in seeking any sort of exemption, one must be extremely careful to stay within the limits that we have already set of humanitarian goods being able to reach people in the country. Help is already going to the Kurds and in the past month new help has been sent to the Iraqis in the south who have been so terribly treated by the Saddam regime. I shall look into the matter to see whether there is any more that we can do. But Britain cannot do it alone. It must be done by the whole international community. Britain is second to none in its efforts to get help to those people.

Lord Boyd-Carpenter: My Lords, is it not painfully clear that the position in this part of the world will not be satisfactory so long as Saddam Hussein is there?

Baroness Chalker of Wallasey: My Lords, my noble friend knows that I have agreed with him on this point many times in the past. It is an easier thing to say than it is to obtain. That is why we have done our best to help the Iraqi people to set up the Iraqi National Congress to give strength to those who are determined to fight. I share my noble friend's view that, as long as Saddam Hussein remains, there will not be an appreciable difference, though we can welcome the fact that there has now been at least the Iraqi recognition of Kuwait, which was long overdue. However, we must remain cautious. Only one month before the Iraqis signed up to recognise Kuwait they had been threatening troops on the Kuwaiti border.

Baroness Blackstone: My Lords, following the question of my noble friend Lord Ennals, does the Minister agree that, while it is right to continue sanctions against Saddam Hussein's regime, we owe it to the Kurds to do all we can to mitigate the effects of those sanctions? Can the Minister tell the House whether the aid that the British Government committed to the Kurds in northern Iraq—I understand that it amounts to £4.7 million mainly for medical assistance and village rehabilitation—is reaching those for whom it is destined?

Baroness Chalker of Wallasey: My Lords, it is certainly true that a high proportion of what is sent is reaching the Kurdish people in the north. Since April 1991 the United Kingdom has contributed over £66 million worth of aid and I have just set aside another £8 million of specific aid to help the plight of the Iraqi people, particularly the Kurds, and the Shia Moslems in the south who are also affected. Aid is getting through, though not 100 per cent. We know that soldiers of Saddam's regime make forages into Kurdish villages to obtain what they can. That does not mean that we shall stop operating and trying to get help to the Kurdish people and to the people from the marshes.

Lord Milverton: My Lords, does the Minister agree that, while we are remembering the Kurds in northern Iraq, some other Kurds also need to know that we are trying to help them? I refer to the Kurds in Turkey. Can my noble friend say that they are being remembered for assistance as well as those living under Saddam Hussein?

Baroness Chalker of Wallasey: My Lords, there is no specific programme of assistance to Kurdish people in Turkey. They live in a society where we constantly remind the government of the needs of all the people of Turkey. Turkey is not only a member of NATO, but

[BARONESS CHALKER OF WALLASEY]
also a member of other organisations. If there is deprivation, it must be handled with the Turkish Government, and that we shall seek to do.

Lord Kennet: My Lords, can the noble Baroness tell us which, in the Government's opinion, is worse in its handling of the Kurdish people—the Iraqi Government or the Turkish Government?

Baroness Chalker of Wallasey: My Lords, there is no comparison between the way in which Saddam Hussein treated innocent Iraqi people—Kurds and Shias—and others who are not Kurds or marsh people. There is no comparison. I am amazed that the noble Lord should ask such a question.

Lord Molloy: My Lords, the noble Baroness is correctly pointing out Saddam Hussein's attitude to anybody who is opposed to him. But is she prepared to accept that those of us who have visited that country and know that what she said is absolutely true, also know that some Kurds are in the pay of Saddam Hussein and are willing to betray their fellow Kurds to any innocent western journalist with whom they may be in contact?

Baroness Chalker of Wallasey: My Lords, in some isolated circumstances the noble Lord may be right. But the majority of Kurds, particularly those who form the Iraqi National Congress, are fighting for their own people and trying to stabilise the Kurdish parts of Iraq.

Defence Cuts

3.28 p.m.

Lord Williams of Elvel asked Her Majesty's Government:

> On what basis they justify defence cuts of £2.5 billion (in constant prices) between 1993-94 and 1997-98 as announced in a "note to editors" accompanying the Budget Statement of 29th November.

The Parliamentary Under-Secretary of State, Ministry of Defence (Lord Henley): My Lords, the 1994 settlement is sufficient to maintain in full the front-line force structures set out in the 1993 and 1994 Defence White Papers. The reductions in the defence budget over this period principally reflect implementation of the final stages of the Options for Change restructuring programme; expected savings from the implementation of Front Line First and the effects of efficiency improvements.

Lord Williams of Elvel: My Lords, I am grateful to the noble Lord, in so far as I can be, for that Answer. Can he confirm that comparing like with like there will be a cut of approximately one-tenth in the defence budget? In fact, in real terms it is slightly over one-tenth. It will go down by 3 per cent. next year, 6.5 per cent. the year after, 1.5 per cent. the year after that and so forth. Is that consistent with what the Secretary of State said to the Conservative Party Conference?

Lord Henley: Yes, my Lords, it is entirely consistent. As I made clear, those were not new announcements, as the noble Lord seems to be implying. They result from Options for Change, the Defence Costs Study and other such reviews. The new plans show a cost programme reducing in real terms by some 11 per cent. I can assure the noble Lord that last year's press release showed a very, very similar reduction. It is, in fact, nothing new.

Lord Ewing of Kirkford: My Lords, these figures contain the belief within the Government that the tender price offered by Devonport for the refitting of Trident submarines will be met. It now seems absolutely clear that there is no stability in the docking facilities at Devonport and that substantial sums of money, running into many millions of pounds, will have to be spent to stabilise the facilities. There are also other serious defects in the facilities at Devonport. Who will have to pay these additional sums of money? Would it not make more sense, even at this date, to transfer the refitting of the Trident submarine fleet from Devonport to where it should have been in the first place, Rosyth?

Lord Henley: My Lords, the noble Lord will understand if I do not allow myself to be drawn into quite such detail on the question of Rosyth. However, I can give him an assurance that my right honourable friend will be answering a question on that subject later today.

Lord Howell: My Lords, is it not the case that, when the Secretary of State for Defence and the Prime Minister made statements to the Conservative Party Conference that there would be no further cuts in defence, they must have known that these further cuts which had not been announced were in preparation for the Budget, one month later in November? Why did that take place? Does the Minister realise that the justification for the change on page 121 of the Red Book is that it is to meet military redundancies and to enhance our front line situation, both of which any normal person would think would require an increase in defence expenditure and not a reduction?

Lord Henley: My Lords, I can assure the noble Lord in no uncertain terms that I have not been misleading the House in saying that these were not new cuts. The reductions were announced in last year's Budget. In fact the 1994 settlement is worth around £220 million more in 1995-96 and £310 million more in 1996-97 than the previous plans allowed. The cash reductions for 1995-96 and 1996-97—some £300 million and £200 million—are more than compensated for by the fall in inflation, which no doubt the noble Lord welcomes. I can assure him that when my right honourable friend the Prime Minister and my right honourable friend the Secretary of State for Defence made their remarks about the need for a further period of stability they knew that we had sufficient resources in this settlement to sustain the range of front-line capabilities described in the recent statements on the Defence Estimates.

Lord Jenkins of Putney: My Lords, is the noble Lord aware that if the Government were to give up Trident they could save much more money than this? There need be no personnel discussions. They could even have more military bands.

Lord Henley: My Lords, we have no intention of giving up Trident. I do not know what the views of the party opposite are but I am very interested to hear the noble Lord's views.

Lord Williams of Elvel: My Lords, does the noble Lord recall that when we debated what was known as Front Line First your Lordships were assured that the savings coming from Front Line First through more efficient administration would go towards the procurement of weapons for the front line? We were assured by no less a person than the present Leader of the House. In the light of the figures which appear to have been slipped out in an appendix to an appendix to an appendix to the Budget Statement, can the noble Lord explain why they told us that the savings from Front Line First were to be used for front-line equipment?

Lord Henley: My Lords, I am sorry but I think that this is entirely unacceptable. The noble Lord is accusing us of what amounts to dishonesty by saying that we were announcing new cuts. We were not. We were repeating the same announcements that we had made in previous years. As my noble friend the Leader of the House said on the occasion of the announcement of the Defence Costs Study—Front Line First—the new plans will mark an end in the upheaval of defence, they will preserve all the front-line capabilities necessary and they will fund necessary enhancements in the equipment programme.

Christmas Recess

Lord Strathclyde: My Lords, it may be for the convenience of the House to know that, subject to the progress of Business, it is expected that the House will adjourn for the Christmas Recess on Friday 16th December. It is expected that the House will sit at 11 a.m. on that day. It may also be for the convenience of the House to know that it is expected that the House will return on Monday 9th January.

Business

Lord Strathclyde: At a convenient moment after 3.30 p.m., my noble friend Lord Henley will, with the leave of the House, repeat a Financial Statement that is to be made in another place.

Financial Statement

3.36 p.m.

Lord Henley: My Lords, with the leave of the House, I shall now repeat a Statement being made in another place by my right honourable friend the Chancellor of the Exchequer. The Statement is as follows:

"With permission, Madam Speaker, I should like to make a Statement. Following the vote on Tuesday night, I told the House that the Government remained committed to taking all the necessary measures to put the public finances on a sound footing. The reductions in the public sector borrowing requirement I announced in my Budget were welcomed at the time by the business community, by the financial markets and by this House. During the course of the Budget debate few right honourable and honourable Members questioned that judgment. To keep these borrowing plans intact, I said I would be bringing forward measures to make good the gap in the public finances from holding the rate of VAT on domestic fuel and power at 8 per cent.

"I can now tell the House what those measures will be. A press note filling out the details of my proposals will be available from the Vote Office as soon as I have sat down.

"Holding the rate of VAT at 8 per cent. will reduce revenue by about £1 billion in 1995-96 and, reflecting the quarterly profile of payments, £1.5 billion in subsequent years. These are the amounts that I have sought to recover.

"Since VAT on fuel will remain at 8 per cent., it would be quite wrong to increase social security expenditure by providing the full compensation package previously announced to help people with VAT at 17.5 per cent. We will adjust the amount that would have been paid if VAT on fuel had been increased, saving around £200 million in 1995-96 and subsequent years. We will of course keep in place the help already given for 8 per cent. VAT on domestic fuel and power. We will increase benefits fully in line with the relevant cost-of-living index, including the component reflecting the impact of last year's VAT increase.

"After these adjustments pensioner couples will receive help of at least £1.05 a week from next April. This will be more than the average weekly cost to pensioners of paying 8 per cent. VAT on fuel. I am also keeping unchanged the increases in cold weather payments and spending on the Home Energy Efficiency Scheme which I announced in the Budget and in last Tuesday's debate.

"This small change in the previously announced pension rates has a knock-on effect to the national insurance system, since the lower earnings limit is automatically linked to the single pension. National insurance contributions will therefore start at £58 rather than £59 a week from April 1995. The upper earnings limit will be unchanged. This will have the effect of raising receipts from National insurance contributions by some £50 million next year.

"The remaining gap for 1995-96 amounts to some £800 million. My first step was to look at public spending. In my last two Budgets I have been able to find savings of £43 billion in public spending over the four survey years. This is much larger than the increases in taxation that we have found it necessary to make to restore healthy public finances after the recession.

[LORD HENLEY]

"We have managed to find these savings while increasing spending in real terms on key public services such as the National Health Service and the police. My objective remains to reduce government spending to below 40 per cent. of total national output. Both of my Budgets have made that objective much more achievable.

"The details of this year's extremely tight public spending settlement have already been announced by the relevant Secretaries of State. I do not consider it practicable or sensible to reopen those settlements today. At the time of my Budget, I struck a balance between spending and revenue designed to ensure that the economy remains on track for steady and sustainable growth. Nothing that has happened since then has led me to change that judgment for this year's settlement.

"The next area I considered to recover the shortfall in revenue was direct taxation. Since 1979, this Government have reduced the basic rate of taxation from 33 pence in the pound to 25 pence. and we also introduced the new lower rate of 20 pence. One-fifth of all taxpayers now pay tax only at this lower rate.

"When seeking to raise revenue in the 1993 Budgets my right honourable friend and I considered it necessary to freeze personal allowances and to reduce the married couple's allowance and the mortgage income relief allowance. I considered then that these increases in direct taxation were a sufficient and reasonable contribution to our revenue needs. That remains my view today. I do not intend to reverse my decisions to index the personal allowances and to over-index above inflation the elderly person's allowance and the 20 pence band.

"I also considered raising additional revenue from business taxation. In my Budget I provided as much help as I could for the business community. The reason was simple. Strong and thriving businesses are essential for a strong and thriving economy.

"I also listened during last week's debate to the Labour Party's proposals for closing loopholes and introducing a windfall tax on utilities and I have done some work on studying them. They are not serious options for revenue raising. This Government have never been a friend to the tax avoidance industry and Conservative Chancellors have changed loopholes year after year. The last two Budgets speak for themselves. I raised nearly £3.5 billion between 1994-95 and 1997-98 by closing loopholes. The honourable gentleman's proposals on loopholes are undesirable changes in taxation on legitimate business.

"I have looked many times at his proposal on executive share options. The policy behind tax relief for executive share options is geared to encouraging companies to motivate key employees and benefit all shareholders. Executives are liable to capital gains tax once they sell their shares. The right honourable gentleman exaggerates the cost of the scheme. He has claimed that I could raise £200 million by 'reforming' it. The actual total cost of this relief is estimated at around £50 million.

"The suggestion of a windfall tax is, by definition, a one-off tax. It could not replace permanent annual loss of a flow of revenue. In any event, it appears to be based on the suggestion of taxing profits on gains which, as the right honourable gentleman appears to have discovered in this morning's press, are already liable to taxation. A windfall tax would simply be another tax on a particular sector of industry. Like other taxes on business, it would inevitably have adverse effects on that business sector's investments and prices.

"My third and remaining option for 1995-96, therefore, has been to look at indirect taxation. As the House has rejected an increase in indirect taxation to which it had previously agreed, it is wholly consistent with my Budget strategy and it preserves the shape of the Budget to fill the hole with increases in indirect taxation. I have decided to bring forward certain increases in taxation in addition to those announced in my Budget to take effect from midnight, 31st December 1994.

"I propose that the duty on tobacco products, with the exception of hand-rolling tobacco, will increase by just under 4 per cent., equivalent to 6 pence on a packet of 20 cigarettes. This further increase in tobacco duty is consistent with our policy of increasing prices to discourage smoking.

"I also propose that the duties on road fuels will rise by a further 1 penny per litre. I have kept these increases to the minimum to limit the burden on business users and the rural motorist. Even after the increases, petrol will still be cheaper in real terms than a decade ago and cheaper than for our main European competitors. The increase will also play a part in our strategy for curbing the emission of CO_2. We remain fully committed to the target of reducing CO_2 emissions to 1990 levels by the year 2000.

"Finally, I propose that duties on alcohol will rise by around 4 per cent. This is equivalent to 1 penny on a pint of beer, 5 pence on a bottle of wine and 26 pence on a bottle of whisky. For the reasons set out in my Budget Statement, I had hoped to spare these industries any increase in duty this year. But in the present circumstances and as a result of my need to raise revenue from sources other than VAT on fuel, I have reluctantly judged it necessary to raise some additional revenue from them.

"Taken together, these increases will raise £180 million in the current year and nearly £800 million in 1995-96. In total this is sufficient to meet the shortfall next year. I expect the public sector borrowing requirement next year to be the same as I announced in my Budget Statement.

"Let me turn now to the following year, 1996-97. For that year I need to raise £1.5 billion. The tax measures that I have announced today will raise an additional £850 million.

"The impact of the higher duties that I have announced today on the RPI will not be as great as the impact would have been from the second stage of VAT on fuel. Inflation will therefore be very slightly lower than expected leading to further public spending savings on benefits of around £160 million in 1996-97 and later years. And there will be savings of around £200 million from the withdrawal of help to compensate for the second stage of VAT.

"There will, however, remain a further gap of around £300 million to be filled in 1996-97. I propose to finance this gap by reducing the public expenditure control totals for those years. For the time being I will score that reduction through a reduction in the provision that I have made for the reserve. The eventual consequence for departmental programmes will be addressed in next year's spending round. I expect the public sector borrowing requirement to be as I announced in my Budget Statement in 1996-97 and in subsequent years.

"Resolutions under the Provisional Collection of Taxes Act to hold VAT on fuel at 8 per cent. with effect from 1st January 1995 will be tabled very shortly. My right honourable friend the Leader of the House will then be arranging a debate before the House rises for the Christmas Recess.

"I said in my Budget speech that the British economy was currently facing the most favourable set of economic circumstances it has seen for many years. Trade figures published only this morning show that exports are up 14 per cent. in the past year and once again at record levels. The trade deficit is the lowest it has been for almost 10 years. The outlook for jobs and future prosperity for men and women in this country is improving day by day.

"This House has an obligation to keep this healthy recovery on track. We have an obligation to act responsibly and not be tempted by short-term populist measures which would undermine confidence in the Government's commitment to sound public finances. The measures I have announced today ensure that that commitment is fulfilled."

My Lords, that concludes the Statement.

3.47 p.m.

Lord Peston: My Lords, I thank the noble Lord for repeating the Statement. I do so most sincerely. But I am bound to say that responding to a Statement, sight unseen, is an absurd way for me and the rest of your Lordships to go on. All of us will respond as best we can. But there is an overwhelming case for dealing with these matters in a different way.

There is certainly an overwhelming case for your Lordships to have some time, as I understand the other place will have, to debate these matters before Christmas. I know that we always say that this is a matter for the usual channels, who will take your Lordships' views into account. But too frequently they do not. Thus even on an important matter like this today, as I understand it, the Back-Benchers will be limited by our usual rule on Statements to 20 minutes after the Front-Benchers have had their say. That will not do. There are great events occurring in our country and your Lordships are placed on the sidelines as spectators. It is about time that we asserted ourselves a bit more and demanded the right to discuss problems like this when they occur and not when the relevant events are history.

We start from a different position from that of the Government because we believe that this policy was mistaken in the first place. What I have not heard from the noble Lord—and I must ask him this question among others—is this. Do the Government still believe that the tax on domestic fuel was a good thing? There has not been a word of withdrawal on that. Do the Government believe that they were right to have had the second tranche of that tax, which they have now had to withdraw, or can we at least be told that in future there will not be a further increase when they feel that they can get away with it? Is that the end of at least the second tranche? We need to have an answer to that.

Before turning to the detail, the other thing that I have to say, very unhappily, is that this is nothing to do with economics or finance; it is all to do with politics. It is all to do with the noble Lord's right honourable friend papering over the cracks in a totally split party. It is also to do with the Government desperately trying to think of a way of taking income away from the public by means of taxes and then giving people a bit back later in order to try to get a few people to vote Tory at the next election. The Government are taking with one hand and giving back with the other. I believe that neither of those political moves has any hope whatever of succeeding. I do not believe that the cracks have been papered over or that the Government can pull off that confidence trick yet again. The Chancellor would have been better advised throughout to stick to serious economic and financial policy-making.

Perhaps I may say *en passant*, since this is my only opportunity that, as I said yesterday, I believe that raising the short-term rate of interest was a mistake. It was a panic measure. It is disturbing to read in the newspapers today that at least some people believe that it is a preliminary to further such increases. To do that would be another example of misplaced policy. Indeed, the whole matter is puzzling because the noble Lord has said, and the Government have claimed, that the economy is doing very well. However, with respect to interest rate increases we have a paradox because the Government are saying, "Yes, we are doing well so we had better stop that and make sure that we do not do too well". To use an expression that we came across not too long ago, the Government are saying, "We can see some 'green shoots' so we had better make sure that there is a bit of winter frost to destroy them".

I shall ask questions in a moment about the details—in so far as I can grasp them—but the other thing that puzzles me is that this whole matter is to do with very little or almost nothing. The way in which we approach the Budget in our country makes it a crisis if any attempt is made to amend it or to deviate from what the Treasury wants. Other countries manage these matters quite differently. Other countries do not regard it as a crisis or a catastrophe if the legislature endeavours to change fiscal proposals. They are discussed rationally and the legislature often get its own way. The Government seem to be placing themselves in peril. Indeed, they are in peril for a good many reasons, but it is absurd for the Government to place themselves at risk in this way.

[LORD PESTON]

I believe that if there could be a free vote in your Lordships' House on this matter, a similar view would result here as in another place, but we are not allowed to have such a vote because of our predecessors' misdemeanours in 1911. There is nothing that I can do about that. I cannot even blame any Member of your Lordships' House for what happened in 1911, but I would certainly like the opportunity to exercise that kind of power. However, unlike what happened in 1911, if I could exercise such power, I would then defer to the other place in due course. As I was saying, it is absurd that the Government should be placed in peril simply because, in my opinion, some sensible people rightly thought that it was a stupid tax.

I turn now to the detail, although it is immensely difficult to do so at the moment. Related to the question of whether the Government really still believe that what they were doing (until they failed to do it) was right is the question: Are the Government now telling us that they truly believe in what they are now doing? Or are the Government about to tell us that if they had the chance they would like to be able to impose the extra VAT on domestic fuel? Are they saying, "We are only doing these things because we can't do what we want"? What is the Government's position? Are they going to defend the tax increases because they believe that they are intrinsically correct or because they do not know what to do?

I ask that because I would certainly prefer one or two of the propositions to increasing the VAT on domestic fuel. Noble Lords opposite know my views on smoking. I believe that one of the best ways to reduce the incidence of smoking is to raise the excise duty on tobacco. I have no difficulty whatever with that. Indeed, I preferred that to what was proposed. My own view is that if we could have approached such matters sensibly, we would never have gone down the path of putting VAT on domestic fuel; instead, we would have done something about tobacco duty.

I know that the alcohol question is a little more difficult. On the one hand, I believe that the Treasury should raise as much revenue as it can from drinking but, on the other hand, I know that there is the problem of competition in a free market in Europe. It is a difficult technical problem. Does the increase in alcohol duty include the reduction in the duty that is being reversed on champagne and other sparkling wines? Perhaps the Minister can tell us about that very important matter.

Lord Stoddart of Swindon: My Lords, what about the champagne socialists?

Lord Peston: Exactly.

I turn to my next point. In taking £200 million away from pensioners, I take it that the noble Lord is saying that pensioners were to get that £200 million to offset the second tranche of the increase in VAT and that he is now saying that, because there is no increase in VAT, the Government are taking back whatever the sum is just to show how generous they are. I take it that it will amount to about 35p per pensioner. Are the Government saying, "Just to show what a caring government we are, we are taking that 35p away from you"? Can the noble Lord confirm that?

I have referred to sitting on the sidelines and I know only what I learn from sitting on the sidelines, but we are told that a great deal of extra money was found as part of a package to buy off the noble Lord's honourable friends who opposed the increase in the second tranche of VAT. I thought that the sum was £100 million. Can the noble Lord tell us what has happened to that £100 million? Has it just disappeared? Indeed, from where was it being found in the first place? It is not for me to advise the Government in their pathetic attempts to try to recapture some popularity, but having got the Treasury to agree to that £100 million, I should have thought that it would be sensible not to let the Treasury pinch it back again. I would have found a way of not taking that sum from the pensioners at least. But that is up to the Government.

Although I am keen to have a debate on this matter, I do not feel that this is the correct time to go through, as did the noble Lord, the main suggestions put forward by the Opposition. There is no hurry for me. Only the others will be made to hurry. The noble Lord did us the honour of telling us that he had considered seriously all the suggestions that had been made by the Labour Party. I must advise him that I am shocked by the Treasury's rejection that it wishes to rule out any intensification of the way in which we deal with loopholes. I am unhappy about that. If we have an opportunity to debate it, I shall explain to the noble Lord how we can deal much more seriously with loopholes than is the case at present.

I take a similar view of executive share options. I am amazed to discover that there is a new Treasury doctrine that we do not care for windfall taxes. I should like to know the date of that Treasury doctrine. The rule in the Treasury used to be, "We'll tax anything we can and keep what we can get away with. The fact that it was a windfall will not bother us at all". Perhaps the noble Lord could reflect on that and tell me whether he would like to consider the matter further.

I have nearly reached my final remarks. What really puzzles me as an economist is that we are heading towards a public sector borrowing requirement of £20 billion with a lower figure still to come. Speaking from memory, I recall that the margin of error in the public sector borrowing requirement is plus or minus £6 billion. That is in the nature of such economic figures. Is it not strange that within a number such as £6 billion we are footling around with £200 million which is of a totally lower order of magnitude? Why does not the Chancellor approach this matter rationally and say, "I wanted to do it, but the economy is doing pretty well, and I wanted it to carry on doing well", and let us forget the whole thing, apart from apologising to the pensioners?

I conclude by echoing the remarks of my right honourable friend the Leader of the Opposition in the other place. He offered to help the Government out of their difficulties in this matter. I should like to echo those remarks. I wish to be as helpful as I possibly can, because I am concerned about the future of our great nation, and my desire is that the economy should not be made worse than it otherwise would be. Will the Minister tell his right honourable friend the Chancellor of the Exchequer that if he feels that he needs my advice, which I feel strongly he does, he has merely to pick up the telephone and ask, and I shall respond as positively as I can?

Lord Ezra: My Lords, I too should like to thank the Minister for having repeated the Statement, and to support what the noble Lord, Lord Peston, has said, that, exceptionally on this occasion, we on this side of the House did not receive a copy of the Statement, something which I regard as rather rare in our proceedings on such an important issue. Furthermore, I hope that we can have time for a longer debate on this matter.

The whole issue raises the question of what is the strategy behind the Budget. The Chancellor has been knocked off course on a relatively small part of the Budget; but that calls into question whether the aim is to support our long-term economy or to build up a reserve to use for a short-term political purpose. If in the next Budget the benefits which have been derived from the improvement in the economy are used purely for short-term purposes, then I should have thought that the thinking was deficient. I should like to have an assurance from the Minister that the intention is to build up the economy; that as we derive greater benefit from the current improvements, they will be ploughed back into the business of Britain in the form of stimulating further investment; to improve our infrastructure; and to ensure that we can overcome the next downturn in the world economy more effectively than we have in the past. That is the first point that I should like to raise.

The second point is one that has already been referred to by the noble Lord, Lord Peston, and that is the interest rate increase. Was the motivation for that increase a feeling that the economy was overheating, and that it would have been imposed in any event, or was it a reaction to the Government's failure to get through their proposal for VAT on fuel? We need to know what led the Government so quickly to introduce an interest rate increase. If it is due to the overheating of the economy, are they concerned about that seriously, and can we expect further increases in interest rates in the near future?

As to the specific measures taken, I believe that most would agree that if additional revenue had to be found, then it would best be found in areas where we should have fiscal disincentives—disincentives on smoking and drinking, and to deal with the problem of pollution from transport. I must say that I concur with the last question posed by the noble Lord, Lord Peston, bearing in mind that this represented such a small proportion of the total revenues about which we are talking, was it necessary to consider raising additional taxes anyway?

Perhaps I may conclude by saying that this has been a most disturbing episode. We are not clear what is the Government's fiscal and financial strategy, and the way in which this has been dealt raises many further doubts.

Lord Henley: My Lords, I start by giving the noble Lord, Lord Ezra, a categoric assurance that obviously we intend to see the economy build up. That is what my right honourable friend the Chancellor of the Exchequer was making clear in his Statement. That is why he made the decisions that he did. I am somewhat surprised by the attitude of the two noble Lords, particularly that of the noble Lord, Lord Peston, a distinguished economist. He seemed to imply that £200 million was a figure which was not worth bothering about. I have to explain to him that we are talking not about £200 million but about £1 billion. That is a fairly large sum, and I suspect that his attitude to those relatively insignificant sums—as he terms them—probably explains why my right honourable friend the Chancellor of the Exchequer is the Chancellor of the Exchequer and why it is exceedingly unlikely that he will be ringing up the noble Lord to seek his advice. It probably goes some way towards explaining why all Chancellors of the Exchequer for the past 15 years have been Conservatives.

I note the noble Lord's request for a debate. He makes such requests on many occasions. I can say only that I am sure that my noble friend the Leader of the House heard his request. I should remind him that we do not debate the Budget, and this is to some extent an offshoot of that. We recently had a debate on the economy during the debates on the Queen's Speech. We normally have an opportunity to have a debate on Second Reading of the Finance Bill.

Perhaps I may move on to the subject of VAT, and whether we thought that it was a good tax, and whether we shall be returning to it at some later stage. We believe in a broadly based tax system. We thought it was therefore sensible to go ahead with the second stage of VAT on fuel, not least because we provided considerable protection for pensioners, disabled people and other vulnerable groups. We should have preferred not to have increased excise duties, but we were left with no option. Obviously it is not without cost.

The most important thing is that we maintain healthy growth by sticking to the path mapped out for public borrowing. I can assure the noble Lord that we shall continue along that line. The noble Lord asked about the £100 million. As that was part of the compensation for the second stage of VAT on fuel and power, it is only right that it should have been withdrawn when the VAT vote was lost.

Both noble Lords asked about the rise in interest rates. Our monetary policy is based on the inflation outlook, and the half point rise yesterday was justified in those terms. We are committed, unlike noble Lords opposite, to avoiding the boom/bust cycle. It is important that we made that increase to maintain confidence in our finances. I do not wish to speculate on any future tax increases.

Perhaps I may deal with one or two small points. The noble Lord, with his Socialist interest in champagne, asked whether the increases announced would apply to it. I can assure him that the earlier reduction will still apply, because sparkling wine was taxed at a rate higher than similar products, including even stronger fortified wines, and that seemed wholly anomalous. Obviously the newly-adjusted downwards rate will be adjusted upwards by the same percentage as other products and

[LORD HENLEY]
therefore the noble Lord will find a small increase of some 7 pence also on his bottle of champagne, but I dare say that he will manage to live with that.

Lastly, perhaps I may repeat that we are as committed as anyone to fighting genuine loopholes fully. We have done so on many occasions, and on occasions the party opposite has voted against those proposals. The Opposition's proposals put forward by the noble Lord's right honourable friend were not loopholes but taxes on business. I hope that that deals with most of the points put to me by the two noble Lords.

4.10 p.m.

Lord Boyd-Carpenter: My Lords, I warmly support the request of the noble Lord, Lord Peston, that your Lordships' House be given an opportunity to debate this Statement in full. It is slightly absurd that, while the two party spokesmen opposite have a reasonable allowance of time, the rest of us are confined within 20 minutes. Given the immense importance of the subject and the wide variety of expertise in this House, it is absurd that we should be so confined. I beg my noble friend seriously to consider arranging a full day's debate on the Statement in order that all Members of your Lordships' House can contribute.

There was little, if any, mention in this Statement of the Government being in the situation in which they were placed as a result of the decision of another place, reducing public expenditure. Surely that would have been the best method of adjusting the balance. I remind my noble friend that this year legal aid is being increased by £100 million. If we are so hard pressed and in such difficulties that we have to increase taxes in order to achieve a balance, surely thought should be given substantially to cutting back on legal aid.

Lord Henley: My Lords, as regard the first point that my noble friend made, I can only express a degree of sympathy. I recognise that there is considerable expertise in this House; we have as Members former Chancellors of the Exchequer, Chief Secretaries and writers of letters to *The Times*. I remember a great letter that was written some 15 years ago. I imagine that many people would care to debate these matters and my noble friend the Leader of the House heard what my noble friend Lord Boyd-Carpenter said. However, there are other occasions on which we can debate them.

My noble friend made a substantive point about reductions in public expenditure. My right honourable friend believed that after going through the public expenditure round it would be invidious to go back to departments to seek further reductions. The Government are committed to seeing a proportion of GNP that is taken up by public expenditure reduced over the years. That is what my right honourable friend the Chancellor of the Exchequer would like to see. I shall not comment on particular departments, although my noble friend raised the question of legal aid. The general point is that it would have been invidious to go back to departments after having achieved a settlement.

Lord Marsh: My Lords, does the Minister accept that many people will agree with the noble Lord, Lord Peston, that the measures that have been outlined are a preferable alternative to the Government's policy. That is not a unique discovery on my part because for some months almost everyone in the country has been saying that. The alternative measures that have been announced are preferable to what was taking place.

Will the Minister accept that the worrying aspect is that £1 billion is a great deal of money as part of a Budget, because a Budget is made up of billions of pounds? The Government got into this situation as a result of their refusal to listen to anything that anyone said in this connection. They were prepared to sacrifice their majority and turn the issue into a major crisis. Does the Minister agree that that is a mixture of stupidity and, even more frightening, a growing level of crass arrogance?

Lord Henley: My Lords, I totally disagree with the noble Lord. He is incorrect in making such assertions. We believed that in a broadly-based taxed system it was right to go ahead with the second stage of VAT on fuel, not least because we were offering the appropriate protection to the various vulnerable groups. Obviously, others thought otherwise and therefore, having lost the vote, my right honourable friend said that he would not go ahead with the increase. However, unlike the noble Lord, Lord Peston, and, I suspect, the noble Lord, Lord Marsh, my right honourable friend considers £1 billion to be a fairly significant sum. That hole had to be plugged and that is why my right honourable friend came forward with the proposals that I announced in the Statement.

Lord Stoddart of Swindon: My Lords, my noble friend said that he wished to help the Government. I assure the Government that the only way in which I wish to help them is out of office, and the sooner that that happens the better things will be for this country and its taxpayers. I must say to my noble friend that if he expects the Government to listen to him, he is living in cloud cuckoo land. They do not even listen to the chairman and vice chairman of the Tory Party. I understand that the chairman advised the Government that the introduction of the further 9.5 per cent. VAT on fuel would amount almost to political suicide. However, the Government went ahead which was, as the noble Lord, Lord Marsh, said, an act of sheer stupidity. Unfortunately, the country is having to reap the whirlwind of the seeds that the Government have sown.

Now the people are faced with a double whammy. First, their taxes are being increased and, secondly, perhaps as a matter of revenge, interest rates are being increased. Let us think about that and understand that, although the Government say that they are in favour of the family, the Budget has hit married couples. There has been a reduction in the married man's allowance and home buyers will be hit a second time by the increase in interest rates. It is all completely unnecessary.

Will the Minister confirm that this year taxation will increase by £26.4 million? Will he also confirm that, if the Chancellor increased the higher tax rate and adopted the measures that were put forward by my noble friend, he would not have to increase the cost of living and put burdens on those in our community who are already worse off?

Lord Henley: My Lords, I agree with the noble Lord in one small particular. He was correct in saying that his noble friend is living in cloud cuckoo land. I totally and utterly reject his allegation that interest rates were increased out of revenge against—I am not sure against whom it was supposed to be. Interest rates were increased for the reasons that I gave and not out of revenge.

I cannot confirm the noble Lord's figures about the increase in taxes. I am grateful to him for pointing to the right page in the Red Book. He knows perfectly well that taxes had to be increased in order to reduce the amount of borrowing. The noble Lord and, for all I know, his party are wedded to the idea of borrowing, borrowing, borrowing. However, that is not the way out. In the end, the gap had to be narrowed and there are two ways of doing that; the first is by having firm control of public expenditure, which we have; and the second is by increasing taxes.

Lord Aldington: My Lords, I too ask the Government—my noble friend the Leader of the House is in his place—to consider an early debate on this matter. I do so not necessarily for the reason given by my noble friend Lord Boyd-Carpenter but because some of us believe that the Government were right about the Budget, right about the interest rate and right about the proposals that they have brought forward today. One would not obtain that impression from listening to these questions.

Lord Henley: My Lords, I can only say that I am very, very grateful to my noble friend for making the point that the Government were right, although misguided people on the other side in the other place voted against certain parts of the Budget. I am sure that my noble friend the Leader of the House will have noted what my noble friend Lord Aldington said; namely, that it might be appropriate for us to have an early debate so that we can make the Government's case loud and clear and can demonstrate that this was a good Budget sadly led astray by others.

Lord Barnett: My Lords, I wonder whether the Minister has read the Government's Red Book. I am glad that he has it with him. Perhaps he will look at paragraph 4.32 of it. It is true that £1 billion is quite a lot of money, but to pretend that you can carry out a Budget with that degree of accuracy is, frankly, misleading.

As we see from the paragraph to which I have referred, the plain fact is that there is an estimated £10.5 billion margin of error in the public sector borrowing requirement. Therefore, is not the real mistake that the Government believed their own Whips and that they could get through the increase in VAT to 17.5 per cent.? They should have asked the Whips whether they can count properly because they obviously counted wrongly. For factual reasons, apart from how damaging it would be to ordinary people, as we have heard, they should not have proposed such an increase. Why on earth did they go ahead with that proposal, given the huge margin of error, when they did not need to?

Lord Henley: My Lords, I am reminded of the saying, "A billion here, a billion there and pretty soon you are spending serious money". I do not agree with the noble Lord. There was a gap there. I accept that there are margins of error; but if one takes out £1 billion, which in effect is what has happened as a result of the vote, it is quite right that the Chancellor should try to put it back and that is what he has tried to do in a manner which is the least damaging possible.

Lord Clark of Kempston: My Lords, does my noble friend not agree that it is essential in running a sound economy to keep control of the public sector borrowing requirement? I hope that my noble friend will agree that my right honourable friend could have increased the public sector borrowing requirement by £1 billion and that would probably have gone through unnoticed. On the other hand, he could have robbed the contingency reserve fund of £1 billion and not increased taxes. But in taking the decision that public sector borrowing is so essential, I believe that my right honourable friend has done the courageous thing and has increased taxation in order to make up that loss of £1 billion. Does my noble friend agree with me that that is a sounder way of running the economy rather than running into debt?

Lord Henley: My Lords, I agree totally with my noble friend. I am sure that he will understand when I say that it is unlikely that noble Lords opposite will agree with my noble friend and me on this matter. As he suggests, they would either have borrowed more or raided this fund or that fund. However, the sensible approach is that adopted by my right honourable friend the Chancellor of the Exchequer.

Lord Howell: My Lords, perhaps I may refer to the reference that was made in the Statement to public expenditure in the year 1996-97? Perhaps I may draw attention to the very serious situation which is affecting most local authorities, whatever their political complexion. They are now finding the greatest difficulty in financing education, housing and social services, which are the services that really affect people living in desperate conditions. Therefore, perhaps I may put in a plea in advance that if the Government are to look again at reducing the public sector borrowing requirement, which I understand, that they take into account the very real difficulties now affecting local authorities and therefore affecting many millions of deserving people in this country.

Lord Henley: My Lords, as my right honourable friend the Chancellor of the Exchequer made quite clear in the Statement, we are committed where possible to keeping down public expenditure. We have a very good record in that regard. But he made it quite clear also that we are committed to providing essential services. That is why he cited just two examples: there has been increased provision for both the police and the National Health Service. I am sure that my right honourable friend will note what the noble Lord has said about anxieties in relation to local authorities. But all parts of

[LORD HENLEY]
government, in one form or another, will be subject to some constraints while we remain committed to providing all essential services.

Lord Skidelsky: My Lords, does my noble friend agree with me that the Chancellor was committed to the VAT increase on fuel by his predecessor and had he not made an attempt to fulfil that commitment, the very same people who now condemn him for stupidity and arrogance would be the first to condemn him for weakness and breaking promises? Failure to attempt to fulfil that commitment would also have had a very damaging effect on the credibility of the Government.

Lord Henley: My Lords, my noble friend is quite correct. Another place had voted on that matter. That VAT increase had been voted through, I believe, on four occasions.

Lord Bruce of Donington: My Lords, many of your Lordships will be rather puzzled by the noble Lord's insistence that £200 million or £300 million are extremely important. I was very struck by that remark because it seems a little odd in view of the fact that the Government had a suicide pact on the necessity for increasing public expenditure to £3.5 billion per annum to be paid out to the European Community. A three-line Whip was put on that vote to increase public expenditure, and indeed it became a vote of confidence. Surely there must be a sense of proportion somewhere. Why do not the Government consider giving a complete rethink to this whole matter, rather than leaving it to a lot of technicians within the Treasury whose errors in the past have been so astronomical that even the Government themselves have found it necessary to reduce their number?

Lord Henley: My Lords, I am afraid that I cannot agree with the noble Lord. The noble Lord will have to accept that I think that the £200 million or £300 million to which the noble Lord referred is a significant sum, as is £1 billion. I shall be delighted if the noble Lord wishes to debate the issue of own resources. There will be ample opportunity to do that in due course. I believe that the decision made in Edinburgh was good. That has kept down the increases and the noble Lord should be grateful for that. Perhaps he will remember that the Commission was seeking something like £1.37 billion; but, as a result of the negotiations of my right honourable friend the Prime Minister, that was kept down to £1.27 billion. That was a decision which was generally welcomed by all sides of both Houses and, for all I know, by the noble Lord himself.

Lord Skelmersdale: My Lords, does my noble friend recall that yesterday my noble friend Lord Trefgarne introduced a debate in your Lordships' House on the subject of small and medium-sized businesses, with special reference to the manufacturing sector? In the course of that debate, my noble friend Lord Ferrers was asked to pass on to my right honourable friend the Chancellor of the Exchequer the view that it would be disastrous for the Government to take the easy option of increasing VAT by 0.5 per cent. across the board. Therefore, the Government are to be congratulated for not taking that easy option.

Secondly, does my noble friend recall that when VAT on domestic fuel and power was originally suggested and introduced at the rate of 8 per cent., part of the rationale for that was that it was a carbon tax? Does my noble friend consider that VAT on domestic fuel and power at 8 per cent. plus the additional taxes on road fuel will be a suitable equivalent to the proposed EC carbon tax?

Lord Henley: My Lords, with regard to the first point raised by my noble friend, I can confirm that my right honourable friend the Chancellor of the Exchequer always takes considerable note of what is said in debates in this House. I am sure that he noted the comments to which my noble friend referred in the debate introduced yesterday by my noble friend Lord Trefgarne.

In relation to his second point, even with the increases now of only 8 per cent. in VAT on fuel, prices for both electricity and gas have come down over the past few years in real terms, even after taking into account that 8 per cent.

Visas and Border Controls: ECC Report

4.30 p.m.

Lord Slynn of Hadley rose to move, That this House takes note of the Report of the European Communities Committee on *Visas and Control of External Borders of the Member States* (14th Report, HL Paper 78).

The noble Lord said: My Lords, the report referred to in the Motion has one unusual feature. Your Lordships are well aware that the European Union now has what are appropriately, or otherwise, called three pillars. The first of those pillars consists of measures adopted by the Council and the Commission of the Community broadly as has been done until now. The second and third of those pillars are very different. They involve agreement by member states dealing with foreign affairs and security matters on the one hand and on the other hand home affairs and justice.

In the report we are concerned with a proposed draft regulation under the Community pillar dealing with visas and a proposal for a convention to be adopted by member states on persons who cross the external frontiers of the Community. That proposed convention is not made under the Community pillar but under Article K.3(2) (c) of the justice and home affairs pillar. This is the first time that the Select Committee has had to consider a proposal under the home affairs and justice pillar.

Our inquiry has shown that there can be difficulties in the overlap between proposals in a related area which comes under the two pillars. I am not sure whether "under" is the right word; there should perhaps be some other word as it is "pillar" and not "pillow". However, I shall use the phrase "under the pillar" in the hope that your Lordships will understand what I mean.

Our inquiry revealed even more a matter which the Select Committee has stressed throughout; namely, that the committee should be able to scrutinise a proposed draft text at an early stage rather than that the committee should be confined to considering proposals at a late stage when the United Kingdom is considering ratifying the conventions. To comment at that stage may well be to whistle in the wind or may lead to the whole process beginning again in a very unsatisfactory way.

Perhaps I may deal, first, with the draft external frontiers convention. It has had a somewhat curious history. Its negotiation began in 1991, but it ran into difficulties because Spain and the United Kingdom were not able to agree about the position of Gibraltar. After the Treaty of Union, it was realised that some of the matters in the proposed convention would have to be transferred to the regulation under the Community pillar.

The basic object of the convention is to lay down rules which will apply to persons who are not Union citizens and who are not, broadly speaking, nationals of a member state who want to cross the external frontiers of the Community. It is broadly agreed that there must be rules based on common criteria to cover such persons and rules which will involve close co-operation among the member states. The target is to strike a balance between eliminating threats to public security and public safety in the member states and at the same time preserving such openness for the rest of the world as is possible.

There are many detailed rules in the draft convention about the establishment of crossing points, the surveillance of frontiers, residence permits and visas. I propose to say nothing about them because I think that it would be wrong to detain your Lordships with a discussion of that kind of detail. Perhaps I may mention just four matters which seem to me to be issues of principle and issues of considerable importance.

One element of the convention, and an important part of it, is the preparation of a joint list for all member states of persons whom all the member states must refuse entry if they seek to come into the Community. That joint list is to consist of names which are notified by the member states and the decision as to whether a person shall be placed on the list is to be based on the threat which that person may represent to the public policy or national security of the member states. The decision to put forward a name is to be taken in accordance with national procedures on account of a number of factors, such as that the person in question has served a custodial sentence of more than one year.

It is obvious that, even now, before the convention is adopted, member states may under their own rules refuse entry to undesirable third-country persons who wish to come into their states. The difference in the new proposal is that, if someone is put on the list, he must be refused entry to all member states. If a businessman now wants to come to Paris and he is on the French exclusion list, he can presumably go to Brussels and his clients will go there to see him. Under the new proposed convention, he would not be able to go anywhere into the Community if he had got on to the list. There is no doubt that, in the view of the committee, the provision of a list is justified when the right people find themselves on the list.

However, the categories of persons who may be put on the list include two matters which gave us concern. The first is where there is information to the effect that the person concerned has committed a serious crime—that is, not a conviction but merely information to the effect that the person has committed a serious crime; and, perhaps even more general, where there are serious grounds for believing that a person is planning to commit a serious crime or that he represents a threat to the public security of a state.

It is idle to pretend that, in the process of people being nominated and their names then being notified to the central list, mistakes could not happen. It cannot be ruled out that names will be put forward by other individuals, even maliciously, with the result that someone may get on to the list who really should not be there at all. A number of our witnesses expressed very serious concern about that possibility. As a result, we think that it is essential that an effective remedy must be provided to give protection against unfair, improper exclusion from the Community and that, at the very least, a person should know which state has put him on the central list.

It is our view that there should also be a remedy in national courts against such wrongful inclusion on the list and against the withdrawal of a residence permit. We do not believe that that should be left to chance. We think that it should either be in the convention or that it should be included in measures adopted to give effect to the convention. It is our recommendation that one of those two courses should be followed.

The second item is very different. Article 6 of the convention provides that, where a passenger comes into Community territory by air from a third state and is going to transfer at the airport where he lands to an aeroplane to take him to another state, he should be subject to entry conditions and entry control at the airport where he first lands. Therefore, if someone comes to London who is going to Paris, the proposal is that he should be controlled in London and if someone is going to Paris and then on to Berlin he should be controlled in Paris.

That may work where intra-Community state flights are treated as domestic flights. It may not work in countries like the United Kingdom, Ireland or Denmark where they are not so treated. But it seems to the Committee that this does not in any view take account of the special position of a hub airport like London where passengers frequently land from all parts of the world in order to transfer to other flights and where they are kept on the air side of immigration controls without any check on their immigration status, and where they are not treated as having entered the United Kingdom.

The Committee considers that this proposal needs radical reconsideration by the Council. It ought to be looked at again in view of the special status of London Airport. It may not be unique, but it is the most striking example of this kind of problem. But even if the proposal is to be maintained, the Committee recommends that adequate time should be given for the very substantial restructuring and changes in the

[LORD SLYNN OF HADLEY]
infrastructure which may have to be adopted at the airport. The proposal at the moment gives far too little notice to the airport authorities.

Thirdly—I can take this more shortly—Article 14 of the convention deals with the responsibility of carriers who bring persons into the United Kingdom or into the Community when they do not have either the necessary travel documents or the necessary visas. The convention proposes to impose penalties upon such carriers even where there is not negligence, and penalties which go beyond the responsibility simply to take them back or to pay for their accommodation in the meantime. It seems to the Committee that that is in conflict with Article 9 of the Chicago Convention which imposes liability only where the carrier has been negligent.

The Committee takes the view that the same should be the position in this draft convention and, moreover, that it is particularly important that airport officials, airline officials and immigration officers should be aware of responsibilities under the European Convention on Human Rights and under the Geneva Convention relating to refugees to ensure that people are not sent back when they are quite genuinely asking to be admitted to a member state because of a well founded fear of persecution for political reasons. What we propose in this area, on the basis of very serious and impressive evidence given to us, was that the appropriate officials and administrators should be made very aware of the dangers which this kind of provision can open up.

Finally, as far as the convention is concerned, I come to a different topic and one of general importance. Because this is a treaty between the member states and not a Community measure, the European Court of Justice does not automatically have jurisdiction to deal with disputes about the interpretation of the convention or disputes which may arise out of its administration. However, there is provision in the treaty for the European Court to be given jurisdiction to interpret and to rule on disputes regarding the application. When this convention was first proposed, there was no proposal to include jurisdiction for the European Court, but the Commission has come to the view that it would be appropriate to provide for a limited jurisdiction; for the power of a national judge, who is dealing with a contention that the convention has been violated if the convention is part of domestic law, to refer that question of interpretation to the European Court, and for both the Commission and member states to take proceedings against other member states in the Community.

We of course understand that this is to be an international treaty and not a Community measure. We also recognise, because of the variety of views on our Committee, that there can be different attitudes to this particular question. But after very considerable discussion, we came to the conclusion that this is the sort of measure in which the European Court of Justice could play a valuable role. All our witnesses took the view that it was desirable that the European Court should have this kind of jurisdiction. Their evidence, I suggest, is not to be disregarded. We were not persuaded—I certainly was not persuaded—by Home Office arguments that the convention is largely Executive and administrative in character and that disputes can be resolved by officials or by the Council of the member states.

As I see it, the European Court is the one way—the best possible way—in which this convention can be most effectively applied uniformly in the Community. This is not to be seen as a way of interfering here; it is to be seen, I submit, as a way of ensuring that all the member states carry out their obligations under the convention in the same way. Without some form of central ruling on interpretation or on disputes, I fail to see how that can happen. It was of notable interest that the witness from the European Parliament was wholly in favour of this proposal and thought it quite absurd that the member states should have to go to the International Court of Justice at the Hague if there was a dispute of that kind. We therefore recommend that the European Court of Justice should have jurisdiction as proposed by the Commission.

Finally, I turn to the regulation which I can deal with much more briefly. There are two important issues of competence and two short matters of practical application. Article 100c of the treaty deals with the approximation of laws, and it provides very specifically that the Council shall determine the third countries whose nationals must be in possession of a visa when they cross one of the external frontiers of the Community.

On the other hand Article K deals generally with asylum policy, the crossing of external borders and with policy dealing with nationals of third countries including conditions of entry and residence. Article 1(1) of the regulation clearly falls inside Article 100c. It provides a list of those third countries whose nationals must have a visa. There can be no challenge, I suspect, to that. Article 1(2), however, gives the Council power to list countries whose nationals are exempted from the need to have visas. In common sense it might be said that the second is a corollary of the first, and if the Council may make a list of those who need visas, it may make a list of those who do not need visas. However, we came to the conclusion that if this had been intended in Article 100c of the treaty, the article would have followed the draft provision in the pre-existing proposed convention where the words were,

"the arrangement shall determine whether or not"

a visa is required by the nationals of a particular member state.

Had that change not taken place, I, for my part, would have accepted that the one was the corollary of the other. But in the light of the change in the language from the earlier convention the Committee came to the conclusion that this was a very specific provision and that if states are to be exempted, this must be put into the convention and not into the regulation.

The other point which I wish to make, and which I believe is of some importance, concerns Article 2. Article 2 provides that member states shall not be entitled to require a visa of a person who seeks to cross their external frontiers and who already holds a visa issued by another member state, if that visa is valid throughout the Community. Therefore, in the United

Kingdom we could not refuse entry to someone who had a visa from Germany or Greece if that visa was valid throughout the Community.

We came to the conclusion that that does not fall within the limited words of Article 100c. That provision was itself a compromise between those who wanted these matters to be under the Community pillar and those who wanted it to be under the home affairs and justice pillar. We do not find it possible to construe Article 100c as allowing Article 2 of the regulation to stand. It may well be a desirable provision, but it should go into the convention.

On that basis, we have come to the view that both those provisions in Article 1(2) and in Article 2 of the proposed regulation are not within the competence of the Community and that they should be put into the convention.

The proposed regulation covers transit visas. We consider that to be wholly inappropriate. We think that the list which has been drawn up of countries whose nationals must have visas is inordinately long. Too much should not be attached to that. There is nothing sinister about it. It was a Commission proposal which was intended to initiate discussion, even though it is somewhat extensive. In the view of the committee there is no doubt that it should be shortened. There seems to be no justification for the inclusion of some Commonwealth countries on the list as countries whose nationals must have visas if they come to the Community, especially as other Commonwealth countries are not on the list.

I am sorry that I have taken some time. However, this is a matter of considerable importance in the Community. My colleagues in Sub-Committee E who conducted the inquiry and I are greatly indebted to our legal adviser, Mrs. Eileen Denza, for her work and guidance in preparing our report, and to our clerk, Mr. Michael Pownall, and those who gave evidence to us. For many of them it involved considerable time and effort, on what are important questions. I beg to move.

Moved, That this House takes note of the report of the European Communities Committee on Visas and Control of External Borders of the Member States (14th Report, H.L. Paper 78).—(*Lord Slynn of Hadley.*)

4.52 p.m.

Baroness Park of Monmouth: My Lords, I have read the committee's admirable report with great interest. Members of the committee are best placed to make informed comment, and I feel rather shy about speaking so early in the debate. However, I wish to make two or three points.

First, I strongly support the last conclusion in paragraph 121 of the report on the question of the negative visa list. The inclusion of Commonwealth countries such as Barbados, Belize, India, Pakistan, the Solomons, Botswana and Zambia, to name only a few, among the countries requiring visas for entry would be deeply damaging to our interests and would be taken as further proof by the Commonwealth that our European dimension is paramount and our Commonwealth membership unimportant. It is also simply not sensible, since so many of our visitors are Commonwealth visitors.

I agree with many of the arguments put forward by the JCWI and the ILPA. The distinctions made between Commonwealth countries seem both invidious and mysterious. It is still more mysterious that, as they point out, no countries in Latin America appear on the list despite their drug culture in some cases (Colombia, for instance) and their abuse of human rights (Guatemala).

In the debate on the European Communities (Amendment) Bill in June 1993 I warned that Article 100c and Articles K.1, K.3 and K.9 would have serious implications for our independence of action. I believe that I was right. I was concerned then about our Commonwealth relationships and about the threat to our national security which the greatly extended powers of the Commission to initiate further action under qualified majority voting after 1996 would pose. I still feel that Article 100c(5), which pays lip service to the need for member states to be able to safeguard internal security, is negated by Article 100c(6) which allows Article 100c to apply to other areas under Article K.9.

I also strongly support paragraphs 109 and 110 of the conclusions. I find it amazing that in the climate of today's Europe, with the spreading activity of, for instance, the Russian mafia and international drug rings, and given the porous and inadequately policed external frontiers in many cases, there should be any serious intention to abolish controls at internal borders, especially in the case of the UK which has no system of internal identity cards, and given the fact that even in 1991, as I said in the 1993 debate, there was and is a thriving trade in the forging of EC passports. Of 591 persons refused entry at one English port alone in 1991 because of forged documents, 524 had forged EC documents.

I agree with the committee that it will still be necessary to control the movement of people across internal frontiers where a member state deems it right to do so. I wish they all did. Equally, I strongly support the recommendation in paragraph 110 that the conventions recommended by the Council:

"should reflect the nature of these conventions as international agreements which individual Member States may choose whether to ratify or not".

Two tendencies have become manifest in the Commission's conduct of affairs, and indeed to some extent that of the Council of member states. The first has been a lack of transparency. For instance, as the committee says in paragraph 74, the inter-governmental negotiations leading to the political agreement of June 1991 on the external frontiers convention took place in secret and the text agreed, which was of obvious importance for European integration, was not laid before the UK Parliament for a further year. The other tendency is towards a creeping assumption of even more powers.

The proposals are now out in the open, and that is good, but we now need to have the political will and the good sense to say in good time whether we agree to what is proposed. Qualified majority voting does not make it easier, but we should retain unequivocally our right not to ratify if necessary. Moreover, we must allow

[BARONESS PARK OF MONMOUTH]
no precedents to be set for this pillar which could have an adverse impact on the 1996 discussions on the defence, security and foreign affairs pillars. Reminding the Commission that we retain our right to ratify and to enter into inter-governmental treaties can only be beneficial. Also, we must not allow the aim of harmonisation to override the individual needs and duties of member countries and the propriety of inter-governmental rather than supragovernmental policies.

4.57 p.m.

Lord Archer of Sandwell: My Lords, I venture to intervene to emphasise one subject about which concern was expressed by the noble and learned Lord, Lord Slynn. I do so lest it be thought that, if no other member of Sub-Committee E were to intervene, we thought of the matter lightly. The fact that I do not echo all that the noble and learned Lord said about the other matters of concern does not entail that we thought lightly about those.

The matter about which I want to express concern and to echo the concern of the noble and learned Lord is the joint list. As I may have mentioned in your Lordships' House previously, I have supported closer integration in Europe for many years —since before the idea was as widely accepted as it is now. I can claim to have been a Christian before Constantine. Therefore, I have no difficulty in supporting the concept of the free movement of persons, although I fully take the point of the noble Baroness, Lady Park, that there are some matters about which we need to exercise control at internal frontiers. If we are to have the free movement of persons, I accept that a necessary consequence is that there should be co-ordination in the control of external borders. But it is simply stating the obvious to point out that the greater the area and the population over which an authority exercises control, the greater the power of that authority over individuals, and the greater the degree to which individuals are at its mercy. It is not simply that an authority exercises power over more individuals; its power over each individual is so much the greater.

We have an example of that. Article 7 of the draft convention provides that a person may be denied entry to the territories of member states if he represents a threat to the public policy, national security or international relations of member states. Article 10 provides for the making of a list of persons who are thought to pose such a threat. It is to be a joint list, and each member state may require that the names of specific persons shall be included in the list. The criteria for including a name on the list are set out in the draft article, Article 7, but the decision whether a particular person falls within those criteria is entirely within the judgment of each member state.

When Mr. de Lobkowicz, head of the unit dealing with the subject in the European Commission, gave evidence to the sub-committee—his evidence is set out at page 61 and the following pages of the minutes of evidence—he made it clear that such a decision was seen as falling within the principle of subsidiarity. Each state would provide such safeguards as it thinks fit against the wrongful inclusion of a person on the list, but if a state submits a name there is no further sieve, and there is no further safeguard.

In effect, the list will be an amalgam of all the national lists. It will represent the exercise of power over more individuals than any national list. But, more importantly, the consequences for any individual will be so much the greater. He will be precluded from entering any of the member states. If France requires an individual to be added to the list, not only will he be precluded from entering France, he will be precluded from entering the United Kingdom or any of the other member states.

Admittedly, there is a proposed exception in relation to visas, as the noble and learned Lord pointed out. If a specific country is persuaded that it is important that an individual on the list should visit its territory for one of the purposes specified, it may issue a visa limited to that territory. But the individual must find means to activate a specific exception, and it is clearly a narrow list of exceptions.

I was surprised to learn that the safeguards against the wrongful inclusion of someone's name are regarded as wholly a matter for the member state which submits the name. It was said to fall within the principle of subsidiarity. It seems a curious application of subsidiarity that France may preclude a United Kingdom national from entering Germany.

The effect of what is proposed is that the authority which exercises that wide power over so many individuals is not the Commission, nor the Council. It is not an authority of the Union at all. If it were, we could address the safeguards which may be required to ensure accountability. I make no secret of the fact that I should like to see the European institutions made more accountable. Because there are those who would like to see the nation states of Europe have more power, and the Union less power, we have arrived at a compromise which probably represents the worst of all worlds. We have institutions which exercise wide powers but a reluctance to entrust the European Parliament and the European Court with the power to control them.

The question of the jurisdiction of the European Court was referred to by the noble and learned Lord, Lord Slynn. I respectfully agree with what he said. But that is not the problem in the case that we are discussing. The authority which exercises such wide power over so many individuals is in fact each nation state. I suspect that that may represent a pattern which we may find in the future in third pillar conventions.

In paragraph 83 of our report, we say that we are concerned at the imprecision of the grounds on which a member state may add a name to the list. I refer in particular to the two grounds mentioned by the noble and learned Lord, Lord Slynn. One ground is,

"information to the effect that the person concerned has committed a serious crime".

It does not even need to be reliable information. There is nothing in the draft convention to indicate that an individual whose name is on the list should be told that his name is on the list. If he applies for a visa, and is refused, he will know that he has been refused a visa.

But he may not require a visa to make the journey that he has in mind. He may arrive at Heathrow at 8.30 for an important meeting in central London at 10.30 and either may be held for two hours while being interrogated or, more probably, simply sent back on the next aircraft. The potential unfairness is exacerbated if the individual is not told what is happening until it is too late to make alternative arrangements.

I understand, as we state in the report, that an individual will be protected by Article 20 of the Convention on the European Information System. However, that leaves him largely at the mercy of the member state, "before which he invokes" his right of access to the information. That may not even be his own state, because the right to be exercised is,

"in accordance with the law of the member state".

For the reasons set out in paragraph 85 of the report, I believe that there is a need for some safeguards within the convention or elsewhere. An individual refused entry because his name is on the list should have a right to be told which member state has required his inclusion and be accorded a right judicially to challenge his inclusion.

These are worrying matters for anyone who cares for civil liberties. But they are particularly worrying as an example of what I believe we may expect from third pillar conventions. There may be a need for co-ordination in a particular area of activity, but it cannot be addressed unless every nation state is carried along, and safeguards for individuals may be the negotiable trade off. What emerges may represent the lowest common denominator among the member states.

I hope that I may transpire to be unduly pessimistic. But so often, it is when I am most pessimistic that I transpire to be right.

5.8 p.m.

Lord Rennell: My Lords, I should like to speak on the issue of short stay visas for non-member nationals visiting the UK. At the moment, a citizen of Tashkent in Uzbekistan who wants to visit the United Kingdom has to apply to Moscow for his visa, with all the appropriate documents. In addition, he is then required to visit the British Embassy in Moscow for an interview. That is a round trip to a foreign country of more than 4,000 miles. It is expensive and time consuming. The United States, France, Germany, and Israel, and other major and minor trading companies have visa issuing facilities in Tashkent. UK companies are at a disadvantage, in particular at a time when trade with Uzbekistan and other Russian and CIS countries is growing quickly.

We have a reputation to uphold. Our embassies and consular offices are a haven for our citizens worldwide. I believe that our foreign friends also have their perception of help and friendliness when they visit our offices abroad. My reason for speaking today is to ask my noble and learned friend on the Front Bench for his consideration that, in addition to the report that we are discussing today, Her Majesty's Government will not forget the high reputation for fairness and efficiency which our diplomatic representatives have. I ask that the Government ensure that our consular visa services retain that reputation.

I should like to give an example of my concern. A British company with offices in Moscow and Tashkent wanted to bring a young Uzbek trainee employee to the UK for basic training and a short English course. Having submitted all the necessary application forms, he visited the consular section of the British Embassy in Moscow—a round trip, as I said before, of 4,000 miles—and was sent back without a visa because, although he had his Russian passport, he did not have his local internal passport. He was given a second appointment a month later. At that stage, three weeks before his next interview, a comprehensive letter was written to the consular section in Moscow by the sponsoring British company stating the full reasons for the visa application, giving the reference number of the application and enclosing a copy of a letter from the English school where the trainee would be studying.

When the unfortunate Mr. Khafizov, who spoke little or no English and had probably never been out of his country before, arrived for the second time in front of the firm but fair immigration officer, he must have had a very hard time. The report of the interview reads as follows:

"Your original application and invitation to the UK"—

this was for a one-month visa—

"was for a business visit, it was changed to short term studies only after you had been invited for a further interview. You state that you do not know why the sponsoring company has invited you to study English, the only reason you could give was that may be the president of the company just liked you. Furthermore you can not explain why you need to study English or why you specifically need to study in the UK other than that you like English. There is no indication that English is necessary for your employment, in fact quite the contrary as you state that your employer is not sending you to the UK and not sponsoring the studies. I also have to take into account the fact that you have not yet applied for leave from your employment to cover the period of your studies. I note that you state that you have no plans for after these studies which indicates to me that you do not intend to return to your current employment, this is further indicated by your statement that you may work for the sponsoring company but you are unable to provide a written offer of employment. Taking account of all the above I am not satisfied that you are a genuine student who will leave the UK after the 1 month period stated.

I am therefore not satisfied that you are genuinely seeking entry for the purpose and for the period as stated by you

I therefore refuse your application".

At the bottom the gentleman has signed the document, which states that the contents have also been explained to him in Russian.

I was rather shocked to read what seemed to me a rather bullying sort of interview. Here was a person who could not speak English; he was not accompanied by a friend or by his own interpreter; and he was probably unaware of the interpretations of the questions that were put to him. One can also only presume that the explanatory letter from the sponsoring company had been mislaid and that it was certainly not read by the interviewing officer.

I am of course aware that it is all too easy to find faults. There is no doubt that the visa office in Moscow is under great pressure. It may be no great consolation to know that we are not alone in this problem. The United States Ambassador in Moscow recently defended his embassy against Russian accusations of rudeness.

[Lord Rennell]

Nonetheless, he promised to increase personnel and space in order to speed up the visa issuing process. In the Soviet era, the US embassy dealt with 3,000 to 4,000 visa applications a year. Today, more than 130,000 applications are filed annually. I have no doubt that our Moscow embassy is faced with a similar huge explosion of applications.

I was very pleased to read in a Written Answer from my noble friend Lady Chalker of Wallasey that there are plans to commence visa services in Uzebekistan soon—indeed, it is hoped no later than the first quarter of 1995. Those plans, together with further visa issuing facilities in Belarus and other CIS countries, will help enormously in relieving the strain on Moscow's resources.

Finally, I ask my noble and learned friend Lord Rodger of Earlsferry that during the careful study of the report that is in front of us today we do not lose sight of the importance of the United Kingdom's good reputation for providing an expanding, efficient and friendly visa issuing facility.

5.15 p.m.

Lord Dubs: My Lords, this report is very useful, and it throws light on an area of policy which is not generally all that well understood. It incidentally also throws light on European decision-making processes. I have long argued that some areas of policy that have hitherto been very much within the national domain are increasingly being determined by Brussels. I refer, for example, to policy on asylum seekers and refugees.

Perhaps I may turn to a number of concerns that are highlighted by this report, and first, the secrecy with which these decisions are made or approached in Brussels. Although today we have a chance to talk about the convention, had it not been for the issue of Gibraltar which gave rise to its delay, it might well have been implemented, signed, sealed and settled before we had had a chance to consider some of the details. The secrecy that surrounds some decision-making by the Council of Ministers is undesirable. It lacks accountability and is essentially undemocratic. We ought to encourage more openness and transparency. Even if we look at measures which I have found undesirable, such as the Asylum and Immigration Appeals Act, at least that had the benefit of procedures which were open, which could be understood and on which every individual citizen of this country could make his or her views known to politicians.

In contrast, the lack of transparency that emanates from Brussels precludes this type of approach. In the past we have had interesting leaks. The *Guardian* occasionally carries very interesting stories about matters which are being kept secret. But surely we should not have to rely on leaks in order to keep ourselves informed as to what is under discussion.

I know that the official answer is that the Government never reveal the details of negotiations concerning international treaties. But I would argue that when we deal with matters which have large elements of human rights in them and which are in effect being dealt with in Brussels instead of being initiated here, then the argument that international treaties should not be, as it were, open to scrutiny, falls down. I suggest that it should not be applied in instances such as this.

Not only is there secrecy and a lack of openness and transparency; the report also makes it clear that some of the procedures are complicated and that indeed there is uncertainty in respect of some of the procedures. Some of the witnesses disagreed with each other about their interpretation of some procedures—they disagreed, for example, on whether it was a treaty or a convention. The report makes clear that there must be doubts about the links between the Dublin Convention; the Schengen Agreement, to which Britain is not a party; the new convention which may or may not be implemented, depending upon the Gibraltar issue; and indeed other matters of policy which European countries have decided, some of which have been implemented through national parliaments.

I would argue that, even if the future course is for the Council of Ministers to play the same part that it does now, —whether that should be the case is a subject for a different debate—I would urge that the Council of Ministers should make itself more open to scrutiny and that it should make its proceedings known to a wider public. I believe that when Denmark took the presidency after the United Kingdom, the Danish Government were quite sympathetic to the idea of more openness, but other countries did not like that idea too much.

I now turn to two specific issues which have already been mentioned in the course of this debate. The first is the joint list. I very much agree with the criticisms that were made of it by my noble and learned friend Lord Archer. Perhaps I may raise one or two further issues in relation to that list. I welcome the fact that the report says that if a person is on the list, he or she will be entitled to speedy judicial remedy in the state which put him or her on the list. It follows that it must be made known to that person which was the state which did so.

But let us consider the United Kingdom. We do not have any remedy. Other countries may be better than we are. My understanding is that we do not have any remedy at all. The last remedy that existed was appeal against a refusal of a visa for visitors or students. That was taken away by the Asylum and Immigration Appeals Act. So we do not have any remedy. The undertaking is rather hollow so far as this country is concerned, even if it is a valid undertaking with regard to other countries of the European Union.

But the criticism goes further than that. If an individual is refused—the previous speaker gave a dramatic instance of such a refusal—he may be refused even if he is not on the stop list but simply because immigration officials have decided that it is not appropriate for him to come to this country. So there is a wider list of people who are refused than the stop list itself. Does such a refusal mean that an individual will automatically be put on the Europe-wide stop list? There is a certain logic which says that that should be the case, but I hope that the answer is otherwise.

In any case, we know very little about our own stop list. I tried to find out about it. I visited Heathrow Airport years ago and was shown round by immigration officials. I saw the black book but I was not allowed to get within three or four feet of it or even allowed to know how many names it contained. But someone told me—I picked it up somewhere—that there are about 6,000 names on our stop list. No doubt the Minister will neither confirm nor deny it. It is a difficult area and one which I believe poses a threat to civil liberties.

I turn to the carriers' liability Act and fines on passengers who arrive without proper documentation. The report says—I welcome it—that primacy should be given to the European Convention on Human Rights and to the refugee convention. But that might be difficult to achieve in practice. I am rather more familiar with the refugee convention. If an individual is living in a country where the government is persecuting him, it is extremely difficult for him to apply for a passport from that government. One only has to think of an Iraqi Kurd applying for a visa to the regime in Baghdad. It is absurd. Many people who are persecuted simply cannot get passports. Even if they happen to have a passport in the first place, it is very difficult when facing persecution or in fear for one's safety to hang about waiting for some other country to issue a visa.

In that situation, individuals do what any Member of this House would do. Let us be honest—if our lives were in peril, we would get forged documents, would we not? Yet, preventing the owner of such a document boarding a plane is precisely what the carriers' liability Act is meant to do. So there is the paradoxical situation that the only way of escape for an individual may be a forged document or a forged visa; but here is legislation intended to stop anyone boarding a plane with such a document. I suggest that there is a Catch-22 situation, and it is hard to argue for the primacy of the refugee convention. I fear that this type of legislation makes it very difficult for people in countries where there is a great deal of persecution to escape and find safety elsewhere.

I conclude by welcoming the Select Committee's proposals with regard to the European Court of Justice. It seems to me that if there is to be secrecy, lack of openness and lack of transparency, then at the very least there should be certain safeguards. There may be other models for safeguards, but I believe that the European Court of Justice represents, in the arguments of the Select Committee, a welcome safeguard. I hope that that is a message that will go from this House to the Government. It is a desirable step forward.

5.26 p.m.

Lord Lester of Herne Hill: My Lords, the Select Committee deserves our gratitude for having produced such a cogent and compelling report. It raises a number of important issues which merit careful consideration. They have been fairly and carefully considered in this concise and well focused debate. There seems to be a wide consensus of view, to which I shall add in my remarks.

The noble and learned Lord, Lord Slynn of Hadley, observed at the outset that this is the first time that the Select Committee has examined a proposal for an international convention under negotiation within the justice and home affairs pillar of the European Union. Previous negotiations regarding external frontiers took place in secret. By contrast, these proposals of the Commission are open to scrutiny by national parliaments and anyone else who is interested. I am sure that all noble Lords will agree that that that is a most welcome development—a more open approach to democratic parliamentary scrutiny of the decision-making process. It originated with the Commission and is a much more open approach than has traditionally been permitted to citizens of this country by successive governments when negotiating treaties in the exercise of their prerogative powers.

The problem of secrecy, to which the noble Lord, Lord Dubs, referred, is surely important. But it is not the fault of the Brussels Commission. It is the responsibility of governments. I am slightly torn on this issue. Much as I press for greater parliamentary scrutiny of the treaty-making power of government, I am reminded that it was Senator Bricker of the United States, whose notorious amendment has led to an extremely insular and reactionary approach in which Congress frequently overscrutinises what the Executive branch does in that area, in a way that liberals like myself deplore. Having said that, I am undoubtedly on the side of those who wish for effective parliamentary scrutiny.

There are obviously many hurdles to clear before either of the measures under discussion comes into force. But the Select Committee's report makes a real and significant contribution to the development of Community policy in an area which affects the basic rights and freedoms of third country nationals seeking to enter the European Union.

The closer integration of Europe will inevitably lead to much greater movement across borders and it will become necessary to have co-ordinated control of the external borders of the member states, as the noble Baroness, Lady Park, emphasised. The Maastricht Treaty created new opportunities for making progress in this area but it is important to ensure that progress is made in the right direction, with adequate safeguards against the misuse of necessary powers exercised by the public authorities of the member states.

Like the noble and learned Lord, Lord Slynn, I want quickly to refer to four of the important issues raised in the report and in this debate: the proposals for a joint list of undesirable immigrants; carriers' liability; the jurisdiction of the European Court of Justice in this area; and the negative list. I shall not comment on the individual case mentioned by the noble Lord, Lord Rennell, about the issuing of student visas in Moscow for Uzbek applicants.

Let me speak first about the joint list. As the noble and learned Lord, Lord Archer of Sandwell, pointed out, the proposed joint list is an amalgam of 12 national lists of undesirable immigrants seeking entry from third states. An individual who has the great misfortune to be on the joint list will be excluded from all 12 member states. A placing on the list is to be based on a decision taken purely in accordance with the national laws of the member states, in accordance with a curious use of the principle of subsidiarity.

[LORD LESTER OF HERNE HILL]

The committee expressed concerns about the proposal for a joint list, concerns which I, like the noble and learned Lord, Lord Archer of Sandwell, and the noble Lord, Lord Dubs, entirely share. Some of the grounds set out in Article 10 for a national decision to place a person on the joint list are vague and imprecise. There is a real and substantial risk that entries may be made by mistake, or through spite or ill will.

To relieve against the possibility of error and serious injustice there must be effective safeguards and affordable remedies for those excluded because their names wrongly appear on the joint list. As suggested by the committee, some protection may be provided by the draft convention on the European information system. But that does not amount to sufficient protection. Under the draft convention, the individual's right of access to personal data held on the European information system is to be exercised in accordance with the law of the member state before which the individual invokes that right. For example, at present the protection of personal privacy in the United Kingdom is mainly contained in the Data Protection Act 1984.

The 1984 Act provides a legal framework for the processing of personal data. But the Act is concerned only with computerised or computer-usable information. It gives no right of access to paper files contained in manual systems. Therefore, any paper records relating to a placing on the joint list will be inaccessible and the denial of such information will severely hamper any appeal which may be made against the decision, if any appeal were allowed. As the noble Lord, Lord Dubs, pointed out, the judicial and other remedies in this country are otherwise extremely limited.

I agree with the committee that there is a need for a separate resolution or amendment to the European information system convention to ensure that member states have in place effective data protection mechanisms which will enable individuals placed on the joint list to access all data relevant to the decision to place them on the list, whether computerised or otherwise. In particular, the committee recommends—and I agree—that the individual refused entry in consequence of inclusion on the joint list should be told which member state placed him on the list and the nature of any allegation said to justify exclusion. The convention should include the requirement of appeals at national level against the decision to place a person on the joint list. Such appeals should take place as quickly as possible. It goes without saying that the list should be regularly updated to remove names no longer relevant or which were placed on the list in error.

I turn briefly to carriers' liability. The imposition of "appropriate penalties" on carriers, as the noble Lord, Lord Dubs, emphasised, is capable of interfering with the ability of asylum seekers to escape from countries where they had a fear of persecution. It would be a grave mistake if carriers were to refuse to carry asylum seekers for fear of penalty under the national legislation. I agree with the committee's recommendation that Article 14 of the draft convention should be modified to conform with Annex 9 to the Chicago Convention and permit the imposition of fines on carriers only where a carrier is negligent. There is also a need for legislation to make clear to carriers their overriding duty not to frustrate the right to seek asylum.

In an effort to avoid penalty, airlines will undoubtedly tighten their procedures. Decisions on immigration control will be delegated to airline staff who are obviously not qualified to take into account the human rights obligations of the member states, both under the Geneva Convention relating to the status of refugees (and protocol) and under the European Convention on Human Rights. As the committee recommends, it would be beneficial if immigration officers and airline staff received instruction so as to ensure full compliance with the UK's obligations under the European Convention and the refugee convention, even though, as the noble Lord, Lord Dubs, explained, the safeguards provided by those conventions in that area are only of limited value.

I turn to the jurisdiction of the European Court of Justice. Again, I agree with the committee which supports the European Commission's proposal to confer on the European Court of Justice jurisdiction to give preliminary rulings concerning the interpretation of the convention and jurisdiction in disputes concerning the implementation of the convention. In my view it involves no violation of pure jurisprudential doctrine that that should be done, even though, as we heard, the convention is an international treaty.

As the committee rightly stated, the European Court would ensure broad uniformity of standards of control and help to give effect to obligations under the European Convention on Human Rights. There would be great benefit in drawing upon the experience of the European Court and its power to interpret and apply general principles of law, not yet fully recognised by the courts of this country, such as the principle of proportionality, so as to ensure, for example, that the penalties required by the external frontiers convention are not disproportionate and do not vary dramatically between member states and so distort control of the external frontiers.

Finally, I come to the negative list. It is a list of countries whose nationals would require visas to enter the territory of the member states. It would impose a visa requirement on a further 45 countries in addition to those the UK requires at present. The noble Baroness, Lady Park of Monmouth, gave powerful reinforcement to the committee's conclusion that the list is inordinately long and would be damaging to the interests of the UK and its visitors. The list should be shortened to remove a number of Commonwealth countries and the 12 member states should seek to formulate coherent criteria common to all.

The Refugee Council was right to point out in the Select Committee hearings that most people fleeing from persecution find it almost impossible to obtain a visa. By imposing the visa requirement so widely, the European Union would be shutting out potential asylum seekers from a large number of countries.

It gives me great pleasure to support the Motion of the noble and learned Lord, Lord Slynn of Hadley, to take note of this admirable report. It is a particular personal pleasure because I have long sat at the noble and learned Lord's feet. When I was an undergraduate at Cambridge I learnt the history of the law of assumpsit from him sitting, as I recall, with Sir Leon Brittan on the end of Queen Victoria's bed in the judges' lodgings at Trinity College, Cambridge. And I have been learning from him ever since. We are fortunate indeed to have such a distinguished former member of the European Court of Justice and serving Law Lord as a main architect of this admirable document.

5.27 p.m.

Lord McIntosh of Haringey: My Lords, I am happy to join with all other noble Lords who expressed their gratitude to the noble and learned Lord, Lord Slynn, and his colleagues for this report on a most important subject. I confess that as a non-lawyer I found a good deal of the argument difficult to follow. I tried to leave aside those parts of the legal argument which did not seem to me to be important or essential for the political and social decisions which arise from the issues. Noble Lords who are legally qualified will therefore forgive me if some of my comments appear to be somewhat simplistic.

The most important thing about the report is the extent to which it is an innovation in the consideration of European draft legislation and conventions. The ability given under Article K for us to consider these conventions in draft and the way in which Article K, and in particular Article K.3, enables them to be dealt with by proposals from the Commission to the Council and by consideration then by the Council, and for the views of the European Parliament to be taken into account, are clearly important for the future of national scrutiny of European directives and legislation. If the advantage which the sub-committee had in dealing with the matter before the text and details are finalised is to be followed in the future, the work of our European Communities Committee will be immensely strengthened.

In this case, however, we obtain little advantage from it because the convention which we are considering this afternoon and which the sub-committee considered is in itself a recycling of a 1991 convention which was arrived at in accordance with the old secretive rules which my noble friend Lord Dubs rightly criticised. It is only before us because of the outstanding disagreement between Spain and the United Kingdom about Gibraltar. Otherwise, as my noble friend said, it would already have been enacted and we would not have been able to say anything at all about it. But the implication that it is a recycled convention, using the new ability of the Commission to raise matters itself when they appear to be in deadlock, means that there has been a self-denying ordinance on the part of almost everybody except the European Parliament and your Lordships' sub-committee to proposing significant changes to the convention. The likelihood is that significant changes will not be made to the conventions. In theory, the way in which we have been able to consider the conventions is hopeful for the future; in practice, the limitations on these particular conventions are rather severe.

I should like to make my comments in the order in which the summary and conclusions in paragraphs 109 to 121 have been presented by the sub-committee. That does not mean that I need comment on all of them but I want to comment on the most important ones. Paragraph 109 refers to internal border controls and expresses the view of the sub-committee, as of previous sub-committees, that it should not be obligatory on the United Kingdom to demolish internal border controls between the United Kingdom and other member states. I do not have very much sympathy with that view, but I do not think it is a matter on which we should excite ourselves too much as the European Court of Justice will be issuing a ruling in the fairly early part of next year. The implications of that ruling, particularly if it is ruled that inter-member state movements cannot be subject to border controls, are very significant indeed.

Paragraph 110 deals with the status of the conventions and brings out the difference between the Home Office view, which is that this is an international agreement which members may sign or not, and the view of the Commission, the wording of which I do not pretend to understand in detail. It may not matter very much except for the fact that the Commission's view—the Article K procedure to which I have already referred—involves a degree of consultation between the Commission, the Council and the European Parliament before a text is finalised. My noble friend Lord Dubs drew attention to the value of that process which would not be available from an international agreement, which needs to be ratified by individual states, produced in the older way.

A further consideration which leads me to greater sympathy with the Commission's view than the sub-committee had is that essentially an agreement of this kind has to be implemented with unanimity. One cannot have an agreement which is ratified by a number of member states but perhaps by not all of them and implemented in different ways. I appreciate that the status of the regulations is quite powerful. Even so, I believe that we have to go into this with a degree of unanimity about both what the conventions contain and the way in which they are to be implemented, even if that means, as was pointed out in evidence to the sub-committee, that very often the result is a compromise which satisfies no one completely.

Paragraph 111 refers to airports. Here I think a little common sense rather than legal argument is called for. It seems to me common sense that the British provision for transit passengers to be treated as airside—in other words, not to go through procedures as they arrive at, in particular, London Airport, but also other airports within the European Union—should be preserved. Noble Lords may know of the procedures facing anyone who enters the United States and wishes to move onto a connecting flight. One goes through immigration procedures in, for example, Seattle before catching a flight to San Francisco, or even worse, one undergoes immigration procedures in San Francisco, where one can wait for two hours before catching a connecting flight to somewhere else. The airside provision for transit passengers, whereby one knows what one's minimum connect time is and that one can catch one's flight and that it is only at one's last destination where one is not catching another flight that one has to go through immigration procedures of perhaps unpredictable length, will

[LORD MCINTOSH OF HARINGEY]

recognise that our system is much better. I hope that all effort will be made by the Government to support that view.

On the other issue of the difference between domestic and international flights, with the extension of domestic flights to include inter-European flights, I think that the airports and the airlines are going a little over the top. After all, Heathrow Airport already has two terminals—Terminal 1 and Terminal 2—which are largely for domestic and European flights and two terminals—Terminal 3 and Terminal 4—which are largely for international flights. Given enough time, I agree, it is not a great problem to redefine domestic flights to include European flights and to make provision for immigration and Customs facilities accordingly. It may be awkward for individual airlines to do both, but it is not a problem of the greatest significance. The worst solution would be if the nine Schengen states were to go ahead with abolishing internal controls and the UK, Ireland and Denmark were to be left on one side. Then we really would be pariahs in Europe.

The most important issue of the joint list has been dealt with by many noble Lords and for very good reason. Inherently, a joint list which is created by bringing together the names of those whom any member state wants to put on but yet which requires the agreement of a large number of member states to get them off will be the lowest common denominator of common sense. It will be the easiest list to get on to and the most difficult list to get off. It does not seem to me that the remedies proposed are adequate for the purpose. The sub-committee uses the phrase "judicial remedy in that state". As has been pointed out, after the Asylum and Immigration Appeals Act 1993, the United Kingdom does not have adequate remedies because we have deliberately abolished them. But I am sure that that is true in other states as well. Surely what we need is not judicial remedy in individual states but common measures accepted throughout the European Union to resolve disputes and appeals.

Exactly the same goes for paragraph 113, which deals with residence permits. The problem is that if a single member state removes the residence permit of an individual the individual cannot get into any of the 12, soon to be 15, member states. That seems to be going over the top. Again, the same principles of common measures to resolve disputes apply.

Paragraph 114 is wholly welcome. It deals with the need for an explicit link with the European information system. This is linked very much into the ability of individuals to appeal against their inclusion on a joint list. I would suggest that it would be desirable to include reference to the European Convention on Data Protection, which deals with the quite sensitive issues of the need to inform individuals about what information is on a list—it will, after all, be a computerised list—without at the same time making information about them available to those who might wish to damage their interests, in particular those in other countries who would wish to persecute them.

The issue of carriers' liability has been a matter of concern to your Lordships over many years. I know that there have been heated debates on the subject. That has been true because the United Kingdom takes perhaps a more extreme view about carriers' liability than almost anyone else. We insist not only on repatriation at the carrier's expense but also on very severe financial penalties, many of which some airlines are still not paying. A considerable amount of money is still outstanding.

We do not make any provision for the recommendations of the sub-committee made by a number of noble Lords that carriers should be liable only if it can be shown that they have been negligent in their procedures. The implications of carriers' liability go far beyond the interests of the individual airlines. They extend to the core of the issue of refugees and asylum seekers, as the noble Lord, Lord Dubs, and others have rightly said. If we are to act in accordance with Article 9 of the Chicago Convention, we shall have to do something about the problem that refugees and asylum seekers have rights only when they are in the country. But they cannot get into the country at all in order to claim those rights if the regulations about carriers' liability go over the top and exclude all those who may, for perfectly understandable and good reasons, be fleeing from persecution in their own country.

I shall deal very briefly with paragraph 116 on the jurisdiction of the European Court of Justice. Without in any way suggesting to the noble Lord, Lord Lester, that I agree with his views about the incorporation of the jurisdiction of the European Court of Justice in United Kingdom law, in general I certainly agree with all that has been said about the jurisdiction of that court as regards the matters concerned with these conventions.

Paragraph 117, 118 and 121 have been very adequately dealt with. They concern visas and the positive and negative lists of countries. I do not remember which film musical it was, but I believe the line is "Accentuate the positive and eliminate the negative".

Baroness Trumpington: My Lords, it continues, I believe, "Latch on to the affirmative".

Lord McIntosh of Haringey: I have no doubt that the noble Baroness is better informed on these matters than I am. I am sure that she can correct me afterwards if I get it wrong.

Lord Graham of Edmonton: And "Don't mess with Mr. In-Between".

Lord McIntosh of Haringey: My Lords, it is important to minimise in particular the grey list which is going to cause confusion for everybody. As the noble Baroness, Lady Park, said, it is true that the actual lists are crazy. That has implications for asylum and for conformity with the Geneva Convention of 1951.

Finally, and very briefly, I agree very much with what has been said, particularly by the noble Lord, Lord Rennell, about short-term visas. It seems to me that a three-month period for a short-term visa is quite inadequate for the United Kingdom for two reasons—

the educational reason which he cites and because as an ex-colonial power we have a very large number of people in this country with families in other parts of the Commonwealth and the former Empire. It is entirely proper that they should wish to be reunited with their families for a period longer than six months. It should not be a complicated matter of getting a European uniform visa and getting a national visa afterwards. We are asking for trouble if we get into that kind of complication. I cannot see what possible damage it can do to the other countries in the European Union if we insist on that point.

I apologise for racing through. The issues raised by this report are of considerable importance. The committee, the chairman and the advisers to the committee are to be congratulated on the way in which they have brought these matters forward, even if they have been unable to penetrate my thick, non-lawyer's skull in many respects.

5.54 p.m.

The Lord Advocate (Lord Rodger of Earlsferry): My Lords, in common with almost everyone who has spoken, I begin by thanking the committee for the work which it has done. I add my thanks to the noble and learned Lord, Lord Slynn, for instigating the debate which we have had this afternoon. I believe that everyone will agree that it has been extremely enlightening. It is one of the hallmarks of a report of this kind that it sheds light on something which can appear to be extremely complex. Sometimes it is very difficult to see the realities which lie behind it. The sub-committee's report and the evidence which was taken by it have done very much to inform your Lordships' House and many beyond it, of the important issues which are involved.

Many of your Lordships have drawn attention to the importance of this report as giving a chance to this House and Parliament to comment on the possible European legislation before it comes into effect. I believe that the noble and learned Lord, Lord Slynn, pointed out that this was in fact the first time that a question of a draft convention of this kind has been subject to a report by the sub-committee. The value of it has been proved.

I noted what was said not only by the noble and learned Lord, Lord Slynn, but by a number of other noble Lords, about the perhaps rather late stage in the proceedings at which this particular remedy of examination by the committee took place. I accept that to some extent it was the hazard of the failure to agree about Gibraltar which allowed that to happen in this case. I believe that the Government will have noted the points which were made in that connection.

Perhaps in addressing some of the topics which have been raised, I can to some extent give your Lordships some information about the events which have happened since the report of the committee in July. Before doing so, I mention one particular matter raised by my noble friend Lord Rennell in connection with visas. Of course I accept that it is a very important function of the Foreign Office that the visa service should be satisfactory. The consular section of the embassy in Moscow has recently been strengthened.

My noble friend drew attention to a particular problem. At present there are no plans to extend consular representation throughout the former Soviet Union. Nonetheless, in the case of Tashkent it is intended that a consular office will be opened there sometime next year as soon as suitable accommodation can be found. My noble friend made an important point and I shall pass it on to Foreign Office Ministers.

Like the noble Lord, Lord McIntosh, I cannot think of a more logical way of dealing with the matter than by going through some of the paragraphs in the same order as they occur in the report. I welcome paragraph 109 where the committee returns to Article 7a which it had dealt with before. It reaffirms its view that no legal obligation is imposed by that article on member states to abolish controls on people at internal community borders. As many noble Lords will know, that has long been the view of the United Kingdom Government. In that connection, as the noble Lord, Lord McIntosh, indicated, it may be—although not necessarily the case—the subject of a ruling by the European Court in connection with the action which the European Parliament has brought against the European Commission for its alleged failure to ensure the complete abolition of frontier controls. The United Kingdom has taken the opportunity of intervening in the case to set out its interpretation of Article 7a. Contrary to what the noble Lord, Lord McIntosh, indicated, our latest information is that the case is unlikely to be heard until the middle of 1995 at the earliest.

In paragraph 110 the committee made a recommendation in connection with the form of the convention. Although it seems a technicality in some ways, this is a matter to which the Government have attached great importance for the kinds of reasons to which the committee referred. I am pleased to be able to tell your Lordships that earlier this year the Council agreed that a final Act drawing up a convention under Title VI should recommend its adoption by member states in accordance with their respective constitutional requirements. Therefore, the convention will be signed by representatives of the heads of government of member states as is consistent with the principles of international law, with the signatures taking place on the same day as that on which the text is formally drawn up. The Government are participating in negotiations on the draft convention with the aim of arriving at a text which has the full character of an international agreement.

From that somewhat esoteric matter, I turn to the reconfiguration of the airport and to the position under the recommendation in paragraph 111. This is a matter of considerable importance. We are all aware of the role of Heathrow and Gatwick airports as hub airports. It is apparent that any change in the present arrangements for routeing airside transit passengers raises important questions about the necessary infrastructure changes and the inconvenience to both carriers and passengers. As your Lordships will appreciate, this matter has been the subject of negotiation. Most of your Lordships do not

[LORD RODGER OF EARLSFERRY] find the provisions particularly attractive. My understanding is that there is no current intention that those provisions in the convention should be amended. Nonetheless, it is correct to have regard to the cost consequences of the changes. Our understanding is that if those convention provisions were to go through, the cost of the necessary adjustments to the infrastructure of the airports would amount to up to £450 million, so it is no small matter. Obviously, if that is to happen, it is important that adequate time should be allowed for the implementation of the changes. The Government will bear that matter fully in mind when negotiating a date for the implementation of the convention. At the moment, officials are liaising with representatives of the industry to arrive at a solution that will, as far as possible, minimise any possible disruption to the airports and their passengers.

It is fair to say that paragraph 112 was of concern to almost all noble Lords who have spoken. It was plainly of great concern to the committee. As I understand it, everybody accepted the basic principle behind the idea of an external frontiers convention and its consequence, having a common list. However, I believe that all noble Lords had apprehensions about the way in which the criteria had been laid down and on the question of appeals.

On the question of exactly what the criteria will be and how they will be put into legislation, the Government cannot at this stage give any indication of our final view. That is because of the provision in Article 10. As some of your Lordships mentioned, although the criteria are set out, the detailed rules have to be determined by measures that are provided for in order to give effect to the convention. Those measures might well require legislation in this country. The final details have not yet been worked out.

In that connection, it is the Government's view at this stage—this goes along with much that has been said by your Lordships—that once a person learns that his name is on the list, he should be informed which country put his name on the list. That is for the obvious reason that unless he is told that, he will have no access to a system whereby he might have some form of redress. As to the form of that redress, the Government do not anticipate that this country will provide for an appeal if somebody's name has been included on the list. Noble Lords may not care for it, but it corresponds to the position that was taken in the 1993 Act. However, that does not mean that those whose names are included on the list are without all judicial remedy because if the inclusion of a name is for some reason unlawful, the person concerned would have a right of judicial review, as in other cases.

On the matter of the European information systems convention, like the committee, the Government fully accept that it would be proper to make a formal link between the convention and the information systems convention.

Lord Lester of Herne Hill: My Lords, I am grateful to the Minister for allowing me to ask a question on that point before he moves on to the next subject. So that I can understand the way in which a judicial review would work, can we assume, so as not to offend any existing member state, that a state called Ruritania becomes a member state of the Union and considers that there are serious grounds for thinking that someone from outside is a threat to Ruritania's public policy on national security? The person is told that it is Ruritania that has put him on the black list. If Ruritania has the kind of limited judicial review that we have in this country, the person concerned will have very little opportunity of obtaining redress in either that country or this country. I wonder, therefore, whether the Minister can indicate a way in which judicial protection can be real rather than symbolic in this area.

Lord Rodger of Earlsferry: My Lords, if Ruritania had the same kind of judicial review as we do, presumably the person would have the same access to remedy in Ruritania as in this country. I am thinking, for example, of a case where the decision to include a person's name on the list was unreasonable, based on a mistake or made on the basis of insufficient evidence. The noble Lord is familiar with such categories. The person concerned would have that kind of remedy. He would not have the remedy of an appeal, as I have made clear.

The matter of carriers' liability has occupied your Lordships on previous occasions also, and some of the points that have been made today can be made in respect of carriers' liability in any context. In this context, we have made it clear that we have invoked the provisions of Annex 9 of the Chicago Convention which allows governments to register a difference between their legislation and that provided for by the convention. We see no conflict with the convention. Indeed, I do not think that such a conflict was suggested.

The carriers' liability legislation is a form of legislation which has been introduced by many countries to meet what is perceived as being a problem with forged and other unsatisfactory documents. The Government have done a great deal to train people at home and abroad in all aspects of the legislation and in detecting forgeries. As I understand it, over 320 training visits have been made to locations in 79 different countries. The programme is continuing. In addition, the Immigration Service is available to give advice on a 24-hour basis. In that way, we hope that the staff involved will have a full understanding of the legislation which they have to implement.

As the noble and learned Lord Lord Slynn recognised, the role of the European Court of Justice is a matter upon which views may be divided. Most noble Lords who spoke were in favour of the ECJ having a role. Despite that recommendation, the Government are opposed to the court having jurisdiction over the interpretation and implementation of this convention. As your Lordships know, Title VI of the treaty does not confer jurisdiction unless the member states agree. In this case the Government consider that jurisdiction should be a matter for national courts.

Much evidence on that matter was laid before the committee. While the Government take the view that it is inappropriate, as this is a third pillar subject, it is fair to say that even some of the witnesses who were broadly in favour of the ECJ could see practical difficulties which, to some extent, are reflected in the committee's recommendations regarding the ECJ's role in taking references on this matter.

Perhaps I may cover the last provisions quickly. We accept fully what the committee said on the competency issues raised under recommendations 117 and 118. They correspond fully with our view.

Finally, the common visa list raises an issue which, again, is of importance to many noble Lords who have noted the extent of the positive list. It is a strange positive list, because it has a negative effect. None the less, your Lordships have noticed that it seems to be extremely long. The Government's position is that it is too long, and that it contains many countries from whose nationals we do not require visas. The system works well without them. We hope that the list can be cut down during the course of negotiations. Of course we are in favour of having a common visa list, because it seems to be a way of minimising variations in national practice and is therefore something which, in general terms, the Community feels is desirable. While, as I say, we are in favour of the idea, we are not happy with the extent of the list at present and hope that when it is finalised it will be shorter.

I have been able to touch on only some of the issues. The debate has raised issues of great importance. It has been a worthwhile debate. I have no doubt that it will be the precursor of many future similar debates.

6.15 p.m.

Lord Slynn of Hadley: My Lords, I thank the Minister for his comprehensive consideration of the most important topics which arise in the report. I thank also other noble Lords who have taken part in the debate. I thank, in particular, the noble Lord, Lord Lester, for his kind personal words. I hope that he remembers more of the history of assumpsit than I do.

This has been an important debate. Your Lordships have made clear how much importance should be attached to the review not just of Community measures but of proposals being discussed by member states under the second and third pillars. Your Lordships made clear too how important it is to protect those who seek asylum and those who may find their names wrongly on a list. I hope that the Government will continue to consider whether there should not be some unified appeal system throughout the Community, if, with experience, they find that persons are being put on the list and are not obtaining an adequate remedy. It is plain that there should be some form of sufficient protection for people who find their names on the list.

I attach great importance to the points made by the noble Baroness, Lady Park of Monmouth, about the difficulty of ensuring that there are to be controls at the external frontiers, even though the committee, as the Minister said, considers that internal border controls do not have to be abolished as a result of the Single European Act.

I have to say—your Lordships will not be surprised about this—that I am disappointed by the Minister's answer as to the role of the ECJ. He will not be offended if I say that I hope that that will not be the Government's standard reaction to proposals under the second and third pillars. We had a witness from a government department on another inquiry last week. We asked, "Should there not here be a role for the European Court?". "No, no, no", came the answer, "The Government do not like this sort of thing going to the European Court of Justice". I ask the Minister to bear in mind that all our witnesses were in favour; the European Parliament is in favour; and all noble Lords who have spoken tonight were in favour.

I am grateful to noble Lords for the attention given to this important topic. Once the regulation and convention are in force, that will lead to some interesting problems.

On Question, Motion agreed to.

Defence Research Agency: Select Committee Report

6.17 p.m.

The Earl of Selborne rose to move, That this House takes note of the Report of the Science and Technology Committee on the *Defence Research Agency* (3rd Report, HL Paper 24).

The noble Earl said: My Lords, perhaps I may say at the outset how grateful was the sub-committee to be able to benefit from the co-option of two noble Lords with considerable knowledge of the Defence Research Agency—my noble friend Lord Trefgarne, who was in the Ministry of Defence at the time of its inception and the noble and gallant Lord, Lord Craig of Radley, from whose expertise we benefited enormously. We were helped greatly by our two specialist advisers, Professor Frank Hartley and Professor Philip Gummett. I must pay tribute also to our Clerk, David Batt, for his crucial contribution.

It was true in my case (and it was possibly true in the case of some other members of the committee) that we were not all familiar with the DRA and its role. Let me say immediately that we were all impressed by the quality of its science and its management. The DRA, as at present constituted, is one of the largest employers of science in the country with 5,000 scientists and a turnover of £795 million. All but 9 per cent. of its work is conducted by the Ministry of Defence. It is a wholly owned agency of the Ministry.

Our report was published in July before the Government produced *Front Line First*, a report on the outcome of the defence cost studies; and as the Government's response to our report states, the report has major implications for the future structure of the agency.

As an outcome of those proposals, it is likely that the DRA will be brought together into a single executive agency with all the other MoD non-nuclear science and technology organisations. That has happened since the publication of our report and I shall deal with it no more.

The DRA was formed in 1991 by amalgamating four research establishments which had formidable reputations. The agency acquired trading fund status in 1993. Our report draws attention to the record of achievement of those defence research establishments

[THE EARL OF SELBORNE]
and how important it has been for the agency to maintain the reputation and momentum in order to retain battle-winning technological advantage. That has been against the background of reducing cost and changing unpredictable risks.

This advantage gained in the past by the provision of technological excellence must now be achieved on greatly reduced funds. The DRA is undergoing a programmed fall in work from the Ministry of Defence of 15 per cent. between 1993 and 1996. That involves the closing of sites, the restructuring of support activities and other cost-cutting measures. At the same time, in common with much other publicly funded work, a market testing programme is being implemented in phases whereby all the work which the DRA carries out for the Defence Procurement Executive of the Ministry will be market tested by 1997. That puts the management of the agency under considerable pressure.

Against these constraints, the DRA has initiated a number of what we describe as positive thrusts into the commercial world by developing closer links with industry through its Pathfinder programme, strategic alignment and dual use technology centres. We recognise that, in spite of its name, research is only one of the agency's two main functions. Sir Ronald Oxburgh pointed out that perhaps its more important role is to be able to offer technical advice to the Ministry. To that end, it engages in strategic and applied research and project support. Its *raison d'etre*—its justification—is that it must acquire and retain an expertise to be able to offer expert advice to the Ministry.

The opportunity to contribute to wealth creation by supporting industry or by expanding its own intellectual property base must not be allowed to detract from its central role by providing a core of technical advice, however important this role might appear to be to industry or, indeed, to other parts of Government. That draws attention to a second serious constraint if the first constraint is funding. Much as the DRA might like to maximise its income, and under its trading fund status it is expected to act commercially, this must always be done in a way that is compatible with the Ministry's requirements. After all, the Ministry is the owner of the agency.

As a wholly owned subsidiary with no mandate to spend money on areas which do not benefit the defence of the country, there are real difficulties in fulfilling the more commercial role that is expected of the agency. To make a difficult situation worse, funding from the DTI is declining. Our report draws attention to the near elimination of DTI grants to Malvern, for example. This puts the DRA into a difficult situation. It is required to meet some very precise targets, yet does not benefit from an equally strong obligation on its shareholder and regulator, the Ministry of Defence.

However, we greatly welcome the increased funding that is to be channelled through the deputy chief scientific adviser. We believe that that will lead to a greater element of stability. If we were critical of the efforts made by the Ministry of Defence to develop its relationship with the DRA it was because we were anxious about the short-term nature of some of the appointments that fulfil the role of customer. That leads to a lack of continuity. That is not true of the deputy chief scientific adviser and his group, who provide a welcome element of stability. In so far as the proportion of funding to the DRA will be increased through this route, we welcome it.

We also drew attention to the concept of the Fraser figure, which we explain in the report, and we believe that the concept needs further development within the Ministry. The DRA needs guidance on the Ministry's long-term requirements. In so far as the Ministry, for reasons which I have acknowledged, is unable to assist adequately in the promotion of wealth creation projects, it must consider closer collaboration with the Office of Science and Technology so that the opportunities to support our industry and to contribute to wealth creation are more effectively exploited. We acknowledge the role of the Office of Science and Technology in the area of defence research in the Technology Foresight programme, which it supervises, and in *Forward Look*.

In a report published last year on priorities for the science base, we made a recommendation that the chief scientific adviser be empowered to expose any inconsistencies in the science plans of departments. We believe that is an obvious example. For reasons of accountability, it is understandable that the Ministry of Defence cannot put as much into wealth creation as perhaps last year's White Paper suggested. We believe that the Office of Science and Technology has a greater input to make in the agency and we recognise that the Ministry of Defence is bound to be protective of its territory.

We looked with interest at the examples of the United States, France and elsewhere where interdepartmental difficulties do not inhibit the development of wealth creating enterprises in defence research establishments—at least not to the same extent. I am sure that the level of parliamentary accountability is different and that it is no good expecting systems that work in one country to be transplanted to another. The concept of economic security is one that the Americans have been able to use to justify the greater flexibility of funding within Ministry of Defence research establishments.

I have dealt at some length with the difficulties and point out that an opportunity to review this delicate relationship within government will occur when the framework document for the DRA is reviewed in 1998. Of course, the Office of Science and Technology will be involved in that review. However, that seems rather a long time to wait.

Having dealt with some of the difficulties encountered by the DRA in fostering industrial links, we were nevertheless impressed by the Pathfinder programme and the concept of dual use technology centres. Since the publication of our report two more such centres have been funded and we greatly welcome that. Both dual use technology centres and Pathfinder programmes will, no doubt, evolve as a track record is established. In particular, we should like to see the Pathfinder programme made more accessible to small manufacturing enterprises.

I have been able to refer only in outline to a few of the recommendations in our report. I wish to emphasise that we believe that before yet more scientists are made redundant and, above all, before unique facilities are lost, we should think carefully about the contribution that these facilities and scientists could make to underpin future economic security.

We believe that the quality of science within the DRA is too high to put at risk and requires some equally high quality solutions from government in order to ensure that we make the best possible use of this expertise. I beg to move.

Moved, That this House takes note of the Report of the Science and Technology Committee on the Defence Research Agency (3rd Report, HL Paper 24).—*(The Earl of Selborne.)*

6.28 p.m.

Lord Carver: My Lords, I should make clear from the start the fact that I am no longer a member of the Science and Technology Committee and am therefore in no way associated with the report. I congratulate the noble Earl and his committee on having produced an interesting and valuable report which illuminates the problems that the Defence Research Agency faces and those that have been created by its formation. The report does not attempt to gloss over the fact that there are unsatisfactory elements in the anomalous situation in which the agency has been placed: its dependence on and tight control by the Ministry of Defence; its remit to contribute as much as possible to fields other than defence, in particular, those considered to be in the national interest; and the demand that it should earn revenue by doing so, affecting its relations with other government departments, with industry, with which in some cases it is competing, and with other research organisations. There is also a delicate problem concerned with relations with similar organisations in allied countries.

The Government's response, published three days ago, underlines those problems. Their defensive arguments, complacently protesting that all the conflicting demands and loyalties can be, are being and will be reconciled in a satisfactory way, illustrate in a repetitive fashion the anomalies inherent in the attempt to make the defence research and development establishments fulfil a number of conflicting purposes.

It would seem to me that the committee had some difficulty in finding solutions to these problems. I doubt whether the noble Earl, its chairman, would claim that its recommendations go very far towards solving them, although they may do something to alleviate them. I believe that that is so because they are not radical enough, and do not go to the heart of the matter. The committee has perhaps been constrained by its acceptance that, as the report states:

"the various structural reorganisations to which the DRA has been subjected in the past few years call for a period of consolidation and stability".

The heart of the matter is that the requirement for re-equipment of our Armed Forces over the foreseeable future does not justify the maintenance of defence research and development establishments of the size and nature of those now left in the DRA. They were built up and endowed with many of their valuable assets in the Second World War. Although much reduced since then, they are out of proportion to the future requirement, certainly in terms of the quantity of equipment which would be produced in this country; and it is not acceptable to justify their existence on the basis of their contribution to the arms export industry.

Because that is the case, the pressure, clearly recognised in the report and in the Government's response, is that greater emphasis should be given to their potential contribution to other fields of national life, particularly to industry, and to their cost to the taxpayer being offset by sale of their services. That produces conflicting demands and loyalties and many other problems, some of which I have already mentioned. The report clearly acknowledges them. Although its recommendations edge in the direction of loosening the Ministry of Defence's tight control and of associating other government departments with the agency, notably the Department of Trade and Industry and the Office of Science and Technology, it treads warily and in my view does not go far enough. The report, in paragraphs 2.34 and 5.14, to which the noble Earl referred, recommends a close study of French and American defence research as examples of directing it towards wider national interests than just the support of a national defence equipment programme. I would urge a study of the German method. As I understand it, the Germans have no defence research establishments as such, controlled by their defence ministry. Their armed forces depend upon a combination of research carried out by their prestigious civil scientific institutes, such as the Max Planck, which also serve industry and other national objectives, and development carried out by the armament firms themselves. One must of course make allowance for all the differences which exist between how science is organised, supported and financed in this country and how it is done in Germany. Nevertheless I believe that a close study of the German solution, which is no less successful than the French and American both in developing military equipment and in supporting broad national objectives, would repay a very careful study.

If we were to move in that direction, my proposal would be to split up the Defence Research Agency into its former four establishments—the Royal Signals and Radar Establishment, the Admiralty Research Establishment, the Royal Aircraft Establishment and the Royal Armament Research and Development Establishment—and detach them, with the probable exception of RARDE, from the Ministry of Defence. The agency, as it now is and as the Ministry of Defence plans it to be, is an uneasy amalgam of establishments of different natures and objectives. I would then convert RSRE at Malvern into a National Electronics Institute, RAE at Farnborough into a National Aerospace Institute and most of ARE into a National Maritime Institute, some elements of it perhaps being absorbed by the Electronics and Aerospace Institutes. In my view, those institutes should have close links with a specific university: perhaps Cambridge for electronics; London, particularly Imperial College, for aerospace; and

[LORD CARVER]
Southampton for maritime. They should also offer shared use on a commercial basis of some of their assets with other research organisations, as has recently been agreed in the case of the ship testing tanks at Haslar between the former Admiralty Research Establishment and British Maritime Technology Ltd. I would envisage those three institutes coming under the aegis of the Engineering and Physical Sciences Research Council.

Parts of RARDE might be amalgamated with other institutes: the former Fighting Vehicle Research and Development Establishment perhaps with what is now the Transport Research Agency; but the weapons and ammunition side, formerly Fort Halstead, should probably remain a Ministry of Defence establishment.

I believe that such a fundamental reorganisation would provide a solution to the problems to which the recommendations of the report, in my view, offer only palliative alleviations. It is unrealistic today, and will be more so in the future, to think of a defence procurement programme based on national research and development and national production. The quantities are too small, the cost too high and the industrial base too narrow. We need to seek a European procurement programme, backed by high quality national science, supporting a thriving British electronic, aerospace, maritime and general engineering industry, working in a European context.

That was the message that the Minister for Defence Procurement gave forcefully yesterday in his address to the Defence Manufacturers Association. I suggest that he should try to persuade his right honourable friend the Defence Secretary to apply it to the Defence Research Agency.

6.37 p.m.

Lord Trefgarne: My Lords, I had the honour to serve on the committee whose report your Lordships are now considering. I wish to start by paying tribute to our chairman, my noble friend Lord Selborne, for the wise and effective way in which he guided our deliberations and which I believe is reflected in the report which we have produced.

I have listened with interest to the speech of the noble and gallant Lord, Lord Carver. I wish that we had had an opportunity, during the course of our deliberations, to know the noble and gallant Lord's views so that they could perhaps have been tested, examined and considered more than they were.

I am wholly supportive of the report which your Lordships are considering. However, there is one matter which is not wholly removed from what the noble and gallant Lord has been talking about today to which I should like to refer; that is, the possibility in due course of moving the Defence Research Agency into the private sector.

We were not charged with considering that proposition. There was no particular support for it among the members of the committee and, indeed, when the Minister, my right honourable friend Mr. Aitken, came to speak to us, he made it clear that there were no government plans for such a move. I am told that the Government's response to our report—and I am sorry to say that my copy arrived only today and I have not yet had an opportunity to study it—refers also to the fact that there are no present government plans for that particular course of action. But I believe that some of the difficulties to which the noble and gallant Lord, Lord Carver, has just referred, which are real and which were identified in our report, would be overcome by moving the Defence Research Agency into the private sector.

Having said that, I agree also with the conclusion which the committee reached to the effect that the DRA has been subjected to all sorts of reorganisations and changes in recent years and now would not be the time for a move into the private sector. The agency deserves and is entitled to a period of consolidation. I recognise the fact that the noble and gallant Lord did not think that that was wholly desirable. However, I certainly believe that to be desirable as, indeed, did the committee.

However, when that period is over in, say, two, three or even four years from now, I believe that it would be right to revisit the question of whether or not the DRA should be privatised. As the noble and gallant Lord said, the fact is that the capacity of the DRA at present exceeds that which can usefully be fully employed by the Ministry of Defence. I am very much attached to the thought that the excellent resources and facilities available within the DRA ought to be more widely available to our national effort in terms of generating more and better technologies for use not only for military purposes, but also for civil purposes, to a much greater extent than they are at present.

As I said, the committee was not charged with examining whether or not the DRA should be privatised; nor, therefore, did we reach any particular, immediate conclusions on that point. But I should like to see the question of the ownership of the DRA revisited after a period of consolidation. I hope that the Government will find it possible to do so.

6.41 p.m.

Lord Craig of Radley: My Lords, this was my first experience of a Select Committee, at least of sitting at the round end of a Select Committee table. I am most grateful for the friendly support that I received from the chairman, the noble Earl, Lord Selborne and from the rest of the committee. As the noble Earl mentioned, the topic of our investigation was not unfamiliar to me. I had some involvement with the work done in the Ministry of Defence which led Ministers to amalgamate the research establishments into the DRA, and the subsequent introduction of a trading fund in 1993. Following the collapse of the Soviet threat, it was also clear that the MoD's research requirements would need to be scrutinised most thoroughly against the background of the post cold war world.

Change in any large and complex organisation is never easy. Those involved in the formation of the DRA faced a double whammy: the amalgamations and restructuring of the former research establishments and the downward pressures on their future budgets. Some argue that in periods of peace and retrenchment, expenditure on the strategic research programme should not be curtailed. Indeed, the Statement on the Defence Estimates 1994 (CM2550 at page 64) said:

"The need to retain battle winning technological advantage is as pressing now as it has ever been in the context of changing unpredictable risks".

If such aspirations are to be realised, it is not only a matter of money but of staff with the right background and motivation to deliver on good ideas. With that in mind, and the unprecedented changes which had already taken place in forming the DRA with its trading fund, our committee called for a period of consolidation and stability. Indeed, several of our witnesses stressed that need.

It was, therefore, with no little surprise that I read in the Defence Costs Study report, *Front Line First*, issued in July 1994 after our review had been completed, that savings estimated at £12 million a year could be expected, subject to further work (I note the reservation implicit in that phrase) if the DRA principles were applied as widely as possible to other MoD organisations which provide scientific and technological services.

It is a fundamental precept of scientific experiment that to get a proper evaluation the introduction of too many variables at the same time will almost certainly distort the conclusions. Fifteen months' experience of the DRA with its trading fund seems perilously short to conclude that it is not only a goer in its present form but that it will be able to absorb new resources and organisations immediately with cost savings and no adverse effects. It was an unfortunate matter of timing that our committee could be given no hint in MoD evidence of such further major changes. Time will tell whether the MoD has got that right or has fallen once more into the trap of piling change upon change to such an extent that quality of output cannot be sustained.

There is just one other aspect of our report that I should like to touch on. We concluded from evidence that Treasury rules place an unnecessarily high burden upon the DRA. I understand that the 6 per cent. risk-free target rate of return set by the Secretary of State for Defence is the same as applied across other government trading funds. They say that it provides a necessary commercial discipline. At the same time, the DRA is said to be free to charge what it deems appropriate for its facilities, provided that it does not disadvantage the MoD. Is there not some inconsistency in those approaches? Why should the DRA be grouped with every other trading fund? Should it not be treated on its own merits? We are told that the DRA is free, but only so long as it charges—at least—what the MoD says it must. Treasury and MoD rules seem to be inflexible, and not always in the best commercial and wealth-creating interests that we would all like to see from the DRA.

The DRA Enterprise fund should be developed to give both the encouragement and the wherewithal to exploit the considerable financial potential of the DRA. While the MoD as sole owner of the DRA must be given priority, and every effort made to meet the MoD's legitimate requirements, it should also be possible for the chief executive and his team to seek to enhance the national wealth-creating potential which lies within the DRA. That may be difficult to achieve in a meaningful way if the MoD insists that any capacity surplus to defence needs must be removed. The DRA seems to be between a rock and the hard place.

Finally, the DRA and its predecessor research establishments have been through a period of unprecedented change, financially, organisationally and functionally. I hope that no "Johnny come lately" will feel that the DRA needs to be reviewed yet again in the near future; for example—and I note what the noble Lord, Lord Trefgarne, said—with a view to privatisation or further restructuring. The agency needs stability to set itself on its new course, to allow time to assess properly the success of the new arrangements and, above all, to allow the scientists and others who have been so personally affected by so much upheaval to plan ahead for their families and themselves. If not, morale and quality of output could be badly hit.

6.48 p.m.

Lord Redesdale: My Lords, I welcome the opportunity to make a few brief comments about the report. I should also like to say that I welcome the Government's reply; indeed, it is extremely comprehensive. However, the area that I most welcome about the Government's reply can be found at the end of paragraph 3. I know that the noble Lord, Lord Trefgarne, will not agree with me in that respect, but I think that those words are most important. They read:

"There continue to be no plans for privatisation".

Like many members of the committee, I believe that privatisation of the Defence Research Agency will not be in the best interests of the country.

When I was considering my speech, I realised that many noble Lords would speak in great detail. As many speakers were members of the committee and know a great deal about the subject, I should like to discuss a few areas that concerned the committee over all.

While thinking about the speech I would make in this debate I received the Defence Research Agency's annual report 1993-94. It is quite an exciting document. The first section of it reads very much like an episode of "Tomorrow's World". I say that with no disrespect at all. The document shows how the Defence Research Agency is at the cutting edge of advanced technologies. I was particularly interested in the work being done on light emission from silicon.

The document almost states why the reforms we are discussing were undertaken. The Defence Research Agency carries out exciting research. The 10 per cent. of it which is directly outside the MoD's control can be used for wealth creation and for the benefit of the country. The report describes the vast areas of expertise that are covered by the Defence Research Agency and many areas which are not limited just to defence.

The second section of the report lists the enormous changes that have taken place within the Defence Research Agency. I believe that these changes are mostly for the good. However, I have one or two points to add on this matter. I believe that one of the driving forces behind the changes is efficiency. But there is a

[LORD REDESDALE]
slight dichotomy as regards pushing for efficiency in research. On the one hand one is trying to limit the money being spent and on the other one is trying to achieve as much with the research as possible.

I have talked with the noble Baroness, Lady Hilton of Eggardon, about the role of efficiency within the DRA. I believe we share the view that one area that has been particularly discussed is that of blue sky research. While there is a strong push for efficiency, that will cut down on the eventual returns from blue sky research. Also, as the research becomes more specialised, that could lead to short-termism. Although I realise that often few benefits are to be gained from pouring vast amounts of money into research without a direct aim in mind, I believe that one area that has to be carefully monitored is that short-termism might become an in-built factor in all the research undertaken by the Defence Research Agency.

I also wish to discuss intellectual property rights. I believe strongly that there is no reason why the country should not benefit from any revenue that may accrue from this work and that intellectual property rights should fund other areas of the Defence Research Agency. However, I disagree with the Government's response in one respect. I believe that, if at all possible, intellectual property rights should be sold to British companies below the rate of return that would normally be expected if they can show that such a course would create jobs in this country and add to the manufacturing base. I believe that that is an important point. One may forget that a small loss of a few million pounds in intellectual property rights could be compensated for if a factory could be established in this country to produce goods as a result of acquiring the intellectual property rights.

I also wish to mention the Treasury rules, as did the noble and gallant Lord, Lord Craig of Radley. They can be inflexible. It seems to be a case of taking from one pocket and putting into another. The Treasury can push for more stringent controls of the Defence Research Agency. However, it is a publicly funded company, and if it can be shown that reducing the Treasury rate of return would benefit the country, I do not believe that one should necessarily have to stick to the 6 per cent. figure, which is an artificial creation.

I wish to end by considering the role of stability. I shall quote from the Defence Research Agency report and the statement of the chief executive, Mr. John Chisholm:

"After two years of preparation, 1993/94 saw the Defence Research Agency launched as a fully trading organisation. It has proved a daunting but so far successful task. The mechanics of making an enterprise of more than 10,000 highly skilled individuals into a disciplined trading entity were sufficiently challenging in themselves; to achieve that transformation while retaining the focus and innovation from DRA's staff has been a rare and important task. Despite many difficulties, some of them relatively major, that task has been by and large accomplished".

There have been massive changes in the Defence Research Agency. I wish to mirror some of the views that have been expressed already by stating that I believe a period of time needs to be set aside to see what effect those changes have had. It would seem to me to be short-sighted to try to attempt major changes in the short term. I believe that a period of stability of perhaps more than two or four years —perhaps six or eight years—should be instituted so that the effects of these changes can be seen. Then, if any further changes are necessary, they can be implemented with the benefit of wisdom.

6.57 p.m.

Lord Graham of Edmonton: My Lords, I begin by extending the apologies of my noble friend Lord Williams, who, as the Minister will know, takes a keen interest in these matters but is unfortunately unable to be here. However, that provided me with the opportunity —in fact the necessity—to do a bit more reading than I might otherwise have done. I must confess that I am an ex-Royal Marine, corporal PLY X112 105, 1943. Ever since then I have taken an interest in defence matters and, on behalf of my party, I have spoken on defence matters from time to time in the past. Therefore it was a pleasure for me to have to do the necessary reading to equip myself for this debate.

I share the commendations of all of us not only to the noble Earl, Lord Selborne, but also to members of his Committee. The Minister normally expresses his gratitude to those colleagues in the House who have served him and the House. He will want to say how grateful we all are to the Committee not merely because it has done a thoroughly worthwhile job but also because it has given the Minister an opportunity to comment on this matter.

The noble Lord, Lord Redesdale, referred to the Ministry's response. There is no need for me to go over the report when the Minister will no doubt do that. If what we have in the report is the response from the Government, that will be the response that we are given from the Government Minister. The debate provides us with an opportunity to state our views before we hear the Minister's response. I certainly hope that he can give a more encouraging response than some previous responses have been. What we have here is an impressive document which has been painstakingly— but I believe expertly and dispassionately—assembled. One hears a great deal about interests, for example Members' interests and declarable interests. "Vested interest" are certainly not dirty words to me.

There has been an impressive investigation into a national asset. Those of us who have been in the House and in politics for a long time, and indeed those individuals whose careers are at stake, recognise that there has been a revolution both in the management and the structure of many hitherto well-established public services. Therefore, I do not believe that there will be any argument about the need for a review.

I listened carefully to the noble and gallant Lord, Lord Carver. He not only told us what is right with the report. He impressed me with the fact that not only had he read the report but he had analysed it, and he presented his ideas on how it could be improved. I am sure that the noble Earl, Lord Selborne, and his committee, will be grateful for that, because it is all grist to the mill.

However, I wish to emphasise immediately a view contrary to that expressed by the noble Lord, Lord Trefgarne. The Government and the Minister have stated repeatedly that they have no plans at present to privatise the industry. The noble Lord nevertheless took the opportunity to say that while he accepted that for the moment, perhaps in two, three or four years' time the question should be revisited. I hesitate to believe that an organisation which has been in turmoil and suffered trauma over the past few years will welcome the fact that, as it is getting to grips with a new role, it can look forward to its entrails being examined yet again in two, three or four years' time. Therefore, I hope that the Minister will be a little more kind to those whose careers are affected and will say that, in the context of the changes, he and his colleagues fully expect the new arrangements to be a success. If they are not successful, then of course the Minister and his colleagues will consider alternatives.

I was very impressed to learn that the DRA is not merely defence oriented or an organisation with a defence capability. There are a number of ways in which an organisation which is established for a limited purpose may develop expertise and then may become a competitor. I understand the delicacy of that situation. There may be resentment. However, I see nothing wrong in a mix of civil and public resources and businesses if it produces a good match. I am very encouraged by that aspect of the report.

Recommendation 4.24 on page 32 states:

"We consider that Treasury rules place an unnecessarily high burden upon DRA. The current target rates of return appear unrealistic, and we consider that DRA should be able to charge customers at marginal costs where appropriate; to do otherwise would place the future of many unique and vital facilities in the United Kingdom in jeopardy".

The committee has had the benefit of hearing the witnesses and questioning them. They have used their great expertise, and their political nous. If it is their view that the present rules could place many unique and vital facilities in the United Kingdom in jeopardy, I should like the Minister either to put that in context or to reassure those who are affected. It would be a nonsense if that were to happen in pursuit of dogma. The noble Lord, Lord Redesdale, also mentioned that point.

It would be in the national interest if there were an understanding or some flexibility in these matters. The noble Earl, Lord Selborne, said that before many more scientists are made redundant and before there is a loss of more unique facilities, one ought to pause and reflect on whether that is necessary. He also said that one must recognise that in the context of the defence of the realm we do not want to find ourselves in a few years' time in a position in which either those facilities have to be recreated or we have to obtain the facilities from other agencies, not only in this country but from abroad.

One of my complaints about this Government is that far too often, in a cavalier fashion, they will sell facilities of this kind in order to boost the Exchequer and provide opportunities for tax cuts. I come from the Enfield and Edmonton area. I believe that the noble Lord, Lord Trefgarne, was the Minister at the time of the sale of the ordnance factories. I find it astounding that the Government keep so few of their eggs in the basket of public ownership. I believe that selling our assets in that way is completely wrong.

Therefore I should be grateful if the Minister could give some reassurance in respect of stability.

In paragraph 5.6 on page 33 the committee recommends that the Government's Chief Scientific Adviser should be:

"specifically empowered to expose any practices which impede closer links between civil and military science and technology".

Perhaps the Minister or the noble Earl, Lord Selborne, can tell us what they have in mind which may cause them to worry about practices which impede such closer links. Are we talking in terms of civil servants and those who guide them resisting the possibility of moving into the civil field? Are we talking in terms of a fight to the last ditch? The noble and gallant Lord, Lord Carver, impressed me with the need to be flexible in these matters. Therefore, I should be grateful if the Minister or the noble Earl, Lord Selborne, could reassure me. I believe that we need a mix of establishments and expertise linking civil and military science.

I was very impressed by the remark in the government report dealing with the need for the DRA to

"seek work from other government departments, some of which have research budgets significantly greater than the MoD's, as well as from the private sector".

Will the Minister indicate to what extent there is co-ordination at government level to ensure that initiatives are not inhibited due to vested interests in other departments?

Perhaps I may give an example from my own experience. A colleague of mine worked for the Coal Board. He was in charge of a body called Minestone Executive, whose function was to sell colliery spoil. That was useful for aggregate. It was not first-class aggregate but second-class aggregate which could be used in, for example, road building. An organisation which was nationally owned had difficulty in selling its product because contracts existed between other departments and other contractors which were not owned by the nation. There was clearly a commercial nexus.

Therefore, I should like the Minister, when he replies, to pay particular attention to paragraph 9 on page 2 of the government report and assure us that the facilities and expertise which rest in the agency are capable of being used by others without too much difficulty.

I was reassured by the words of the noble Earl, Lord Selborne. I noted the reference in the report to the decline in DTI funding. The noble Earl seemed to lay great store on an alternative, secondary source of funding. Perhaps he may say when he replies how he is assured that money is available from that other source.

Reference has been made to short termism, a subject of which the Minister is well aware. We are talking about a vital public interest in every sense of the word. The Minister and I will differ on our attitudes in general to the public and private sectors. However, I believe that the DRA needs to be protected. The agency must not

[LORD GRAHAM OF EDMONTON]
disintegrate for short-term reasons, with parts of it sold off. Five thousand scientists and many other employees who serve the nation well are involved.

I had intended to say how useful the report is for people such as myself. I read it with a great deal of interest. However, perhaps I may say to the noble Earl, Lord Selborne, and others that paragraph 2.22 on page 17 almost put me off. It states:

"DRA already seeks European (EC and non-EC) collaboration, involving itself in EC Framework Programme projects and in EUCLID, BRITE/EURAM, ESPRIT, SCIENCE, and MAST".

We are supposed to understand that. It seems gobbledegook. The report is full of initials. This report clearly has a great value to those people who prepared it; they will use it. But it could be improved if so many initials were not used. However, the House is indebted to the noble Earl, Lord Selborne, and to those who contributed to the report. On this side of the Chamber, we pay a warm tribute to their work and look forward to the continuation of the valuable national service given by those men and women.

7.12 p.m.

Lord Henley: My Lords, the noble Lord the Opposition Chief Whip says that we often differ, and he is certainly right. However, there is one matter on which I am in full agreement with him: it is regarding the problems with and frequency of acronyms. As one who has only recently come to the Ministry of Defence, I am having great difficulties in getting to know and understand the vast number of acronyms which proliferate in that department.

I had also hoped on this occasion to be able to agree with the noble Lord on one other matter. He, like me, always welcomes brevity in speeches. I had thought for the first time ever that I would be able to congratulate every speaker in an untimed debate on keeping their speeches to within 10 minutes. However, the noble Lord himself broke that rule. I shall seek to keep within 10 minutes myself; but I do not know whether I can. I shall certainly not respond at the same length as our response which was published last week, to which other noble Lords have referred.

I start by extending my thanks to the noble Earl, Lord Selborne, for calling this debate on the Select Committee's report and offering my thanks to him, the members of the committee and its staff for their work in producing the report. I wish to say how grateful I am for the tribute that he paid to the Defence Research Agency and the excellence of its work.

As the House is aware, the publication of the committee's report coincided with the publication of our own report, *Front Line First*, which included a proposal to enlarge the DRA. We have been engaged in considering that proposal. As I have already mentioned, our response to the Select Committee's report was published this week.

I think that I would reject the allegations from the noble and gallant Lord, Lord Carver—for whom I have the greatest respect—that the report was complacent. I rest to some extent on the remarks of the noble Lord, Lord Redesdale, who welcomed the report. I hope that he will offer a similar welcome to other announcements that my department may make from time to time.

We value the scrutiny given by the Select Committee to the DRA's role in the relationship between the agency and the department. We are pleased that the committee speaks highly of the DRA management and staff to the extent that it considers achievable the DRA's aim for international pre-eminence. We were disappointed, however, that similar acknowledgement was not given to the efforts made within my department to develop that relationship. The DRA is our principal scientific and technical knowledge base, and as its principle customer my department uses the trading fund regime to derive the best value for money from that knowledge base for the taxpayer's benefit. This will be even more the case when the trading fund is enlarged, and new streamlined procedures governing our relationship will help the DRA to plan ahead and improve the cost-effectiveness of the research programme.

The relationship between the DRA and its MoD customers is one of a trusted partnership in which the DRA has substantial knowledge of our future equipment needs and joins with us in planning the research programme. The *Front Line First* proposals on the restructuring of the MoD research programme into corporate research and contract research will allow us and the DRA to build a more coherent research programme to the benefit of my department and the wider economy.

Obviously I understand the committee's call—it was referred to by my noble friend Lord Selborne and the noble and gallant Lord, Lord Craig of Radley—for a period of consolidation and stability in the DRA's affairs. I have to say that there was no case to exempt the DRA from the rigours of the Defence Costs Study which looked at all aspects of support to the front line. We are determined to drive down costs to the taxpayer. The broad framework of the DRA structure and operating processes will remain in place.

The proposal in *Front Line First*, as my noble friend Lord Selborne, made clear, is to bring together the DRA, the Chemical and Biological Defence Establishment, the Defence Operational Analysis Centre, the Director of Test and Evaluation, and other MoD scientific staff into a single, enlarged executive agency. This will enhance the ability of those organisations to meet, through the existing trading fund, the demands placed on them by my department. The proposal in principle has been the subject of consultation with the trade unions and nothing in the comments received on the consultative document leads us to believe that it is not right to go ahead and prepare to launch the enlarged agency on 1st April next year. Nor do I believe that that will affect the stability of the DRA.

No evidence has been presented in favour of privatising the DRA—a matter to which my noble friend Lord Trefgarne referred. The *Front Line First* report—I believe that my noble friend mentioned it—specifically recommended that it should not be a candidate for privatisation. Indeed, in his evidence to the committee, the then Minister for Defence Procurement, my right honourable friend Mr. Jonathan Aitken urged caution in the light of our international commitments. However, I can assure my noble friend Lord Trefgarne that those are matters which should be and will be kept under review. Should it be a suitable candidate for privatisation in the future, that is certainly a matter that we can look to. However, I must express the caution that my right honourable friend expressed in his evidence to the committee: that it is certainly not a matter for the immediate or foreseeable future.

We welcome the importance that the committee attaches to the wealth-creating activity of the DRA. Last year's White Paper on science, engineering and technology, *Realising Our Potential*, emphasised the Government's commitment to harnessing all publicly funded science and technology more effectively to support wealth creation and improve the quality of life. The DRA has an important role in delivering our increased efforts to realise the wealth creation potential of its research and development activities. I can give an assurance to the House that the DRA is working closely with both the Office of Science and Technology and the DTI to take forward its wealth creation initiatives. The exchange of information with the civil sector is an important part of that process.

We rejected the idea that was advocated in the report and repeated both by my noble friend and by the noble and gallant Lord, Lord Carver. Lord Carver went on to suggest looking at the German solution to these problems. Certainly, again, as someone who is new to the department that is something—without making any commitments—that I would be more than willing to do. As I said, we rejected the idea in the report that the Office of Science and Technology and the DTI should share in ownership of the DRA, as that would undermine ministerial accountability without creating any clear benefits.

However, my department will invite the Government's Chief Scientific Adviser, Sir William Stewart, to become an external member of the Defence Research Agency Council.

Perhaps I may say a word or two about the Treasury rules that were referred to by the noble and gallant Lord, Lord Craig, the noble Lord, Lord Graham, and, I believe, the noble Lord, Lord Redesdale. We reject the contention that such rules place an unnecessarily high burden on the DRA. The present 6 per cent. target rate of return set by the Secretary of State as owner of the DRA is the same risk-free rate that applies across similar Government trading funds and provides the necessary commercial discipline. The DRA is free to charge what it considers appropriate for its facilities provided that it does not disadvantage the Ministry of Defence. It is merely constrained by the willingness and ability of its customers collectively to pay the full cost. I do not accept the noble and gallant Lord's arguments that those are contradictory. Nor do I accept the argument that those impose excessive constraints.

We also consider that the—

Lord Trefgarne: My Lords, I wonder if I may intervene. I hope my noble friend understands that the views to which he just referred and rejected so firmly were held almost universally throughout the committee, not just by my noble and gallant friend Lord Craig.

Lord Henley: Obviously, my Lords, I take note particularly of what the noble and gallant Lord, Lord Craig, said, and also of what the committee said. If my noble friend—a former colleague on this Front Bench—also forcefully makes those remarks, I will take even greater note of them. I am afraid, however, that I do not accept the arguments that have been put forward. I hope that my noble friend will therefore bear with me in that respect.

We also consider that the present arrangements provide sufficient commercial freedom for the DRA to contribute to the activities of British industry more widely. The important issue is for the DRA to use these effectively without affecting its capacity to meet the needs of the Ministry of Defence and the Armed Forces. The "trusted partnership" allows the agency to identify how the research programme might be modified to meet its wider remit while still meeting the MoD's needs.

In conclusion, perhaps I may remind the House that the Ministry of Defence is concerned first with defence objectives. That is our prime role. We require that the DRA should support that objective. However, such a mutually beneficial relationship does not rule out a wider remit for the agency, and we believe that within the overall defence framework it is possible for the DRA to operate flexibly and to make a very real contribution to the wider role of wealth creation. These are objectives that this Government support, and we shall continue to encourage in what has undoubtedly become a flagship among agencies for service delivery and efficiency.

7.23 p.m.

The Earl of Selborne: My Lords, I thank all those who have contributed to what I have found to be a very interesting debate, and I thank particularly my noble friend the Minister for his contribution and for the government response to our report.

Perhaps I may very briefly—because indeed the brevity of the speeches throughout this debate has been exemplary—make two or three points. In his stimulating contribution, the noble and gallant Lord, Lord Carver, referred to the German model. I think the committee would have had a lot of sympathy with that had we produced the report in 1991 or thereabouts. Instead, we are looking at the DRA four years into its existence, and that is very different. If the radical solution of which the noble and gallant Lord urges at least consideration and which he feels we should have looked at more carefully had been the answer, it should have been an answer four years ago, not now. We looked very carefully at the quality of the science and the need to try to ensure that that science delivers relevant research, particularly for its own purposes and the Ministry of Defence. We were not sure that yet another uprooting would be helpful.

My noble friend Lord Trefgarne referred to the issue of privatisation and seemed to imply that there was a self-denying ordinance on the committee not to look at this issue. That is far from the case. A number of people gave evidence on the ownership of the agency, and that

[THE EARL OF SELBORNE] was mainly in terms of whether it should remain in the ownership of the Ministry of Defence. Our terms of reference were as wide as you like: we were simply conducting an inquiry into the Defence Research Agency. This is very much a case of the dog that did not bark. Very few people referred to privatisation—although it is true that the Minister himself did so. And Sir Peter Kemp in his written evidence reminded us that at the time when the DRA was created privatisation had been quite a live issue. However, throughout all the written evidence that we received—and it was a large amount—there simply was no request for privatisation. That is why we did not take that line of inquiry very far.

Lastly, a very forceful and valid point was made by the noble Lord, Lord Graham of Edmonton, when he referred politely to the "Alphabet soup" throughout this report. I refer the noble Lord to page 41 where, I am horrified to count, the number of acronyms comes to 60. I am afraid that that is the culture in which the Ministry of Defence lives. The noble Lord will remember from his days in the services just how widespread initials were, and they remain so. All I can say is that he read out to great effect one particularly awful paragraph.

However, if he looks, for instance, at what SCIENCE (which you would think was a perfectly good word) really means—it is referred to on page 41—he will realise that in real life it is even worse than as an acronym, so perhaps we were wise to keep to the acronym in that respect.

The noble Lord asked me to refer to another point, and perhaps with your Lordships' indulgence I may briefly do so. If the DTI is not funding the research establishments within the Defence Research Agency as much as we would wish—and it is not—we look then to the Office of Science and Technology. The problem with the Office of Science and Technology is that it does not have the money. Nevertheless, it was set up two (or is it three?) years ago with the remit to try to co-ordinate research throughout government. We believe that there is a job to be done. I listened with great interest to what my noble friend the Minister said. I still believe that perhaps his ministry and the Office of Science and Technology could look carefully at this point. I therefore obviously welcome the appointment of Sir William Stewart to which my noble friend referred.

On Question, Motion agreed to.

House adjourned at twenty-seven minutes past seven o'clock.

Written Answers

Thursday 8th December 1994

IRAQ: TROOP DEPLOYMENTS

Lord Kennet asked Her Majesty's Government:

What, if any, is the status in international law, and what is their opinion, of the "understanding" that any moment of Iraqi troops south of the 32nd parallel beyond "pre-crisis levels" would "trigger American action" against Iraqi forces, reported in the 24 October 1994 issue of *Aviation Week and Space Technology,* particularly in the light of the same journal's report, in its issue of 14 October: "Iraqi invasion threat reassessed by military: . . . US field commanders . . . say they now suspect . . . the big movement of Iraqi troops . . . may have been triggered by fear and panic, caused by intense, around-the-clock allied air operation"; and whether such operations did in fact take place.

The Minister of State, Foreign and Commonwealth (Baroness Chalker of Wallasey): Following the deployment of Iraqi troops near the Kuwaiti border in October, the UN Security Council unanimously adopted Resolution 949, placing clear requirements on Iraq. It demanded the complete withdrawal of recently deployed troops, and warned that Iraq should not use its forces to threaten neighbours or UN personnel.

At the time that Iraq began these deployments, there had been no increase in allied air operations.

UKRAINE: ACCESSION TO NON-PROLIFERATION TREATY

Lord Kennet asked Her Majesty's Government:

Whether any problems remain concerning the adherence of Ukraine to the NPT, given the presence of nuclear weapons on its soil and its claimed ownership of them.

Baroness Chalker of Wallasey: No. Ukraine acceded to the Nuclear Non-Proliferation Treaty on 5th December.

UKRAINE: SECURITY ASSURANCES

Lord Kennet asked Her Majesty's Government:

What are the written security assurances which they have agreed to extend to Ukraine, in the context of Ukraine adhering to the Non-Proliferation Treaty (NPT), and in what way they differ from the security assurances currently extended to other signatories of the NPT.

Baroness Chalker of Wallasey: Copies of the Memorandum on Security Assurances in connection with Ukraine's accession to the Nuclear Non-Proliferation Treaty shall be placed in the Libraries of the House.

The assurances that we have given concern our commitment to seek immediate Security Council action in certain circumstances involving the use or threat of use of nuclear weapons against Ukraine and the circumstances in which we will not use nuclear weapons against Ukraine as a non-nuclear-weapons state party to the NPT. These assurances are substantially similar to those currently extended by ourselves to other non-nuclear weapons states parties to the NPT.

NON-NUCLEAR STATES: SECURITY ASSURANCES

Lord Kennet asked Her Majesty's Government:

Whether it is now their intention (and that of the United States of America and Russia) to extend written security assurances like those extended to Ukraine to any other non-nuclear state signatory of the treaty that requests them.

Baroness Chalker of Wallasey: The United Kingdom (and the United States of America and Russia) provided similar security assurances to Belarus and Kazakhstan on 5 December.

US NUCLEAR WEAPONS: REMOVAL FROM SOUTH KOREA

Lord Kennet asked Her Majesty's Government:

Whether the United States of America will now allow the removal of its nuclear weapons from South Korea to be verified, given that the removal of ex-Soviet nuclear weapons from Ukraine is to be verified.

Baroness Chalker of Wallasey: That is a matter for the Government of the United States of America.

RWANDA: EU AID

Lord Judd asked Her Majesty's Government:

Whether they have received any reports of moves by the Government of France to block the transmission of aid from the European Union to Rwanda; and, if so, what sums are involved and what is their response.

Baroness Chalker of Wallasey: The EU Development Council agreed unanimously, on 25 November, to an action programme costing 67 mecu (£53 million), which focuses on immediate rehabilitation needs in Rwanda.

EMERGENCY PROVISIONS (NORTHERN IRELAND) ACT 1991: REVIEW REPORT

Lord Lyell asked Her Majesty's Government:

Whether they have yet received the report of Mr. J. J. Rowe's fundamental review of the Emergency Provisions (Northern Ireland) Act 1991.

Baroness Miller of Hendon: My right honourable and learned friend the Secretary of State for Northern Ireland has received the report and is giving it careful consideration.

MARRIED QUARTERS ESTATE: PRIVATISATION STUDY

Viscount Davidson asked Her Majesty's Government:

What progress they are making with the development of plans for transfer of the married quarters estate to the private sector?

The Parliamentary Under-Secretary of State, Ministry of Defence (Lord Henley): It is too early to be confident that such a transfer will be possible on terms which will satisfy our requirements. Nonetheless, the initial work undertaken for us by NatWest Markets, the investment bank, has been productive and encouraging. We therefore now intend to progress to development of comprehensive proposals aimed at achieving the transfer in financial year 1995–96. A decision on whether or not to proceed will not be taken until worked-out proposals are available in the first part of next year. Meanwhile, however, following completion of the initial study, we are proceeding to competitive selection of financial and other advisers to help us prepare for and effect the transfer.

OPERATION GRANBY: PROTECTION AGAINST BOTULINUM

The Countess of Mar asked Her Majesty's Government:

Why members of HM Armed Forces were not vaccinated against botulinum when they were aware that Iraq had the capability to manufacture and use biological weapons including anthrax and botulinum prior to Operation Granby (as stated on page ix, paragraph 18 of *Lessons Learned from Operation Granby*).

Lord Henley: Details of specific medical countermeasures employed by British Forces against the potential biological warfare threat during Operation Granby remain classified.

FUMING NITRIC ACID

The Countess of Mar asked Her Majesty's Government:

What is the colour of fuming nitric acid observed by the naked eye; whether fuming nitric acid contains phosgene (ca) and phosgene oxine (cx); and what signs and symptoms they would expect to observe in an individual exposed to a few droplets of liquid nitric acid within five minutes of exposure.

Lord Henley: This is a matter for the Chief Executive of the Chemical and Biological Defence Establishment. I have therefore asked him to reply.

Letter to the Countess of Mar from the Chief Executive of the Chemical and Biological Defence Establishment, Dr. Graham Pearson, dated 8 December 1994:

1. Your Parliamentary Question to Her Majesty's Government asking what is the colour of fuming nitric acid observed by the naked eye; whether fuming nitric acid contains phosgene (ca) and phosgene oxime (cx); and what signs and symptoms would they expect to observe in an individual exposed to a few droplets of liquid nitric acid within five minutes of exposure has been passed to me to answer as Chief Executive of the Chemical and Biological Defence Establishment.

2. Fuming nitric acid is yellowish in colour and produces yellow brown fumes on exposure to the air. Nitric acid is normally produced by reaction of nitrogen dioxide with water and contains no carbon containing molecules. It does not contain phosgene (for which the code is CG) or phosgene oxime (CX). Neither of these would be stable in fuming nitric acid.

3. A few droplets of liquid nitric acid on the skin will cause immediate pain and blistering. The fumes from nitric acid will cause immediate irritation and pain in the eye, airway irritation, cough and possibly chest pain.

The Countess of Mar asked Her Majesty's Government:

Whether three colour detector paper would respond to exposure to fuming nitric acid, and if so, what colour will it show.

Lord Henley: Three colour detector paper is designed to respond to liquid CW agent by turning red (blister), yellow (non persistent nerve) or green (persistent nerve) depending on the agent; it will not respond to vapour. Application of liquid concentrated nitric or liquid "fuming" nitric acid to the paper would result only in a darkening of the area contaminated by the liquid which would not be interpreted as an agent response.

The Countess of Mar asked Her Majesty's Government:

Whether Computer-Aided Measurement and Control (CAM) monitors are designed to detect nitric acid, and if so, what reading would they expect to find on a CAM monitor directed at fuming nitric acid.

Lord Henley: We have no record of a Computer Aided Measurement and Control instrument in the inventory of any United Kingdom Service; it is assumed that the question refers to the Chemical Agent Monitor (CAM). CAM is not designed to detect fuming nitric acid. Laboratory tests have, however, shown that if the instrument is exposed to the concentrated brown fumes from fuming nitric acid then a reading might be achieved indicating the presence of a low concentration of H (blister) agent.

MUSTARD GAS

The Countess of Mar asked Her Majesty's Government:

What is the colour of mustard gas observed by the naked eye, and what signs and symptoms they would expect to observe in an individual exposed to a few droplets of liquid mustard gas agent within five minute of exposure.

Lord Henley: This is a matter for the Chief Executive of the Chemical and Biological Defence Establishment. I have therefore asked him to reply.

Letter to the Countess of Mar from the Chief Executive of the Chemical and Biological Defence

Establishment, Dr. Graham Pearson, dated 8 December 1994:

1. Your Parliamentary Question to Her Majesty's Government asking what is the colour of mustard gas observed by the naked eye, and what signs and symptoms would they expect to observe in an individual exposed to a few droplets of liquid mustard gas agent within five minutes of exposure has been passed to me to answer as Chief Executive of the Chemical and Biological Defence Establishment.

2. The colour of liquid mustard gas varies slightly according to the production process and the degree of purity. When chemically pure it is colourless but is generally yellowish in colour when produced for use in weapons.

3. No symptoms or signs would be observed in the first five minutes after exposure to a few drops of liquid mustard. Eye and skin effects are typically delayed by several hours after exposure. A very high concentration of mustard gas may cause immediate cough and irritation, but such a concentration would not be produced following exposure to a few droplets.

PROTECTIVE VACCINES AND DRUGS: REFUSAL BY SERVICE PERSONNEL

The Countess of Mar asked Her Majesty's Government:

Under what circumstances members of Her Majesty's Armed Forces may find themselves liable to disciplinary action for refusing drugs or vaccines in a war situation, and whether such action would contravene an individual's human or civil rights.

Lord Henley: In operational circumstances where it is regarded as reasonable to issue an order for Service personnel to receive vaccines or drugs to protect them against the threat of biological or chemical warfare agents, refusal of such a lawful order might render members of the Armed Forces liable to disciplinary action. Whether the order was reasonable, and therefore lawful, could be raised as an issue in the disciplinary proceedings, and the individual's rights would be taken into account. Each case would turn on its own facts and merits, including the fact such drugs and vaccines could be life saving in operational circumstances.

STUDENT LOANS

Earl Russell asked Her Majesty's Government:

What is the average delay in the payment of student loans, whether there are any plans to improve this figure, and whether the Student Loans Company has given efficiency priority over effectiveness.

Lord Lucas: In its recently published annual report, the Student Loans Company reported that, in the academic year 1993–94, it had paid 91 per cent. of loans within 21 days of receipt of the application.

For the academic year 1994–95 my right honourable friend the Secretary of State for Education has set a target of payment of 92 per cent. of loans within 21 days. The Student Loans Company estimates its performance as at 30 November at 88 per cent. As at the same date the company had issued over 180,000 loans for the academic year 1994–95, as compared with 120,000 at the same time last year. Over 111,000 have been paid to existing borrowers, and over 69,000 to new borrowers.

The company has been experiencing difficulties associated with the introduction of a new repeat application procedure intended to increase efficiency and effectiveness. Forms were sent in May 1994 to existing borrowers to enable those who wished to take out another loan this academic year to make a simplified application before the start of term. Out of 320,000 students eligible for this procedure, only 60,000 returned their forms during the summer. The company made arrangements to process the large volume of outstanding applications which they expected to arrive when the academic year began. Plans were also made to deal with students who had lost or misplaced the simplified application forms.

In the event, many more students had lost or misplaced their forms than anticipated. Many telephoned the company for replacement forms, exceeding the normal call handling capacity. The company accelerated the normal programme of recruitment of temporary staff, moved staff from other areas of activity, doubled the telephone answering capacity, extended the hours of business into the evening and weekends, and gave priority to loans processing.

The company has written to all higher education institutions (HEIs) to apologise to all students, their parents and HEIs for the inconvenience caused. It has explained how the difficulties arose, and has informed them that the backlog should be cleared by Christmas.

The company's letter also explains how it proposes to prevent a recurrence of these difficulties in the future. I am sending a copy to the noble Earl and I have placed a copy in the Library.

ORGANOPHOSPHORUS SHEEP DIPS: UNAUTHORISED PURCHASERS

The Countess of Mar asked Her Majesty's Government:

How many irregularities under the Medicines (Veterinary Drugs) (Pharmacy and Merchants' List) (Amendment) Order 1994 have been detected, and whether there are any prosecutions pending.

The Parliamentary Secretary, Minister of Agriculture, Fisheries and Food (Earl Howe): Inspectors of the Royal Pharmaceutical Society of Great Britain are responsible for monitoring compliance with this order.

I understand that since 1 April 1994, seven instances of sales of OP sheep dips to unregistered purchasers have been formally reported to the Society. A further nine cases of possible breaches have been noted. The inspectors have, in addition, given informal advice to suppliers of OP sheep dips, but the numbers are not recorded for this activity. No prosecutions are currently pending.

ORGANOPHOSPHORUS SHEEP DIPS: ADVERSE REACTIONS

The Countess of Mar asked Her Majesty's Government:

How many reports of suspected adverse reactions to exposure to organophosphate sheep dips were recorded by the Veterinary Medicines Directorate in 1993 and 1994 to date.

Earl Howe: The information requested, relating to human exposure to organophosphorus sheep dips, is as follows:

1993	181
1994[1]	47

[1] to 30 November

ORGANOPHOSPHORUS PESTICIDE AND HERBICIDES: LOW LEVEL EXPOSURE

The Countess of Mar asked Her Majesty's Government:

Whether they are conducting any research into the effects of chronic low level exposure to organophosphate pesticides and herbicides on workers and residents in market gardening and fruit growing districts with a record of high usage of these chemicals; and

Whether they are conducting any research into the health effects on people of long term, low level exposure to organophosphate pesticides used in domestic or workplace premises for pest control.

Earl Howe: We are not conducting any research into these precise areas. However, the possibility that cumulative exposure could carry a risk to health is taken into account when considering applications for pesticides approval.

SHEEP ANNUAL PREMIUM AND ENVIRONMENTALLY SENSITIVE AREAS SCHEMES

Lord Stanley of Alderley asked Her Majesty's Government:

Whether they have discretion to refuse an application for *(a)* the Sheep Annual Premium Scheme; *(b)* the Environmentally Sensitive Scheme; and, if so, on what grounds.

Earl Howe: Sheep Annual Premium Scheme claims are subject to Community rules which are directly applicable in the UK. Member states may take steps to protect the environment and the Government have recently introduced measures to reduce or withhold payments from producers who overgraze their land or who use unsuitable supplementary feeding methods. Otherwise the Government have no discretion to refuse a claim which is properly made.

Agreements under the Environmentally Sensitive Areas scheme are generally available to anyone who has an interest in agricultural land within a designated ESA such that they can ensure that the conditions of the agreement are met. However Section 18(3) of the Agriculture Act 1986 gives the Minister of Agriculture, Fisheries and Food discretion to refuse an application for an agreement. Situations in which this discretion is exercised include where he considers that the proposed agreement is unlikely to facilitate the objectives of the scheme or offer a cost-effective use of public money; where an applicant has carried out work contrary to the objectives of the scheme shortly before applying to join or rejoin; and where an applicant has acted in a manner which would be in breach of the proposed agreement before it has been signed.

NATIONAL LOTTERY

The Marquess of Ailesbury asked Her Majesty's Government:

Whether they accept that the public was led to believe that 50 per cent. of the National Lottery's receipts would be paid out in prizes every week.

The Parliamentary Under-Secretary of State, Department of National Heritage (Viscount Astor): Over the course of Camelot's seven-year licence to run the National Lottery, the prize payout percentage is expected to be 56.5 per cent. of net sales after deduction of lottery duty. At current levels of duty (12 per cent. of gross sales) this is indeed equivalent to 50 per cent. of gross sales. The percentage being paid out in different years and on individual games promoted during that period will, however, vary. Almost two million people won prizes in the first two weeks of the lottery.

ISBN 0-10-701395-9